Texas
Pattern Jury Charges

Business • Consumer • Insurance • Employment

TEXAS

PATTERN JURY CHARGES

Business • Consumer

Insurance • Employment

Prepared by the

COMMITTEE

on

PATTERN JURY CHARGES

of the

STATE BAR OF TEXAS

Austin 2008

The State Bar of Texas, through its TexasBarBooks Department, publishes practice books prepared and edited by knowledgeable authors to give practicing lawyers as much assistance as possible. The competence of the authors ensures outstanding professional products, but, of course, neither the State Bar of Texas, the editors, nor the authors make either express or implied warranties in regard to their use. Each lawyer must depend on his or her own knowledge of the law and expertise in the use or modification of these materials.

IRS CIRCULAR 230 NOTICE: To ensure compliance with requirements imposed by the IRS, we inform you that (1) this written material was not intended or written by the author(s) to be used for the purpose of avoiding federal penalties that may be imposed on a taxpayer; (2) this written material cannot be used by a taxpayer for the purpose of avoiding penalties that may be imposed on the taxpayer; (3) this written material cannot be used in promoting, marketing, or recommending to another party any tax-related transaction or matter; and (4) a taxpayer should seek advice based on the taxpayer's particular circumstances from an independent tax advisor.

The use of the masculine gender throughout this publication is purely for literary convenience and should, of course, be understood to include the feminine gender as well.

International Standard Book Number: 978-1-892542-56-4
Library of Congress Control Number: 2008937182

Printed in the United States of America

Texas Pattern Jury Charges—Business, Consumer, Insurance & Employment was formerly titled *Texas Pattern Jury Charges, Volume 4*.

COMMITTEE ON PATTERN JURY CHARGES

Business • Consumer • Insurance • Employment

2007–2008

KAREN S. PRECELLA, *Chair*
MARK L. KINCAID, *Vice-Chair*

HON. JANE BLAND
QUENTIN BROGDON
J. BRETT BUSBY
LADAWN H. CONWAY
DAVID H. DONALDSON, JR.
HON. GRANT DORFMAN
SARAH ANN DUCKERS
HON. JENNIFER WALKER ELROD
JOHN GRIFFIN, JR.
DAVID E. HARRELL, JR.
CHARLES L. HENKE, JR.
THOMAS S. LEATHERBURY
PHILIP K. MAXWELL
RENÉE FORINASH MCELHANEY
RICHARD G. MUNZINGER
HON. BRIAN PATRICK QUINN
DANIEL L. RENTFRO, JR.
CRISTINA ESPINOSA RODRIGUEZ
HON. REBECCA SIMMONS
SCOTT PATRICK STOLLEY

COMMITTEE ON PATTERN JURY CHARGES—OVERSIGHT

2007–2008

HON. TRACY KEE CHRISTOPHER, *Chair*
HON. KENT C. SULLIVAN, *Vice-Chair*
HON. SCOTT A. BRISTER, *Supreme Court Liaison*
HON. HARRIET O'NEILL, *Supreme Court Liaison*

ALEXANDRA W. ALBRIGHT
RICHARD R. BRANN
SHARON E. CALLAWAY
TIM CHOVANEC
NORTON A. COLVIN
RON FRANKLIN
MARK K. GLASSER
JOHN BLAISE GSANGER
HON. DWIGHT E. JEFFERSON
HON. CYNTHIA S. KENT
HON. ELIZABETH LANG-MIERS
PENELOPE E. NICHOLSON
HON. DAVID PEEPLES
DANIEL V. POZZA
THOMAS C. RINEY
HON. GUADALUPE RIVERA
WAYNE C. SCHIESS
HON. PHYLIS J. SPEEDLIN
MOLLY STEELE

COMMITTEE ON PATTERN JURY CHARGES

Business • Consumer • Insurance • Employment

1989–2006

Chairs

MIKE M. TABOR, 1989–1993
PHILIP K. MAXWELL, 1993–1997
SHARON E. CALLAWAY, 1997–2004
TIMOTHY G. CHOVANEC, 2004–2006

Vice-Chairs

PHILIP K. MAXWELL, 1991–1993
GEORGE WALTER BRAMBLETT, JR., 1993–1995
SHARON E. CALLAWAY, 1995–1997
TIMOTHY G. CHOVANEC, 1997–2004
KAREN S. PRECELLA, 2003–2004

Members

HON. MARILYN ABOUSSIE
BEN L. ADERHOLT
C. MARK BAKER
DAVID BATSON
ASIM BHANSALI
MICHAEL ALLEN BIRRER
THOMAS BLACK
HON. JANE BLAND
SAMUEL L. BOYD
KATHERINE BUTLER BREM
ARTHUR J. BRENDER, JR.
KAMELA BRIDGES
J. BRETT BUSBY
ROBERT L. RUSSELL BUSH
STEPHEN ASHON CHAN
WILLIAM J. CHRISS
DAVID S. COALE
HON. ANN T. COCHRAN
DOUGLAS G. CORNWELL
PETER M. CURRY, JR.
HON. MARK D. DAVIDSON
DON C. DENNIS
HARISH C. DHINGRA
MARTIN DIES, JR.
DAVID H. DONALDSON, JR.
HON. JENNIFER WALKER ELROD
EDWIN R. FLEURIET
HON. HENRY ROBERT FROST
MARILYN D. GARNER
BERNARDO S. GARZA
JOHN GRIFFIN, JR.
LAWRENCE BRADLEY HANCOCK
WILLIAM T. HANKINSON
JAMES A. HERRMANN

Members

Mark F. Howell
Charles W. Hurd
Teresa Rhonda Jones
Jeffrey R. Jury
David E. Keltner
Andrew L. Kerr
Mark L. Kincaid
Jerome M. Kolander, Jr.
Hon. Douglas S. Lang
John G. Lewis
Peter Linzer
Jack W. London
David T. Lopez
Mark E. Lowes
C. Robert Mace
Margaret M. Maisel
Renée Forinash McElhaney
Mark McQuality
Sterling Minor
Frank W. Mitchell
Hon. Frank Montalvo
Richard G. Munzinger
Sara Murray
Keith B. O'Connell
Kemnagum Ken Okorie
Dudley Oldham
Carrin F. Patman
Katrina Shana Patrick
Timothy Patton
Terri Curry Peace
Hon. Brian Patrick Quinn
Barbara Radnofsky
Hon. Jorge Cantu Rangel
Hon. Rose Guerra Reyna
Susan Rafferty Richardson
Cristina Espinosa Rodriguez
Gregg M. Rosenberg
Yona Rozen
Anthony J. Sadberry
Hon. Rebecca Simmons
Greg A. Sivinski
Jeffrey D. Small
Lawrence David Smith
Craig Smyser
Rosemary T. Snider
Carlos Ramon Soltero
Clifton A. Vaughn
Robert Blake Wallis
William E. Walton
Thomas H. Watkins
Charles R. Watson, Jr.
Timothy Webb
Terry Weldon
Hon. W. David West
Hon. Mark L. Whittington
T. J. Wray
James L. "Larry" Wright
Eric Lyf Yollick

COMMITTEE ON PATTERN JURY CHARGES

Civil

1990–1991

J. Hadley Edgar, *Chair*
Hon. William L. Hughes, Jr., *Vice-Chair*

Blake Bailey
R. Doak Bishop
George E. Chandler
Stephen C. Dillard
Robert L. Gibbins, Jr.
Douglass D. Hearne
Karen M. Kacir
Stephen R. Lewis
Wayne H. Prescott
Thomas T. Rogers

CONTENTS

PREFACE

The Pattern Jury Charges (volume 4) Committee has worked for over five years to produce this addition to the Pattern Jury Charges series. During most of that period the Committee met once a month and spent additional time between meetings doing research and writing drafts of the various questions, instructions, and comments that make up this volume.

The Committee gratefully acknowledges the instrumental role of Chief Justice Thomas R. Phillips, who chaired the Committee from 1985–87. It is also grateful for the help and support of five State Bar presidents: Charles L. Smith (1985–86), Bill Whitehurst (1986–87), Joe H. Nagy (1987–88), James B. Sales (1988–89), and Darrell Jordan (1989–90).

In every successful enterprise there can be found a few key people who make things happen. The chair is particularly grateful for the attendance, participation, and hard work of Tom Black, Ann Cochran, Don Dennis, John Lewis, Peter Linzer, Phil Maxwell, Frank Mitchell, Richard Munzinger, and Dudley Oldham. We are also indebted to numerous other lawyers and judges who read the drafts and offered ideas for improvement—ranging from matters of substantive law to those having to do with style, format, and utility.

Our project legal editor, Vickie Tatum, deserves special recognition for her work on this volume. The State Bar Books and Systems staff has provided invaluable support, and we are also grateful for the advice and counsel of J. Hadley Edgar, chairman of the State Bar standing Committee on Pattern Jury Charges.

—Mike Tabor, *Chair*

PREFACE TO THE 2008 EDITION

With this edition of *Texas Pattern Jury Charges—Business, Consumer, Insurance & Employment*, the book includes a new defamation and business disparagement chapter that builds upon the collective work of the many men and women who have contributed to its pages over the years. This new chapter would not have come to fruition without the initiative, perseverance, and hard work of many Committee members—both past and present.

More than four years ago, former Chairs Sharon Callaway and Tim Chovanec appointed a defamation subcommittee that consisted of Richard Munzinger, David Donaldson, Tim Chovanec, and Karen Precella. After much research and work, Richard prepared an extensive draft on which the subcommittee worked for the following year. Guided by the in-depth defamation knowledge and experience of Richard and David, the full Committee gave the new chapter its usual rigorous review, and practitioners were asked to comment on the proposed patterns. With the completion of the chapter, members returned to their more mundane work, leaving behind the levity of Richard's humorous illustrations of potentially defamatory scenarios.

Each Committee member volunteered countless hours not just to creating the new chapter but to reviewing the entire book. These lawyers have a passion for the law, an attention to detail, and a mission to conform the book to the law as it currently exists. Virtually no detail is too small to debate. We always emerge from this collaborative process with mutual respect and admiration among each other and a new set of friends.

In addition to the Committee members, we would like to thank Sharon Sandle, our State Bar liaison, and the staff of TexasBarBooks for their assistance and guidance in bringing this edition to print.

—Karen Precella, *Chair*
Mark L. Kincaid, *Vice-Chair*

CHANGES IN THE 2008 EDITION

The 2008 edition of *Texas Pattern Jury Charges—Business, Consumer, Insurance & Employment* includes the following changes from the 2006 edition:

1. Admonitory Instructions—Added instruction concerning parallel theories on damages (100.13)

2. Contracts—

    a. Revised the comment on an agreement contemplating further negotiations or writings (101.1)

    b. Added a new comment on UCC cases and anticipatory repudiation (101.23)

    c. Revised the comment on the source of the definition of undue influence (101.27)

3. Fiduciary Duty—

    a. Revised the comment concerning the presumption of unfairness and its effect on the burden of proof (104.2)

    b. Added a comment on knowing participation in another's breach of fiduciary duty (104.2)

4. Interference with Existing and Prospective Contract—Added a brief discussion of contracts that are merely delayed (106.2)

5. Employment—

    a. Revised the question on retaliation (107.9)

    b. Revised the comment discussing the causation standard in retaliation cases (107.9)

6. Piercing the Corporate Veil—

    a. Revised the discussion concerning statutory modification of the standard for piercing the corporate veil set out in *Castleberry v. Branscum* (108.2–.7)

    b. Revised the discussion of "actual fraud" (108.2–.7)

    c. Added a comment on the adoption of the Business Organizations Code (108.2–.7)

7. Defamation—Added chapter 110 covering questions and instructions for use in defamation and business disparagement cases

8. Damages—

   a. Chapter renumbered from 110 to 115

   b. Revised the comments concerning damages in breach of fiduciary duty cases to include discussion of what issues constitute jury questions and a list of the statutory remedies available (115.15)

   c. Added damages questions for use in defamation cases (115.33, 115.34)

   d. Revised the proportionate responsibility question (115.35)

   e. Added a comment concerning additional instructions to address the risk that a jury may award exemplary damages for a constitutionally improper reason (115.37)

   f. Revised the comment concerning the recovery of attorney's fees under chapter 38 of the Texas Civil Practice and Remedies Code (115.46)

   g. Revised the comment concerning segregating claims when attorney's fees are not recoverable for one or more claims (115.46)

INTRODUCTION

1. Purpose of Publication

The purpose of this volume, like those of the others in this series, is to assist the bench and bar in preparing the court's charge in jury cases. It provides definitions, instructions, and questions needed to submit jury charges in the following cases:

- contract cases, both common-law and UCC sale of goods;
- actions under the Texas Deceptive Trade Practices–Consumer Protection Act (DTPA) and the Texas Insurance Code;
- actions against insurers for violation of the duty of good faith and fair dealing;
- breach of fiduciary duty;
- fraud, both common-law and statutory (Tex. Bus. & Com. Code § 27.01), and negligent misrepresentation;
- tortious interference with existing contracts and prospective contractual relations;
- employment actions;
- actions to hold shareholders personally liable for the liabilities of a corporation ("piercing the corporate veil");
- civil conspiracy; and
- defamation and business disparagement.

It also contains questions and comments pertaining to defenses to the above actions and a section on damages.

The pattern charges are suggestions and guides to be used by a trial court if they are applicable and proper in a specific case. The Committee hopes that this volume will prove as worthy as have the earlier *Texas Pattern Jury Charges* volumes.

2. Scope of Pattern Charges

The infinite combinations of possible facts in contract, consumer, employment, and other business cases make it impracticable for the Committee to offer questions suitable for every occasion. The Committee has tried to prepare charges to serve as guides for the usual litigation encountered in these types of cases. However, a charge should conform to the pleadings and evidence of a case, and occasions will arise for the use of questions and instructions not specifically addressed here.

3. Use of Accepted Precedents

Like its predecessors, this Committee has avoided recommending changes in the law and has based this material on what it perceives the present law to be. It has attempted to foresee theories and objections that might be made in a variety of circumstances but not to express favor or disfavor for particular positions. In unsettled areas, the Committee generally has not taken a position on the exact form of a charge. However, it has provided guidelines in some areas in which there is no definitive authority. Of course, trial judges and attorneys should recognize that these recommendations may be affected by future appellate decisions and statutory changes.

4. PRINCIPLES OF STYLE

a. *Preference for broad-form questions.* Tex. R. Civ. P. 277 provides that "the court shall, whenever feasible, submit the cause upon broad-form questions." Accordingly, the basic questions are designed to be accompanied by one or more instructions. *See Texas Department of Human Services v. E.B.*, 802 S.W.2d 647 (Tex. 1990). Three recent cases on proportionate responsibility, damages, and liability, however, indicate that broad-form submission may not be feasible in a variety of circumstances depending on the law, the theories, and the evidence in a given case. *See Romero v. KPH Consolidation, Inc.*, 166 S.W.3d 212 (Tex. 2005) (single broad-form proportionate responsibility question may not be feasible if one theory is legally invalid or not supported by sufficient evidence); *Harris County v. Smith*, 96 S.W.3d 230 (Tex. 2002) (broad-form submission of multiple elements of damage may cause harmful error if one or more of the elements is not supported by sufficient evidence); *Crown Life Insurance Co. v. Casteel*, 22 S.W.3d 378 (Tex. 2000) (broad-form submission combining valid and invalid theories of liability cause of harmful error). As a result, although some modifications to the pattern jury charges have been made where a lack of feasibility appears to be the rule rather than the exception, the court and parties should evaluate all submissions to determine whether broad-form submission is feasible.

b. *Simplicity.* The Committee has sought to be as brief as possible and to use language that is simple and easy to understand.

c. *Definitions and instructions.* The supreme court has disapproved the practice of embellishing standard definitions and instructions, *Lemos v. Montez*, 680 S.W.2d 798 (Tex. 1984), or of adding unnecessary instructions, *First International Bank v. Roper Corp.*, 686 S.W.2d 602 (Tex. 1985). The Committee has endeavored to adhere to standard definitions and instructions stated in general terms rather than terms of the particular parties and facts of the case. If an instruction in general terms would be unduly complicated and confusing, however, reference to specific parties and facts is suggested.

d. *Placement of definitions and instructions in the charges.* Definitions and instructions that apply to a number of questions should be given immediately after the general instructions required by Tex. R. Civ. P. 226a. *See Woods v. Crane Carrier Co.*, 693 S.W.2d 377 (Tex. 1985). However, if a definition or instruction applies to only one question or cluster of questions (e.g., damages questions), it should be placed with that question or cluster. Specific guidance for placement of definitions and instructions can be found in the individual PJCs and comments.

e. *Burden of proof.* As authorized by Tex. R. Civ. P. 277, it is recommended that the burden of proof be placed by instruction rather than by inclusion in each question.

When the burden is placed by instruction, it is not necessary that each question begin: "Do you find from a preponderance of the evidence that . . ." The admonitory instructions contain the following instruction, applicable to all questions:

> Answer "Yes" or "No" to all questions unless otherwise instructed. A "Yes" answer must be based on a preponderance of the evidence unless you are otherwise instructed. If you do not find that a preponderance of the evidence supports a "Yes" answer, then answer "No." The term "preponderance of the evidence" means the greater weight of credible evidence admitted in this case. A preponderance of the evidence is not measured by the number of witnesses or by the number of documents admitted in evidence. For a fact to be proved by a preponderance of the evidence, you must find that the fact is more likely true than not true. Whenever a question requires an answer other than "Yes" or "No," your answer must be based on a preponderance of the evidence unless you are otherwise instructed.

f. *Hypothetical examples.* The names of hypothetical parties and facts have been italicized to indicate that the names and facts of the particular case should be substituted. In general, the name *Paul Payne* has been used for the plaintiff and *Don Davis* for the defendant. Some PJCs use other hypothetical parties (see, e.g., PJC 115.35). Their use is explained in the comments.

5. Comments and Citations of Authority

The comments to each PJC provide a ready reference to the law that serves as a foundation for the charge. The primary authority cited is Texas (or, for employment law, federal) case law. In some instances, secondary authority—for example, *Restatement (Second) of Contracts*—is also cited. The Committee wishes to emphasize that secondary authority is cited solely as additional guidance to the reader and not as legal authority for the proposition stated. Some comments also include variations of the recommended forms and additional questions or instructions for special circumstances.

6. Using the Pattern Charges

Matters on which the evidence is undisputed should not be submitted by either instruction or question. Conversely, questions, instructions, and definitions not included in this book may sometimes become necessary. Finally, preparation of a proper charge requires careful legal analysis and sound judgment.

7. FUTURE REVISIONS

The contents of questions, instructions, and definitions in the court's charge depend on the underlying substantive law relevant to the case. The Committee expects to publish updates as needed to reflect changes and new developments in the law.

CHAPTER 100 ADMONITORY INSTRUCTIONS

PJC 100.1 Instructions to Jury Panel before Voir Dire Examination

LADIES AND GENTLEMEN OF THE JURY PANEL:

The case that is now on trial is *Paul Payne* vs. *Don Davis*. This is a civil action which will be tried before a jury. Your duty as jurors will be to decide the disputed facts. It is the duty of the judge to see that the case is tried in accordance with the rules of law. In this case, as in all cases, the actions of the judge, parties, witnesses, attorneys and jurors must be according to law. The Texas law permits proof of any violation of the rules of proper jury conduct. By this I mean that jurors and others may be called upon to testify in open court about acts of jury misconduct. I instruct you, therefore, to follow carefully all instructions which I am now going to give you, as well as others which you will receive while this case is on trial. If you do not obey the instructions I am about to give you, it may become necessary for another jury to re-try this case with all of the attendant waste of your time here and the expense to the litigants and the taxpayers of this county for another trial. These instructions are as follows:

1. Do not mingle with nor talk to the lawyers, the witnesses, the parties, or any other person who might be connected with or interested in this case, except for casual greetings. They have to follow these same instructions and you will understand it when they do.

2. Do not accept from, nor give to, any of those persons any favors however slight, such as rides, food or refreshments.

3. Do not discuss anything about this case, or even mention it to anyone whomsoever, including your wife or husband, nor permit anyone to mention it in your hearing until you are discharged as jurors or excused from this case. If anyone attempts to discuss the case, report it to me at once.

4 The parties through their attorneys have the right to direct questions to each of you concerning your qualifications, background, experiences and attitudes. In questioning you, they are not meddling in your personal affairs, but are trying to select fair and impartial jurors who are free from any bias or prejudice in this particular case.

a. Do not conceal information or give answers which are not true. Listen to the questions and give full and complete answers.

b. If the attorneys ask some questions directed to you as a group which require an answer on your part individually, hold up your hand until you have answered the questions.

Do you understand these instructions? If not, please let me know now.

Whether you are selected as a juror for this case or not, you are performing a significant service which only free people can perform. We shall try the case as fast as possible consistent with justice, which requires a careful and correct trial. If selected on the jury, unless I instruct you differently, you will be permitted to separate at recesses and for meals, and at night.

The attorneys will now proceed with their examination.

COMMENT

When to use. The foregoing oral instructions are prescribed in Tex. R. Civ. P. 226a. The instructions, "with such modifications as the circumstances of the particular case may require," are to be given to the jury panel "after they have been sworn as provided in Rule 226 and before the voir dire examination."

Caveat. As this edition went to press, the Supreme Court Advisory Committee was considering changes in the admonitory instructions for recommendation to the Supreme Court of Texas. For updates on the status of these recommendations, any changes to the approved instructions under rule 226a of the Texas Rules of Civil Procedure adopted by the Supreme Court, and any new pattern jury charges promulgated in response to such changes, visit **Update.TexasBarBooks.com** (book ID: 6454).

PJC 100.2 Instructions to Jury after Jury Selection

[Oral Instructions]

LADIES AND GENTLEMEN:

By the oath which you take as jurors, you become officials of this court and active participants in the public administration of justice. I now give you further instructions which you must obey throughout this trial.

It is your duty to listen to and consider the evidence and to determine fact issues later submitted to you, but I, as judge, will decide matters of the law. You will now receive written instructions which you will observe during this trial, together with such other instructions as I may hereafter give, or as heretofore I have given to you.

[A copy of the written instructions set out below shall thereupon be handed to each juror.]

As you examine the instructions which have just been handed to you, we will go over them briefly together. The first three instructions have previously been stated, and you will continue to observe them throughout the trial. These and the other instructions just handed to you are as follows:

[The written instructions set out below shall thereupon be read by the court to the jury.]

Counsel, you may proceed.

[Written Instructions]

1. Do not mingle with nor talk to the lawyers, the witnesses, the parties, or any other person who might be connected with or interested in this case, except for casual greetings. They have to follow these same instructions and you will understand it when they do.

2. Do not accept from, nor give to, any of those persons any favors however slight, such as rides, food or refreshments.

3. Do not discuss anything about this case, or even mention it to anyone whomsoever, including your wife or husband nor permit anyone to mention it in your hearing until you are discharged as jurors or excused from this case. If anyone attempts to discuss the case, report it to me at once.

4. Do not even discuss this case among yourselves until after you have heard all of the evidence, the court's charge, the attorneys' arguments and until I have sent you to the jury room to consider your verdict.

5. Do not make any investigation about the facts of this case. Occasionally we have a juror who privately seeks out information about a case on trial. This is improper. All evidence must be presented in open court so that each side may question the witnesses and make proper objection. This avoids a trial based upon secret evidence. These rules apply to jurors the same as they apply to the parties and to me. If you know of, or learn anything about, this case except from the evidence admitted during the course of this trial, you should tell me about it at once. You have just taken an oath that you will render a verdict on the evidence submitted to you under my rulings.

6. Do not make personal inspections, observations, investigations, or experiments nor personally view premises, things or articles not produced in court. Do not let anyone else do any of these things for you.

7. Do not tell other jurors your own personal experiences nor those of other persons, nor relate any special information. A juror may have special knowledge of matters such as business, technical or professional matters or he may have expert knowledge or opinions, or he may know what happened in this or some other lawsuit. To tell the other jurors any of this information is a violation of these instructions.

8. Do not discuss or consider attorney's fees unless evidence about attorney's fees is admitted.

9. Do not consider, discuss, nor speculate whether or not any party is or is not protected in whole or in part by insurance of any kind.

10. Do not seek information contained in law books, dictionaries, public or private records or elsewhere, which is not admitted in evidence.

At the conclusion of all the evidence, I may submit to you a written charge asking you some specific questions. You will not be asked, and you should not consider, whether one party or the other should win. Since you will need to consider all of the evidence admitted by me, it is important that you pay close attention to the evidence as it is presented.

The Texas law permits proof of any violation of the rules of proper jury conduct. By this I mean that jurors and others may be called upon to testify in open court about acts of jury misconduct. I instruct you, therefore, to follow carefully all instructions which I have given you, as well as others which you later receive while this case is on trial.

You may keep these instructions and review them as the case proceeds. A violation of these instructions should be reported to me.

COMMENT

When to use. The foregoing instructions are prescribed in Tex. R. Civ. P. 226a. The instructions, "with such modifications as the circumstances of the particular case may require," are to be given to the jury "immediately after the jurors are selected for the case."

If no tort claim is involved. Item 9 should be deleted from the foregoing instructions unless a tort claim is involved in the case.

Caveat. As this edition went to press, the Supreme Court Advisory Committee was considering changes in the admonitory instructions for recommendation to the Supreme Court of Texas. For updates on the status of these recommendations, any changes to the approved instructions under rule 226a of the Texas Rules of Civil Procedure adopted by the Supreme Court, and any new pattern jury charges promulgated in response to such changes, visit **Update.TexasBarBooks.com** (book ID: 6454).

PJC 100.3 Charge of the Court

LADIES AND GENTLEMEN OF THE JURY:

This case is submitted to you by asking questions about the facts, which you must decide from the evidence you have heard in this trial. You are the sole judges of the credibility of the witnesses and the weight to be given their testimony, but in matters of law, you must be governed by the instructions in this charge. In discharging your responsibility on this jury, you will observe all the instructions which have previously been given you. I shall now give you additional instructions which you should carefully and strictly follow during your deliberations.

1. Do not let bias, prejudice or sympathy play any part in your deliberations.

2. In arriving at your answers, consider only the evidence introduced here under oath and such exhibits, if any, as have been introduced for your consideration under the rulings of the court, that is, what you have seen and heard in this courtroom, together with the law as given you by the court. In your deliberations, you will not consider or discuss anything that is not represented by the evidence in this case.

3. Since every answer that is required by the charge is important, no juror should state or consider that any required answer is not important.

4. You must not decide who you think should win, and then try to answer the questions accordingly. Simply answer the questions, and do not discuss nor concern yourselves with the effect of your answers.

5. You will not decide the answer to a question by lot or by drawing straws, or by any other method of chance. Do not return a quotient verdict. A quotient verdict means that the jurors agree to abide by the result to be reached by adding together each juror's figures and dividing by the number of jurors to get an average. Do not do any trading on your answers; that is, one juror should not agree to answer a certain question one way if others will agree to answer another question another way.

6. Unless otherwise instructed, you may answer a question upon the vote of ten or more jurors. If you answer more than one question upon the vote of ten or more jurors, the same group of at least ten of you must agree upon the answers to each of those questions.

These instructions are given you because your conduct is subject to review the same as that of the witnesses, parties, attorneys and the judge. If it should be found that you have disregarded any of these instructions, it will be jury misconduct and it may require another trial by another jury; then all of our time will have been wasted.

The presiding juror or any other who observes a violation of the court's instructions shall immediately warn the one who is violating the same and caution the juror not to do so again.

When words are used in this charge in a sense that varies from the meaning commonly understood, you are given a proper legal definition, which you are bound to accept in place of any other meaning.

Answer "Yes" or "No" to all questions unless otherwise instructed. A "Yes" answer must be based on a preponderance of the evidence unless you are otherwise instructed. If you do not find that a preponderance of the evidence supports a "Yes" answer, then answer "No." The term "preponderance of the evidence" means the greater weight of credible evidence admitted in this case. A preponderance of the evidence is not measured by the number of witnesses or by the number of documents admitted in evidence. For a fact to be proved by a preponderance of the evidence, you must find that the fact is more likely true than not true. Whenever a question requires an answer other than "Yes" or "No," your answer must be based on a preponderance of the evidence unless you are otherwise instructed.

[Definitions, questions, and special instructions given to the jury will be transcribed here.]

After you retire to the jury room, you will select your own presiding juror. The first thing the presiding juror will do is to have this complete charge read aloud and then you will deliberate upon your answers to the questions asked.

It is the duty of the presiding juror—

1. to preside during your deliberations,
2. to see that your deliberations are conducted in an orderly manner and in accordance with the instructions in this charge,
3. to write out and hand to the bailiff any communications concerning the case that you desire to have delivered to the judge,
4. to vote on the questions,
5. to write your answers to the questions in the spaces provided, and

6. to certify to your verdict in the space provided for the presiding juror's signature or to obtain the signatures of all the jurors who agree with the verdict if your verdict is less than unanimous.

You should not discuss the case with anyone, not even with other members of the jury, unless all of you are present and assembled in the jury room. Should anyone attempt to talk to you about the case before the verdict is returned, whether at the courthouse, at your home, or elsewhere, please inform the judge of this fact.

When you have answered all the questions you are required to answer under the instructions of the judge and your presiding juror has placed your answers in the spaces provided and signed the verdict as presiding juror or obtained the signatures, you will inform the bailiff at the door of the jury room that you have reached a verdict, and then you will return into court with your verdict.

____

JUDGE PRESIDING

[If none of the jury's answers must be unanimous, use the following certificate.]

Certificate

We, the jury, have answered the above and foregoing questions as herein indicated, and herewith return same into court as our verdict.

(To be signed by the presiding juror if the jury is unanimous.)

____

PRESIDING JUROR

____

Printed Name of Presiding Juror

(To be signed by those rendering the verdict if the jury is not unanimous.)

Jurors' Signatures | Jurors' Printed Names

[Insert appropriate number of lines.]

____________________ ____________________

____________________ ____________________

____________________ ____________________

____________________ ____________________

____________________ ____________________

____________________ ____________________

____________________ ____________________

____________________ ____________________

____________________ ____________________

____________________ ____________________

____________________ ____________________

[If some of the jury's answers must be unanimous and others need not be, use the following certificate.]

Certificate

We, the jury, have answered the above and foregoing questions as herein indicated, and herewith return same into court as our verdict.

I certify that the jury was unanimous in answering the following questions:

Answer "All" or list questions: ____________________

____

PRESIDING JUROR

____
Printed Name of Presiding Juror

(If the answers to some questions were not unanimous, the jurors who agreed to those answers must certify as follows:)

We agree to the answers to the following questions:

List questions: ______________________

Jurors' Signatures | Jurors' Printed Names

[Insert appropriate number of lines.]

______________________________ ______________________________

______________________________ ______________________________

______________________________ ______________________________

______________________________ ______________________________

______________________________ ______________________________

______________________________ ______________________________

______________________________ ______________________________

______________________________ ______________________________

______________________________ ______________________________

______________________________ ______________________________

______________________________ ______________________________

COMMENT

When to use. The above charge of the court includes the written instructions required by the supreme court's January 27, 2005, order under Tex. R. Civ. P. 226a. The paragraph beginning with "Answer 'Yes' or 'No'" has been added to the form prescribed under rule 226a and is necessary to place the burden of proof by instruction. The paragraph beginning with "When words are used in this charge" and all the language from "It is the duty of the presiding juror" to the end of the charge have also been added to the form prescribed under rule 226a. It is the Committee's view that these additional instructions are desirable.

Alternative format. The court's order also provides:

> The court may also determine that a clearer way of obtaining the required certificate is to segregate the questions to which the jury's answers must be unanimous and request a certificate for each part of the charge.

Tex. R. Civ. P. 226a, Approved Instructions (Order of the Supreme Court of Texas dated Jan. 27, 2005, Misc. Docket No. 05-9022).

Caveat. As this edition went to press, the Supreme Court Advisory Committee was considering changes in the admonitory instructions for recommendation to the Supreme Court of Texas. For updates on the status of these recommendations, any changes to the approved instructions under rule 226a of the Texas Rules of Civil Procedure adopted by the Supreme Court, and any new pattern jury charges promulgated in response to such changes, visit **Update.TexasBarBooks.com** (book ID: 6454).

PJC 100.4 Additional Instruction for Bifurcated Trial

LADIES AND GENTLEMEN OF THE JURY:

In discharging your responsibility on this jury, you will observe all the instructions that have been previously given you.

____

JUDGE PRESIDING

Certificate

We, the jury, have answered the above and foregoing question[*s*] as herein indicated, and herewith return same into court as our verdict.

I certify that the jury was unanimous in answering the following question[*s*]:

Answer "All" or list questions: ________________________

____

PRESIDING JUROR

____

Printed Name of Presiding Juror

COMMENT

When to use. PJC 100.4 should be used as an instruction for the second phase of a bifurcated trial pursuant to *Transportation Insurance Co. v. Moriel*, 879 S.W.2d 10, 29–30 (Tex. 1994), or Tex. Civ. Prac. & Rem. Code § 41.009.

Source of instruction. The instruction comes from the supreme court's January 27, 2005, order under Tex. R. Civ. P. 226a. *See also* Tex. Civ. Prac. & Rem. Code § 41.003(d), (e).

Actions filed before September 1, 2003. For actions filed before September 1, 2003, add the following instruction derived from *Hyman Farm Service, Inc. v. Earth Oil*

& *Gas Co.*, 920 S.W.2d 452 (Tex. App.—Amarillo 1996, no writ), along with signature lines for jurors to use if the verdict is not unanimous:

> I shall now give you additional instructions that you should carefully and strictly follow during your deliberations.
>
> All jurors have the right and the responsibility to deliberate on [*this*] [*these*] question[*s*], but at least ten of those who agreed to the verdict in the first phase of this trial must agree to this answer and sign this verdict accordingly. If your first verdict was unanimous, this second verdict may be rendered by the vote of at least ten of you.

Caveat. As this edition went to press, the Supreme Court Advisory Committee was considering changes in the admonitory instructions for recommendation to the Supreme Court of Texas. For updates on the status of these recommendations, any changes to the approved instructions under rule 226a of the Texas Rules of Civil Procedure adopted by the Supreme Court, and any new pattern jury charges promulgated in response to such changes, visit **Update.TexasBarBooks.com** (book ID: 6454).

PJC 100.5 Instructions to Jury after Verdict

The court has previously instructed you that you should observe strict secrecy during the trial and during your deliberations, and that you should not discuss this case with anyone except other jurors during your deliberations. I am now about to discharge you. After your discharge, you are released from your secrecy. You will then be free to discuss the case and your deliberations with anyone. However, you are also free to decline to discuss the case and your deliberations if you wish.

After you are discharged, it is lawful for the attorneys or other persons to question you to determine whether any of the standards for jury conduct which I have given you in the course of this trial were violated and to ask you to give an affidavit to that effect. You are free to discuss or not to discuss these matters and to give or not to give an affidavit.

COMMENT

When to use. The foregoing instructions are prescribed in Tex. R. Civ. P. 226a. The instructions are to be given orally to the jury "after the verdict has been accepted by the court and before the jurors are discharged."

Caveat. As this edition went to press, the Supreme Court Advisory Committee was considering changes in the admonitory instructions for recommendation to the Supreme Court of Texas. For updates on the status of these recommendations, any changes to the approved instructions under rule 226a of the Texas Rules of Civil Procedure adopted by the Supreme Court, and any new pattern jury charges promulgated in response to such changes, visit **Update.TexasBarBooks.com** (book ID: 6454).

PJC 100.6 Instruction to Jury If Permitted to Separate

You are again instructed that it is your duty not to converse with, or permit yourselves to be addressed by, any other person on any subject connected with this trial.

COMMENT

When to use. The foregoing instruction is required by Tex. R. Civ. P. 284, which states, "If permitted to separate, either during the trial or after the case is submitted to them, the jury shall be admonished by the court that it is their duty not to converse with, or permit themselves to be addressed by any other person, on any subject connected with the trial."

Caveat. As this edition went to press, the Supreme Court Advisory Committee was considering changes in the admonitory instructions for recommendation to the Supreme Court of Texas. For updates on the status of these recommendations, any changes to the approved instructions under rule 226a of the Texas Rules of Civil Procedure adopted by the Supreme Court, and any new pattern jury charges promulgated in response to such changes, visit **Update.TexasBarBooks.com** (book ID: 6454).

PJC 100.7 Instruction If Jury Disagrees about Testimony

MEMBERS OF THE JURY:

You have made the following request in writing:

[Insert copy of request.]

Your request is governed by the following rule:

> "If the jury disagree as to the statement of any witness, they may, upon applying to the court, have read to them from the court reporter's notes that part of such witness' testimony on the point in dispute . . . ."

If you report that you disagree concerning the statement of a witness and specify the point on which you disagree, the court reporter will search his notes and read to you the testimony of the witness on the point.

____
JUDGE PRESIDING

COMMENT

When to use. This written instruction is based on Tex. R. Civ. P. 287 and is to be used if the jurors request that testimony from the court reporter's notes be read to them.

Caveat. As this edition went to press, the Supreme Court Advisory Committee was considering changes in the admonitory instructions for recommendation to the Supreme Court of Texas. For updates on the status of these recommendations, any changes to the approved instructions under rule 226a of the Texas Rules of Civil Procedure adopted by the Supreme Court, and any new pattern jury charges promulgated in response to such changes, visit **Update.TexasBarBooks.com** (book ID: 6454).

PJC 100.8 Circumstantial Evidence

A fact may be established by direct evidence or by circumstantial evidence or both. A fact is established by direct evidence when proved by documentary evidence or by witnesses who saw the act done or heard the words spoken. A fact is established by circumstantial evidence when it may be fairly and reasonably inferred from other facts proved.

COMMENT

When to use. PJC 100.8 may be used if there is circumstantial evidence in the case. It would be placed in the charge of the court (PJC 100.3) after the instruction on preponderance of the evidence and immediately before the definitions, questions, and special instructions. For cases defining circumstantial evidence, see *Blount v. Bordens, Inc.*, 910 S.W.2d 931, 933 (Tex. 1995) (per curiam); and *Russell v. Russell*, 865 S.W.2d 929, 933 (Tex. 1993). It is not error to give or to refuse an instruction on circumstantial evidence. *Larson v. Ellison*, 217 S.W.2d 420 (Tex. 1949); *Johnson v. Zurich General Accident & Liability Insurance Co.*, 205 S.W.2d 353 (Tex. 1947); *Adams v. Valley Federal Credit Union*, 848 S.W.2d 182, 188 (Tex. App.—Corpus Christi 1992, writ denied).

Caveat. As this edition went to press, the Supreme Court Advisory Committee was considering changes in the admonitory instructions for recommendation to the Supreme Court of Texas. For updates on the status of these recommendations, any changes to the approved instructions under rule 226a of the Texas Rules of Civil Procedure adopted by the Supreme Court, and any new pattern jury charges promulgated in response to such changes, visit **Update.TexasBarBooks.com** (book ID: 6454).

PJC 100.9 Proximate Cause

"Proximate cause" means that cause which, in a natural and continuous sequence, produces an event, and without which cause such event would not have occurred. In order to be a proximate cause, the act or omission complained of must be such that a person using the degree of care required of him would have foreseen that the event, or some similar event, might reasonably result therefrom. There may be more than one proximate cause of an event.

COMMENT

Caveat. In *Ford Motor Co. v. Ledesma*, 242 S.W.3d 32, 46 (Tex. 2007), the court held that the definition of "producing cause" should contain the "substantial factor" language. In light of that holding and previous supreme court cases discussing the similarities between producing and proximate cause (*see, e.g., Union Pump Co. v. Allbritton*, 898 S.W.2d 773, 775 (Tex. 1995)), the definition of "proximate cause" may need to be modified to include the "substantial factor" language as follows:

"Proximate cause" has two parts:

1. a proximate cause is a substantial factor that [*in a natural and continuous sequence*] brings about an event and without which the event would not have occurred; and

2. a proximate cause is foreseeable. "Foreseeable" means that a person using ordinary care would have reasonably anticipated that his acts or failure to act would have caused the event or some similar event.

There may be more than one proximate cause of an event.

The phrase "in a natural and continuous sequence" is bracketed because it is unclear whether those words remain necessary in light of the "substantial factor" language and the apparent deletion of "in a natural sequence" from the analysis of "producing cause" in *Ledesma*. *Ledesma*, 242 S.W.3d at 46. The Committee has also attempted to make the language more understandable to the average juror.

When to use. PJC 100.9 should be used in every case in which a finding of proximate cause is required. It is based on the definition approved by the court in *Rudes v. Gottschalk*, 324 S.W.2d 201, 207 (Tex. 1959). For a discussion of the element of "foreseeability," see *Motsenbocker v. Wyatt*, 369 S.W.2d 319, 323 (Tex. 1963); and *Carey v. Pure Distributing Corp.*, 124 S.W.2d 847, 849 (Tex. 1939).

Caveat. As this edition went to press, the Supreme Court Advisory Committee was considering changes in the admonitory instructions for recommendation to the Supreme Court of Texas. For updates on the status of these recommendations, any changes to the approved instructions under rule 226a of the Texas Rules of Civil Procedure adopted by the Supreme Court, and any new pattern jury charges promulgated in response to such changes, visit **Update.TexasBarBooks.com** (book ID: 6454).

PJC 100.10 Instructions to Deadlocked Jury

I have your note that you are deadlocked. In the interest of justice, if you could end this litigation by your verdict, you should do so.

I do not mean to say that any individual juror should yield his or her own conscience and positive conviction, but I do mean that when you are in the jury room, you should discuss this matter carefully, listen to each other, and try, if you can, to reach a conclusion on the questions. It is your duty as a juror to keep your mind open and free to every reasonable argument that may be presented by your fellow jurors so that this jury may arrive at a verdict that justly answers the consciences of the individuals making up this jury. You should not have any pride of opinion and should avoid hastily forming or expressing an opinion. At the same time, you should not surrender any conscientious views founded on the evidence unless convinced of your error by your fellow jurors.

If you fail to reach a verdict, this case may have to be tried before another jury. Then all of our time will have been wasted.

Accordingly, I return you to your deliberations.

COMMENT

Source. The foregoing instructions are modeled on the charge in *Stevens v. Travelers Insurance Co.*, 563 S.W.2d 223 (Tex. 1978), and on Tex. R. Civ. P. 226a.

Caveat. As this edition went to press, the Supreme Court Advisory Committee was considering changes in the admonitory instructions for recommendation to the Supreme Court of Texas. For updates on the status of these recommendations, any changes to the approved instructions under rule 226a of the Texas Rules of Civil Procedure adopted by the Supreme Court, and any new pattern jury charges promulgated in response to such changes, visit **Update.TexasBarBooks.com** (book ID: 6454).

PJC 100.11 Instructions on Jurors' Note-Taking (Comment)

A number of trial judges permit jurors to take notes during the presentation of evidence. *See Manges v. Willoughby*, 505 S.W.2d 379 (Tex. Civ. App.—San Antonio 1974, writ ref'd n.r.e.). The Committee expresses no opinion on this practice. If, however, jurors are allowed to take notes during the trial, they should be instructed, both after jury selection and before retiring to deliberate, on how the notes are to be taken and used. Some of the points a judge may wish to cover are contained in the following sample instructions.

[To be included in PJC 100.2 (instructions to jury after jury selection):]

During trial, if taking notes will help focus your attention on the evidence, you may take notes. If taking notes will distract your attention from the evidence, you should not take notes. Any notes you take are for your own personal use, and you may not share them with other jurors. Your personal recollection of the evidence takes precedence over any notes you have taken. A juror may not rely on the notes of another juror.

[To be included in PJC 100.3 (charge of the court):]

During trial it was permissible for you to take notes. You may carry those notes to the jury room for your personal use during deliberation on the court's charge. You may not share these notes with other jurors. Your personal recollection of the evidence takes precedence over any notes you have taken. A juror may not rely on the notes of another juror. If you disagree about the evidence, the presiding juror may apply to the court and have the court reporter's notes read to the jury.

Caveat. As this edition went to press, the Supreme Court Advisory Committee was considering changes in the admonitory instructions for recommendation to the Supreme Court of Texas. For updates on the status of these recommendations, any changes to the approved instructions under rule 226a of the Texas Rules of Civil Procedure adopted by the Supreme Court, and any new pattern jury charges promulgated in response to such changes, visit **Update.TexasBarBooks.com** (book ID: 6454).

PJC 100.12 Privilege—No Adverse Inference

You are instructed that you may not draw an adverse inference from [*name of party*]'s claim of [*privilege asserted*] privilege.

COMMENT

When to use. On request by any party against whom the jury might draw an adverse inference from a claim of privilege, the court shall instruct the jury that no inference may be drawn therefrom. Tex. R. Evid. 513(d). The court is not required by rule 513(d) to submit such an instruction regarding the privilege against self-incrimination. Tex. R. Evid. 513(c), (d). *See also Wilz v. Flournoy*, 228 S.W.3d 674 (Tex. 2007).

Scope of assertion of privilege. The Committee expresses no opinion as to the propriety of such an instruction on the assertion of a privilege by a nonparty witness.

Caveat. As this edition went to press, the Supreme Court Advisory Committee was considering changes in the admonitory instructions for recommendation to the Supreme Court of Texas. For updates on the status of these recommendations, any changes to the approved instructions under rule 226a of the Texas Rules of Civil Procedure adopted by the Supreme Court, and any new pattern jury charges promulgated in response to such changes, visit **Update.TexasBarBooks.com** (book ID: 6454).

PJC 100.13 Parallel Theories on Damages

In answering questions about damages, answer each question separately. Do not increase or reduce the amount in one answer because of your answer to any other question about damages. Do not speculate about what any party's ultimate recovery may or may not be. Any recovery will be determined by the court when it applies the law to your answers at the time of judgment.

COMMENT

When to use. If several theories of recovery are submitted in the charge and any theory has a different legal measure of damages to be applied to a factually similar claim for damages, the Committee recommends that a separate damages question for each theory be submitted and that the above additional instruction be included earlier in the charge.

Caveat. As this edition went to press, the Supreme Court Advisory Committee was considering changes in the admonitory instructions for recommendation to the Supreme Court of Texas. For updates on the status of these recommendations, any changes to the approved instructions under rule 226a of the Texas Rules of Civil Procedure adopted by the Supreme Court, and any new pattern jury charges promulgated in response to such changes, visit **Update.TexasBarBooks.com** (book ID: 6454).

CHAPTER 101 CONTRACTS

PJC 101.1 Basic Question—Existence

QUESTION ______

Did *Paul Payne* and *Don Davis* agree [*insert all disputed terms*]?

[Insert instructions, if appropriate.]

Answer: _______________

COMMENT

When to use. PJC 101.1 submits the issue of the existence of an agreement. It should be used if there is a dispute about the existence of an agreement or its terms and a specific factual finding is necessary to determine whether the agreement constitutes a legally binding contract. (See the discussion of consideration and essential terms below.) Usually PJC 101.1 will apply in cases involving oral agreements, oral modification of written agreements, and agreements based on several written instruments.

Broad-form submission. The broad form of this question follows the mandate of Tex. R. Civ. P. 277, which states: "In all jury cases the court shall, whenever feasible, submit the cause upon broad-form questions."

In some cases an even broader question that combines issues of both existence and breach of an agreement may be appropriate. For example:

Did *Don Davis* fail to comply with the agreement, if any?

In such a case, however, care should be taken that the submission does not ask the jury to decide questions of law, which must be determined by the court alone. *Lone Star Steel Co. v. Scott*, 759 S.W.2d 144, 157 (Tex. App.—Texarkana 1988, writ denied) (whether agreement constitutes binding contract and interpretation of that contract are questions of law).

Accompanying instructions. In cases involving straightforward factual disputes about the existence of an agreement, no definition of "agreement" is required. *Texaco, Inc. v. Pennzoil Co.*, 729 S.W.2d 768, 814 (Tex. App.—Houston [1st Dist.] 1987, writ ref'd n.r.e.), *cert. dismissed*, 485 U.S. 994 (1988) (applying New York law); *Mann v. Fender*, 587 S.W.2d 188, 199 (Tex. Civ. App.—Waco 1979, writ ref'd n.r.e.); *West Texas State Bank v. Tri-Service Drilling Co.*, 339 S.W.2d 249, 256 (Tex. Civ. App.—Eastland 1960, writ ref'd n.r.e.). If questions relating to contract formation are involved, however, additional instructions will be required. See PJC 101.3.

Essential terms. To form a valid contract, the parties must have the same understanding of the subject matter of the contract and all its essential terms. *Smulcer v. Rog-*

ers, 256 S.W.2d 120, 121–22 (Tex. Civ. App.—Fort Worth 1953, writ ref'd n.r.e.). To be enforceable, a contract must be reasonably definite and certain. *T.O. Stanley Boot Co. v. Bank of El Paso*, 847 S.W.2d 218, 221 (Tex. 1992); *Kirkwood & Morgan, Inc. v. Roach*, 360 S.W.2d 173, 175 (Tex. Civ. App.—San Antonio 1962, writ ref'd n.r.e.). Failure to agree on or include an essential term renders a contract unenforceable. *T.O. Stanley Boot Co.*, 847 S.W.2d at 221; *Wheeler v. White*, 398 S.W.2d 93 (Tex. 1965); *Weitzman v. Steinberg*, 638 S.W.2d 171, 175 (Tex. App.—Dallas 1982, no writ); *Estate of Eberling v. Fair*, 546 S.W.2d 329, 333–34 (Tex. Civ. App.—Dallas 1976, writ ref'd n.r.e.). The court should include in PJC 101.1, therefore, all disputed terms essential to create an enforceable agreement. A disputed nonessential term should also be included if it is the basis of the plaintiff's claim for damages.

Some omitted terms supplied by law. Some omitted terms, however, will be supplied by application of law, and the failure to include those terms will not render the agreement invalid. See, e.g., PJC 101.10 (instruction on time of compliance) and 101.13 (instruction on price). In such cases it is not necessary to secure a jury finding on the parties' agreement to those terms, and they should not be included in PJC 101.1 unless their absence will be confusing to the jury. The circumstances of each case will determine whether it is appropriate to include instructions such as those contemplated by PJC 101.10 and 101.13.

Agreement contemplating further negotiations or writings. During negotiations, the parties may agree to some terms of the agreement with the expectation that other terms are to be agreed on later. In many instances, such an expectation does not prevent the agreement already made from being an enforceable agreement. *Scott v. Ingle Bros. Pacific, Inc.*, 489 S.W.2d 554, 555 (Tex. 1972); *see also Simmons & Simmons Construction Co. v. Rea*, 286 S.W.2d 415 (Tex. 1955); *but see Ski River Development, Inc. v. McCalla*, 167 S.W.3d 121, 134 (Tex. App.—Waco 2005, pet. denied) (when contract left material and essential terms for future negotiation, agreement was not definite and specific and, therefore, was not enforceable). In such a case, the basic issue submitted in PJC 101.1 should be modified to inquire whether the parties intended to bind themselves to an agreement that includes the terms initially agreed on. *Scott*, 489 S.W.2d at 555. Case law suggests the following question:

Did *Paul Payne* and *Don Davis* intend to bind themselves to an agreement that included the following terms:

[Insert disputed terms.]

See Scott, 489 S.W.2d at 555; *see also Texaco, Inc.*, 729 S.W.2d at 812.

A similar issue is presented if the parties reach preliminary agreement on certain material terms yet also contemplate a future written document. Whether the parties intended to be bound in the absence of execution of the final written document is ordinarily a question of fact. *Foreca, S.A. v. GRD Development Co.*, 758 S.W.2d 744 (Tex. 1988). The *Foreca* opinion approves the following submission in such a case:

> Do you find that the writings of *September 2, 1983*, and *October 19, 1983*, constituted an agreement whereby [*insert disputed terms*]?

The court cited comment c to section 27 of the *Restatement (Second) of Contracts* (1981) as setting forth circumstances that may be helpful in determining whether a contract has been formed. *Foreca, S.A.*, 758 S.W.2d at 746 n.2. The court did not make it clear, however, whether these considerations should be included in the jury instructions.

PJC 101.2 Basic Question—Compliance

QUESTION ______

Did *Don Davis* fail to comply with *the agreement*?

[Insert instructions, if appropriate.]

Answer: _______________

COMMENT

When to use. If breach is the only issue in dispute, no predicate is required. Otherwise, PJC 101.2 should be submitted predicated on an affirmative answer to PJC 101.1.

Broad-form submission. Tex. R. Civ. P. 277 mandates broad-form submission whenever feasible. *See Ryan Mortgage Investors v. Fleming-Wood*, 650 S.W.2d 928, 932–33 (Tex. App.—Fort Worth 1983, writ ref'd n.r.e.) (approving broad question in written contract case); *Jon-T Farms, Inc. v. Goodpasture, Inc.*, 554 S.W.2d 743, 750–51 (Tex. Civ. App.—Amarillo 1977, writ ref'd n.r.e.) (approving broad question in UCC sale-of-goods case). If there is legal uncertainty on one or more theories of recovery, broad-form submission may not be feasible and separate questions may be required. *See Crown Life Insurance Co. v. Casteel*, 22 S.W.3d 378, 388–89 (Tex. 2000) (broad-form submission combining valid and invalid theories was harmful error). For further discussion, see Introduction 4(a). When a broad-form submission is not feasible, the cause may be submitted on more limited fact-specific questions, such as—

Did *Don Davis* fail [*insert alleged failure*]?

Disjunctive question for competing claims of material breach. If both parties allege a breach of contract against one another, the court can ask the breach-of-contract question disjunctively, together with an appropriate instruction directing the jury to decide who committed the first material breach. *Mustang Pipeline Co. v. Driver Pipeline Co.*, 134 S.W.3d 195, 200 (Tex. 2004). An alternative way to submit competing claims of breach of an agreement is set forth below.

QUESTION 1

Did *Don Davis* fail to comply with *the agreement*?

[Insert instructions, if appropriate.]

Answer: _______________

QUESTION 2

Did *Paul Payne* fail to comply with *the agreement*?

[Insert instructions, if appropriate.]

Answer: _______________

If you answered "Yes" to both Question 1 and Question 2, then answer Question 3. Otherwise, do not answer Question 3.

QUESTION 3

Who failed to comply with *the agreement* first?

Answer "*Don Davis*" or "*Paul Payne.*"

Answer: _______________

The Committee believes that this conditional submission satisfies the supreme court's instruction in *Mustang Pipeline Co.*, 134 S.W.3d at 200, to have the jury determine which party breached first and thereby excused performance by the other party. *See Mustang Pipeline Co.*, 134 S.W.3d at 200.

Material breach. If the parties dispute whether the alleged breach is a material one, the court should insert any or all of the following instructions regarding materiality, as appropriate:

A failure to comply must be material. The circumstances to consider in determining whether a failure to comply is material include:

(a) the extent to which the injured party will be deprived of the benefit which he reasonably expected;

(b) the extent to which the injured party can be adequately compensated for the part of that benefit of which he will be deprived;

(c) the extent to which the party failing to perform or to offer to perform will suffer forfeiture;

(d) the likelihood that the party failing to perform or to offer to perform will cure his failure, taking into account the circumstances including any reasonable assurances;

(e) the extent to which the behavior of the party failing to perform or to offer to perform comports with standards of good faith and fair dealing.

Mustang Pipeline Co., 134 S.W.3d at 199 (adopting *Restatement (Second) of Contracts* § 241 (1981)). See also PJC 101.22.

Integrated written document. If the dispute arises from an integrated written document, a phrase identifying the agreement should be substituted for the words *the agreement. See Ryan Mortgage Investors*, 650 S.W.2d at 932–33.

Implied terms. If the alleged breach involves an omitted term, such as time of compliance, an additional instruction is necessary. See, e.g., PJC 101.10 and 101.13.

Interpretation. Construction of an unambiguous term is an issue for the court. *J.M. Davidson, Inc. v. Webster*, 128 S.W.3d 223, 229 (Tex. 2003). If appropriate, an instruction should be included giving the jury the correct interpretation of that term. See PJC 101.7. If the court determines that a particular provision is ambiguous, an instruction on resolving that ambiguity should be included. See PJC 101.8.

Caveat. Care must be taken to ensure that the question is appropriate under the facts of the particular case. Many contract disputes focus entirely on issues such as defenses, damages, promissory estoppel, quantum meruit, or agency, which are addressed in other parts of this volume. In such cases the parties may not need any form of PJC 101.2. If the only jury question is the validity of a defense, PJC 101.2 is not appropriate, and the instruction appropriate to that defense (e.g., PJC 101.21–.33) may be rewritten as the question.

UCC good-faith obligation. Every contract or duty governed by the Uniform Commercial Code imposes an obligation of good faith in its performance or enforcement. Tex. Bus. & Com. Code § 1.304 (Tex. UCC); *Printing Center of Texas, Inc. v. Supermind Publishing Co.*, 669 S.W.2d 779, 784 (Tex. App.—Houston [14th Dist.] 1984, no writ). The failure to act in good faith under the UCC does not create an independent cause of action. *Adolph Coors Co. v. Rodriguez*, 780 S.W.2d 477, 482 (Tex. App.—Corpus Christi 1989, writ denied) (to be actionable, bad-faith conduct must relate to some aspect of performance under terms of contract).

Except as otherwise provided in chapter 5 of the Code, "'Good faith' . . . means honesty in fact and the observance of reasonable commercial standards of fair dealing." Tex. UCC § 1.201(b)(20).

If the transaction is covered by the Code, the following instruction would be appropriate to submit with the basic question:

> In addition to the language of the agreement, the law imposes on a party to a contract a duty to [*perform*] [*enforce*] [*perform or enforce*] the contract in good faith. In that connection, good faith means honesty in fact and the observance of reasonable commercial standards of fair dealing.

Depending on the pleadings and evidence in the particular case, the court may instruct on performance or enforcement or both.

If a party contends that the agreement defines the standards for good-faith performance, the jury should be instructed as follows:

> The parties to the agreement may by agreement determine the standards by which the performance of the obligation of good faith is to be measured if such standards are not manifestly unreasonable.

Tex. UCC § 1.302(b). The Committee is not aware of any Texas case supporting a departure from the language of section 1.302(b) (formerly section 1.102(c)).

Good and workmanlike manner. In some cases involving construction, repairs, and some services, there is an obligation to perform in a good and workmanlike manner. For instructions and comments, see PJC 102.12.

PJC 101.3 Instruction on Formation of Agreement

In deciding whether the parties reached an agreement, you may consider what they said and did in light of the surrounding circumstances, including any earlier course of dealing. You may not consider the parties' unexpressed thoughts or intentions.

COMMENT

When to use. If appropriate, PJC 101.3 should be submitted with the question of the existence of a contract (PJC 101.1) to confine the jury's deliberations on the issue of contract formation to legally appropriate factors.

Source of instruction. Only the parties' objective manifestations of intent may be considered. *Adams v. Petrade International, Inc.*, 754 S.W.2d 696, 717 (Tex. App.—Houston [1st Dist.] 1988, writ denied); *Slade v. Phelps*, 446 S.W.2d 931, 933 (Tex. Civ. App.—Tyler 1969, no writ). An agreement may be implied from and evidenced by the parties' conduct in the light of the surrounding circumstances, including any earlier course of dealing. *Haws & Garrett General Contractors, Inc. v. Gorbett Bros. Welding Co.*, 480 S.W.2d 607, 609–10 (Tex. 1972); *Calvin V. Koltermann, Inc. v. Underream Piling Co.*, 563 S.W.2d 950, 956 (Tex. Civ. App.—San Antonio 1977, writ ref'd n.r.e.). Generally, silence and inaction cannot be construed as an assent to an offer. *Texas Ass'n of Counties County Government Risk Management Pool v. Matagorda County*, 52 S.W.3d 128, 132 (Tex. 2000) (applying 2 *Williston on Contracts* § 6.49 (4th ed. 1991)).

UCC article 2 cases. Tex. Bus. & Com. Code § 1.201(b)(3) (Tex. UCC) defines "agreement" and includes those factors that may be considered in determining the existence of an agreement. *See also* Tex. UCC § 1.303 (course of performance, course of dealing, and usage of trade), § 2.202 (final written expression: parol evidence), § 2.204 (formation in general).

PJC 101.4 Instruction on Authority

A party's conduct includes the conduct of another who acts with the party's authority or apparent authority.

Authority for another to act for a party must arise from the party's agreement that the other act on behalf and for the benefit of the party. If a party so authorizes another to perform an act, that other party is also authorized to do whatever else is proper, usual, and necessary to perform the act expressly authorized.

Apparent authority exists if a party (1) knowingly permits another to hold himself out as having authority or, (2) through lack of ordinary care, bestows on another such indications of authority that lead a reasonably prudent person to rely on the apparent existence of authority to his detriment. Only the acts of the party sought to be charged with responsibility for the conduct of another may be considered in determining whether apparent authority exists.

COMMENT

When to use. PJC 101.4 may be appropriate if the evidence raises a question of express, implied, or apparent authority. It is to be used only to determine whether a party is contractually bound by the conduct of another. In common-law tort and statutory actions, where the issue is a party's vicarious liability for the wrongful conduct of another, different rules of law may apply. For the rules relating to deceptive trade practices and insurance actions, see the comments titled "Vicarious liability" at PJC 102.1, 102.7, 102.8, and 102.14.

Express authority. Express authority arises from the principal's agreement that the agent act on the principal's behalf and for his benefit. *Clark's-Gamble, Inc. v. State*, 486 S.W.2d 840, 845 (Tex. Civ. App.—Amarillo 1972, writ ref'd n.r.e.).

Implied authority. Implied authority arises by implication from a grant of express authority. A grant of express authority implies authority to do those acts proper, usual, and necessary to perform the act expressly authorized. *Employers Casualty Co. v. Winslow*, 356 S.W.2d 160, 168 (Tex. Civ. App.—El Paso 1962, writ ref'd n.r.e.).

Apparent authority. Apparent authority arises if a principal either intentionally or negligently induces parties to believe that a person is the principal's agent even though the principal has conferred no authority on that person. *Roberts v. Capitol City Steel Co.*, 376 S.W.2d 771, 775 (Tex. Civ. App.—Austin 1964, writ ref'd n.r.e.). Apparent authority, which is based partly on estoppel, may arise from two sources: first, from the principal's knowingly allowing an agent to claim authority; and second, from the principal's negligently bestowing on the agent such indications of authority that a reasonably prudent person is led to rely on the existence of that authority. *Gaines v. Kelly*, 235 S.W.3d 179, 182–84 (Tex. 2007); *Ames v. Great Southern Bank*, 672 S.W.2d 447, 450 (Tex. 1984); *Hall v. F.A. Halamicek Enterprises*, 669 S.W.2d 368, 375 (Tex. App.—Corpus Christi 1984, no writ); *Sorenson v. Shupe Bros. Co.*, 517 S.W.2d 861, 864 (Tex. Civ. App.—Amarillo 1974, no writ).

Because apparent authority is based on estoppel, the principal's conduct must be that which would lead a reasonably prudent person to believe that authority exists. *Douglass v. Panama, Inc.*, 504 S.W.2d 776, 778–79 (Tex. 1974); *Campbell v. C.D. Payne & Geldermann Securities, Inc.*, 894 S.W.2d 411, 422 (Tex. App.—Amarillo 1995, writ denied).

If apparent authority is not an issue, the phrase *or apparent authority* should be deleted from the first paragraph of the instruction, along with the definition of apparent authority.

PJC 101.5 Instruction on Ratification

A party's conduct includes conduct of others that the party has ratified. Ratification may be express or implied.

Implied ratification occurs if a party, though he may have been unaware of unauthorized conduct taken on his behalf at the time it occurred, retains the benefits of the transaction involving the unauthorized conduct after he acquired full knowledge of the unauthorized conduct. Implied ratification results in the ratification of the entire transaction.

COMMENT

When to use. PJC 101.5 may be appropriate if a party seeks to avoid liability on the basis that the act of a purported agent was unauthorized or if a party seeks to hold another responsible for unauthorized but ratified conduct.

Source of instruction. The instruction is derived from *Land Title Co. v. F.M. Stigler, Inc.*, 609 S.W.2d 754 (Tex. 1980) (ratification occurs if principal retains benefits of transaction after full knowledge of unauthorized acts of person acting on principal's behalf). Ratification, rather than any type of authority, binds the principal in these cases. *Land Title Co.*, 609 S.W.2d at 756–58.

Not applicable to fraud. PJC 101.5 does not apply in situations involving ratification of fraud.

PJC 101.6 Conditions Precedent (Comment)

Conditions precedent defined. "A condition precedent may be either a condition to the formation of a contract or to an obligation to perform an existing agreement. Conditions may, therefore, relate either to the formation of contracts or to liability under them." *Hohenberg Bros. Co. v. George E. Gibbons & Co.*, 537 S.W.2d 1, 3 (Tex. 1976).

Conditions precedent to an obligation to perform are acts or events that are to occur after the contract is made and that must occur before there is a right to immediate performance and before there can be a breach of contractual duty. *Hohenberg Bros. Co.*, 537 S.W.2d at 3.

Creation of condition precedent. Although no particular words are necessary to create a condition, terms such as "if," "provided that," and "on condition that" usually connote a condition rather than a covenant or promise. Absent such a limiting clause, whether a provision represents a condition or a promise must be gathered from the contract as a whole and from the intent of the parties. *Hohenberg Bros. Co.*, 537 S.W.2d at 3.

Conditions not favored. To prevent forfeitures, courts are inclined to construe provisions as covenants rather than as conditions. *Rogers v. Ricane Enterprises*, 772 S.W.2d 76, 79 (Tex. 1989); *Henshaw v. Texas Natural Resources Foundation*, 216 S.W.2d 566, 570 (Tex. 1949); *Ogilvie v. Hill*, 563 S.W.2d 846, 849 (Tex. Civ. App.—Texarkana 1978, writ ref'd n.r.e.).

PJC 101.7 Court's Construction of Provision of Agreement (Comment)

Court's construction should be included in charge. If the construction of a provision of the agreement is in dispute and the court resolves the dispute by interpreting the provision according to the rules of construction, the court should include that interpretation in submitting PJC 101.2.

Court's duty to interpret unambiguous contract. If an instrument is unambiguous or if it is ambiguous but parol evidence of circumstances is undisputed, construction of the instrument is an issue for the court. *Friendswood Development Co. v. McDade + Co.*, 926 S.W.2d 280, 282 (Tex. 1996); *Brown v. Payne*, 176 S.W.2d 306, 308 (Tex. 1943). An instrument is ambiguous if, after application of the pertinent rules of construction, it remains reasonably susceptible of more than one meaning, taking into consideration the circumstances present when the instrument was executed. *Towers of Texas, Inc. v. J&J Systems, Inc.*, 834 S.W.2d 1, 2 (Tex. 1992); *Coker v. Coker*, 650 S.W.2d 391, 393–94 (Tex. 1983).

PJC 101.8 Instruction on Ambiguous Provisions

It is your duty to interpret the following language of the agreement:

[Insert ambiguous language.]

You must decide its meaning by determining the intent of the parties at the time of the agreement. Consider all the facts and circumstances surrounding the making of the agreement, the interpretation placed on the agreement by the parties, and the conduct of the parties.

COMMENT

When to use. If the court determines that the contract contains ambiguous language, PJC 101.8 should accompany PJC 101.1.

If an instrument is unambiguous or if it is ambiguous but parol evidence of circumstances is undisputed, construction of the instrument is an issue for the court. *Seagull Energy E&P, Inc. v. Eland Energy, Inc.*, 207 S.W.3d 342, 345 (Tex. 2006); *Friendswood Development Co. v. McDade + Co.*, 926 S.W.2d 280, 282 (Tex. 1996); *Brown v. Payne*, 176 S.W.2d 306, 308 (Tex. 1943). "Whether a contract is ambiguous is a question of law for the court to decide." *Lopez v. Munoz, Hockema & Reed, L.L.P.*, 22 S.W.3d 857, 861 (Tex. 2000). If the court determines that the contract is ambiguous, the parties' intent is a fact issue. *Columbia Gas Transmission Corp. v. New Ulm Gas, Ltd.*, 940 S.W.2d 587, 589 (Tex. 1996); *Trinity Industries, Inc. v. Ashland, Inc.*, 53 S.W.3d 852, 860 (Tex. App.—Austin 2001, pet. denied). However, if an insurance contract is ambiguous, the court "must resolve the uncertainty by adopting the construction most favorable to the insured." *State Farm Fire & Casualty Co. v. Reed*, 873 S.W.2d 698, 699 (Tex. 1993); *see also Glover v. National Insurance Underwriters*, 545 S.W.2d 755, 761 (Tex. 1977).

Intent must be understandable. Parties to a contract must express their intentions understandably. To be enforceable, a contract must be sufficiently certain to enable the court to determine the legal obligations of the parties. *T.O. Stanley Boot Co. v. Bank of El Paso*, 847 S.W.2d 218, 221 (Tex. 1992); *Bendalin v. Delgado*, 406 S.W.2d 897, 899 (Tex. 1966).

Parties' interpretation given great weight. The most significant rule of contractual interpretation is that great, if not controlling, weight should be given to the parties' interpretation. The court and the jury should assume that parties to a contract are in the best position to know what they intended by the language used. *James Stewart & Co. v. Law*, 233 S.W.2d 558, 561 (Tex. 1950); *see also Trinity Universal Insurance Co. v. Ponsford Bros.*, 423 S.W.2d 571, 575 (Tex. 1968). One factor to be considered in determining the parties' interpretation is their conduct. *Consolidated Engineering Co. v. Southern Steel Co.*, 699 S.W.2d 188, 192–93 (Tex. 1985).

PJC 101.9 Trade Custom (Comment)

Instruction may be appropriate. Texas law is not clear on whether trade custom is merely evidentiary and not appropriate for jury instruction or whether it may in fact form the basis for a proper instruction. Such an instruction would be used to augment or modify PJC 101.1 or 101.2. It could inquire whether a particular custom or usage existed and, if it existed, whether the parties intended that it would affect a contract term. *Lambert v. H. Molsen & Co.*, 551 S.W.2d 151, 154 (Tex. Civ. App.—Waco 1977, writ ref'd n.r.e.) ("The [trial] court instructed the jury . . . that if it found . . . that the custom and usage actually existed, then it could be considered by the jury toward determining the parties' contractual intent."). The court in *Lambert* did not expressly approve the instruction used by the trial court, but the opinion does provide an example of the form of a trade-custom instruction. *See also Tennell v. Esteve Cotton Co.*, 546 S.W.2d 346 (Tex. Civ. App.—Amarillo 1976, writ ref'd n.r.e.); *Englebrecht v. W.D. Brannan & Sons, Inc.*, 501 S.W.2d 707 (Tex. Civ. App.—Amarillo 1973, no writ) (discussing submission of instructions on custom).

Evidence of trade custom may aid interpretation of ambiguous contract. Evidence of custom may be admitted to aid in the interpretation of a contract if the contract is ambiguous, imprecise, incomplete, or inconsistent, but such evidence is not admissible to contradict, restrict, or enlarge what otherwise needs no explanation. *Miller v. Gray*, 149 S.W.2d 582, 583–84 (Tex. 1941); *Energen Resources MAQ, Inc. v. Dalbosco*, 23 S.W.3d 551, 557 (Tex. App.—Houston [1st Dist.] 2000, pet. denied); *PGP Gas Products, Inc. v. Reserve Equipment, Inc.*, 667 S.W.2d 604, 607–08 (Tex. App.—Austin 1984, writ ref'd n.r.e.).

UCC article 2 cases. Trade custom, course of dealing, and course of performance are relevant in determining the meaning of the agreement. *See* Tex. Bus. & Com. Code §§ 1.303, 2.202 (Tex. UCC).

PJC 101.10 Instruction on Time of Compliance

Compliance with an agreement must occur within a reasonable time under the circumstances unless the parties agreed that compliance must occur within a specified time and the parties intended compliance within such time to be an essential part of the agreement.

In determining whether the parties intended time of compliance to be an essential part of the agreement, you may consider the nature and purpose of the agreement and the facts and circumstances surrounding its making.

COMMENT

When to use. PJC 101.10 is appropriate if a party contends that failure to comply by the date specified in the agreement constitutes a material breach, even though the agreement itself does not expressly state that time is of the essence. *See Siderius, Inc. v. Wallace Co.*, 583 S.W.2d 852, 863–64 (Tex. Civ. App.—Tyler 1979, no writ); *Laredo Hides Co. v. H&H Meat Products Co.*, 513 S.W.2d 210, 216–18 (Tex. Civ. App.—Corpus Christi 1974, writ ref'd n.r.e.).

UCC article 2 cases. If the time for delivery or shipment is not specified in the contract, the time shall be reasonable. Tex. Bus. & Com. Code § 2.309(a) (Tex. UCC). "Whether a time for taking an action required by this title is reasonable depends on the nature, purpose, and circumstances of the action" and on any prior dealing between the parties. Tex. UCC § 1.205(a) & cmt. 2; *see also* Tex. UCC §§ 2.504, 2.601, 2.612.

PJC 101.11 Instruction on Offer and Acceptance

In attempting to reach an agreement, one party may specifically prescribe the time, manner, or other requirements for the other party's acceptance of the offer. If the offer is not accepted as prescribed, there is no agreement.

COMMENT

When to use. PJC 101.11 submits a common offer-and-acceptance instruction and may be used in an appropriate case with PJC 101.1.

Waiver. The offeror can waive limitations on manner of acceptance, and the above instruction should be modified to incorporate waiver in an appropriate case. *See Town of Lindsay v. Cooke County Electric Cooperative Ass'n*, 502 S.W.2d 117 (Tex. 1973).

Acceptance by performance. The supreme court has adopted sections 32 and 62 of the *Restatement (Second) of Contracts* (1981). These sections state that under some circumstances performance of an act that the offeree is requested to promise to perform may constitute a valid acceptance. *United Concrete Pipe Corp. v. Spin-Line Co.*, 430 S.W.2d 360, 364 (Tex. 1968) (citing 1964 tentative draft, with different section numbers).

Time for acceptance. If no time for acceptance of an offer is specified, the law implies a reasonable time. *Moore v. Dodge*, 603 S.W.2d 236, 239 (Tex. Civ. App.—El Paso 1980, writ ref'd n.r.e.).

PJC 101.12 Instruction on Withdrawal or Revocation of Offer

There is no agreement unless the party to whom an offer is made accepts it before knowing that the offer has been withdrawn.

COMMENT

When to use. PJC 101.12 should be included with PJC 101.1 only if one party claims the offer was withdrawn before it was accepted.

Acceptance by performance. The supreme court has adopted sections 32 and 62 of the *Restatement (Second) of Contracts* (1981). These sections state that under some circumstances performance of an act that the offeree is requested to promise to perform may constitute a valid acceptance. *United Concrete Pipe Corp. v. Spin-Line Co.*, 430 S.W.2d 360, 364 (Tex. 1968) (citing 1964 tentative draft, with different section numbers).

Revocable offers. Ordinarily, the party making an offer may revoke it anytime before the offeree accepts it in the manner prescribed. *See Bowles v. Fickas*, 167 S.W.2d 741, 742–43 (Tex. 1943). The offeror can effectively revoke an offer by doing some act inconsistent with the offer, but the offeree must have actual knowledge of the revocation. *Antwine v. Reed*, 199 S.W.2d 482, 485 (Tex. 1947). After making an irrevocable offer, however, the offeror cannot unilaterally vary or revoke it. *Wall v. Trinity Sand & Gravel Co.*, 369 S.W.2d 315, 317 (Tex. 1963). A common type of irrevocable offer is an option contract where the offer is supported by independent consideration.

UCC cases. *See* Tex. Bus. & Com. Code § 2.206(b) (Tex. UCC).

PJC 101.13 Instruction on Price

If *Paul Payne* and *Don Davis* agreed to other essential terms but failed to specify price, it is presumed a reasonable price was intended.

COMMENT

When to use. PJC 101.13 should accompany PJC 101.1 or 101.2 in appropriate cases.

Source of instruction. The above instruction is derived from *Bendalin v. Delgado*, 406 S.W.2d 897, 900 (Tex. 1966).

UCC cases. Tex. Bus. & Com. Code § 2.305(a) (Tex. UCC) states:

> (a) The parties if they so intend can conclude a contract for sale even though the price is not settled. In such a case the price is a reasonable price at the time for delivery if
>
> (1) nothing is said as to price; or
>
> (2) the price is left to be agreed by the parties and they fail to agree; or
>
> (3) the price is to be fixed in terms of some agreed market or other standard as set or recorded by a third person or agency and it is not so set or recorded.

PJC 101.14 Consideration (Comment)

Consideration essential. Consideration is essential to a contract. *Unthank v. Rippstein*, 386 S.W.2d 134, 137 (Tex. 1964). Whether a particular matter constitutes adequate legal consideration is a question of law for the court. *Williams v. Hill*, 396 S.W.2d 911, 913 (Tex. Civ. App.—Dallas 1965, no writ). The court's determination, however, may be based on facts found by the jury. *See, e.g.*, *Schepps Grocery Co. v. Burroughs Corp.*, 635 S.W.2d 606, 608 (Tex. App.—Houston [14th Dist.] 1982, no writ).

Burden of proof. In suits on a written contract, the burden of proof rests on the party alleging a lack of consideration. *Simpson v. MBank Dallas, N.A.*, 724 S.W.2d 102, 107 (Tex. App.—Dallas 1987, writ ref'd n.r.e.). In actions on an oral contract, the burden is on the plaintiff to prove the existence of consideration. *Okemah Construction, Inc. v. Barkley-Farmer, Inc.*, 583 S.W.2d 458, 460 (Tex. Civ. App.—Houston [1st Dist.] 1979, no writ) (collecting cases).

Failure of consideration. The doctrine of failure of consideration does not involve issues relating to contract formation but is usually an affirmative defense based on a claim that the party seeking to recover on the contract has breached it in a manner sufficient to excuse the other party's noncompliance. For appropriate instructions, see PJC 101.22.

[PJC 101.15–.20 are reserved for expansion.]

PJC 101.21 Defenses—Basic Question

If your answer to Question ______ [*101.1*] is "Yes," then answer the following question. Otherwise, do not answer the following question.

QUESTION ______

Was *Don Davis*'s failure to comply excused?

[Insert instructions; see PJC 101.22–.33.]

Answer: _______________

COMMENT

When to use. PJC 101.21 poses the controlling question for cases where a defendant asserts one or more defenses to a contract suit.

Broad-form submission. The broad form of this question follows the mandate of Tex. R. Civ. P. 277. When feasible, the courts are urged to submit the controlling issues of a case in broad terms in order to simplify the charge. *Island Recreational Development Corp. v. Republic of Texas Savings Ass'n*, 710 S.W.2d 551, 555 (Tex. 1986). A single broad question may include one or more independent grounds. *Island Recreational Development Corp.*, 710 S.W.2d at 554–55. The dissenting opinions agree but would require instructions referring to the grounds. *Island Recreational Development Corp.*, 710 S.W.2d at 557–58, 561. If there is legal uncertainty on one or more theories of recovery, broad-form submission may not be feasible and separate questions may be required. *See Crown Life Insurance Co. v. Casteel*, 22 S.W.3d 378, 388–89 (Tex. 2000) (broad-form submission combining valid and invalid theories was harmful error).

Instructions on grounds of defense required. In the absence of one or more independent grounds of defense, the jury is not permitted to excuse the defendant from complying with the agreement. Standing alone, PJC 101.21 does not encompass any grounds of defense, so it is mandatory that grounds raised by the pleadings and evidence be submitted by including instructions such as PJC 101.22–.33. *See, e.g.*, *Traeger v. Lorenz*, 749 S.W.2d 249 (Tex. App.—San Antonio 1988, no writ) (separate grounds of waiver and abandonment should have been submitted in deed restriction case).

PJC 101.22 Defenses—Instruction on Plaintiff's Material Breach (Failure of Consideration)

Failure to comply by *Don Davis* is excused by *Paul Payne*'s previous failure to comply with a material obligation of the same agreement.

COMMENT

When to use. PJC 101.22 may accompany PJC 101.21 if the defendant raises the affirmative defense of the plaintiff's material breach of the agreement. Generally, when one party to a contract commits a material breach of that contract, the other party is discharged or excused from further performance. *Mustang Pipeline Co. v. Driver Pipeline Co.*, 134 S.W.3d 195, 196 (Tex. 2004); *see also Dobbins v. Redden*, 785 S.W.2d 377 (Tex. 1990) (party in default on contract cannot maintain suit for its breach).

Form of instruction. The instruction is suggested by *Huff v. Speer*, 554 S.W.2d 259, 262 (Tex. Civ. App.—Houston [1st Dist.] 1977, writ ref'd n.r.e.), and *King Title Co. v. Croft*, 562 S.W.2d 536, 537 (Tex. Civ. App.—El Paso 1978, no writ).

If the alleged failure to comply by the complaining party involves timeliness of performance and if no date for completion is specified in the agreement, the following instruction should be added to PJC 101.22:

> Delay in compliance beyond a reasonable period is a failure to comply.

See Cannan v. Varn, 591 S.W.2d 583 (Tex. Civ. App.—Corpus Christi 1979, writ ref'd n.r.e.).

Material breach versus failure of consideration. Although designated here as plaintiff's material breach, the issue is commonly referred to as failure or partial failure of consideration. The Committee considers the latter designation inappropriate and confusing, however, because it suggests issues relating to contract formation. See PJC 101.3; see also PJC 101.14. The facts involved usually pertain instead to the affirmative defense that the party seeking to recover on a contract has breached it in a manner sufficient to excuse the defendant's noncompliance. *See National Bank of Commerce v. Williams*, 84 S.W.2d 691, 692 (Tex. 1935); *Austin Lake Estates, Inc. v. Meyer*, 557 S.W.2d 380, 384 (Tex. Civ. App.—Austin 1977, no writ).

Failure to comply with provisions of a bilateral contract may be excused by the unjustifiable failure of the other party to comply with provisions binding on him. *Jordan Drilling Co. v. Starr*, 232 S.W.2d 149, 159 (Tex. Civ. App.—El Paso 1949, writ ref'd n.r.e.). The breach need not be total for rescission to be proper; a partial breach is sufficient if it affects a material part of the agreement. *Hausler v. Harding-Gill Co.*, 15

S.W.2d 548, 549 (Tex. Comm'n App. 1929, judgm't adopted); *Ennis v. Interstate Distributors, Inc.*, 598 S.W.2d 903, 906 (Tex. Civ. App.—Dallas 1980, no writ). Partial failure of consideration involves breach of a nonmaterial provision of the contract and does not support rescission but merely damages. *Gensco, Inc. v. Transformaciones Metalurgicias Especiales, S.A.*, 666 S.W.2d 549, 553 (Tex. App.—Houston [14th Dist.] 1984, writ dism'd).

Whether a breach is so material as to support this defense is a question of fact for the jury. *Hudson v. Wakefield*, 645 S.W.2d 427, 430 (Tex. 1983). "In determining the materiality of a breach, courts will consider, among other things, the extent to which the nonbreaching party will be deprived of the benefit that it could have reasonably anticipated from full performance." *Hernandez v. Gulf Group Lloyds*, 875 S.W.2d 691, 693 (Tex. 1994); *see also Restatement (Second) of Contracts* § 241(a) (1981); *Hernandez*, 875 S.W.2d at 693 n.2; *Advance Components, Inc. v. Goodstein*, 608 S.W.2d 737, 739–40 (Tex. Civ. App.—Dallas 1980, writ ref'd n.r.e.) (listing other factors for determining the materiality of a breach).

PJC 101.23 Defenses—Instruction on Anticipatory Repudiation

Failure to comply by *Don Davis* is excused by *Paul Payne*'s prior repudiation of the same agreement.

A party repudiates an agreement when *he* indicates, by *his* words or actions, that *he* is not going to perform *his* obligations under the agreement in the future, showing a fixed intention to abandon, renounce, and refuse to perform the agreement.

COMMENT

When to use. PJC 101.23 submits the doctrine of anticipatory repudiation as a defensive measure. It may also be appropriate, in slightly different form, as an element of the plaintiff's cause of action. Upon a party's repudiation of a contract, the nonrepudiating party may treat the repudiation as a breach or may continue to perform under the contract and await the time of the agreed-upon performance. *Ingersoll-Rand Co. v. Valero Energy Corp.*, 997 S.W.2d 203, 211 (Tex. 1999).

Source of instruction. The elements in the instruction are adapted from the discussion of the doctrine in *Group Life & Health Insurance Co. v. Turner*, 620 S.W.2d 670, 672–73 (Tex. Civ. App.—Dallas 1981, no writ).

"Without just excuse." To excuse a failure to comply, the repudiation must have been "without just excuse." *Group Life & Health Insurance Co.*, 620 S.W.2d at 673 (quoting *Universal Life & Accident Insurance Co. v. Sanders*, 102 S.W.2d 405 (Tex. 1937)).

UCC cases. In cases involving the sale of goods, the instruction defining anticipatory repudiation may need to be revised. *See* Tex. Bus. & Com. Code § 2.610 (Tex. UCC).

PJC 101.24 Defenses—Instruction on Waiver

Failure to comply by *Don Davis* is excused if compliance is waived by *Paul Payne*.

Waiver is an intentional surrender of a known right or intentional conduct inconsistent with claiming the right.

COMMENT

When to use. PJC 101.24 is appropriate to submit the affirmative defense of waiver. It may also be appropriate, in slightly different form, as an element of the plaintiff's cause of action, because waiver is an independent ground of recovery. *See Middle States Petroleum Corp. v. Messenger*, 368 S.W.2d 645, 654 (Tex. Civ. App.—Dallas 1963, writ ref'd n.r.e.). The Committee believes that an instruction on waiver should be submitted if the issue is raised by the evidence. *But see Island Recreational Development Corp. v. Republic of Texas Savings Ass'n*, 710 S.W.2d 551 (Tex. 1986) (affirming judgment notwithstanding lack of submission of waiver).

Source of definition. The definition is adapted from *United States Fidelity & Guaranty Co. v. Bimco Iron & Metal Corp.*, 464 S.W.2d 353, 357 (Tex. 1971); *see also Gage v. Langford*, 582 S.W.2d 203, 207 (Tex. Civ. App.—Eastland 1979, writ ref'd n.r.e.) (definition of waiver incorrectly omitted "intentionally" from phrase "giving up, relinquishment, or surrender of some known right").

Distinguished from estoppel. The supreme court has emphasized the unilateral character of waiver and distinguished it from estoppel:

> [W]aiver is essentially unilateral in its character; it results as a legal consequence from some act or conduct of the party against whom it operates; no act of the party in whose favor it is made is necessary to complete it. It need not be founded upon a new agreement or be supported by consideration, nor is it essential that it be based upon an estoppel.

Massachusetts Bonding & Insurance Co. v. Orkin Exterminating Co., 416 S.W.2d 396, 401 (Tex. 1967).

UCC article 2 cases. A waiver affecting an executory portion of the agreement may be retracted on reasonable notification that strict performance will be required. Tex. Bus. & Com. Code § 2.209(e) (Tex. UCC).

PJC 101.25 Defenses—Instruction on Equitable Estoppel

Failure to comply by *Don Davis* is excused if all the following circumstances occurred:

1. *Paul Payne*

   a. by words or conduct made a false representation or concealed material facts,

   b. with knowledge of the facts or with knowledge or information that would lead a reasonable person to discover the facts, and

   c. with the intention that *Don Davis* would rely on the false representation or concealment in acting or deciding not to act; and

2. *Don Davis*

   a. did not know and had no means of knowing the real facts and

   b. relied to *his* detriment on the false representation or concealment of material facts.

COMMENT

When to use. PJC 101.25 submits the affirmative defense of equitable estoppel.

Source of definition. The elements of estoppel are adapted from *Gulbenkian v. Penn*, 252 S.W.2d 929, 932 (Tex. 1952); *see also Nelson v. Jordan*, 663 S.W.2d 82, 87 (Tex. App.—Austin 1983, writ ref'd n.r.e.) (listing elements). For a general discussion of equitable estoppel, see *Barfield v. Howard M. Smith Co. of Amarillo*, 426 S.W.2d 834 (Tex. 1968).

Equitable estoppel distinguished from other types of estoppel. Equitable estoppel differs from other types of estoppel because it requires some deception practiced on a party who was misled to his injury. *Bocanegra v. Aetna Life Insurance Co.*, 605 S.W.2d 848, 851 (Tex. 1980). That party, however, must show his justifiable reliance on the representation. *Kuehne v. Denson*, 219 S.W.2d 1006, 1008–09 (Tex. 1949).

Estoppel based on silence. Estoppel may also be based on silence or inaction, rather than on affirmative misrepresentations, if one under a duty to speak or act has by his silence or inaction misled the opposing party to his detriment. *Smith v. National Resort Communities, Inc.*, 585 S.W.2d 655, 658 (Tex. 1979); *Scott v. Vandor*, 671 S.W.2d 79, 87 (Tex. App.—Houston [1st Dist.] 1984, writ ref'd n.r.e.). If estoppel is based on something other than affirmative misrepresentations, a different instruction should be substituted for PJC 101.25.

PJC 101.26 Defenses—Instruction on Duress

Failure to comply by *Don Davis* is excused if the agreement was made under duress caused by *Paul Payne*.

Duress is the mental, physical, or economic coercion of another, causing that party to act contrary to his free will and interest.

COMMENT

When to use. PJC 101.26 is appropriate if one party claims the agreement is voidable because it was made under duress. It may also be used in slightly different language to submit an affirmative claim for rescission. As a general rule, a party seeking cancellation or rescission must do equity by restoring the other party to his original status. *Texas Co. v. State*, 281 S.W.2d 83, 91 (Tex. 1955); *Freyer v. Michels*, 360 S.W.2d 559, 562 (Tex. Civ. App.—Dallas 1962, writ dism'd). It is not clear whether this rule applies if the doctrine is asserted as a defense.

Source of definition. The definition is derived from *Black Lake Pipe Line Co. v. Union Construction Co.*, 538 S.W.2d 80, 85 n.2 (Tex. 1976), *overruled on other grounds by Sterner v. Marathon Oil Co.*, 767 S.W.2d 686 (Tex. 1989); *Brooks v. Taylor*, 359 S.W.2d 539, 542 (Tex. Civ. App.—Amarillo 1962, writ ref'd n.r.e.); and *Housing Authority of City of Dallas v. Hubbell*, 325 S.W.2d 880, 905 (Tex. Civ. App.—Dallas 1959, writ ref'd n.r.e.).

Caveat. Unless the alleged coercion can legally constitute duress, PJC 101.26 should not be submitted. "It is never duress to threaten to do that which a party has a legal right to do." *Ulmer v. Ulmer*, 162 S.W.2d 944, 947 (Tex. 1942). Filing or threatening to file a civil suit cannot, as a matter of law, constitute duress. *Continental Casualty Co. v. Huizar*, 740 S.W.2d 429, 430 (Tex. 1987). The vice arises only if extortive measures are employed or if improper demands are made in bad faith. *Matthews v. Matthews*, 725 S.W.2d 275, 279 (Tex. App.—Houston [1st Dist.] 1986, writ ref'd n.r.e.); *Sanders v. Republic National Bank*, 389 S.W.2d 551, 555 (Tex. Civ. App.—Tyler 1965, no writ); *see also Mitchell v. C.C. Sanitation Co.*, 430 S.W.2d 933 (Tex. Civ. App.—Houston [14th Dist.] 1968, writ ref'd n.r.e.). *State National Bank v. Farah Manufacturing Co.*, 678 S.W.2d 661 (Tex. App.—El Paso 1984, judgm't dism'd by agr.) gives a general overview of this topic. A threat to file criminal prosecution may constitute duress even if the threatened party is guilty of the crime. *Eggleston v. Humble Pipe Line Co.*, 482 S.W.2d 909, 916 (Tex. Civ. App.—Houston [14th Dist.] 1972, writ ref'd n.r.e.); *Pierce v. Estate of Haverlah*, 428 S.W.2d 422, 425 (Tex. Civ. App.—Tyler 1968, writ ref'd n.r.e.).

Economic duress. If economic duress is alleged, this instruction should be submitted only if the party against whom duress is charged was responsible for the other party's financial distress. *Simpson v. MBank Dallas, N.A.*, 724 S.W.2d 102, 109 (Tex. App.—Dallas 1987, writ ref'd n.r.e.); *Griffith v. Geffen & Jacobsen, P.C.*, 693 S.W.2d 724, 728 (Tex. App.—Dallas 1985, no writ).

Imminence of harm. The threat of harm must be imminent, and the threatened party must have no present means of protection. It must cause the threatened person to do what there was no legal obligation to do. *Dale v. Simon*, 267 S.W. 467, 470 (Tex. Comm'n App. 1924, judgm't adopted); *Creative Manufacturing, Inc. v. Unik, Inc.*, 726 S.W.2d 207, 211 (Tex. App.—Fort Worth 1987, writ ref'd n.r.e.).

PJC 101.27 Defenses—Instruction on Undue Influence

Failure to comply by *Don Davis* is excused if the agreement was made as the result of undue influence by *Paul Payne*.

"Undue influence" means that there was such dominion and control exercised over the mind of the person executing the agreement, under the facts and circumstances then existing, as to overcome his free will. In effect, the will of the party exerting undue influence was substituted for that of the party entering the agreement, preventing him from exercising his own discretion and causing him to do what he would not have done but for such dominion and control.

COMMENT

When to use. PJC 101.27 is appropriate when one party disputes the existence of the agreement because it was made under undue influence. As a general rule, a party seeking cancellation or rescission must do equity by restoring the other party to his original status. *Texas Co. v. State*, 281 S.W.2d 83, 91 (Tex. 1955); *Freyer v. Michels*, 360 S.W.2d 559, 562 (Tex. Civ. App.—Dallas 1962, writ dism'd). It is not clear whether this rule applies if the doctrine is asserted as a defense.

Source of definition. The definition is adapted from *Rothermel v. Duncan*, 369 S.W.2d 917, 922 (Tex. 1963). Although that case concerns a will contest, the definition for undue influence used in *Rothermel* is often used in cases involving disputes over agreements. *See Decker v. Decker*, 192 S.W.3d 648, 651 (Tex. App.—Fort Worth 2006, no pet.) (dispute over agreement to transfer deed); *Seymour v. American Engine & Grinding Co.*, 956 S.W.2d 49, 59 (Tex. App.—Houston [14th Dist.] 1996, pet. denied) (dispute involving stock purchase agreement).

"Undue influence." Not every influence exerted on the will of another is undue. *Rothermel*, 369 S.W.2d at 922. The exertion of undue influence is usually a subtle thing involving an extended course of dealings and circumstances, and it may be proved by circumstantial as well as direct evidence. *Rothermel*, 369 S.W.2d at 922. Influence is not undue merely because it is persuasive and effective, and the law does not condemn all persuasion, entreaty, importunity, or intercession. *B.A.L. v. Edna Gladney Home*, 677 S.W.2d 826, 830 (Tex. App.—Fort Worth 1984, writ ref'd n.r.e.).

PJC 101.28 Defenses—Instruction on Mutual Mistake of Fact

Failure to comply is excused if the agreement was made as the result of a mutual mistake.

A mutual mistake results from a mistake of fact common to both parties if both parties had the same misconception concerning the fact in question. A mistake by one party but not the other is not a mutual mistake.

COMMENT

When to use. PJC 101.28 is appropriate when a party disputes terms of the agreement on the basis that they were established by mutual mistake of fact. See PJC 101.29 for an instruction on mutual mistake due to a scrivener's error.

Mistake must relate to same subject matter. To prove a mutual mistake, evidence must show that both parties had the same misunderstanding of the same material fact. *A.L.G. Enterprises v. Huffman*, 660 S.W.2d 603, 606 (Tex. App.—Corpus Christi 1983), *aff'd & remanded for mutual mistake issue only*, 672 S.W.2d 230 (Tex. 1984).

Excuses failure to perform. Mutual mistake is an equitable defense that, if proved, excuses a party's failure to perform a contract. *A.L.G. Enterprises*, 660 S.W.2d at 606; *but see Geodyne Energy Income Production Partnership I-E v. Newton Corp.*, 161 S.W.3d 482, 491 (Tex. 2005) ("[a] person who intentionally assumes the risk of unknown facts cannot escape a bargain by alleging mistake or misunderstanding" (footnote omitted)). The question of mutual mistake is for the jury. *See, e.g.*, *Davis v. Grammer*, 750 S.W.2d 766, 767 (Tex. 1988) (illustrating that mutual mistake is submitted to the jury); *see also James T. Taylor & Son, Inc. v. Arlington Independent School District*, 335 S.W.2d 371, 376 (Tex. 1960). This instruction may also be used, in slightly different language, to submit an affirmative claim for rescission.

Caveat: unilateral mistake. Case law has drawn a distinction between unilateral and mutual mistake. Evidence may give rise to a defense based on unilateral mistake but fail to raise a defense based on mutual mistake. *See Durham v. Uvalde Rock Asphalt Co.*, 599 S.W.2d 866, 870 (Tex. Civ. App.—San Antonio 1980, no writ). For a discussion of issues involved in cases of unilateral mistake, see *Monarch Marking System Co. v. Reed's Photo Mart, Inc.*, 485 S.W.2d 905 (Tex. 1972).

PJC 101.29 Defenses—Instruction on Mutual Mistake—Scrivener's Error

Failure to comply is excused if the agreement was made as the result of a mutual mistake.

A mutual mistake arises when parties to an agreement have identical intent and understanding of the terms to be embodied in a proposed written agreement, but, in the effort to reduce the agreement to writing, a mistake is made so that the writing does not present the intended agreement.

COMMENT

When to use. PJC 101.29 is appropriate if a party disputes terms of the agreement because they resulted from a mutual mistake in recording the agreement. For an instruction on mutual mistake of fact, see PJC 101.28.

True agreement of the parties. If a scrivener or typist makes a mistake, "an instrument may be reformed and modified by a court to reflect the true agreement of the parties, if the mistake was a mutual mistake." *Henderson v. Henderson*, 694 S.W.2d 31, 34 (Tex. App.—Corpus Christi 1985, writ ref'd n.r.e.).

Requirements for reformation. "Reformation of an instrument is a proper remedy when two requirements are satisfied; (1) the true agreement of the parties is shown; and (2) the provision erroneously written into the instrument is there by mutual mistake." *Parker v. HNG Oil Co.*, 732 S.W.2d 754, 755 (Tex. App.—Corpus Christi 1987, no writ). "[K]nowledge by one party of another's mistake in the expression of the contract is equal to mutual mistake." *Goff v. Southmost Savings & Loan Ass'n*, 758 S.W.2d 822, 826 (Tex. App.—Corpus Christi 1988, writ denied).

PJC 101.30 Defenses—Instruction on Novation

Failure to comply with one agreement is excused if the parties agreed that a new agreement would take its place.

COMMENT

When to use. PJC 101.30 may be used to submit the affirmative defense of novation. Novation occurs when the rights of the parties are determined by a new agreement that extinguishes the previous one. *See Flanagan v. Martin*, 880 S.W.2d 863, 867 (Tex. App.—Waco 1994, writ dism'd w.o.j.); *DoAll Dallas Co. v. Trinity National Bank*, 498 S.W.2d 396, 400–01 (Tex. Civ. App.—Texarkana 1973, writ ref'd n.r.e.). A novation may also be the substitution of new for old parties to an agreement. *See Russell v. Northeast Bank*, 527 S.W.2d 783, 786 (Tex. Civ. App.—Houston [1st Dist.] 1975, writ ref'd n.r.e.).

If reasonable minds differ on the evidence of a new express agreement, novation is a question of law for the court. Absent an express agreement, novation is a question of fact. *Chastain v. Cooper & Reed*, 257 S.W.2d 422, 424 (Tex. 1953).

Accord and satisfaction distinguished from novation. The defense of accord and satisfaction "rests upon a new contract, express or implied, in which the parties agree to the discharge of an existing obligation in a manner otherwise than originally agreed." *Harris v. Rowe*, 593 S.W.2d 303, 306 (Tex. 1979).

"An accord and satisfaction may or may not be also a novation, but where the new promise itself is accepted as satisfaction the transaction is more properly termed a novation." *DoAll Dallas Co.*, 498 S.W.2d at 400.

PJC 101.31 Defenses—Instruction on Modification

Failure to comply with a term in an agreement is excused if the parties agreed that a new term would take its place.

COMMENT

When to use. PJC 101.31 is appropriate if the defendant claims he was excused from complying with a term of the agreement because the parties had agreed to modify the agreement by substituting a new term for an old term. *See Mandril v. Kasishke*, 620 S.W.2d 238, 244 (Tex. Civ. App.—Amarillo 1981, writ ref'd n.r.e.) (parties have power to make and modify contracts). The question of whether a modification has taken place is one of fact and depends on the intent of the parties. *Hathaway v. General Mills, Inc.*, 711 S.W.2d 227, 228–29 (Tex. 1986).

UCC article 2 cases. An agreement modifying a sales contract needs no consideration to be binding, but any modification must meet the test of good faith imposed by the Code. Tex. Bus. & Com. Code § 2.209(a) & cmt. 2 (Tex. UCC).

Accord and satisfaction and novation. For instructions on accord and satisfaction and novation, see PJC 101.32 and 101.30.

PJC 101.32 Defenses—Instruction on Accord and Satisfaction

Failure to comply with an agreement is excused if a different performance was accepted as full satisfaction of performance of the original obligations of the agreement.

COMMENT

When to use. PJC 101.32 is appropriate to submit the affirmative defense of accord and satisfaction. This defense is raised by pleading and evidence that the plaintiff agreed to and accepted performance different from that of the original agreement, in full satisfaction of the original obligation. *Jenkins v. Henry C. Beck Co.*, 449 S.W.2d 454, 455 (Tex. 1969); *see also Pileco, Inc. v. HCI, Inc.*, 735 S.W.2d 561 (Tex. App.—Houston [1st Dist.] 1987, writ ref'd n.r.e.). If the plaintiff refuses to accept the differing performance as he has agreed to do, the original obligation is not discharged and the defendant may bring an action against the plaintiff for specific performance of the accord. *Alexander v. Handley*, 146 S.W.2d 740, 743 (Tex. Comm'n App. 1941, holding approved).

If existence of accord is disputed. If existence of the accord is disputed, the above instruction should be accompanied by an instruction on the elements of agreement, mutual assent, and, if appropriate, other elements of contract formation as suggested in PJC 101.3–.8.

PJC 101.33 Defenses—Instruction on Mental Capacity

Failure to comply is excused if *Don Davis* lacked sufficient mind and memory to understand the nature and consequences of *his* acts and the business *he* was transacting.

COMMENT

When to use. PJC 101.33 is appropriate if a party defends on the basis of lack of mental capacity. It may also be used, in slightly different language, to submit an affirmative claim for rescission.

Source of instruction. The instruction is derived from *Mandell & Wright v. Thomas*, 441 S.W.2d 841, 845 (Tex. 1969); *see also Bach v. Hudson*, 596 S.W.2d 673, 675–76 (Tex. Civ. App.—Corpus Christi 1980, no writ).

Burden of proof. The burden of proof falls on the party seeking to show lack of mental capacity. *Walker v. Eason*, 643 S.W.2d 390, 391 (Tex. 1982).

[PJC 101.34–.40 are reserved for expansion.]

PJC 101.41 Question on Promissory Estoppel

QUESTION ______

Did *Paul Payne* substantially rely to *his* detriment on *Don Davis*'s promise, if any, and was this reliance foreseeable by *Don Davis*?

Answer: _______________

COMMENT

When to use. The doctrine of promissory estoppel may be invoked as a cause of action. It is appropriate if a promisee has acted to his detriment in reasonable reliance on an otherwise unenforceable promise. The theory supplies a remedy enabling an injured party to be compensated for "foreseeable, definite and substantial reliance." *Wheeler v. White*, 398 S.W.2d 93, 96–97 (Tex. 1965).

Source of question. *Wheeler*, 398 S.W.2d at 96–97; *see also Restatement (Second) of Contracts* § 90 (1981); *English v. Fischer*, 660 S.W.2d 521, 524 (Tex. 1983) (requisites of promissory estoppel are "(1) a promise, (2) foreseeability of reliance thereon by the promisor, and (3) substantial reliance by the promisee to his detriment").

Limited remedy. Recovery under the doctrine of promissory estoppel is limited to restoring the promisee to the position he would have been in had he not acted in reliance on the promise. See PJC 115.5. Lost profits may not be recovered. *Fretz Construction Co. v. Southern National Bank*, 626 S.W.2d 478, 483 (Tex. 1981).

Exception to statute of frauds. A more limited application of this doctrine has been used as an exception to the statute of frauds. *See "Moore" Burger, Inc. v. Phillips Petroleum Co.*, 492 S.W.2d 934, 937–40 (Tex. 1972). PJC 101.41 is not intended to cover such situations.

PJC 101.42 Question and Instruction on Quantum Meruit

QUESTION ______

Did *Paul Payne* perform compensable work for *Don Davis*?

One party performs compensable work if valuable services are rendered or materials furnished for another party who knowingly accepts and uses them and if the party accepting them should know that the performing party expects to be paid for the work.

Answer: ______________

COMMENT

When to use. If one party receives a benefit by accepting the services of another, the accepting party is obligated by principles of equity to pay the reasonable value of those services. *Colbert v. Dallas Joint Stock Land Bank*, 150 S.W.2d 771, 773 (Tex. 1941). The elements of a quantum meruit claim are set out in *Bashara v. Baptist Memorial Hospital System*, 685 S.W.2d 307, 310 (Tex. 1985). If a valid express contract covering the subject matter exists, recovery on quantum meruit generally is not allowed under Texas law. *Truly v. Austin*, 744 S.W.2d 934, 936 (Tex. 1988); *see also Woodard v. Southwest States, Inc.*, 384 S.W.2d 674, 675 (Tex. 1964). Recovery in quantum meruit is allowed for partial performance of a contract if (1) the defendant's breach prevents the plaintiff's completion, (2) the contract is unilateral and requires no performance by the plaintiff, or (3) the contract involves building or construction. *Truly*, 744 S.W.2d at 936–37. See PJC 115.6 for a question on quantum meruit recovery.

Construction contracts. The existence of an express contract does not, however, preclude recovery in quantum meruit for the reasonable value of work performed and accepted but not covered by the contract. *Black Lake Pipe Line Co. v. Union Construction Co.*, 538 S.W.2d 80, 86 (Tex. 1976), *overruled on other grounds by Sterner v. Marathon Oil Co.*, 767 S.W.2d 686 (Tex. 1989). The right to recover in quantum meruit is based on a promise "implied by law to pay for beneficial services rendered and knowingly accepted." *Davidson v. Clearman*, 391 S.W.2d 48, 50 (Tex. 1965).

A building contractor who has not substantially performed his contract may have quantum meruit as an alternate ground of recovery. *Dobbins v. Redden*, 785 S.W.2d 377 (Tex. 1990); *Truly*, 744 S.W.2d at 937; *see also Beeman v. Worrell*, 612 S.W.2d 953, 956 (Tex. Civ. App.—Dallas 1981, no writ); *Coon v. Schoeneman*, 476 S.W.2d 439, 442–43 (Tex. Civ. App.—Dallas 1972, writ ref'd n.r.e.). For further discussion on construction contracts, see PJC 101.46.

Construction contract and quantum meruit issues may be submitted in the same charge. *See City of Galveston v. Heffernan*, 155 S.W.2d 912 (Tex. 1941) (dispute concerned both subject matter of express contract and additional work done outside confines of contract); *see also Chapa v. Reilly*, 733 S.W.2d 236, 237 (Tex. App.—Corpus Christi 1986, writ ref'd n.r.e.).

[PJC 101.43–.45 are reserved for expansion.]

PJC 101.46 Construction Contracts Distinguished from Ordinary Contracts (Comment)

Doctrine of substantial performance. In ordinary contract cases, a party who is himself in default cannot maintain a suit for its breach. *Gulf Pipe Line Co. v. Nearen*, 138 S.W.2d 1065, 1068 (Tex. 1940). This strict rule has been relaxed in the law of construction contracts by the doctrine of substantial performance, which allows recovery to a building contractor who has breached but substantially performed his contract. *Dobbins v. Redden*, 785 S.W.2d 377 (Tex. 1990); *Vance v. My Apartment Steak House of San Antonio, Inc.*, 677 S.W.2d 480, 481 (Tex. 1984); *Atkinson v. Jackson Bros.*, 270 S.W. 848, 850 (Tex. Comm'n App. 1925, holding approved).

Quantum meruit as alternate ground. A building contractor who has not substantially performed may have quantum meruit as an alternate ground of recovery. *Dobbins*, 785 S.W.2d at 378; *Truly v. Austin*, 744 S.W.2d 934, 937 (Tex. 1988); *see also Beeman v. Worrell*, 612 S.W.2d 953, 956 (Tex. Civ. App.—Dallas 1981, no writ); *Coon v. Schoeneman*, 476 S.W.2d 439, 442–43 (Tex. Civ. App.—Dallas 1972, writ ref'd n.r.e.). For questions on quantum meruit, see PJC 101.42 and 115.6.

Construction contracts and quantum meruit questions may be submitted in the same charge. *See City of Galveston v. Heffernan*, 155 S.W.2d 912 (Tex. 1941) (dispute concerned both subject matter of express contract and additional work done outside contract); *see also Chapa v. Reilly*, 733 S.W.2d 236, 237 (Tex. App.—Corpus Christi 1986, writ ref'd n.r.e.).

Recovery. A contractor who has substantially performed may recover the contract price less the cost of completion and remedying any defects. *Vance*, 677 S.W.2d at 481.

The doctrine of substantial performance also comes into play when the owner sues the contractor. If the contractor has substantially performed, the owner can recover the cost of completion less the unpaid balance on the contract price, known as the remedial measure of damages. If the contractor has not substantially performed, the measure of the owner's damages is the difference between the value of the building as constructed and its value had it been constructed in accordance with the contract. *Turner, Collie & Braden, Inc. v. Brookhollow, Inc.*, 642 S.W.2d 160, 164 (Tex. 1982).

Jury submissions in these suits are complicated if both the owner and the contractor seek affirmative recovery. *See, e.g., Fidelity & Deposit Co. of Maryland v. Stool*, 607 S.W.2d 17 (Tex. Civ. App.—Tyler 1980, no writ); *Greene v. Bearden Enterprises, Inc.*, 598 S.W.2d 649 (Tex. Civ. App.—Fort Worth 1980, writ ref'd n.r.e.).

Property Code requirements for suits filed after September 1, 1989. Chapter 27 of the Texas Property Code contains defenses, notice requirements, and opportunities to cure or settle in suits over residential construction defects filed after September 1, 1989. Tex. Prop. Code ch. 27. Chapter 27 was amended during the 2003 legislative session. The 2003 amendments apply only to causes of action that accrue on or after September

1, 2003, or, in some cases, contracts entered into after September 1, 2003. Acts 2003, 78th Leg., R.S., ch. 458, § 2.07 (H.B. 730), eff. Sept. 1, 2003.

PJC 102.1 Question and Instruction on False, Misleading, or Deceptive Act or Practice (DTPA § 17.46(b))

QUESTION ______

Did *Don Davis* engage in any false, misleading, or deceptive act or practice that *Paul Payne* relied on to *his* detriment and that was a producing cause of damages to *Paul Payne*?

"Producing cause" means an efficient, exciting, or contributing cause that, in a natural sequence, produced the damages, if any. There may be more than one producing cause.

"False, misleading, or deceptive act or practice" means any of the following:

[Insert appropriate instructions.]

Answer: ______________

COMMENT

When to use. PJC 102.1 is a basic question that should be appropriate in most cases brought under section 17.46(b) of the Texas Deceptive Trade Practices–Consumer Protection Act (Tex. Bus. & Com. Code §§ 17.41–.63) (DTPA). Questions for other causes of action based on the DTPA or the Insurance Code may be found at PJC 102.7 (unconscionable action), 102.8 (warranty), 102.14 (Insurance Code), and 102.21 (knowing or intentional conduct).

Accompanying instructions. Instructions to accompany PJC 102.1, informing the jury what type of conduct should be considered under the question, are at PJC 102.2–.6. If more than one instruction is used, each must be separated by the word or, because a finding of any one of the acts or practices defined in the instructions would support recovery under the DTPA.

"Producing cause." A consumer may maintain an action where any act or omission violating the DTPA constitutes a *producing cause* of actual damages. DTPA § 17.50(a). The definition of "producing cause" is from *Rourke v. Garza*, 530 S.W.2d 794, 801 (Tex. 1975).

Broad-form submission. PJC 102.1 is a broad-form question designed to be accompanied by one or more appropriate instructions. Tex. R. Civ. P. 277 requires that "the court shall, whenever feasible, submit the cause upon broad-form questions." *See also Brown v. American Transfer & Storage Co.*, 601 S.W.2d 931, 937 (Tex. 1980) (approving broad question in deceptive trade practice case). If there is legal uncertainty on one or more theories of recovery, broad-form submission may not be feasible, and separate questions may be required. *See Romero v. KPH Consolidation, Inc.*, 166 S.W.3d 212, 215 (Tex. 2005); *Crown Life Insurance Co. v. Casteel*, 22 S.W.3d 378, 388–89 (Tex. 2000) (broad-form submission combining valid and invalid theories was harmful error).

Knowing or intentional conduct. If the defendant is found to have knowingly or intentionally engaged in any false, misleading, or deceptive conduct, the DTPA provides for additional damages. DTPA § 17.50(b)(1). See PJC 102.21 for a question on knowing or intentional conduct and PJC 115.11 for a question on additional damages.

Vicarious liability. If the issue is the vicarious liability of one for another's conduct, see *Celtic Life Insurance Co. v. Coats*, 885 S.W.2d 96, 98–99 (Tex. 1994); *Royal Globe Insurance Co. v. Bar Consultants, Inc.*, 577 S.W.2d 688, 693–95 (Tex. 1979) (discussing principal's liability for acts of agent in DTPA and Insurance Code case); and *Southwestern Bell Telephone Co. v. Wilson*, 768 S.W.2d 755, 759 (Tex. App.—Corpus Christi 1988, writ denied) (company liable for unreasonable collection efforts of outside attorneys that "were committed for the purpose of accomplishing the mission entrusted to the attorneys").

PJC 102.2 Description of Goods or Services or Affiliation of Persons (DTPA § 17.46(b)(5))

Representing that *goods* [*or services*] had or would have *characteristics* that they did not have [*or*]

COMMENT

When to use. PJC 102.2 is designed to accompany the question in PJC 102.1 to submit a cause of action based on Tex. Bus. & Com. Code § 17.46(b)(5) (DTPA).

Use of "or." If used with other instructions (see PJC 102.3–.6), PJC 102.2 must be followed by the word *or*, because a finding of any one of the acts or practices defined in the instructions would support recovery under the DTPA.

Source of instruction. DTPA § 17.46(b)(5) prohibits "representing that goods or services have sponsorship, approval, characteristics, ingredients, uses, benefits, or quantities which they do not have or that a person has a sponsorship, approval, status, affiliation, or connection which he does not."

Use of statutory language. The supreme court has held that jury submissions of section 17.46(b) cases should follow the language of the statute as closely as possible but may be altered somewhat to conform to the evidence of the case. *Spencer v. Eagle Star Insurance Co. of America*, 876 S.W.2d 154, 157 (Tex. 1994); *Brown v. American Transfer & Storage Co.*, 601 S.W.2d 931, 937 (Tex. 1980). Thus, if appropriate, the word *characteristics* may be replaced with the words *sponsorship*, *approval*, *ingredients*, *uses*, *benefits*, or *quantities*. *See Brown*, 601 S.W.2d at 937; DTPA § 17.46(b)(5). Material terms, however, should not be omitted or substituted. *See Transport Insurance Co. v. Faircloth*, 898 S.W.2d 269, 273 (Tex. 1995) (construing DTPA section 17.46(b)(23), renumbered in 2001 as DTPA § 17.46(b)(24)).

Affiliation of person. If deception regarding a person's affiliation is claimed, PJC 102.2 may be reworded as follows:

> Representing that a *person* had or would have *a sponsorship* that the *person* does not or will not have.

A. *Substitutions for "sponsorship."* In an appropriate case, the word *sponsorship* may be replaced with *status*, *affiliation*, *approval*, or *connection*. *See* DTPA § 17.46(b)(5).

B. *"Person" includes business entity.* Under the DTPA, the word *person* includes a business entity. DTPA § 17.45(3). In a case in which a business entity is involved, however, it may be advisable either to include the statutory definition in the charge or to substitute the name of the entity for the word *person*.

"Goods" includes real estate. The use of the word *goods* in PJC 102.2 is intended to cover real property. *See* DTPA § 17.45(1). If real estate is involved, however, it may be advisable either to include the statutory definition in the charge or to substitute a reference to the real estate in question for the word *goods*.

Misrepresentations about future characteristics, uses, or benefits. Although not appearing in the statute, the words *would have* are used in PJC 102.2. The Committee believes this use to be appropriate under *Brown*, 601 S.W.2d at 937, and *Smith v. Baldwin*, 611 S.W.2d 611, 614–16 (Tex. 1980) (representation need not be untrue when made: DTPA § 17.46(b) applies to misrepresentations about the future as well as about the present).

PJC 102.3 Quality of Goods or Services (DTPA § 17.46(b)(7))

Representing that *goods* [*or services*] are or will be of a particular *quality* if they were of another [*or*]

COMMENT

When to use. PJC 102.3 should be used with PJC 102.1 to submit a cause of action under Tex. Bus. & Com. Code § 17.46(b)(7) (DTPA).

Use of "or." If used with other instructions (see PJC 102.2 and 102.4–.6), PJC 102.3 must be followed by the word *or*, because a finding of any one of the acts or practices defined in the instructions would support recovery under the DTPA.

Source of instruction. DTPA § 17.46(b)(7) prohibits "representing that goods or services are of a particular standard, quality, or grade, or that goods are of a particular style or model, if they are of another."

Use of statutory language. The supreme court has held that jury submissions of section 17.46(b) cases should follow the language of the statute as closely as possible but may be altered somewhat to conform to the evidence of the case. *Spencer v. Eagle Star Insurance Co. of America*, 876 S.W.2d 154, 157 (Tex. 1994); *Brown v. American Transfer & Storage Co.*, 601 S.W.2d 931, 937 (Tex. 1980). Thus, if appropriate, the word *quality* may be replaced with the words *standard* or *grade*, and, if only goods and not services are involved, the words *style* or *model* may replace the word *quality*. *See Brown*, 601 S.W.2d at 937; DTPA § 17.46(b)(7). Material terms, however, should not be omitted or substituted. *See Transport Insurance Co. v. Faircloth*, 898 S.W.2d 269, 273 (Tex. 1995) (construing DTPA section 17.46(b)(23), renumbered in 2001 as DTPA § 17.46(b)(24)).

"Goods" includes real estate. The use of the word *goods* in PJC 102.3 is intended to cover real property. *See* DTPA § 17.45(1). If real estate is involved, however, it may be advisable either to include the statutory definition in the charge or to substitute a reference to the real estate in question for the word *goods*.

Misrepresentations about future quality. Although not appearing in the statute, the words *will be* are used in PJC 102.3. The Committee believes this use to be appropriate under *Brown*, 601 S.W.2d at 937, and *Smith v. Baldwin*, 611 S.W.2d 611, 614–16 (Tex. 1980) (representation need not be untrue when made: DTPA § 17.46(b) applies to misrepresentations concerning both present and future quality of goods or services).

PJC 102.4 Misrepresented and Unlawful Agreements (DTPA § 17.46(b)(12))

Representing that an agreement confers or involves *rights* that it did not have or involve [*or*]

COMMENT

When to use. PJC 102.4 should be used with PJC 102.1 to submit a cause of action under Tex. Bus. & Com. Code § 17.46(b)(12) (DTPA).

Use of "or." If used with other instructions (see PJC 102.2–.3 and 102.5–.6), PJC 102.4 must be followed by the word *or*, because a finding of any one of the acts or practices defined in the instructions would support recovery under the DTPA.

Source of instruction. DTPA § 17.46(b)(12) prohibits "representing that an agreement confers or involves rights, remedies, or obligations which it does not have or involve, or which are prohibited by law."

Use of statutory language. The supreme court has held that jury submissions of section 17.46(b) cases should follow the language of the statute as closely as possible but may be altered somewhat to conform to the evidence of the case. *Spencer v. Eagle Star Insurance Co. of America*, 876 S.W.2d 154, 157 (Tex. 1994); *Brown v. American Transfer & Storage Co.*, 601 S.W.2d 931, 937 (Tex. 1980). In an appropriate case, the words *remedies* and/or *obligations* may be added to or substituted for the word *rights* in the above instruction. *See Brown*, 601 S.W.2d at 937; DTPA § 17.46(b)(12). Material terms, however, should not be omitted or substituted. *See Transport Insurance Co. v. Faircloth*, 898 S.W.2d 269, 273 (Tex. 1995) (construing DTPA section 17.46(b)(23), renumbered in 2001 as DTPA § 17.46(b)(24)).

Misrepresentations about the future. A representation need not be untrue when made. Because DTPA § 17.46(b) applies to misrepresentations about the future as well as about the present, misrepresentations of present and future rights are covered by this instruction. *See Smith v. Baldwin*, 611 S.W.2d 611, 614–16 (Tex. 1980).

Unlawful agreement. DTPA § 17.46(b)(12) also prohibits representing that an agreement has terms that are "prohibited by law." Because the Committee believes that the question of what is prohibited by law would be for the court, the jury would be asked only whether the representation occurred. In such a case, the question might include:

> Representing that an agreement confers or involves [*insert particular right, remedy, or obligation found to be unlawful*].

PJC 102.5 Failure to Disclose Information (DTPA § 17.46(b)(24))

Failing to disclose information about *goods* [*or services*] that was known at the time of the transaction with the intention to induce *Paul Payne* into a transaction *he* otherwise would not have entered into if the information had been disclosed [*or*]

COMMENT

When to use. PJC 102.5 should be used with PJC 102.1 to submit a cause of action under Tex. Bus. & Com. Code § 17.46(b)(24) (DTPA).

Use of "or." If used with other instructions (see PJC 102.2–.4 and 102.6), PJC 102.5 must be followed by the word *or*, because a finding of any one of the acts or practices defined in the instructions would support recovery under the DTPA.

Source of instruction. DTPA § 17.46(b)(24) makes it a deceptive trade practice to fail "to disclose information concerning goods or services which was known at the time of the transaction if such failure to disclose such information was intended to induce the consumer into a transaction into which the consumer would not have entered had the information been disclosed."

Use of statutory language. The supreme court has held that jury submissions of section 17.46(b) cases should follow the language of the statute as closely as possible but may be altered somewhat to conform to the evidence of the case. *Spencer v. Eagle Star Insurance Co. of America*, 876 S.W.2d 154, 157 (Tex. 1994); *Brown v. American Transfer & Storage Co.*, 601 S.W.2d 931, 937 (Tex. 1980). Material terms, however, should not be omitted or substituted. *See Transport Insurance Co. v. Faircloth*, 898 S.W.2d 269, 273 (Tex. 1995) (construing DTPA section 17.46(b)(23), renumbered in 2001 as DTPA § 17.46(b)(24)).

"Goods" includes real estate. The use of the word *goods* in PJC 102.5 is intended to cover real property. *See* DTPA § 17.45(1). If real estate is involved, however, it may be advisable either to include the statutory definition in the charge or to substitute a reference to the real estate in question for the word *goods*.

PJC 102.6 Other "Laundry List" Violations (DTPA § 17.46(b)) (Comment)

PJC 102.2–.5 provide patterns for submitting the most frequently litigated claims under section 17.46(b). *See* Tex. Bus. & Com. Code § 17.46(b)(5), (7), (12), (24) (DTPA). However, a claim arising under any other subsection of section 17.46(b) may be handled in the same manner—for example, by adapting the statutory language to the facts of the case in the form of an instruction to be submitted with PJC 102.1.

PJC 102.7 Question and Instruction on Unconscionable Action or Course of Action (DTPA §§ 17.50(a)(3) and 17.45(5))

QUESTION ______

Did *Don Davis* engage in any unconscionable action or course of action that was a producing cause of damages to *Paul Payne*?

"Producing cause" means a cause that was a substantial factor in bringing about the damages, if any, and without which the damages would not have occurred. There may be more than one producing cause.

An unconscionable action or course of action is an act or practice that, to a consumer's detriment, takes advantage of the lack of knowledge, ability, experience, or capacity of the consumer to a grossly unfair degree.

Answer: _______________

COMMENT

When to use. PJC 102.7 is to be used with PJC 102.1 to submit a claim based on Tex. Bus. & Com. Code § 17.50(a)(3) (DTPA). This statute gives a consumer a cause of action for "any unconscionable action or course of action by any person." The definition of "unconscionable action or course of action" is derived from DTPA § 17.45(5). Questions for other causes of action based on the DTPA or the Insurance Code may be found at PJC 102.1 (false, misleading, or deceptive act), 102.8 (warranty), 102.14 (Insurance Code), and 102.21 (knowing or intentional conduct).

"Producing cause." Under section 17.50(a) of the DTPA, a "consumer may maintain an action where any of the following constitute a *producing cause*" of actual damages. DTPA § 17.50(a) (emphasis added). The definition of "producing cause" is from *Ford Motor Co. v. Ledesma*, 242 S.W.3d 32, 46 (Tex. 2007). Both "contributing" and "in a natural sequence" are omitted from the definition of "producing cause" above. The supreme court did not retain those words in its analysis. *See Ledesma*, 242 S.W.3d at 46. However, the court did not criticize either of those concepts, and it may be appropriate to retain one or both of those concepts in an appropriate case.

Broad-form submission. PJC 102.7 is a broad-form question designed to be accompanied by one or more appropriate instructions. Tex. R. Civ. P. 277 requires that "the court shall, whenever feasible, submit the cause upon broad-form questions." *See also Brown v. American Transfer & Storage Co.*, 601 S.W.2d 931, 937 (Tex. 1980) (approving broad question in deceptive trade practice case). If there is legal uncertainty on one or more theories of recovery, broad-form submission may not be feasible, and separate questions may be required. *See Romero v. KPH Consolidation, Inc.*, 166 S.W.3d 212, 215 (Tex. 2005); *Crown Life Insurance Co. v. Casteel*, 22 S.W.3d 378, 389 (Tex. 2000) (broad-form submission combining valid and invalid theories was harmful error).

Knowing or intentional conduct. If the defendant is found to have knowingly or intentionally engaged in any false, misleading, or deceptive conduct, the DTPA provides for additional damages. DTPA § 17.50(b)(1). See PJC 102.21 for a question on knowing or intentional conduct and PJC 115.11 for a question on additional damages.

Vicarious liability. If the issue is the vicarious liability of one for another's conduct, see *Celtic Life Insurance Co. v. Coats*, 885 S.W.2d 96, 98–99 (Tex. 1994); *Royal Globe Insurance Co. v. Bar Consultants, Inc.*, 577 S.W.2d 688, 693–95 (Tex. 1979) (discussing principal's liability for acts of agent in DTPA and Insurance Code case); and *Southwestern Bell Telephone Co. v. Wilson*, 768 S.W.2d 755, 759 (Tex. App.—Corpus Christi 1988, writ denied) (company liable for unreasonable collection efforts of outside attorneys that "were committed for the purpose of accomplishing the mission entrusted to the attorneys").

PJC 102.8 Question and Instruction on Warranty (DTPA § 17.50(a)(2); Tex. UCC §§ 2.313–.315)

QUESTION ______

Was the failure, if any, of *Don Davis* to comply with a warranty a producing cause of damages to *Paul Payne*?

> "Producing cause" means a cause that was a substantial factor in bringing about the damages, if any, and without which the damages would not have occurred. There may be more than one producing cause.
>
> "Failure to comply with a warranty" means any of the following:

[Insert appropriate instructions.]

Answer: _______________

COMMENT

When to use. PJC 102.8 is a basic question that should be appropriate in most cases brought under Tex. Bus. & Com. Code § 17.50(a)(2) (DTPA). *See also* Tex. Bus. & Com. Code §§ 2.313–.315 (Tex. UCC). Questions for other causes of action based on the DTPA or the Insurance Code may be found at PJC 102.1 (false, misleading, or deceptive act), 102.7 (unconscionable action), 102.14 (Insurance Code), and 102.21 (knowing or intentional conduct).

Creation of warranty. The DTPA does not define "warranty." Nor does it create any warranties; therefore, any warranty must be established independently of the Act. *La Sara Grain Co. v. First National Bank*, 673 S.W.2d 558, 565 (Tex. 1984).

"Producing cause." Under section 17.50(a) of the DTPA, a "consumer may maintain an action where any of the following constitute a *producing cause*" of actual damages. DTPA § 17.50(a) (emphasis added). The definition of "producing cause" is from *Ford Motor Co. v. Ledesma*, 242 S.W.3d 32, 46 (Tex. 2007). Both "contributing" and "in a natural sequence" are omitted from the definition of "producing cause" above. The supreme court did not retain those words in its analysis. *See Ledesma*, 242 S.W.3d at 46. However, the court did not criticize either of those concepts, and it may be appropriate to retain one or both of those concepts in an appropriate case.

Accompanying instructions. Instructions to accompany PJC 102.8, informing the jury what type of conduct should be considered under the question, are at PJC 102.9–.13. If more than one instruction is used, each must be separated by the word *or*, because a finding of any one of the acts or practices defined in the instructions would support recovery under the DTPA.

Broad-form submission. PJC 102.8 is a broad-form question designed to be accompanied by one or more appropriate instructions. Tex. R. Civ. P. 277 requires that "the court shall, whenever feasible, submit the cause upon broad-form questions." *See also Brown v. American Transfer & Storage Co.*, 601 S.W.2d 931, 937 (Tex. 1980) (approving broad question in deceptive trade practice case). If there is legal uncertainty on one or more theories of recovery, broad-form submission may not be feasible, and separate questions may be required. *See Romero v. KPH Consolidation, Inc.*, 166 S.W.3d 212, 215 (Tex. 2005); *Crown Life Insurance Co. v. Casteel*, 22 S.W.3d 378, 389 (Tex. 2000) (broad-form submission combining valid and invalid theories was harmful error).

Knowing or intentional conduct. If the defendant is found to have knowingly or intentionally engaged in any false, misleading, or deceptive conduct, the DTPA provides for additional damages. DTPA § 17.50(b)(1). See PJC 102.21 for a question on knowing or intentional conduct and PJC 115.11 for a question on additional damages.

Vicarious liability. If the issue is the vicarious liability of one for another's conduct, see *Celtic Life Insurance Co. v. Coats*, 885 S.W.2d 96, 98–99 (Tex. 1994); *Royal Globe Insurance Co. v. Bar Consultants, Inc.*, 577 S.W.2d 688, 693–95 (Tex. 1979) (discussing principal's liability for acts of agent in DTPA and Insurance Code case); and *Southwestern Bell Telephone Co. v. Wilson*, 768 S.W.2d 755, 759 (Tex. App.—Corpus Christi 1988, writ denied) (company liable for unreasonable collection efforts of outside attorneys that "were committed for the purpose of accomplishing the mission entrusted to the attorneys").

PJC 102.9 Express Warranty—Goods or Services (DTPA § 17.50(a)(2); Tex. UCC § 2.313)

Failing to comply with an express warranty.

An express warranty is any affirmation of fact or promise made by *Don Davis* that relates to the [*describe particular goods*] and becomes part of the basis of the bargain. It is not necessary that formal words such as "warrant" or "guarantee" be used or that there be a specific intent to make a warranty.

[*or*]

COMMENT

When to use. PJC 102.9 may be used with PJC 102.8 to submit a claim of breach of express warranty involving the sale of goods. *See* Tex. Bus. & Com. Code § 17.50(a)(2) (DTPA); *see also* Tex. Bus. & Com. Code § 2.313 (Tex. UCC) (creation of express warranty).

Use of "or." If used with other instructions (see PJC 102.10–.13), PJC 102.9 must be followed by the word *or*, because a finding of any one of the acts or practices defined in the instructions would support recovery under the DTPA.

Creation of warranty. The DTPA does not define "warranty." Nor does it create any warranties; therefore, any warranty must be established independently of the Act. *La Sara Grain Co. v. First National Bank*, 673 S.W.2d 558, 565 (Tex. 1984).

Goods or services. The Uniform Commercial Code defines and creates warranties in the sale of goods. Tex. UCC § 2.313. It defines "goods" as "all things . . . movable at the time of identification to the contract for sale . . . . [and] the unborn young of animals and growing crops and other identified things attached to realty." Tex. UCC § 2.105. The DTPA, however, has a broader definition of "goods" in that it includes real estate. DTPA § 17.45(1) ("goods" means tangible chattels or real property purchased or leased for use). The DTPA also includes services. DTPA § 17.45(2).

There are no decisions compelling the use of the UCC definition of express warranty set forth in PJC 102.9 in a nongoods case. In *Southwestern Bell Telephone Co. v. FDP Corp.*, 811 S.W.2d 572, 574 (Tex. 1991), the supreme court stated that because "sale of advertising is predominantly a service transaction, not a sale of goods, the warranty provisions of Article Two of the [UCC] do not explicitly govern this case." The court also stated that "although the case at bar involves a service transaction, reference to the Code is instructive." *Southwestern Bell Telephone Co.*, 811 S.W.2d at 575. The Committee expresses no opinion on whether the above definition should be used in nongoods cases.

Affirmation merely of value of goods. A mere affirmation of the value of the goods or a statement purporting to be merely the seller's opinion or commendation of the goods does not create a warranty. Tex. UCC § 2.313.

Superior knowledge. If the seller has knowledge superior to that of the consumer, however, such an affirmation may create a warranty. *Valley Datsun v. Martinez*, 578 S.W.2d 485, 490 (Tex. Civ. App.—Corpus Christi 1979, no writ) (seller's knowledge, in conjunction with buyer's ignorance, operated to "make the slightest divergence from mere praise into representations of fact" and create warranty). In a case in which the issue is in dispute, the jury might be asked whether the defendant *had* such knowledge:

> Did *Don Davis* have, or purport to have, superior knowledge of the subject matter of any misrepresentation that you have found was a producing cause of *Paul Payne*'s damages?
>
> *Don Davis* had superior knowledge of the subject matter if *his* knowledge or information regarding that subject matter was superior to that possessed by *Paul Payne* and *Paul Payne* did not have equal access to such knowledge or information.
>
> *Don Davis* purported to have superior knowledge if *he* had the appearance of having such knowledge or implied, professed outwardly, or claimed that *he* had such knowledge regarding a matter that was not equally open to *Paul Payne.*

For discussions of the "superior knowledge" rule, see *Trenholm v. Ratcliff*, 646 S.W.2d 927, 930 (Tex. 1983); *United States Pipe & Foundry Co. v. City of Waco*, 108 S.W.2d 432, 435–37 (Tex. 1937); *Valley Datsun*, 578 S.W.2d at 490; and *General Supply & Equipment Co. v. Phillips*, 490 S.W.2d 913, 917 (Tex. Civ. App.—Tyler 1972, writ ref'd n.r.e.).

PJC 102.10 Implied Warranty of Merchantability—Goods (DTPA § 17.50(a)(2); Tex. UCC § 2.314(b)(3))

Furnishing goods that, because of a lack of something necessary for adequacy, were not fit for the ordinary purposes for which such goods are used [*or*]

COMMENT

When to use. PJC 102.10 may be used with PJC 102.8 to submit a cause of action for breach of an implied warranty of merchantability under Tex. Bus. & Com. Code § 2.314(b)(3) (Tex. UCC). *See also* Tex. Bus. & Com. Code § 17.50(a)(2) (DTPA); *Plas-Tex, Inc. v. U.S. Steel Corp.*, 772 S.W.2d 442 (Tex. 1989).

Use of "or." If used with other instructions (see PJC 102.9 and 102.11–.13), PJC 102.10 must be followed by the word *or*, because a finding of any one of the acts or practices defined in the instructions would support recovery under the DTPA.

Caveat. Note that the above instruction is appropriate *only* for a case brought under Tex. UCC § 2.314(b)(3). *See Plas-Tex, Inc.*, 772 S.W.2d at 444–45. *Plas-Tex, Inc.* defined "defect" as "a condition of the goods that renders them unfit for the ordinary purposes for which they are used because of a lack of something necessary for adequacy." *Plas-Tex, Inc.*, 772 S.W.2d at 444. For simplicity and clarity, the Committee has included only the definition itself in the above instruction. The Committee expresses no opinion about the above definition's applicability if the evidence shows a *presence*, rather than a *lack*, of something that makes the goods unfit.

Other elements of merchantability. For cases involving other elements of merchantability, the instruction should be modified to delete the reference to "defect" and to include the relevant elements raised by the evidence. The elements are as follows:

> Furnishing fungible goods not of fair average quality within the description;
>
> Furnishing goods that did not run, within the variations permitted by the agreement, of even kind, quality, and quantity within each unit and among all units involved;
>
> Furnishing goods that were not adequately contained, packaged, and labeled as the agreement required;
>
> Furnishing goods that did not conform to the promises or affirmations of fact made on the container or label.

Tex. UCC § 2.314(b)(2), (4)–(6); *see also* Tex. UCC § 2.314(b)(1).

Seller must be merchant. The implied warranty arises only if the seller is a "merchant" as defined in Tex. UCC § 2.104(a). Tex. UCC § 2.314(a). Whether the seller is subject to the statute has been held to be a jury issue. *Nelson v. Union Equity Co-operative Exchange*, 536 S.W.2d 635, 641 (Tex. Civ. App.—Fort Worth 1976), *aff'd on other grounds*, 548 S.W.2d 352 (Tex. 1977).

PJC 102.11 Implied Warranty of Fitness for Particular Purpose—Goods (DTPA § 17.50(a)(2); Tex. UCC § 2.315)

Furnishing or selecting goods that were not suitable for a particular purpose if *Don Davis* had reason to know the purpose and also had reason to know that *Paul Payne* was relying on *Don Davis*'s skill or judgment to furnish or select suitable goods [*or*]

COMMENT

When to use. PJC 102.11 may be used with PJC 102.8 to submit a claim of breach of an implied warranty of fitness for a particular purpose. *See* Tex. Bus. & Com. Code § 17.50(a)(2) (DTPA); Tex. Bus. & Com. Code § 2.315 (Tex. UCC).

Use of "or." If used with other instructions (see PJC 102.10 and 102.12–.13), PJC 102.11 must be followed by the word *or*, because a finding of any one of the acts or practices defined in the instructions would support recovery under the DTPA.

Defendant need not be merchant. Note that this warranty does not require the defendant to be a "merchant," as does the implied warranty of merchantability in Tex. UCC § 2.314. See PJC 102.10.

PJC 102.12 Implied Warranty of Good and Workmanlike Performance—Services (DTPA § 17.50(a)(2))

Failing to perform services in a good and workmanlike manner.

A good and workmanlike manner is that quality of work performed by one who has the knowledge, training, or experience necessary for the successful practice of a trade or occupation and performed in a manner generally considered proficient by those capable of judging such work.

[*or*]

COMMENT

When to use. PJC 102.12, when used with PJC 102.8, submits the claim of a breach of an implied warranty to perform services in a good and workmanlike manner. *See* Tex. Bus. & Com. Code § 17.50(a)(2) (DTPA); *Melody Home Manufacturing Co. v. Barnes*, 741 S.W.2d 349, 354 (Tex. 1987) (implied warranty to repair or modify goods or property in good and workmanlike manner); *Humber v. Morton*, 426 S.W.2d 554 (Tex. 1968) (implied warranty of construction of new home in good and workmanlike manner). In *Parkway Co. v. Woodruff*, 901 S.W.2d 434, 439 (Tex. 1995), the supreme court announced that this service warranty (1) "will not be judicially imposed unless there is a demonstrated need for it"; and (2) "extends only to services provided to remedy defects existing at the time of the relevant consumer transaction."

Use of "or." If used with other instructions (see PJC 102.9–.11 and 102.13), PJC 102.12 must be followed by the word *or,* because a finding of any one of the acts or practices defined in the instructions would support recovery under the DTPA.

Source of instruction. The above instruction is from *Melody Home Manufacturing Co.*, 741 S.W.2d at 354.

Independent of warranty of habitability. The warranty covered by PJC 102.12 is independent of the implied warranty of habitability. *Evans v. J. Stiles, Inc.*, 689 S.W.2d 399, 400 (Tex. 1985). There is no need for additional language in the instruction, such as "and suitable for human habitation." *Cocke v. White*, 697 S.W.2d 739, 744 (Tex. App.—Corpus Christi 1985, writ ref'd n.r.e.). See PJC 102.13 for the implied warranty of habitability.

PJC 102.13 Implied Warranty of Habitability (DTPA § 17.50(a)(2))

Selling a home that was not suitable for human habitation [*or*]

COMMENT

When to use. PJC 102.13 may be used with PJC 102.8 to submit a claim of breach of implied warranty of habitability. *See* Tex. Bus. & Com. Code § 17.50(a)(2) (DTPA); *Humber v. Morton*, 426 S.W.2d 554 (Tex. 1968) (implied warranty of habitability in new home construction); *see also Gupta v. Ritter Homes, Inc.*, 646 S.W.2d 168, 169 (Tex. 1983) (warranty extends to all subsequent purchasers); *but see PPG Industries v. JMB/Houston Centers Partners Ltd. Partnership*, 146 S.W.3d 79, 88 n.37 (Tex. 2004) (asserting that *Gupta v. Ritter Homes, Inc.* has been overruled on this issue).

Use of "or." If used with other instructions (see PJC 102.9–.12), PJC 102.13 must be followed by the word *or*, because a finding of any one of the acts or practices defined in the instructions would support recovery under the DTPA.

Habitability in residential leases. In *Kamarath v. Bennett*, 568 S.W.2d 658, 660–61 (Tex. 1978), the court found an implied warranty of habitability applicable to a rented apartment. However, legislation has since been passed setting forth the specific duties of a landlord "to repair and remedy" residential premises. Tex. Prop. Code § 92.052. These duties are in lieu of existing common-law and statutory warranties. Tex. Prop. Code § 92.061.

Suitability in commercial leases. In *Davidow v. Inwood North Professional Group—Phase I*, 747 S.W.2d 373, 377 (Tex. 1988), the court held that an implied warranty of suitability had been breached in the commercial lease of a doctor's office. In an appropriate case, the language of PJC 102.13 may be adapted to cover the breach of this warranty.

Distinguished from "good and workmanlike" warranty. The *Humber* warranty contains two distinct elements: (1) warranty of good and workmanlike manner of construction of a new home and (2) warranty of habitability. *Evans v. J. Stiles, Inc.*, 689 S.W.2d 399, 400 (Tex. 1985). For the warranty of good and workmanlike manner of construction, see PJC 102.12.

PJC 102.14 Question on Insurance Code Chapter 541

QUESTION ______

Did *Don Davis* engage in any unfair or deceptive act or practice that caused damages to *Paul Payne*?

"Unfair or deceptive act or practice" means any of the following:

[Insert appropriate instructions.]

Answer: _______________

COMMENT

When to use. PJC 102.14 is a basic question that should be appropriate in most cases brought under Tex. Ins. Code ch. 541 (formerly Tex. Ins. Code art. 21.21). Code section 541.003 also prohibits "unfair methods of competition," and in such a case PJC 102.14 should be modified as appropriate. Questions for causes of action based on the DTPA may be found at PJC 102.1 (false, misleading, or deceptive act), 102.7 (unconscionable action), and 102.8 (warranty). See also PJC 102.21 (knowing or intentional conduct).

Accompanying instructions. Instructions to accompany PJC 102.14, informing the jury what type of conduct should be considered under the question, are at PJC 102.16–.19. If more than one instruction is used, each must be separated by the word *or*, because a finding of any one of the acts or practices defined in the instructions would support recovery under the Insurance Code.

Broad-form submission. PJC 102.14 is a broad-form question designed to be accompanied by one or more appropriate instructions. Tex. R. Civ. P. 277 requires that "the court shall, whenever feasible, submit the cause upon broad-form questions." *See also Brown v. American Transfer & Storage Co.*, 601 S.W.2d 931, 937 (Tex. 1980) (approving broad question in deceptive trade practice case). If there is legal uncertainty on one or more theories of recovery, broad-form submission may not be feasible, and separate questions may be required. *See Romero v. KPH Consolidation, Inc.*, 166 S.W.3d 212, 215 (Tex. 2005); *Crown Life Insurance Co. v. Casteel*, 22 S.W.3d 378, 389 (Tex. 2000) (broad-form submission combining valid and invalid theories was harmful error).

Knowing conduct. If the defendant is found to have knowingly engaged in an unfair or deceptive act or practice, the Insurance Code provides for additional damages. Tex. Ins. Code § 541.152(b). See PJC 102.21 for a question on knowing conduct and PJC 115.11 for a question on additional damages.

Additional damages. An award of additional damages is discretionary with the trier of fact if the defendant acted knowingly. To seek additional damages, the plaintiff should submit the question on knowing conduct as in PJC 102.21 and then should ask the jury to determine the amount of additional damages as in PJC 115.11.

Causation. Unlike the DTPA questions (PJC 102.1, 102.7, and 102.8), PJC 102.14 does not contain the term "producing cause," because the Insurance Code does not refer to "producing cause" as an element. Instead, the Code grants a cause of action to a person who has sustained actual damages "caused by" another's engaging in a prohibited act. *See* Tex. Ins. Code § 541.151 (formerly Tex. Ins. Code art. 21.21, § 16(a)). The Committee believes that "producing cause" need not be submitted to obtain actual damages as long as the damages question inquires about damages that were caused by the prohibited conduct. The insurance damages question, PJC 115.13, contains such an inquiry. For a discussion of the special causation issues relating to recovery of policy benefits as damages, see the Comment to PJC 115.13.

Vicarious liability. If the issue is the vicarious liability of one for another's conduct, see *Celtic Life Insurance Co. v. Coats*, 885 S.W.2d 96, 98–99 (Tex. 1994); *Royal Globe Insurance Co. v. Bar Consultants, Inc.*, 577 S.W.2d 688, 693–95 (Tex. 1979) (discussing principal's liability for acts of agent in DTPA and Insurance Code case); and *Southwestern Bell Telephone Co. v. Wilson*, 768 S.W.2d 755, 759 (Tex. App.—Corpus Christi 1988, writ denied) (company liable for unreasonable collection efforts of outside attorneys that "were committed for the purpose of accomplishing the mission entrusted to the attorneys").

[PJC 102.15 is reserved for expansion.]

PJC 102.16 Misrepresentations or False Advertising of Policy Contracts—Insurance (Tex. Ins. Code § 541.051(1))

Making or causing to be made any statement misrepresenting the terms, benefits, or advantages of an insurance policy [*or*]

COMMENT

When to use. PJC 102.16 may be used with PJC 102.14 to submit a claim of misrepresentation or false advertising of an insurance policy. *See* Tex. Ins. Code § 541.051(1) (formerly Tex. Ins. Code art. 21.21, § 4(1)); *Royal Globe Insurance Co. v. Bar Consultants, Inc.*, 577 S.W.2d 688 (Tex. 1979). A claim may also be brought under Tex. Bus. & Com. Code § 17.50(a)(4) (DTPA).

Use of "or." If used with other instructions (see PJC 102.17–.19), PJC 102.16 must be followed by the word *or*, because a finding of any one of the acts or practices defined in the instructions would support recovery.

Use of statutory language. The supreme court has held that jury submission in this type of case should follow the statutory language as closely as possible but may be altered somewhat to conform to the evidence of the case. *Spencer v. Eagle Star Insurance Co. of America*, 876 S.W.2d 154, 157 (Tex. 1994); *Brown v. American Transfer & Storage Co.*, 601 S.W.2d 931, 937 (Tex. 1980). Material terms, however, should not be omitted or substituted. *See Transport Insurance Co. v. Faircloth*, 898 S.W.2d 269, 273 (Tex. 1995) (construing DTPA section 17.46(b)(23), renumbered in 2001 as DTPA § 17.46(b)(24)).

Adapt instruction for other claims. Other kinds of conduct are outlawed by chapter 541, subchapter B, of the Insurance Code, all of which are actionable under DTPA § 17.50(a)(4) and Tex. Ins. Code ch. 541, subch. D, and the instruction should be adapted to include the kind involved in the case. *See, e.g.*, Tex. Ins. Code § 541.054 ("Boycott, Coercion and Intimidation"). For sample instructions submitting other claims under chapter 541, subchapter B, see PJC 102.17–.19. For other conduct prohibited by other subparts of subchapter B, instructions may be drafted using the above instruction or the forms at PJC 102.16–.19.

PJC 102.17 False Information or Advertising—Insurance (Tex. Ins. Code § 541.052)

Making, or directly or indirectly causing to be made, an assertion, representation, or statement with respect to insurance that was untrue, deceptive, or misleading [*or*]

COMMENT

When to use. PJC 102.17 should be used with PJC 102.14 to submit a claim under Tex. Ins. Code § 541.052 (formerly Tex. Ins. Code art. 21.21, § 4(2)), which prohibits false information in advertising generally. *See Royal Globe Insurance Co. v. Bar Consultants, Inc.*, 577 S.W.2d 688 (Tex. 1979). A claim may also be brought under Tex. Bus. & Com. Code § 17.50(a)(4) (DTPA).

Use of "or." If used with other instructions (see PJC 102.16 and 102.18–.19), PJC 102.17 must be followed by the word *or*, because a finding of any one of the acts or practices defined in the instructions would support recovery.

Use of statutory language. The supreme court has held that jury submission in this type of case should follow the statutory language as closely as possible but may be altered somewhat to conform to the evidence of the case. *Spencer v. Eagle Star Insurance Co. of America*, 876 S.W.2d 154, 157 (Tex. 1994); *Brown v. American Transfer & Storage Co.*, 601 S.W.2d 931, 937 (Tex. 1980). Material terms, however, should not be omitted or substituted. *See Transport Insurance Co. v. Faircloth*, 898 S.W.2d 269, 273 (Tex. 1995) (construing DTPA section 17.46(b)(23), renumbered in 2001 as DTPA § 17.46(b)(24)).

Adapt instruction for other claims. Other kinds of conduct are outlawed by chapter 541, subchapter B, of the Insurance Code, all of which are actionable under DTPA § 17.50(a)(4) and Tex. Ins. Code ch. 541, subch. D, and the instruction should be adapted to include the kind involved in the case. *See, e.g.*, Tex. Ins. Code § 541.054 ("Boycott, Coercion and Intimidation"). For sample instructions submitting other claims under chapter 541, subchapter B, see PJC 102.16, 102.18, or 102.19. For other conduct prohibited by other subparts of chapter 541, subchapter B, instructions may be drafted using the above instruction or the forms at PJC 102.16–.19.

PJC 102.18 Unfair Insurance Settlement Practices (Tex. Ins. Code § 541.060)

Misrepresenting to a claimant a material fact or policy provision relating to the coverage at issue [*or*]

Failing to attempt in good faith to effectuate a prompt, fair, and equitable settlement of a claim when the insurer's liability has become reasonably clear [*or*]

Failing to attempt in good faith to effectuate a prompt, fair, and equitable settlement under one part of a policy, when the insurer's liability has become reasonably clear, if the failure to settle was in order to influence *Paul Payne* to settle an additional claim under another part of the policy [*or*]

Failing to provide promptly to *Paul Payne* a reasonable explanation of the factual and legal basis in the policy for an insurer's denial of the claim [or the insurer's offer of a compromise settlement of the claim] [*or*]

Failing to affirm or deny coverage of a claim within a reasonable time [*or*]

Failing to submit a reservation of rights letter to *Paul Payne* within a reasonable time [*or*]

Refusing [failing or unreasonably delaying] a settlement offer under *Paul Payne*'s policy, because other coverage may have been available, [or because other parties may be responsible for the damages *Paul Payne* suffered] [*or*]

Trying to enforce a full and final release of a claim by *Paul Payne*, when only a partial payment had been made, unless the release was for a doubtful or disputed claim [*or*]

Refusing to pay a claim without conducting a reasonable investigation of the claim [*or*]

Delaying [or refusing] to settle *Paul Payne*'s claim solely because there was other insurance available to satisfy all or any part of the loss that formed the basis of *his* claim [*or*]

Requiring that *Paul Payne* produce *his* federal income tax returns for inspection or investigation, as a condition of settling *his* claim [*or*]

COMMENT

When to use. PJC 102.18 may be used with PJC 102.14 to submit a cause of action for unfair settlement practices under Tex. Ins. Code § 541.060 (formerly Tex. Ins. Code art. 21.21, § 4(10)). Use only the subpart(s) raised by the pleadings and the evidence.

Use of "or." If used with other instructions (see PJC 102.16–.17 and 102.19), or if more than one subpart is used, each subpart used from PJC 102.18 must be followed by the word *or*, because a finding of any one of the acts or practices defined in the instructions would support recovery.

Source of instruction. PJC 102.18 is based on Tex. Ins. Code § 541.060, which prohibits unfair settlement practices.

Use of statutory language. The supreme court has held that jury submission in this type of case should follow the statutory language as closely as possible but may be altered somewhat to conform to the evidence of the case. *Spencer v. Eagle Star Insurance Co. of America*, 876 S.W.2d 154, 157 (Tex. 1994); *Brown v. American Transfer & Storage Co.*, 601 S.W.2d 931, 937 (Tex. 1980). Material terms, however, should not be omitted or substituted. *See Transport Insurance Co. v. Faircloth*, 898 S.W.2d 269, 273 (Tex. 1995) (construing Texas Business and Commerce Code section 17.46(b)(23) (DTPA), renumbered in 2001 as DTPA § 17.46(b)(24)). Several of the subsections in Tex. Ins. Code § 541.060 contain additional terms that may be added to the instruction or that may preclude submission of a particular practice.

Liability insurance cases. In *Rocor International, Inc. v. National Union Fire Insurance Co.*, 77 S.W.3d 253, 260 (Tex. 2002), the supreme court held that a liability insurer may be liable to an insured under Tex. Ins. Code art. 21.21 (now codified as Tex. Ins. Code ch. 541) for failing to settle when the insurer's liability becomes reasonably clear. The court held that the insurer's liability becomes reasonably clear when "(1) the policy covers the claim, (2) the insured's liability is reasonably clear, (3) the claimant has made a proper settlement demand within policy limits, and (4) the demand's terms are such that an ordinarily prudent insurer would accept it." *Rocor International, Inc.*, 77 S.W.3d at 262. Element (1), in most cases, will be a question of law or will require resolution of a separate fact question. Element (3), in most cases, will involve a question of law. The following instruction would be appropriate to submit elements (2) and (4):

> You are instructed that an "insurer's liability has become reasonably clear" when the insured's liability to the claimant in the underlying case is reasonably clear and the claimant's settlement demand to the insured is such that an ordinarily prudent insurer would accept it.

PJC 102.19 Misrepresentation—Insurance (Tex. Ins. Code § 541.061)

Making any misrepresentation relating to an insurance policy by:

a. making any untrue statement of a material fact; or

b. failing to state a material fact that is necessary to make other statements not misleading, considering the circumstances under which the statements are made; or

c. making any statement in such a manner as to mislead a reasonably prudent person to a false conclusion of a material fact; or

d. stating that [*insert any misstatement of law*]; or

e. failing to disclose [*insert matters required by law to be disclosed*].

[*or*]

COMMENT

When to use. PJC 102.19 may be used with PJC 102.14 to submit a cause of action for any misrepresentation relating to an insurance policy. *See* Tex. Ins. Code § 541.061 (formerly Tex. Ins. Code art. 21.21, § 4(11)).

Use of "or." If used with other instructions (see PJC 102.16–.18), PJC 102.19 must be followed by the word *or*, because a finding of any one of the acts or practices defined in the instructions would support recovery.

Source of instruction. PJC 102.19 is based on Tex. Ins. Code § 541.061, which prohibits misrepresentation.

Use of statutory language. The supreme court has held that jury submission in this type of case should follow the statutory language as closely as possible but may be altered somewhat to conform to the evidence of the case. *Spencer v. Eagle Star Insurance Co. of America*, 876 S.W.2d 154, 157 (Tex. 1994); *Brown v. American Transfer & Storage Co.*, 601 S.W.2d 931, 937 (Tex. 1980). Material terms, however, should not be omitted or substituted. *See Transport Insurance Co. v. Faircloth*, 898 S.W.2d 269, 273 (Tex. 1995) (construing Texas Business and Commerce Code section 17.46(b)(23) (DTPA), renumbered in 2001 as DTPA § 17.46(b)(24)). Subparts *d* and *e* of PJC 102.19 submit questions relating to misstatements of law and failures to disclose information required by law. It is the Committee's opinion that these prohibitions require a preliminary determination by the trial court about whether the conduct was a misstatement of law or nondisclosure of information required by law to be disclosed, before the jury decides whether the conduct occurred. Therefore, the instruction should be adapted to conform to the specific conduct found by the trial court.

[PJC 102.20 is reserved for expansion.]

PJC 102.21 Question and Instruction on Knowing or Intentional Conduct

If your answer to Question ______ [*102.1, 102.7, 102.8, or 102.14*] is "Yes," then answer the following question. Otherwise, do not answer the following question.

QUESTION ______

Did *Don Davis* engage in any such conduct *knowingly* [*intentionally*]?

> "Knowingly" means actual awareness, at the time of the conduct, of the falsity, deception, or unfairness of the conduct in question or actual awareness of the conduct constituting a failure to comply with a warranty. Actual awareness may be inferred where objective manifestations indicate that a person acted with actual awareness.

[And/or insert definition of "intentionally."]

In answering this question, consider only the conduct that you have found *was a producing cause of* damages to *Paul Payne.*

Answer: ______________

COMMENT

When to use. PJC 102.21 is to be used if there is evidence that the defendant knowingly or intentionally engaged in conduct that violates the DTPA or Insurance Code. *See* Tex. Bus. & Com. Code § 17.50(b)(1) (DTPA); Tex. Ins. Code § 541.152(b) (formerly Tex. Ins. Code art. 21.21, § 16(b)(1)).

The Insurance Code allows the jury to award up to three times the plaintiff's actual damages if the defendant acted "knowingly." Tex. Ins. Code § 541.152(b). In contrast, the DTPA distinguishes between economic damages and mental anguish damages. A finding that the defendant acted "knowingly" allows discretionary trebling only of the plaintiff's economic damages. Discretionary trebling of both economic damages and mental anguish damages is allowed only if the defendant acted intentionally. DTPA § 17.50(b)(1).

Definition of "knowingly." The definition of "knowingly" comes from DTPA § 17.45(9). The definition is different under Tex. Ins. Code § 541.002(1). In a suit brought under that statute, the definition should read:

> "Knowingly" means actual awareness of the falsity, unfairness, or deceptiveness of the act or practice on which a claim for damages is based. Actual awareness may be inferred if objective manifestations indicate that a person acted with actual awareness.

Tex. Ins. Code § 541.002(1).

Definition and use of "intentionally." The difference between "knowledge" and "intent" is that under "intent" the defendant specifically intended that the consumer act in detrimental reliance. *Compare* DTPA § 17.45(9) *with* § 17.45(13). A finding that the defendant acted knowingly allows discretionary trebling only of economic damages under the DTPA, whereas a finding of intentional conduct allows discretionary trebling of both economic and mental anguish damages. DTPA § 17.50(b)(1). If both economic damages and mental anguish damages are sought, the consumer may choose to submit separate questions on the defendant's knowledge and intent, or a single question on intent.

If the defendant's intent is submitted, the following definition should be used in addition to, or instead of, the definition of "knowingly":

> "Intentionally" means actual awareness of the falsity, deception, or unfairness of the conduct in question or actual awareness of the conduct constituting a failure to comply with a warranty, coupled with the specific intent that the consumer act in detrimental reliance on the falsity or deception [or *detrimental ignorance of the unfairness*]. Specific intent may be inferred where objective manifestations indicate that a person acted intentionally [or *may be inferred from facts showing that the person acted with such flagrant disregard of prudent and fair business practices that the person should be treated as having acted intentionally*].

DTPA § 17.45(13). The bracketed language should be added or substituted to conform to the evidence in the case. *See Spencer v. Eagle Star Insurance Co. of America*, 876 S.W.2d 154, 157 (Tex. 1994); *Brown v. American Transfer & Storage Co.*, 601 S.W.2d 931, 937 (Tex. 1980).

Additional damages for knowing or intentional conduct. See PJC 115.11 for a question on additional damages that may be used if PJC 102.21 is answered "Yes."

Actual awareness of failure to comply with a warranty. If the case does not involve a breach of warranty, the phrase *or actual awareness of the conduct constituting a failure to comply with a warranty* should be deleted from the above definition of "knowingly." If the case does involve a breach of warranty, the words *condition*, *defect*, or *failure* may be substituted for the word *conduct* in the definition. DTPA § 17.45(9).

Producing cause. For cases brought under Tex. Ins. Code ch. 541, subch. D, the phrase *resulted in* should be substituted for the phrase *was a producing cause of* in the limiting instruction above. *Compare* Tex. Ins. Code § 541.151 *with* DTPA § 17.50(a).

PJC 102.22 Defenses to Deceptive Trade Practices Act and Insurance Code Chapter 541 Claims (Comment)

Common-law defenses. A primary purpose of the enactment of the DTPA was to provide consumers a cause of action for deceptive trade practices without the burden of proof and numerous defenses encountered in a common-law fraud or breach-of-warranty suit. *Smith v. Baldwin*, 611 S.W.2d 611, 614 (Tex. 1980) (common-law defense of "substantial performance" no defense to DTPA action); *see also Alvarado v. Bolton*, 749 S.W.2d 47, 48 (Tex. 1988) (doctrine of merger not applicable in warranty suit brought under DTPA); *Ojeda de Toca v. Wise*, 748 S.W.2d 449 (Tex. 1988) (imputed notice under real property recording statute not a defense to DTPA action for damages); *Weitzel v. Barnes*, 691 S.W.2d 598, 600 (Tex. 1985) (parol evidence rule will not bar proof of violation of DTPA section 17.46(b)). Thus it is generally true that common-law defenses are unavailable in a DTPA suit.

The above reasoning has been extended to Insurance Code suits. *See Frank B. Hall & Co. v. Beach, Inc.*, 733 S.W.2d 251, 264 (Tex. App.—Corpus Christi 1987, writ ref'd n.r.e.) (contributory negligence could not defeat recovery on Insurance Code claims).

For cases discussing the applicability of "as is" language to the DTPA, see *Prudential Insurance Co. of America v. Jefferson Associates*, 896 S.W.2d 156 (Tex. 1995), and *Smith v. Levine*, 911 S.W.2d 427 (Tex. App.—San Antonio 1995, writ denied).

Statutory defenses.

A. *Third-party information.* A defendant's reliance on third-party information in making the false representation may be a defense to a claim brought under DTPA section 17.50. Tex. Bus. & Com. Code § 17.506(a)–(c) (DTPA).

B. *Complete tender.* The defense of complete tender may apply if the defendant proves that he tendered to the plaintiff, within thirty days after receiving written notice of the complaint, the amount of actual damages claimed and the expenses, including attorney's fees, if any, reasonably incurred by the plaintiff in asserting his claim. DTPA § 17.506(d).

C. *Waiver.* The following elements must be proved: (1) the waiver was in writing, signed by the consumer, and in the form prescribed by DTPA § 17.42(c); (2) the consumer was not in a significantly disparate bargaining position; and (3) in seeking or acquiring the goods or services, the consumer was represented by legal counsel who was not directly or indirectly identified, suggested, or selected by the defendant or an agent of the defendant. DTPA § 17.42(a).

D. *Comparative or proportionate responsibility.* DTPA claims are subject to the proportionate responsibility provisions of chapter 33 of the Texas Civil Practice and Remedies Code. Tex. Civ. Prac. & Rem. Code § 33.002(a)(2). Insurance Code claims are not mentioned in the statute. For a discussion and a sample submission of a proportionate responsibility claim, see PJC 115.35.

E. *Notice and tender of settlement under DTPA.* Though technically not a "defense," the presuit notice provisions of the DTPA can limit or delay a DTPA suit. *See* DTPA § 17.505. The notice must state the "specific complaint" and the amount of actual damages and expenses incurred. DTPA § 17.505(a). The defendant then has a statutorily prescribed time to tender a written settlement offer, which, if rejected by the consumer, may be filed with the court. At trial, if the court finds the offer is "substantially the same" as the actual damages found, the consumer may not recover any amount greater than that of the offer or the amount of actual damages. DTPA § 17.5052. Issues pertaining to notice and tender are to be decided by the court, not by the jury, so no submission is necessary. DTPA § 17.5052(g); *see also Hines v. Hash*, 843 S.W.2d 464, 466–67 (Tex. 1992).

In addition, the defendant has an opportunity to tender a settlement offer within certain times after suit is filed. *See* DTPA § 17.5052(b)–(g). Procedures for comparing the settlement offer to the amount awarded for damages and fees are also set out.

For the requirements of the notice, the timeliness and the method of objection to lack of notice, and the court action required when no notice has been given, see *Hines*, 843 S.W.2d at 467–68.

F. *Notice and tender under Insurance Code.* Actions brought under Insurance Code chapter 541, subchapter D, also require notice. The notice must state the "specific complaint" and the amount of actual damages and expenses incurred. Tex. Ins. Code § 541.154(b) (formerly Tex. Ins. Code art. 21.21, § 16(e)). The defendant may file a rejected offer of settlement with the court, and if the court finds the offer is the same as, "substantially the same" as, or more than the actual damages found, the consumer may not recover any amount greater than the lesser of the offer or the amount of actual damages. Tex. Ins. Code §§ 541.158–.159 (formerly Tex. Ins. Code art. 21.21, § 16A).

G. *Warranty defenses under UCC.* The supreme court has stated that section 17.42 of the DTPA makes invalid a limitation or waiver of liability for violations of section 17.46 but does not do so to warranty disclaimers authorized by the UCC or common law. *Southwestern Bell Telephone Co. v. FDP Corp.*, 811 S.W.2d 572, 576–77 (Tex. 1991). If the consumer pleads a DTPA cause of action alleging violation of warranties arising under UCC article 2, several statutory defenses based on article 2 have been held to apply, including—

- buyer's waiver of implied warranties. *FDP Corp.*, 811 S.W.2d at 576–77; *Mercedes-Benz of North America, Inc. v. Dickenson*, 720 S.W.2d 844, 852 (Tex. App.—Fort Worth 1986, no writ).

- buyer's failure to give notice to seller of breach of warranty as required by Tex. Bus. & Com. Code § 2.607(c)(1) (Tex. UCC). *Import Motors, Inc. v. Matthews*, 557 S.W.2d 807, 809 (Tex. Civ. App.—Austin 1977, writ ref'd n.r.e.).

- contractual limitation of damages in an express warranty. *Rinehart v. Sonitrol of Dallas, Inc.*, 620 S.W.2d 660, 663–64 (Tex. Civ. App.—Dallas 1981, writ ref'd n.r.e.).

H. *Professional services exemption.* The DTPA exempts certain claims for damages based on professional services, "the essence of which is the providing of advice, judgment, opinion, or similar professional skill." The exemption does not apply to—

1. "an express misrepresentation of a material fact that cannot be characterized as advice, judgment, or opinion";
2. "a failure to disclose information in violation of [DTPA] Section 17.46(b)(24)";
3. "an unconscionable action or course of action that cannot be characterized as advice, judgment, or opinion";
4. "breach of an express warranty that cannot be characterized as advice, judgment, or opinion"; or
5. "a violation of [DTPA] Section 17.46(b)(26)."

DTPA § 17.49(c). The term "professional services" is not defined in the statute.

I. *Negotiated contract exemption.* The DTPA also exempts claims for damages based on a written contract with a total consideration of $100,000, if in negotiating the contract the consumer is represented by legal counsel not "directly or indirectly identified, suggested, or selected by the defendant" or the defendant's agent, and the cause of action does not involve a consumer's residence. DTPA § 17.49(f).

J. *Transaction limit.* The DTPA exempts causes of action "arising from a transaction, a project, or a set of transactions relating to the same project, involving total consideration by the consumer of more than $500,000, other than a cause of action involving a consumer's residence." DTPA § 17.49(g).

K. *Personal injury exemption.* Except as specifically provided in DTPA § 17.50(b), (h), damages for bodily injury or death or for the infliction of mental anguish are exempted from DTPA coverage. DTPA § 17.49(e).

PJC 102.23 Statute of Limitations (DTPA § 17.565; Tex. Ins. Code § 541.162)

If your answer to Question ______ [*102.1, 102.7, 102.8, or 102.14*] is "Yes," then answer the following question. Otherwise, do not answer the following question.

QUESTION ______

By what date should *Paul Payne*, in the exercise of reasonable diligence, have discovered all the *false, misleading, or deceptive acts or practices* of *Don Davis*?

Answer with a date in the blank below.

Answer: ______________

COMMENT

When to use. PJC 102.23 is used to determine if the suit is barred by the statute of limitations. Tex. Bus. & Com. Code § 17.565 (DTPA) incorporates the "discovery rule." *See Eshleman v. Shield*, 764 S.W.2d 776 (Tex. 1989); *see also* Tex. Ins. Code § 541.162(a) (formerly Tex. Ins. Code art. 21.21, § 16(d)). Even if the act occurred more than two years before suit was filed, the limitations defense will not apply if the plaintiff did not discover or could not reasonably have discovered the act until a date within two years before the suit was filed. To prevail, a plaintiff need prove only one act or practice that is not time-barred. Therefore, the question asks when the plaintiff discovered or should have discovered the latest act that was a producing cause of damages. If the date is within the two-year period, the limitations defense does not apply.

Source of question. The question is derived from *Willis v. Maverick*, 760 S.W.2d 642, 647 (Tex. 1988); *see also KPMG Peat Marwick v. Harrison County Housing Finance Corp.*, 988 S.W.2d 746, 749–50 (Tex. 1999).

Insurance Code cases. In cases brought under the Insurance Code, the phrase *unfair or deceptive acts or practices* should be used instead of the phrase *false, misleading, or deceptive acts or practices* in the above question. *See* Tex. Ins. Code § 541.162(a)(2).

Breach-of-warranty cases. In cases involving a breach of warranty, the phrase *failures to comply with a warranty* should be used in lieu of the phrase *false, misleading, or deceptive acts or practices* in the above question.

Distinct damages claims. If the plaintiff has two claims involving distinctly different damages caused by distinctly different conduct and the limitations defense is raised, the Committee recommends that separate liability, damages, and limitations questions be submitted.

Extra 180 days. Both DTPA § 17.565 and Tex. Ins. Code § 541.162(b) provide for an extra 180 days to be tacked onto the two-year period if the plaintiff can show he was induced by the defendant to refrain from filing suit. If that exception is raised, the jury would need to be asked:

> Was *Paul Payne*'s failure to file suit by [*insert date two years after date of occurrence or of plaintiff's actual or deemed discovery*] caused by *Don Davis*'s knowingly engaging in conduct solely calculated to induce *Paul Payne* to refrain from or postpone filing suit?

PJC 102.24 Counterclaim—Bad Faith or Harassment (DTPA § 17.50(c); Tex. Ins. Code ch. 541, subch. D) (Comment)

Statutory remedies. A defendant may recover attorney's fees and court costs from a plaintiff who files a groundless, bad-faith, or harassing lawsuit. Tex. Bus. & Com. Code § 17.50(c) (DTPA); Tex. Ins. Code § 541.153 (formerly Tex. Ins. Code art. 21.21, § 16(c)).

A number of courts of appeals have interpreted DTPA § 17.50(c) to mean that the jury determines bad faith and harassment whereas the court determines groundlessness (*see, e.g., Fichtner v. Richardson*, 708 S.W.2d 479 (Tex. App.—Dallas 1986, writ ref'd n.r.e.); *Parks v. McDougall*, 659 S.W.2d 875 (Tex. App.—San Antonio 1983, no writ); *LaChance v. McKown*, 649 S.W.2d 658 (Tex. App.—Texarkana 1983, writ ref'd n.r.e.)). The supreme court has held, however, that the court, not the jury, must decide the issues of groundlessness, bad faith, and harassment. *Donwerth v. Preston II Chrysler-Dodge, Inc.*, 775 S.W.2d 634, 637 (Tex. 1989).

PJC 103.1 Tort Duty of Good Faith and Fair Dealing—Question and Instruction on Insurance Claim Denial or Delay in Payment

QUESTION ______

Did *Don Davis Insurance Company* fail to comply with its duty of good faith and fair dealing to *Paul Payne*?

An insurer fails to comply with its duty of good faith and fair dealing by—

Failing to attempt in good faith to effectuate a prompt, fair, and equitable settlement of a claim when the insurer's liability has become reasonably clear [*or*]

Refusing to pay a claim without conducting a reasonable investigation of the claim [*or*]

Canceling an insurance policy without a reasonable basis.

Answer: _______________

COMMENT

When to use. PJC 103.1 may be used to submit a breach of the common-law duty of good faith and fair dealing by an insurer.

Source of duty. The supreme court has held, as a matter of law, that a special relationship exists between an insurer and the insured arising out of the parties' unequal bargaining power and the exclusive control that the insurer exercises over the processing of claims and the canceling of insurance contracts. *Union Bankers Insurance Co. v. Shelton*, 889 S.W.2d 278, 283 (Tex. 1994); *Aranda v. Insurance Co. of North America*, 748 S.W.2d 210, 212 (Tex. 1988); *Arnold v. National County Mutual Fire Insurance Co.*, 725 S.W.2d 165, 167 (Tex. 1987). The supreme court has held that the duty does not extend past the rendition of a money judgment against an insurer. *Mid-Century Insurance Co. of Texas v. Boyte*, 80 S.W.3d 546, 548 (Tex. 2002).

This duty is nondelegable. Therefore, agents and contractors providing claims-handling services cannot be liable to an insured for breach of this duty. *Natividad v. Alexis, Inc.*, 875 S.W.2d 695, 698 (Tex. 1994).

The supreme court has refused to apply the duty to a liability insurer investigating and defending claims by a third party against its insured. *Maryland Insurance Co. v. Head*

Industrial Coatings & Services, Inc., 938 S.W.2d 27, 28–29 (Tex. 1996). However, an insured may have a statutory claim against the insurer in this context. See PJC 102.18.

Source of instruction. In *Arnold* and *Aranda*, the supreme court held that an insurer breaches its duty by denying a claim without a reasonable basis or by failing to conduct a reasonable investigation. *Aranda*, 748 S.W.2d at 213; *Arnold*, 725 S.W.2d at 167. In *Shelton*, the supreme court extended the duty to include an insurer's unreasonable cancellation of an insurance policy. *Shelton*, 889 S.W.2d at 283. PJC 103.1 submits each of these elements of the duty. In *Universe Life Insurance Co. v. Giles*, 950 S.W.2d 48 (Tex. 1997), the supreme court revised the common-law duty to track the statutory prohibition on unfair refusal to settle. *Giles*, 950 S.W.2d at 55–56; Tex. Ins. Code § 541.060(a)(2)(A) (formerly Tex. Ins. Code art. 21.21, § 4(10)(a)(ii)). The first definition is taken from this statutory language and parallels PJC 102.18. By extension, the duty of good faith and fair dealing with respect to failing to conduct a reasonable investigation has been recast in the statutory language of Tex. Ins. Code § 541.060(a)(7) (formerly Tex. Ins. Code art. 21.21, § 4(10)(a)(viii)). This language also parallels the statutory submission in PJC 102.18. The third definition is based on *Shelton* and has no statutory counterpart.

Modification of instruction for worker's compensation claims. The 1991 revisions to the worker's compensation statutes substantially changed the manner in which worker's compensation claims can be resolved. Unlike other first-party insurance claims, worker's compensation claims accruing after January 1, 1991, cannot be settled by payment of specific dollar amounts or limitations on duration of medical care. Resolution of worker's compensation claims under the 1991 revisions must be framed in terms of resolving disputed issues, must be approved by the Texas Workers' Compensation Commission (TWCC), and is specifically governed by statutes and rules. *See* Tex. Lab. Code § 408.005; 28 Tex. Admin. Code §§ 147.1–.11.

In *Giles*, the supreme court adopted the standard found in Tex. Ins. Code § 541.060(a)(2) (formerly Tex. Ins. Code art. 21.21, § 4(10)(a)(ii)) for establishing a breach of the duty of good faith and fair dealing as "failing to attempt . . . to effectuate a prompt, fair, and equitable settlement." *Giles*, 950 S.W.2d at 55. In *United States Fire Insurance Co. v. Williams*, 955 S.W.2d 267 (Tex. 1997), the *Giles* standard was applied to worker's compensation claims. Under the 1991 revisions to the worker's compensation statutes, a carrier is required to "pay" health-care providers or "initiate" income benefits, rather than attempt to settle. Because the carrier's statutory duty is to pay or initiate benefits, with the right to dispute claims through the TWCC dispute resolution system, there appears to be no affirmative duty to attempt to settle a worker's compensation claim, unlike other first-party insurance claims. The supreme court held that, because the question of entitlement to worker's compensation benefits is within the exclusive jurisdiction of the TWCC, there can be no breach of duty of good faith and fair dealing for failing to pay or initiate benefits to which a claimant is not entitled. *American Motorists Insurance Co. v. Fodge*, 63 S.W.3d 801, 804 (Tex. 2001).

The Committee believes that the *Giles* standard is not in harmony with the statutes and rules that now govern the handling of worker's compensation claims. It therefore recommends the following instruction for good faith and fair dealing cases arising out of worker's compensation claims originating after January 1, 1991:

> An insurer fails to comply with its duty of good faith and fair dealing by—
>
> > Failing to [*pay*] [*initiate*] benefits when the insurer's liability has become reasonably clear [*or*]
> >
> > Refusing to [*pay*] [*initiate*] benefits without conducting a reasonable investigation.

Causation. A finding of a breach of the common-law duty of good faith and fair dealing entitles a plaintiff to recovery of all damages proximately caused by the wrongful conduct. *Aranda*, 748 S.W.2d at 215; *Chitsey v. National Lloyds Insurance Co.*, 738 S.W.2d 641, 643 (Tex. 1987). Causation is incorporated into the damages instruction. See PJC 115.14.

Exemplary damages. Exemplary damages are allowed for breach of the duty of good faith and fair dealing and are governed by the same principles applicable to other tort actions. *Transportation Insurance Co. v. Moriel*, 879 S.W.2d 10, 23 & n.16 (Tex. 1994); *Arnold*, 725 S.W.2d at 168. Fraud, malice, and gross negligence are grounds for recovery of exemplary damages. Tex. Civ. Prac. & Rem. Code § 41.003(a). For questions submitting exemplary damages, see PJC 115.36 and 115.37 and the Comments accompanying those questions.

Noninsurance cases. The courts have been reluctant to impose a special relationship on parties to an arm's-length business transaction outside the insurance area. *See, e.g., City of Midland v. O'Bryant*, 18 S.W.3d 209, 215–16 (Tex. 2000) (employer-employee relationship); *FDIC v. Coleman*, 795 S.W.2d 706, 708–09 (Tex. 1990) (secured creditor/guarantor and receiver/guarantor); *Texstar North America, Inc. v. Ladd Petroleum Corp.*, 809 S.W.2d 672, 678 (Tex. App.—Corpus Christi 1991, writ denied) (working-interest owners/parties to joint operating agreement); *Nautical Landings Marina, Inc. v. First National Bank*, 791 S.W.2d 293, 299 (Tex. App.—Corpus Christi 1990, writ denied) (lender/borrower); *Adolph Coors Co. v. Rodriguez*, 780 S.W.2d 477, 481 (Tex. App.—Corpus Christi 1989, writ denied) (supplier/distributor); *City of San Antonio v. Forgy*, 769 S.W.2d 293, 296–98 (Tex. App.—San Antonio 1989, writ denied) (city/contractor); *Lovell v. Western National Life Insurance Co.*, 754 S.W.2d 298, 303 (Tex. App.—Amarillo 1988, writ denied) (mortgagor/mortgagee). *But see Subaru of America, Inc. v. David McDavid Nissan*, 84 S.W.3d 212, 225–26 (Tex. 2002) (statutory special relationship existed in automobile dealership franchise agreement); *Sanus/New York Life Health Plan, Inc. v. Dube-Seybold-Sutherland Management, Inc.*, 837 S.W.2d

191, 199 (Tex. App.—Houston [1st Dist.] 1992, writ denied) (special relationship existed between health maintenance organization and health-care provider).

PJC 103.2 Duty of Good Faith under the Uniform Commercial Code (Comment)

The basic question in PJC 101.2 should be used with one of the appropriate instructions set out in the comment titled "UCC good-faith obligation."

PJC 103.3 Duty of Good Faith by Express Contract (Comment)

Parties may create a duty of good faith and fair dealing by the express terms of a contract not governed by the Uniform Commercial Code. The basic question in PJC 101.2 should be used to submit all contractual provisions including the express duty of good faith and fair dealing.

PJC 104.1 Question and Instruction—Existence of Relationship of Trust and Confidence

QUESTION ______

Did a relationship of trust and confidence exist between *Don Davis* and *Paul Payne*?

> A relationship of trust and confidence existed if *Paul Payne* justifiably placed trust and confidence in *Don Davis* to act in *Paul Payne*'s best interest. *Paul Payne*'s subjective trust and feelings alone do not justify transforming arm's-length dealings into a relationship of trust and confidence.

Answer: _______________

COMMENT

When to use. This question and instruction submit the existence of an informal fiduciary relationship, commonly referred to as a "relationship of trust and confidence" or a "confidential relationship." This relationship may arise from moral, social, domestic, or purely personal relationships. *Meyer v. Cathey*, 167 S.W.3d 327, 330–31 (Tex. 2005) (quoting *Associated Indemnity Corp. v. CAT Contracting, Inc.*, 964 S.W.2d 276, 287 (Tex. 1998)); *Thigpen v. Locke*, 363 S.W.2d 247, 253 (Tex. 1962); *MacDonald v. Follett*, 180 S.W.2d 334, 337 (Tex. 1944). In this regard, informal fiduciary relationships are distinguished from technical or formal fiduciary relationships such as attorney-client, principal-agent, partner-partner, trustee–cestui que trust, or guardian-ward, which as a matter of law are relationships of trust and confidence. *Thigpen*, 363 S.W.2d at 253. The existence of an informal relationship of trust and confidence is usually a question of fact. *Crim Truck & Tractor Co. v Navistar International Transportation Corp.*, 823 S.W.2d 591, 594 (Tex. 1992).

If the existence of a formal fiduciary relationship is disputed, a question should be submitted inquiring whether the formal fiduciary relationship exists with respect to the occurrence or transaction at issue. *See Johnson v. Brewer & Pritchard, P.C.*, 73 S.W.3d 193, 200–03 (Tex. 2002); *Schiller v. Elick*, 240 S.W.2d 997, 999–1000 (Tex. 1951); see also the current edition of State Bar of Texas, *Texas Pattern Jury Charges—Malpractice, Premises & Products*, PJC 61.3.

When the issue is a question of law. Although the existence of an informal relationship of trust and confidence is ordinarily a question of fact, if the issue is one of no evidence, it becomes a question of law. *Crim Truck & Tractor Co.*, 823 S.W.2d at 594. Similarly, if the facts are undisputed, the question is one of law. *Meyer*, 167 S.W.3d at

330. The supreme court has held that the following situations, for example, do not rise to the level of a relationship of trust and confidence:

- One businessman trusts another and relies on his promise to perform a contract. *Consolidated Gas & Equipment Co. v. Thompson*, 405 S.W.2d 333, 336 (Tex. 1966); *Thigpen*, 363 S.W.2d at 253.
- The relationship has been a cordial one and of long duration. *Thigpen*, 363 S.W.2d at 253.
- People have had prior dealings with each other and one party subjectively trusts the other. *Meyer*, 167 S.W.3d at 331; *Schlumberger Technology Corp. v. Swanson*, 959 S.W.2d 171, 177 (Tex. 1997); *Consolidated Gas & Equipment Co.*, 405 S.W.2d at 336; *Thigpen*, 363 S.W.2d at 253.
- The plaintiff has always done everything requested by the defendant. *Crim Truck & Tractor Co.*, 823 S.W.2d at 596 n.6.

If commencement or termination of relationship is at issue. If there is a dispute about whether the relationship had begun or had terminated at the time of the alleged breach, the Committee suggests adding to the question the phrases, *on* [*date*] or *at the time of the* [*occurrence or transaction*]. *See Meyer*, 167 S.W.3d at 331 (quoting *Associated Indemnity Corp.*, 964 S.W.2d at 287); *Swanson*, 959 S.W.2d at 177 (in a business transaction, the special relationship of trust and confidence must have existed before, and apart from, the agreement made the basis of the suit); *Schiller*, 240 S.W.2d at 1000 (the relationship must not have been terminated before the time of the occurrence or transaction giving rise to the cause of action).

Source of question and instruction. PJC 104.1 is derived from *Thigpen*, 363 S.W.2d at 253 (confidential relationship exists if beneficiary is justified in placing trust and confidence in fiduciary to act in beneficiary's best interest); *Crim Truck & Tractor Co.*, 823 S.W.2d at 594–95 (subjective trust alone does not transform arm's-length transaction into fiduciary relationship); and *Fitz-Gerald v. Hull*, 237 S.W.2d 256, 261 (Tex. 1951) (informal relationship may arise where one person trusts and relies on another).

PJC 104.2 Question and Instruction—Breach of Fiduciary Duty

QUESTION ______

Did *Don Davis* comply with *his* fiduciary duty to *Paul Payne*?

[*Because a relationship of trust and confidence existed between them*,] [*As Paul Payne's attorney*,] [*Because they were partners*,] [*As Paul Payne's agent*,] *Don Davis* owed *Paul Payne* a fiduciary duty. To prove *he* complied with *his* duty, *Don Davis* must show:

a. the transaction[*s*] in question [*was/were*] fair and equitable to *Paul Payne*;

b. *Don Davis* made reasonable use of the confidence that *Paul Payne* placed in *him*;

c. *Don Davis* acted in the utmost good faith and exercised the most scrupulous honesty toward *Paul Payne*;

d. *Don Davis* placed the interests of *Paul Payne* before *his* own, did not use the advantage of *his* position to gain any benefit for *himself* at the expense of *Paul Payne*, and did not place *himself* in any position where *his* self-interest might conflict with *his* obligations as a fiduciary; and

e. *Don Davis* fully and fairly disclosed all important information to *Paul Payne* concerning the transaction[*s*].

Answer: _______________

COMMENT

When to use. PJC 104.2 submits the question of breach of a fiduciary duty, whether the duty is based on a formal or an informal relationship, where it is alleged that the fiduciary has profited or benefited from a transaction with the beneficiary.

If the existence of a formal fiduciary relationship is disputed, a preliminary question should be submitted. *Schiller v. Elick*, 240 S.W.2d 997, 999 (Tex. 1951) (dispute whether defendant was plaintiff's agent); *see also Johnson v. Brewer & Pritchard, P.C.*, 73 S.W.3d 193, 202–03 (Tex. 2002) (whether to impose fiduciary duty on employee depends on whether he was agent with respect to particular transaction). See also the current edition of State Bar of Texas, *Texas Pattern Jury Charges—Malpractice, Premises & Products*, PJC 61.3. PJC 104.1 submits the existence of an informal fiduciary relationship. PJC 104.2 should be conditioned on an affirmative answer to either PJC 104.1 or the preliminary question asking whether the formal fiduciary relationship exists.

Source of question and instruction. The question and instruction are derived from *Stephens County Museum, Inc. v. Swenson*, 517 S.W.2d 257, 261 (Tex. 1974) (material issues are whether fiduciary made reasonable use of the trust and confidence placed in him and whether the transactions were ultimately fair and equitable to the beneficiary); *Fitz-Gerald v. Hull*, 237 S.W.2d 256, 264–65 (Tex. 1951) (persons engaged in joint adventure owe to each other the utmost good faith and the most scrupulous honesty); *Crim Truck & Tractor Co. v. Navistar International Transportation Corp.*, 823 S.W.2d 591, 594 (Tex. 1992) (fiduciary duty requires a party to place the interest of the other party before his own); *Slay v. Burnett Trust*, 187 S.W.2d 377, 387–88 (Tex. 1945) (duty of loyalty prohibits trustee from using the advantage of his position to gain any benefit for himself at the expense of his cestui que trust and from placing himself in any position where his self-interest will or may conflict with his obligations as trustee); *Kinzbach Tool Co. v. Corbett-Wallace Corp.*, 160 S.W.2d 509, 512–14 (Tex. 1942) (it is the duty of a fiduciary to deal openly and to make full disclosure to the party with whom he stands in such relationship); and *Johnson v. Peckham*, 120 S.W.2d 786, 787 (Tex. 1938) (partners required to make full disclosure of all material facts within their knowledge relating to partnership affairs; it is necessary to make disclosure of all important information).

Presumption of unfairness shifts burden of proof. When a fiduciary profits or benefits in any way from a transaction with the beneficiary, a presumption of unfairness arises that shifts the burden of persuasion to the fiduciary or the party claiming the validity or benefits of the transaction to show that the transaction was fair and equitable to the beneficiary. *Keck, Mahin & Cate, Grant Cook v. National Union Fire Insurance Co. of Pittsburgh*, 20 S.W.3d 692, 699 (Tex. 2000); *Texas Bank & Trust Co. v. Moore*, 595 S.W.2d 502, 509 (Tex. 1980); *Archer v. Griffith*, 390 S.W.2d 735, 739 (Tex. 1964).

The presumption may be rebutted by the fiduciary. *Stephens County Museum, Inc.*, 517 S.W.2d at 261; *see also Texas Bank & Trust Co.*, 595 S.W.2d at 509. Normally, a rebuttable presumption shifts the burden of producing evidence to the party against whom it operates but does not shift the burden of persuasion to that party. *General Motors Corp. v. Saenz*, 873 S.W.2d 353, 359 (Tex. 1993). In fiduciary duty cases, however, the presumption of unfairness operates to shift both the burden of producing evidence and the burden of persuasion to the fiduciary. *Sorrell v. Elsey*, 748 S.W.2d 584, 586 (Tex. App.—San Antonio 1988, writ denied); *Miller v. Miller*, 700 S.W.2d 941, 945–46 (Tex. App.—Dallas 1985, writ ref'd n.r.e.); *Gum v. Schaefer*, 683 S.W.2d 803, 806 (Tex. App.—Corpus Christi 1984, no writ) (per curiam); *Fillion v. Troy*, 656 S.W.2d 912, 914 (Tex. App.—Houston [1st Dist.] 1983, writ ref'd n.r.e.); *Cole v. Plummer*, 559 S.W.2d 87, 89 (Tex. Civ. App.—Eastland 1977, writ ref'd n.r.e.); *see also Peckham*, 120 S.W.2d at 788 (issue of whether beneficiary of fiduciary relationship relied on fiduciary to perform his duties was immaterial).

If there is no evidence rebutting the presumption, no breach of fiduciary duty question is necessary. *Texas Bank & Trust Co.*, 595 S.W.2d at 509.

Liability questions normally place the burden of proof on the plaintiff, who is required to obtain an affirmative finding. When the burden is shifted to the fiduciary, however, a "No" answer supports liability. Thus, when the burden is on the fiduciary to prove compliance with his fiduciary duties, subsequent questions that depend on a finding of breach of fiduciary duty may need to be conditioned on a "No" answer to PJC 104.2. See, e.g., PJC 115.15–.18.

Question where burden does not shift. In those cases where the presumption of unfairness does not arise and the burden of persuasion does not shift to the fiduciary, the question in PJC 104.2 should be modified to read:

> Did *Don Davis* fail to comply with *his* fiduciary duty to *Paul Payne*?

The instruction should also be modified to place the burden of persuasion on *Paul Payne*.

Modification of instruction. The instruction in PJC 104.2 may need to be modified to include additional duties imposed by statute, contract, or common law on a particular fiduciary relationship. Conversely, if a statute or contract limits the scope of fiduciary duties, the instruction should be modified to conform to those limitations. *See National Plan Administrators, Inc. v. National Health Insurance Co.*, 235 S.W.3d 695, 700–04 (Tex. 2007); *Sterling Trust Co. v. Adderley*, 168 S.W.3d 835, 846–47 (Tex. 2005). Consult the Texas Revised Partnership Act regarding duties applicable to partners. *See* Tex. Bus. Orgs. Code § 152.204(d); Tex. Rev. Civ. Stat. art. 6132b–4.04(f) & Comment of Bar Committee—1943.

Knowing participation. An additional question or instruction may be required when the plaintiff alleges that a defendant is liable because it knowingly participated in another's breach of fiduciary duty. *See Kinzbach Tool Co.*, 160 S.W.2d at 513–14.

Caveat. If the burden of persuasion is on the fiduciary, it is unclear which party bears the burden of requesting the compliance question. *Compare Moore v. Texas Bank & Trust Co.*, 576 S.W.2d 691, 695 (Tex. Civ. App.—Eastland 1979), *rev'd on other grounds*, 595 S.W.2d 502 (Tex. 1980) (burden to properly request issue rests on plaintiff-beneficiary because it "is an element of the plaintiff's theory of recovery"), *with Cole*, 559 S.W.2d at 89 (fiduciary has burden of "securing a finding the confidential relationship was not breached").

Remedies. See PJC 115.15 regarding equitable remedies and damages for breach of fiduciary duty; PJC 115.16 for a question on the amount of profit disgorgement; PJC 115.17 for a question on the amount of fee forfeiture; and PJC 115.18 for a question on actual damages for breach of fiduciary duty.

PJC 105.1 Question on Common-Law Fraud—Intentional Misrepresentation

QUESTION ______

Did *Don Davis* commit fraud against *Paul Payne*?

[Insert appropriate instructions.]

Answer: _______________

COMMENT

When to use. PJC 105.1 is a broad-form question. *See* Tex. R. Civ. P. 277. It should be appropriate in most cases involving claims for fraud and can be used to submit both affirmative claims for damages and affirmative defenses.

Accompanying instructions and definitions. PJC 105.1 should be accompanied by appropriate instructions and definitions. See PJC 105.2–.4.

Damages. Damages questions are set out in chapter 115. PJC 115.19 submits direct damages in fraud cases, and PJC 115.20 submits consequential damages in such cases. For recovery of exemplary damages, see PJC 115.36 and 115.37.

PJC 105.2 Instruction on Common-Law Fraud—Intentional Misrepresentation

Fraud occurs when—

a. a party makes a material misrepresentation,

b. the misrepresentation is made with knowledge of its falsity or made recklessly without any knowledge of the truth and as a positive assertion,

c. the misrepresentation is made with the intention that it should be acted on by the other party, and

d. the other party relies on the misrepresentation and thereby suffers injury.

"Misrepresentation" means:

[Insert appropriate definitions from PJC 105.3A–.3E.]

COMMENT

When to use. PJC 105.2 should be used in a common-law fraud case if there is a claim of intentional misrepresentation.

Accompanying question, definitions. PJC 105.2 is designed to follow PJC 105.1 and to be accompanied by one or more of the definitions of misrepresentation at PJC 105.3A–.3E.

Use of "or." If more than one definition is used, each must be separated by the word *or*, because a finding of any one type of misrepresentation would support recovery.

Source of instruction. The supreme court has repeatedly identified these elements of common-law fraud. *Johnson v. Brewer & Pritchard, P.C.*, 73 S.W.3d 193, 211 n.45 (Tex. 2002); *In re FirstMerit Bank, N.A.*, 52 S.W.3d 749, 758 (Tex. 2001); *Wal-Mart Stores v. Sturges*, 52 S.W.3d 711, 727 (Tex. 2001); *Johnson & Higgins of Texas, Inc. v. Kenneco Energy, Inc.*, 962 S.W.2d 507, 524 (Tex. 1998); *Formosa Plastics Corp. USA v. Presidio Engineers & Contractors, Inc.*, 960 S.W.2d 41, 47 (Tex. 1998); *Sears, Roebuck & Co. v. Meadows*, 877 S.W.2d 281, 282 (Tex. 1994); *Trenholm v. Ratcliff*, 646 S.W.2d 927, 930 (Tex. 1983); *Stone v. Lawyers Title Insurance Corp.*, 554 S.W.2d 183, 185 (Tex. 1977); *see also Oilwell Division, United States Steel Corp. v. Fryer*, 493 S.W.2d 487, 491 (Tex. 1973) (fraudulent inducement as affirmative defense).

Reliance. In *Koral Industries v. Security-Connecticut Life Insurance Co.*, 802 S.W.2d 650, 651 (Tex. 1990), the supreme court rejected the argument that a party's failure to use due diligence barred a claim of fraud. *See also Trenholm*, 646 S.W.2d at 933 (defendant in fraud case cannot complain that plaintiff failed to discover truth through exercise of care). Generally, therefore, the jury should be asked only to consider the plaintiff's reliance and not asked to find whether that reliance was justified. *But see Ernst & Young, L.L.P. v. Pacific Mutual Life Insurance Co.*, 51 S.W.3d 573, 577 (Tex. 2001) (in cases not involving representations made to induce a specific party, the reliance element may need to include "actually and justifiably relied upon the representation"); *see also Texas First National Bank v. Ng*, 167 S.W.3d 842, 856 n.24 (Tex. App.—Houston [14th Dist.] 2005, pet. granted, judgm't vacated & remanded by agr.) (noting apparent disagreement among Texas courts on whether reliance must be justifiable).

PJC 105.3 Definitions of Misrepresentation—Intentional Misrepresentation

PJC 105.3A Factual Misrepresentation

A false statement of fact [*or*]

COMMENT

When to use. PJC 105.3A should be used in cases involving an allegation that the defendant made an affirmative statement of fact that was false. *See Trenholm v. Ratcliff*, 646 S.W.2d 927, 930 (Tex. 1983) (false statement of fact actionable as fraud).

Accompanying question and instruction. PJC 105.3A is designed to accompany the broad-form fraud question at PJC 105.1 and the basic elements of fraud at PJC 105.2. For other definitions of misrepresentation, see PJC 105.3B–.3E.

Use of "or." If more than one definition is used, each must be separated by the word *or*, because a finding of any one type of misrepresentation would support recovery.

PJC 105.3B Promise of Future Action

A promise of future performance made with an intent, at the time the promise was made, not to perform as promised [*or*]

COMMENT

When to use. PJC 105.3B should be used if the alleged fraud is a promise made with intent not to perform. *Formosa Plastics Corp. USA v. Presidio Engineers & Contractors, Inc.*, 960 S.W.2d 41, 46–48 (Tex. 1998); *T.O. Stanley Boot Co. v. Bank of El Paso*, 847 S.W.2d 218, 222 (Tex. 1992); *Spoljaric v. Percival Tours, Inc.*, 708 S.W.2d 432, 434–35 (Tex. 1986).

Accompanying question and instruction. PJC 105.3B is designed to accompany the broad-form fraud question at PJC 105.1 and the basic elements of fraud at PJC 105.2. For other definitions of misrepresentation, see PJC 105.3A and 105.3C–.3E.

Use of "or." If more than one definition is used, each must be separated by the word *or*, because a finding of any one type of misrepresentation would support recovery.

PJC 105.3C Opinion Mixed with Fact

A statement of opinion based on a false statement of fact [*or*]

COMMENT

When to use. PJC 105.3C should be used in cases involving an allegation that the defendant represented to the plaintiff an opinion based on a fact that the defendant knew was false. This type of statement constitutes an exception to the general rule that only false statements of fact can be actionable as fraud. *Trenholm v. Ratcliff*, 646 S.W.2d 927, 930 (Tex. 1983).

Accompanying question and instruction. PJC 105.3C is designed to accompany the broad-form fraud question at PJC 105.1 and the basic elements of fraud at PJC 105.2. For other definitions of misrepresentation, see PJC 105.3A–.3B and 105.3D–.3E.

Use of "or." If more than one definition is used, each must be separated by the word *or*, because a finding of any one type of misrepresentation would support recovery.

PJC 105.3D False Statement of Opinion

A statement of opinion that the maker knows to be false [*or*]

COMMENT

When to use. PJC 105.3D should be used in cases involving an allegation that the defendant represented to the plaintiff an opinion that the defendant knew to be false. This type of statement constitutes an exception to the general rule that only false statements of fact can be actionable as fraud. *Transport Insurance Co. v. Faircloth*, 898 S.W.2d 269, 276 (Tex. 1995); *Trenholm v. Ratcliff*, 646 S.W.2d 927, 930 (Tex. 1983).

Accompanying question and instruction. PJC 105.3D is designed to accompany the broad-form fraud question at PJC 105.1 and the basic elements of fraud at PJC 105.2. For other definitions of misrepresentation, see PJC 105.3A–.3C and 105.3E.

Use of "or." If more than one definition is used, each must be separated by the word *or*, because a finding of any one type of misrepresentation would support recovery.

PJC 105.3E Opinion Made with Special Knowledge

An expression of opinion that is false, made by one claiming or implying to have special knowledge of the subject matter of the opinion.

> "Special knowledge" means knowledge or information superior to that possessed by the other party and to which the other party did not have equal access.

[*or*]

COMMENT

When to use. PJC 105.3E should be used in cases involving an allegation that the defendant purported to have special knowledge of facts that would occur or exist in the future and represented to the plaintiff an opinion based on that special knowledge. *Trenholm v. Ratcliff*, 646 S.W.2d 927, 930 (Tex. 1983); *see also Fina Supply, Inc. v. Abilene National Bank*, 726 S.W.2d 537, 540 (Tex. 1987); *United States Pipe & Foundry Co. v. City of Waco*, 108 S.W.2d 432, 435–37 (Tex. 1937); *Wright v. Carpenter*, 579 S.W.2d 575, 580 (Tex. Civ. App.—Corpus Christi 1979, writ ref'd n.r.e.); *Bell v. Bradshaw*, 342 S.W.2d 185, 189–90 (Tex. Civ. App.—Dallas 1960, no writ).

Accompanying question and instruction. PJC 105.3E is designed to accompany the broad-form fraud question at PJC 105.1 and the basic elements of fraud at PJC 105.2. For other definitions of misrepresentation, see PJC 105.3A–.3D.

Use of "or." If more than one definition is used, each must be separated by the word *or*, because a finding of any one type of misrepresentation would support recovery.

PJC 105.4 Instruction on Common-Law Fraud—Failure to Disclose When There Is Duty to Disclose

Fraud occurs when—

a. a party fails to disclose a material fact within the knowledge of that party,

b. the party knows that the other party is ignorant of the fact and does not have an equal opportunity to discover the truth,

c. the party intends to induce the other party to take some action by failing to disclose the fact, and

d. the other party suffers injury as a result of acting without knowledge of the undisclosed fact.

COMMENT

When to use. PJC 105.4 should accompany PJC 105.1 if the court finds that there is a duty to disclose.

Source of instruction. PJC 105.4 is based on an instruction approved in *New Process Steel Corp. v. Steel Corp. of Texas*, 703 S.W.2d 209, 214 (Tex. App.—Houston [1st Dist.] 1985, writ ref'd n.r.e.). *See also Custom Leasing, Inc. v. Texas Bank & Trust Co.*, 516 S.W.2d 138, 142 (Tex. 1974); *GXG, Inc. v. Texacal Oil & Gas*, 977 S.W.2d 403, 409 (Tex. App.—Corpus Christi 1998, pet. denied). Instruction *d* submits the reliance element of fraud. *See Schlumberger Technology Corp. v. Swanson*, 959 S.W.2d 171, 181–82 (Tex. 1997); *Custom Leasing*, 516 S.W.2d at 143.

Fiduciary duty. Subsection *d* reliance should not be submitted as an element in a case involving failure to disclose by a fiduciary who profits or benefits in any way from a transaction with the beneficiary. *See Schlumberger*, 959 S.W.2d at 177–81; *see also* PJC 104.2. PJC 105.4 may need to be further modified to submit fraud by a fiduciary.

Silence as misrepresentation. "As a general rule, a failure to disclose information does not constitute fraud unless there is a duty to disclose the information." *Bradford v. Vento*, 48 S.W.3d 749, 755 (Tex. 2001). "Whether such a duty exists is a question of law." *Bradford*, 48 S.W.3d at 755. The supreme court has concluded that a duty to disclose arises when there is a confidential or fiduciary relationship. *Insurance Co. of North America v. Morris*, 981 S.W.2d 667, 674–75 (Tex. 1998). The court has also held that a duty to disclose arises in other circumstances. *See Spoljaric v. Percival Tours, Inc.*, 708 S.W.2d 432, 435 (Tex. 1986) (specific representations about bonus plan gave rise to duty to disclose adoption of an alternate plan); *Smith v. National Resort Communities, Inc.*,

585 S.W.2d 655, 658 (Tex. 1979) (seller of real estate has duty to disclose material facts not reasonably discoverable by purchaser).

Courts of appeals have concluded that a duty to disclose may arise when (1) there is a special or fiduciary relationship, (2) a person voluntarily discloses partial information but fails to disclose the whole truth, (3) a person makes a representation but fails to disclose new information that makes the earlier representation misleading or untrue, or (4) a person makes a partial disclosure and conveys a false impression. *See, e.g., Columbia/HCA Healthcare Corp. v. Cottey*, 72 S.W.3d 735, 744–45 (Tex. App.—Waco 2002, no pet.); *Anderson, Greenwood & Co. v. Martin*, 44 S.W.3d 200, 212–13 (Tex. App.—Houston [14th Dist.] 2001, pet. denied); *Lesikar v. Rappeport*, 33 S.W.3d 282, 299 (Tex. App.—Texarkana 2000, pet. denied); *Hoggett v. Brown*, 971 S.W.2d 472, 487 (Tex. App.—Houston [14th Dist.] 1997, pet. denied).

Section 551 of the *Restatement (Second) of Torts* (1977) recognizes a general duty to disclose facts in a commercial setting. In *Bradford*, however, the supreme court stated "[w]e have never adopted section 551." *Bradford*, 48 S.W.3d at 756; *see also SmithKline Beecham Corp. v. Doe*, 903 S.W.2d 347, 352 (Tex. 1995).

Rescission. If rescission is sought, the intent requirement may be lessened. *See Calloway v. Manion*, 572 F.2d 1033, 1039 (5th Cir. 1978); *Chase, Inc. v. Bostick*, 551 S.W.2d 116, 119 (Tex. Civ. App.—Tyler 1977, writ ref'd n.r.e.). Mere failure to disclose material information may give rise to rescission. *Smith*, 585 S.W.2d at 658.

Concealment. Active concealment of material facts may also be as actionable as false statements. *Campbell v. Booth*, 526 S.W.2d 167, 172 (Tex. Civ. App.—Dallas 1975, writ ref'd n.r.e.). PJC 105.4 element *a* may need to be modified to include concealment. *See GXG, Inc.*, 977 S.W.2d at 409.

PJC 105.5 Question on Statute of Limitations—Common-Law Fraud

If you answered Question ______ [*105.1*] "Yes," then answer the following question. Otherwise, do not answer the following question.

QUESTION ______

By what date should *Paul Payne*, in the exercise of reasonable diligence, have discovered the fraud of *Don Davis*?

Answer with a date in the blank below.

Answer: _______________

COMMENT

When to use. PJC 105.5 is to be used to determine if a cause of action for common-law fraud is barred by the statute of limitations. Actions for fraud are governed by a four-year limitations period. Tex. Civ. Prac. & Rem. Code § 16.004(a)(4); *see also Williams v. Khalaf*, 802 S.W.2d 651, 654–58 (Tex. 1990).

Source of question. PJC 105.5 is derived from *KPMG Peat Marwick v. Harrison County Housing Finance Corp.*, 988 S.W.2d 746, 750 (Tex. 1999), and *Computer Associates International, Inc. v. Altai, Inc.*, 918 S.W.2d 453, 456 (Tex. 1994).

Continuing fraud. In a case involving continuing fraud resulting in a continuing or ongoing injury, PJC 105.5 may need to be modified to ask when the plaintiff should have discovered the latest fraudulent act. See PJC 102.23 and its Comment.

Distinct damages claims. If the plaintiff has two claims involving distinctly different conduct and the limitations defense is raised, the Committee recommends that separate liability, damages, and limitations questions be submitted.

Caveat. The supreme court has identified two categories of litigation in which the accrual of a cause of action may be deferred for limitations purposes: (1) cases involving allegations of fraud or fraudulent concealment and (2) all other cases. In cases involving fraud or fraudulent concealment, "accrual is deferred because a person cannot be permitted to avoid liability for his actions by deceitfully concealing wrongdoing until limitations has run." *S.V. v. R.V.*, 933 S.W.2d 1, 6 (Tex. 1996). In the second category of cases, accrual is deferred when "the nature of the injury incurred is inherently undiscoverable and the evidence of injury is objectively verifiable." *S.V.*, 933 S.W.2d at 6 (quoting *Computer Associates International, Inc.*, 918 S.W.2d at 456). Although the term "discovery rule" has been applied to both categories, that term is properly used only when referring to the deferred accrual of a cause of action in the second category of cases, i.e., cases not involving fraud or fraudulent concealment. *See S.V.*, 933 S.W.2d at 5–6; *Computer Associates International, Inc.*, 918 S.W.2d at 456.

The supreme court has not addressed the appropriate jury submission for the discovery rule in nonfraud cases. Its opinions discussing the elements of the discovery rule have used varying language. The supreme court has most often defined the discovery rule as deferring the accrual of a cause of action until the plaintiff knew or should have known of its injury and that it was likely caused by the wrongful acts of another. *See KPMG Peat Marwick*, 988 S.W.2d at 749; *Childs v. Haussecker*, 974 S.W.2d 31, 37, 40 (Tex. 1998). If the discovery rule is submitted in terms of the plaintiff's discovery of a wrongfully caused injury, it may be necessary to define "injury" and "wrongful acts"; otherwise, the jury might be impermissibly allowed to speculate on the meaning of those terms. Because Texas courts have not consistently defined the elements of fraudulent concealment for limitations purposes, the Committee expresses no opinion on the appropriate submission.

[PJC 105.6 is reserved for expansion.]

PJC 105.7 Question on Statutory Fraud (Real Estate or Stock Transaction)

QUESTION ______

Did *Don Davis* commit [*statutory*] fraud against *Paul Payne*?

[*Insert appropriate instructions.*]

Answer: _______________

COMMENT

When to use. PJC 105.7 is a broad-form question. *See* Tex. R. Civ. P. 277. It should be appropriate in most cases involving claims for fraud in connection with a stock or real estate transaction under Tex. Bus. & Com. Code § 27.01. The Committee recommends obtaining independent findings when there are allegations of both common-law and statutory fraud because of the different remedies available.

Accompanying instructions and definitions. PJC 105.7 should be accompanied by appropriate instructions and definitions. See PJC 105.8 and 105.9.

Damages. Damages questions are set out in chapter 115. PJC 115.19 submits direct damages in fraud cases, and PJC 115.20 submits consequential damages in such cases. Although the statute does not require actual awareness of the falsity to recover actual damages, actual awareness of the falsity must be established in order to recover exemplary damages. Tex. Bus. & Com. Code § 27.01; *Woodlands Land Development Co., L.P. v. Jenkins*, 48 S.W.3d 415, 426 (Tex. App.—Beaumont 2001, no pet.). For recovery of exemplary damages, see Tex. Bus. & Com. Code § 27.01(c), (d); see also PJC 105.11 and 115.36–.37.

Actual awareness. The statute does not require actual awareness of the falsity for the recovery of actual damages. *Kerrville HRH, Inc. v. City of Kerrville*, 803 S.W.2d 377, 384 (Tex. App.—San Antonio 1990, writ denied); *Wright v. Carpenter*, 579 S.W.2d 575, 579 (Tex. Civ. App.—Corpus Christi 1979, writ ref'd n.r.e.); *Speer v. Pool*, 210 S.W.2d 423, 426 (Tex. Civ. App.—El Paso 1947, no writ). *But see Crofford v. Bowden*, 311 S.W.2d 954, 956 (Tex. Civ. App.—Fort Worth 1958, writ ref'd) (requiring scienter under prior statute).

PJC 105.8 Instruction on Statutory Fraud—Factual Misrepresentation

Fraud occurs when—

a. there is a false representation of a past or existing material fact,

b. the false representation is made to a person for the purpose of inducing that person to enter into a contract, and

c. the false representation is relied on by that person in entering into that contract.

[*or*]

COMMENT

When to use. PJC 105.8 is based on Tex. Bus. & Com. Code § 27.01(a)(1), which applies only to fraud in a transaction involving real estate or stock in a corporation or joint stock company. If there is a dispute about whether the transaction involves real estate or stock in a corporation or joint stock company, additional instructions may be necessary.

Accompanying question. PJC 105.8 is designed to follow PJC 105.7.

Use of "or." If more than one instruction is used, each must be separated by the word *or*, because a finding of any one type of misrepresentation would support recovery.

PJC 105.9 Instruction on Statutory Fraud—False Promise

Fraud occurs when—

a. a party makes a false promise to do an act,

b. the promise is material,

c. the promise is made with the intention of not fulfilling it,

d. the promise is made to a person for the purpose of inducing that person to enter into a contract, and

e. that person relies on the promise in entering into that contract.

[*or*]

COMMENT

When to use. PJC 105.9 is based on Tex. Bus. & Com. Code § 27.01(a)(2), which applies only to fraud in a transaction involving real estate or stock in a corporation or joint stock company. If there is a dispute about whether the transaction involves real estate or stock in a corporation or joint stock company, additional instructions may be necessary.

Accompanying question. PJC 105.9 is designed to accompany the broad-form question at PJC 105.7 in cases involving an allegation of a false promise to perform an act with the present intent not to perform it.

Use of "or." If more than one instruction is used, each must be separated by the word *or*, because a finding of any one type of misrepresentation would support recovery.

PJC 105.10 Question and Instruction on Benefiting from Statutory Fraud

If your answer to Question ______ [*105.7 used with 105.8 or 105.9*] is "Yes," then answer the following question. Otherwise, do not answer the following question.

QUESTION ______

Did *Deborah Dennis* commit fraud against *Paul Payne*?

Fraud occurs when—

a. a person has actual awareness of the falsity of a representation or promise made by another person, and

b. fails to disclose the falsity of the representation or promise to the person defrauded, and

c. benefits from the false representation or promise.

Actual awareness may be inferred where objective manifestations indicate a person acted with actual awareness.

"Representation or promise" means the representation or promise you found to be fraud in response to Question ______ [*105.7 used with 105.8 or 105.9*].

Answer: ______________

COMMENT

When to use. PJC 105.10 submits liability under Tex. Bus. & Com. Code § 27.01(d) when the fraud of another person is separately submitted. If the underlying fraud of another person is not separately submitted under Tex. Bus. & Com. Code § 27.01(a), additional instructions for finding a false representation or promise under Tex. Bus. & Com. Code § 27.01(a) are required as part of this submission.

PJC 105.11 Question and Instruction on Actual Awareness of Statutory Fraud

If you unanimously answered Question ______ [*105.7 used with 105.8 or 105.9*] "Yes," then answer the following question. Otherwise, do not answer the following question.

QUESTION ______

Did *Don Davis* have actual awareness of the falsity of the representation or promise you found to be fraud in Question ______ [*105.7 used with 105.8 or 105.9*]?

> Actual awareness may be inferred where objective manifestations indicate a person acted with actual awareness.

Answer: _______________

COMMENT

When to use. Tex. Bus. & Com. Code § 27.01(c) provides for recovery of exemplary damages if the person making the false representation or promise does so with actual awareness of its falsity. For the appropriate question on exemplary damages, see PJC 115.37. PJC 105.11 should not be used in connection with the question or instruction regarding benefiting from statutory fraud at PJC 105.10.

Actions filed before September 1, 2003. Unanimity is not required in actions filed before September 1, 2003. In such cases, substitute the following conditioning instruction:

> If your answer to Question ______ [*105.7 used with 105.8 or 105.9*] is "Yes," then answer the following question. Otherwise, do not answer the following question

[PJC 105.12–.15 are reserved for expansion.]

PJC 105.16 Question and Instruction on Negligent Misrepresentation

QUESTION ______

Did *Don Davis* make a negligent misrepresentation on which *Paul Payne* justifiably relied?

Negligent misrepresentation occurs when—

a. a party makes a representation in the course of his business or in a transaction in which he has a pecuniary interest,

b. the representation supplies false information for the guidance of others in their business, and

c. the party making the representation did not exercise reasonable care or competence in obtaining or communicating the information.

Answer: ______________

COMMENT

When to use. PJC 105.16 is a broad-form question that should be appropriate in most cases involving a claim of negligent misrepresentation if the court, as a matter of law, or the jury, as a matter of fact, has found that the plaintiff is within the class of persons allowed to bring this cause of action. *See Federal Land Bank Ass'n of Tyler v. Sloane*, 825 S.W.2d 439, 442 (Tex. 1991) (adopting *Restatement (Second) of Torts* § 552 (1977), tort of negligent misrepresentation); *see also McCamish, Martin, Brown & Loeffler v. F.E. Appling Interests*, 991 S.W.2d 787, 791 (Tex. 1999).

Source of question and instruction. The question and instruction are patterned after the supreme court's opinion in *Sloane*, 825 S.W.2d at 442.

Damages. Economic damages for negligent misrepresentation are limited to those necessary to compensate the party for the pecuniary loss caused by the misrepresentation. Benefit-of-the-bargain and lost-profit damages are not available. *Sloane*, 825 S.W.2d at 442–43 (adopting *Restatement (Second) of Torts* § 552B (1977)); *see also D.S.A., Inc. v. Hillsboro Independent School District*, 973 S.W.2d 662, 663–64 (Tex. 1998). In *D.S.A., Inc.*, the court also recognized that under *Restatement (Second) of Torts* § 311 (1965), "[a] party may recover for negligent misrepresentations involving a risk of physical harm only if actual physical harm results." *D.S.A., Inc.*, 973 S.W.2d at 664; *accord*, *Sloane*, 825 S.W.2d at 443 n.4. For submission of negligent misrepresentation damages, see PJC 115.21.

PJC 106.1 Question and Instruction—Intentional Interference with Existing Contract

QUESTION ______

Did *Don Davis* intentionally interfere with [*identify contract*]?

Interference is intentional if committed with the desire to interfere with the contract or with the belief that interference is substantially certain to result.

Answer: _______________

COMMENT

When to use. An existing contract is a necessary element of a claim of intentional interference with contract. PJC 106.1 should be used in cases involving claims for intentional interference with a contract if the existence of the contract is not in dispute. If the existence of the contract is in dispute, additional jury questions or instructions may be required. See chapter 101.

Source of question and instruction. The four elements of intentional interference with a contract are (1) a contract subject to interference, (2) an act of interference that was willful and intentional, (3) the act being a proximate cause of the plaintiff's damage, and (4) actual damage or loss. *Prudential Insurance Co. of America v. Financial Review Services, Inc.*, 29 S.W.3d 74, 77 (Tex. 2000); *ACS Investors, Inc. v. McLaughlin*, 943 S.W.2d 426, 430 (Tex. 1997); *Holloway v. Skinner*, 898 S.W.2d 793, 795–96 (Tex. 1995); *Victoria Bank & Trust Co. v. Brady*, 811 S.W.2d 931, 939 (Tex. 1991); *see also Southwestern Bell Telephone Co. v. John Carlo Texas, Inc.*, 843 S.W.2d 470 (Tex. 1992). The third and fourth elements are submitted together with the question and instructions on damages in PJC 115.22.

Interference. Interference can include conduct that prevents performance of a contract or makes performance of a contract impossible, more burdensome, or more difficult or of less or no value to the one entitled to performance. *See International Union UAW v. Johnson Controls, Inc.*, 813 S.W.2d 558, 568 (Tex. App.—Dallas 1991, writ denied); *Tippett v. Hart*, 497 S.W.2d 606, 610 (Tex. Civ. App.—Amarillo), *writ ref'd n.r.e. per curiam*, 501 S.W.2d 874 (Tex. 1973).

Damages. Damages questions are set forth in chapter 115. PJC 115.22 submits actual damages in cases involving existing contracts and in cases involving prospective contractual relations.

Exemplary damages. For questions submitting exemplary damages, see PJC 115.36 and 115.37 and the Comments accompanying those questions.

PJC 106.2 Wrongful Interference with Prospective Contractual or Business Relations (Comment)

The supreme court has recognized the existence of the cause of action of tortious interference with a prospective contract or business relationship. *See Wal-Mart Stores v. Sturges*, 52 S.W.3d 711 (Tex. 2001). Furthermore, the elements consistently have been described as (1) the existence of a reasonable probability that the parties would have entered into a contractual or business relationship, (2) the actor committed an independently tortious or unlawful act that was a substantial factor in preventing the contractual or business relationship from occurring, (3) the actor acted with a conscious desire to prevent the relationship from occurring or knew that the interference was certain or substantially certain to occur as a result of his conduct, and (4) the complainant suffered actual harm or damage as a result of the interference. *Texas Disposal Systems Landfill, Inc. v. Waste Management Holdings, Inc.*, 219 S.W.3d 563 (Tex. App.—Austin 2007, pet. denied); *Brown v. Swett & Crawford of Texas, Inc.*, 178 S.W.3d 373, 381–82 (Tex. App.—Houston [1st Dist.] 2005, no pet.); *Bright v. Addison*, 171 S.W.3d 588, 598 (Tex. App.—Dallas 2005, pet. dism'd); *Community Initiatives, Inc. v. Chase Bank of Texas, N.A.*, 153 S.W.3d 270, 283–84 (Tex. App.—El Paso 2004, no pet.); *Finlan v. Dallas Independent School District*, 90 S.W.3d 395, 412 (Tex. App.—Eastland 2002, pet. denied); *Allied Capital Corp. v. Cravens*, 67 S.W.3d 486, 491 (Tex. App.—Corpus Christi 2002, no pet.); *Baty v. ProTech Insurance Agency*, 63 S.W.3d 841, 860 (Tex. App.—Houston [14th Dist.] 2001, pet. denied); *Ash v. Hack Branch Distributing Co.*, 54 S.W.3d 401, 414–15 (Tex. App.—Waco 2001, pet. denied); *Pecos Petroleum Co. v. McMillan*, Not reported in S.W.3d, 2003 WL 1823389 (Tex. App.—San Antonio April 9, 2003, pet. denied). Where a contract or business relationship is delayed but eventually arises, there can be no claim for tortuous interference with prospective contracts or business relationships. *Texas Disposal Systems Landfill, Inc.*, 219 S.W.3d at 590–91.

As with the claim of intentional interference with an existing contract, interference as contemplated by this cause is intentional if committed with the desire to interfere with the contract or with the belief that interference is substantially certain to result. *Bradford v. Vento*, 48 S.W.3d 749, 757 (Tex. 2001) (quoting *Restatement (Second) of Torts* § 766B cmt. d (1979)). However, according to the supreme court, if the actor had no desire to effectuate the interference by his conduct but knew that interference would be a mere incidental result, then the interference may not be improper. *Bradford*, 48 S.W.3d at 757.

The applicable damages questions are set forth in PJC 115.22, 115.36, and 115.37.

PJC 106.3 Question—Defense of Legal Justification

If your answer to Question ______ [*106.1*] is "Yes," then answer the following question. Otherwise, do not answer the following question.

QUESTION ______

Did *Don Davis* interfere because he had a good-faith belief that he had a right to do so?

Answer: ______________

COMMENT

When to use. PJC 106.3 submits the affirmative defense of justification. The justification defense applies to intentional interference with an existing contract. *Texas Beef Cattle Co. v. Green*, 921 S.W.2d 203, 211 (Tex. 1996).

Source of question and instruction. PJC 106.3 is derived from *Texas Beef Cattle Co.*, 921 S.W.2d at 211, and *Southwestern Bell Telephone Co. v. John Carlo Texas, Inc.*, 843 S.W.2d 470, 472 (Tex. 1992). *See also Victoria Bank & Trust Co. v. Brady*, 811 S.W.2d 931, 939 (Tex. 1991); *Sterner v. Marathon Oil Co.*, 767 S.W.2d 686, 689–91 (Tex. 1989).

Burden of proof. The defendant has the burden of proof on a justification defense. *Texas Beef Cattle Co.*, 921 S.W.2d at 211; *see also Wal-Mart Stores v. Sturges*, 52 S.W.3d 711, 725 (Tex. 2001).

Questions of law or fact. Whether the defendant has established a legal right to interfere is a question of law for the court. If no legal right exists as a matter of law, the court must then make a threshold determination if a mistaken but colorable legal right was asserted. If a colorable legal right was asserted, then the jury is to determine whether the defendant exercised that colorable legal right in good faith. *Texas Beef Cattle Co.*, 921 S.W.2d at 211.

Scope of instruction. Interference may be justified under circumstances other than those addressed in PJC 106.3. *See, e.g.*, *Eloise Bauer & Associates v. Electronic Realty Associates*, 621 S.W.2d 200, 203 (Tex. Civ. App.—Texarkana 1981, writ ref'd n.r.e.) (employee acting in good faith to further interests of employer); *see also Russell v. Edgewood Independent School District*, 406 S.W.2d 249, 252 (Tex. Civ. App.—San Antonio 1966, writ ref'd n.r.e.); *Restatement (Second) of Torts* §§ 769–772 (1977). Although *Texas Beef Cattle Co.* omitted reference to "interests that a party possesses in the subject matter equal or superior to that of the other party," the Committee believes that such interests are subsumed in the term "colorable legal right." *Compare Texas Beef Cattle*

Co., 921 S.W.2d at 211 (citing *Sakowitz, Inc. v. Steck*, 669 S.W.2d 105, 107 (Tex. 1984), *overruled on other grounds by Sterner*, 767 S.W.2d at 690), *with John Carlo Texas, Inc.*, 843 S.W.2d at 472.

Defenses to interference with prospective business relations. In *Sturges*, the supreme court held that "[j]ustification and privilege are defenses in a claim for tortious interference with prospective relations only to the extent that they are defenses to the independent tortiousness of the defendant's conduct. Otherwise, the plaintiff need not prove that the defendant's conduct was not justified or privileged, nor can a defendant assert such defenses." *Sturges*, 52 S.W.3d at 727.

Exercise of privilege by illegal or tortious means. "A party may not exercise an otherwise legitimate privilege by resort to illegal or tortious means." *Prudential Insurance Co. of America v. Financial Review Services, Inc.*, 29 S.W.3d 74, 81 (Tex. 2000). Thus, even if a defendant establishes a legal right or privilege, "if the plaintiff pleads and proves methods of interference that are tortious in themselves, then the issue of privilege or justification never arises." *Prudential Insurance Co. of America*, 29 S.W.3d at 81; *see also Butnaru v. Ford Motor Co.*, 84 S.W.3d 198, 207 (Tex. 2002) (exercise of contractual right of first refusal that violates statutory prohibition may establish lack of justification). The Committee expresses no opinion on whether in the context of a claim for intentional interference with an existing contract a defendant may nevertheless raise "defenses to the wrongfulness of the alleged [tortious or wrongful] conduct." *Sturges*, 52 S.W.3d at 727.

CHAPTER 107 EMPLOYMENT

PJC 107.1 Breach of Employment Agreement (Comment)

Subject to general contract rules. PJC chapter 101 governs the submission of breach of employment agreement cases. An express agreement limiting the employer's right to discharge an employee at will is subject to general rules governing contracts. *See, e.g., Mansell v. Texas & Pacific Railway Co.*, 137 S.W.2d 997, 999–1000 (Tex. 1940) (agreement that employment could not be terminated without a fair investigation); *Morgan v. Jack Brown Cleaners, Inc.*, 764 S.W.2d 825, 827 (Tex. App.—Austin 1989, writ denied) (oral agreement that plaintiff would be transferred to another position and not terminated if her department were shut down); *Ramos v. Henry C. Beck Co.*, 711 S.W.2d 331, 336 (Tex. App.—Dallas 1986, no writ) (agreement that plaintiff would not be discharged absent good cause). The supreme court has expressly reserved the question of whether an oral agreement is sufficient to modify an employment-at-will relationship. *Goodyear Tire & Rubber Co. v. Portilla*, 879 S.W.2d 47, 51–52 n.8 (Tex. 1994).

If an express agreement exists between an employer and an employee limiting the employer's right to discharge an employee and breach of that agreement is alleged, PJC 101.2 should be submitted. If there is a dispute about the existence of an agreement or its terms, PJC 101.1 should be submitted, with PJC 101.2 predicated on an affirmative answer to PJC 101.1. Any defense to breach of the employment agreement should be submitted under PJC 101.21.

If there is no specific contract term or express agreement to the contrary, the rule that either party may terminate the employment relationship at will with or without cause will control. *Montgomery County Hospital District v. Brown*, 965 S.W.2d 501, 502 (Tex. 1998); *Federal Express Corp. v. Dutschmann*, 846 S.W.2d 282, 283 (Tex. 1993); *East Line & R.R.R. Co. v. Scott*, 10 S.W. 99, 102 (Tex. 1888).

Property interest. A "for cause" or "good cause" limitation on dismissal of a public employee creates a property right in continued employment that is protected under the Constitution's Due Process Clause. *Bexar County Sheriff's Civil Service Commission v. Davis*, 802 S.W.2d 659, 661 & n.2 (Tex. 1990), *cert. denied*, 502 U.S. 811 (1991); *Brandy v. City of Cedar Hill*, 884 S.W.2d 913, 915 (Tex. App.—Texarkana 1994, no writ). If a property interest in not being discharged without good cause exists, the Committee suggests the following jury question with a modified definition of PJC 107.2's "good cause":

Did *Don Davis* terminate *Paul Payne* without good cause?

Accompanying instructions. Depending on the nature of the specific contract terms or any defenses, additional instructions may be necessary for use with PJC 101.2 and 101.21. See PJC 107.2 (instruction on good cause as defense to early discharge) and chapter 101 (general instructions on contracts).

PJC 107.2 Instruction on Good Cause as Defense to Early Discharge

Failure to comply by *Don Davis* is excused if there was good cause for discharging *Paul Payne* before the agreed term of employment expired. "Good cause" means that the employee failed to perform those duties in the scope of his employment as a person of ordinary prudence would have done under the same or similar circumstances, or that the employee committed acts in the scope of his employment that a person of ordinary prudence would not have done under the same or similar circumstances.

COMMENT

When to use. PJC 107.2 submits the defense of "good cause" to breach of an agreement to employ for a definite term. *See, e.g.*, *Lee-Wright, Inc. v. Hall*, 840 S.W.2d 572, 578 (Tex. App.—Houston [1st Dist.] 1992, no writ); *Watts v. St. Mary's Hall, Inc.*, 662 S.W.2d 55, 58–59 (Tex. App.—San Antonio 1983, writ ref'd n.r.e.); *Lone Star Steel Co. v. Wahl*, 636 S.W.2d 217, 220 (Tex. App.—Texarkana 1982, no writ). This instruction should be used with PJC 101.21, the basic contract defense question.

Source of instruction. PJC 107.2 is derived from *Winograd v. Willis*, 789 S.W.2d 307, 311 (Tex. App.—Houston [14th Dist.] 1990, writ denied); *see also Dixie Glass Co. v. Pollak*, 341 S.W.2d 530, 541–42 (Tex. Civ. App.—Houston 1960) (defining "good cause"), *writ ref'd n.r.e. per curiam*, 347 S.W.2d 596 (Tex. 1961).

"Good cause" defined in agreement. If "good cause" or a similar term, such as "just cause" or "proper cause," is explicitly defined in the agreement or if specific grounds for termination are recited in the agreement, PJC 107.2 should not be submitted.

PJC 107.3 Question on Wrongful Discharge for Refusing to Perform an Illegal Act

QUESTION ______

Was *Paul Payne* discharged for the sole reason that *he* refused to perform an illegal act?

As used in this question, an "illegal act" means any of the following:

[Insert appropriate instructions.]

Answer: _______________

COMMENT

When to use. PJC 107.3 should be used for a claim that the employee was discharged for the sole reason that he refused to perform an illegal act.

Source of question. PJC 107.3 is derived from *Sabine Pilot Service, Inc. v. Hauck*, 687 S.W.2d 733, 735 (Tex. 1985), and *Paul v. P.B.-K.B.B., Inc.*, 801 S.W.2d 229, 230 (Tex. App.—Houston [14th Dist.] 1990, writ denied). *Burt v. City of Burkburnett*, 800 S.W.2d 625, 627 (Tex. App.—Fort Worth 1990, writ denied), interpreted *Sabine Pilot*'s use of the word *refused* to include a requirement that the employer, in some manner, must order, require, or request the employee to commit an illegal act.

Illegal act. The trial court should make a threshold determination as a matter of law whether the act the employee refused to commit was illegal. In *Hancock v. Express One International, Inc.*, 800 S.W.2d 634, 636–37 (Tex. App.—Dallas 1990, writ denied), the court refused to extend the *Sabine Pilot* exception to illegal acts that carry only civil penalties.

After-acquired evidence of employee misconduct. If the employer has pleaded the discovery of evidence of employee misconduct acquired only after the employee's employment was terminated, see PJC 107.7 for the applicable question.

PJC 107.4 Question and Instruction on Retaliation under Texas Whistleblower Act

QUESTION ______

Was *Paul Payne*'s report [*insert matter reported*] made in good faith and a cause of *Don Davis*'s [*terminating, suspending, or (describe other discriminatory action)*] *Paul Payne* when *he* [*terminated, suspended, or (describe other discriminatory action)*] *Paul Payne*?

"Good faith" means that (1) *Paul Payne* believed that the conduct reported was a violation of law and (2) *his* belief was reasonable in light of *his* training and experience.

Answer: ______________

COMMENT

When to use. PJC 107.4 should be used if a violation of Tex. Gov't Code § 554.002 is alleged. If the existence of an adverse personnel action is in dispute, a finding in addition to PJC 107.4 is necessary.

Source of question and instruction. PJC 107.4 is derived from Tex. Gov't Code § 554.002; *Texas Department of Human Services v. Hinds*, 904 S.W.2d 629 (Tex. 1995); and *Texas Department of Human Services v. Green*, 855 S.W.2d 136, 150–51 (Tex. App.—Austin 1993, writ denied). The instruction was adopted by the supreme court in *Wichita County, Texas v. Hart*, 917 S.W.2d 779, 784–85 (Tex. 1996). The question specifically requires the jury to find causation. *See City of Fort Worth v. Zimlich*, 29 S.W.3d 62 (Tex. 2000).

Provisions of Whistleblower Act. The Texas Whistleblower Act is found at Tex. Gov't Code §§ 554.001–.010. A state or local governmental body may not terminate, suspend, or otherwise discriminate against a public employee who in good faith reports a violation of law to an appropriate law enforcement authority. Tex. Gov't Code § 554.002 (formerly Tex. Rev. Civ. Stat. art. 6252–16(a)); *see also Winters v. Houston Chronicle Publishing Co.*, 795 S.W.2d 723 (Tex. 1990) (declining to extend Whistleblower Act to private sector employees); *accord*, *Austin v. Healthtrust, Inc.—The Hospital Co.*, 967 S.W.2d 400 (Tex. 1998) (reaffirming *Winters*'s refusal to recognize common-law whistleblower action).

Appropriate law enforcement authority. Whether the person or entity to which the employee made the report is "an appropriate law enforcement authority" is a question of law. *Texas Department of Transportation v. Needham*, 82 S.W.3d 314, 318–20 (Tex. 2002); *City of Beaumont v. Bouillion*, 896 S.W.2d 143, 145–46 (Tex. 1995); *see* *also Town of Flower Mound v. Teague*, 111 S.W.3d 742, 753 (Tex. App.—Fort Worth 2003, pet. denied) (citing PJC 107.4). However, an employee may pursue a cause of action if he had a good-faith belief that the governmental entity to which he reported a violation of law was the appropriate law enforcement authority as the statute defines the terms even if the entity, as a matter of law, is not an appropriate law enforcement authority. Tex. Gov't Code § 554.002; *Needham*, 82 S.W.3d at 320–21. If a fact question exists about whether the employee had such a good-faith belief, the Committee recommends that the following question and instruction be submitted to the jury:

QUESTION _____

Did *Paul Payne* have a good-faith belief that the governmental entity to which *he* reported a violation of a law was an appropriate law enforcement authority?

"Good-faith belief" in this question means that—

1. *Paul Payne* believed that the governmental entity was authorized to (a) regulate under or enforce the law alleged to be violated in the report or (b) investigate or prosecute a violation of criminal law; and

2. *his* belief was reasonable in light of *his* training and experience.

Answer "Yes" or "No."

Answer: _______________

See City of Houston v. Levingston, 221 S.W.3d 204, 218–19 (Tex. App.—Houston [1st Dist.] 2006, no pet.) (citing *Needham*, 82 S.W.3d at 321, and discussing the requirements for establishing a good-faith belief that the governmental entity to which an employee reported a violation of law was an appropriate law enforcement authority in the context of Tex. Gov't Code § 554.002(b)).

Good faith. PJC 107.4 specifically applies to lawsuits against public employers pursuant to the Texas Whistleblower Act, which provides that a "state or local governmental entity may not suspend or terminate the employment of, or take other adverse personnel action against, a public employee who in good faith reports a violation of law by the employing governmental entity or another public employee to an appropriate law enforcement authority." Tex. Gov't Code § 554.002(a). Actions may be brought against private employers pursuant to statutes such as the Texas Commission on Human Rights Act, the Texas Workers' Compensation Act, and the Texas Health and Safety Code. *See* Tex. Lab. Code § 21.055 (Texas Commission on Human Rights Act); Tex. Lab. Code §§ 451.001–.003 (Texas Workers' Compensation Act); Tex. Health & Safety Code

§§ 161.134, 242.133. However, these statutes do not contain the "good faith" language. There is a split of authority about whether "good faith" is required in a whistleblower action against private employers. *Compare Goodman v. Page*, 984 S.W.2d 299, 303 (Tex. App.—Fort Worth 1998, pet. denied) (listing elements of section 242.133 of Texas Health and Safety Code without "good faith" requirement), *with Tomhave v. Oaks Psychiatric Hospital*, 82 S.W.3d 381, 385 (Tex. App.—Austin 2002, pet. denied) (listing "good faith" reporting as element of cause of action under section 161.134 of Texas Health and Safety Code), *overruled on other grounds by Binur v. Jacobo*, 135 S.W.3d 646, 651 (Tex. 2004); *see also Dallas Metrocare v. Pratt*, 124 S.W.3d 147 (Tex. 2003); *Healthtrust, Inc.*, 967 S.W.2d at 401–02; *Winters*, 795 S.W.2d at 724; *Simmons Airlines v. Lagrotte*, 50 S.W.3d 748, 751–52 n.5 (Tex. App.—Dallas 2001, pet. denied).

Other retaliation statutes. The Committee has not provided pattern jury charges for every statutory prohibition against retaliatory discharge. Other such statutes include—

- Tex. Agric. Code § 125.013(b) (agricultural laborer for reporting violation of Agricultural Hazard Communication Act);
- Tex. Civ. Prac. & Rem. Code § 122.001 (jury duty; criminal statute);
- Tex. Elec. Code § 276.001 (voting for certain candidate or proposition or refusing to reveal how one voted);
- Tex. Fam. Code § 158.209 (child support or child custody order or writ relating to an employee);
- Tex. Gov't Code § 431.006 (training or duty in state military forces);
- Tex. Health & Safety Code § 161.134 (employees of hospital, mental health facility, or treatment facility reporting violation of law or rule);
- Tex. Health & Safety Code § 242.133 (employees of an institution reporting violations of law);
- Tex. Lab. Code § 52.041 (employee refusing to make purchases from a specific place or store or refusing to engage in dealings with a specific person or business; criminal statute);
- Tex. Lab. Code § 52.051 (compliance with subpoena);
- Tex. Lab. Code § 101.052 (union membership or nonmembership);
- Tex. Lab. Code §§ 411.082–.083 (using telephone service to report in good faith a violation of occupational health or safety law);
- Tex. Loc. Gov't Code § 160.006 (county employee exercising right or participating in grievance procedures established under Local Government Code);
- Tex. Occ. Code § 160.012 (physician reporting acts of another physician that pose threat to public welfare); *see also* Tex. Occ. Code §§ 160.002–.004;

- 29 U.S.C. § 158(a)(1), (3), (4) (engaging in union activities);
- 29 U.S.C. § 215(a)(3) (exercising rights to a minimum wage and overtime compensation);
- 29 U.S.C. § 1140 (exercising rights under employee benefit plan);
- 42 U.S.C. § 5851 (federal whistleblower provision).

Caveat: causes of action accruing on or after June 15, 1995. If the adverse personnel action occurred on or after June 15, 1995, it is an affirmative defense to a Whistleblower Act suit that the state or local governmental entity would have taken the action against the employee "based solely on information, observation, or evidence that is not related to the fact that the employee made a report" of a violation of law. Tex. Gov't Code § 554.004(b). In *Hinds*, 904 S.W.2d at 637, the supreme court noted that it expressed no opinion on whether the amended statute shifted the burden of proof.

After-acquired evidence of employee misconduct. If the employer has pleaded the discovery of evidence of employee misconduct acquired only after the employee's employment was terminated, see PJC 107.7 for the applicable question.

PJC 107.5 Question and Instruction on Retaliation for Seeking Worker's Compensation Benefits

QUESTION ______

Did *Don Davis* [*discharge or (describe other discriminatory action)*] *Paul Payne* because *he* [*filed a worker's compensation claim in good faith, hired a lawyer to represent him in a worker's compensation claim, instituted or caused to be instituted a worker's compensation claim in good faith, testified or is about to testify in a worker's compensation proceeding*]?

> There may be more than one cause for an employment decision. An employer does not [*discharge or (describe other discriminatory action)*] an employee for [*filing a worker's compensation claim in good faith, hiring a lawyer to represent him in a worker's compensation claim, instituting or causing to be instituted a worker's compensation claim in good faith, testifying or intending to testify in a worker's compensation proceeding*] if the employer would have [*insert employment decision—e.g., discharged*] the employee when he did even if the employee had not [*filed a worker's compensation claim in good faith, hired a lawyer to represent him in a worker's compensation claim, instituted or caused to be instituted a worker's compensation claim in good faith, testified or was about to testify in a worker's compensation proceeding*].

Answer: _______________

COMMENT

When to use. PJC 107.5 should be used for a claim that the employer has committed an unlawful practice under Tex. Lab. Code § 451.001 (formerly Tex. Rev. Civ. Stat. art. 8307c).

Source of question and instruction. PJC 107.5 is derived from Tex. Lab. Code § 451.001 (formerly Tex. Rev. Civ. Stat. art. 8307c) and *Azar Nut Co. v. Caille*, 720 S.W.2d 685, 687 (Tex. App.—El Paso 1986), *aff'd*, 734 S.W.2d 667 (Tex. 1987); *see also Southwestern Bell Telephone Co. v. Garza*, 164 S.W.3d 607, 615–16 (Tex. 2004) (discussing PJC 107.5 and noting that the court's charge would have been more accurate if it had asked whether the defendant discriminated against the plaintiff, thereby retaining the statutory language). The instruction is derived from *Continental Coffee Products Co. v. Cazarez*, 937 S.W.2d 444, 450–51 (Tex. 1996) (citing *Investment Properties Management, Inc. v. Montes*, 821 S.W.2d 691, 694 (Tex. App.—El Paso 1991, no writ)), and

Texas Department of Human Services v. Hinds, 904 S.W.2d 629, 637 (Tex. 1995). *See also Dallas County v. Holmes*, 62 S.W.3d 326, 332–33 (Tex. App.—Dallas 2001, no pet.); *Wyler Industrial Works, Inc. v. Garcia*, 999 S.W.2d 494, 511 (Tex. App.—El Paso 1999, no pet.).

Institution of proceeding. If an employee has been discharged after injury, but before claim paperwork has been filed, the following instruction may be given:

> "Instituting or causing to be instituted a worker's compensation proceeding" includes reporting an injury to *Don Davis*, being furnished with medical benefits, or receiving weekly compensation benefits.

See Worsham Steel Co. v. Arias, 831 S.W.2d 81, 84 (Tex. App.—El Paso 1992, no writ); *Mid-South Bottling Co. v. Cigainero*, 799 S.W.2d 385, 389 (Tex. App.—Texarkana 1990, writ denied); *Texas Steel Co. v. Douglas*, 533 S.W.2d 111, 116 (Tex. Civ. App.—Fort Worth 1976, writ ref'd n.r.e.).

After-acquired evidence of employee misconduct. If the employer has pleaded the discovery of evidence of employee misconduct acquired only after the employee's employment was terminated, see PJC 107.7 for the applicable question.

PJC 107.6 Question and Instruction on Unlawful Employment Practices

QUESTION ______

Was [*race, color, disability, religion, sex, national origin, or age*] a motivating factor in *Don Davis*'s decision to [*fail or refuse to hire, discharge, or (describe other discriminatory action)*] *Paul Payne*?

A "motivating factor" in an employment decision is a reason for making the decision at the time it was made. There may be more than one motivating factor for an employment decision.

Answer: ______________

COMMENT

When to use. PJC 107.6 should be used for a claim that the employer has committed an unlawful employment practice as set out in the Texas Commission on Human Rights Act, Tex. Lab. Code §§ 21.001–.556 (TCHRA). PJC 107.6 applies to employment practices prohibited by Tex. Lab. Code § 21.051(1) and will need to be modified according to the facts of the case. If there is a fact issue concerning the existence of an adverse employment action, an additional finding is necessary.

PJC 107.6 and the questions and instructions that follow are drafted for TCHRA cases but may also be used in federal law claims, because the TCHRA conforms substantially to title VII of the 1964 Civil Rights Act, 42 U.S.C. §§ 2000e to e-17; the Age Discrimination in Employment Act (ADEA), 29 U.S.C. §§ 621–634; and the Americans with Disabilities Act (ADA), 42 U.S.C. §§ 12101–12213. The TCHRA is not, however, always identical to federal law. Therefore, before using these submissions in cases based on federal law, the practitioner should compare the language of the TCHRA with the language of the applicable federal statute and the cases construing those statutes.

Use of federal case law. The TCHRA is expressly intended to implement policies of title VII of the Civil Rights Act of 1964. Tex. Lab. Code § 21.001(1); *Schroeder v. Texas Iron Works, Inc.*, 813 S.W.2d 483, 485 (Tex. 1991). Because one of the purposes behind the TCHRA is the "correlation of state law with federal law in the area of discrimination in employment," federal case law interpreting title VII serves as a guide for interpretation of cases brought under chapter 21 of the Labor Code. *Schroeder*, 813 S.W.2d at 485; *see also Specialty Retailers, Inc. v. DeMoranville*, 933 S.W.2d 490, 492 (Tex. 1996) (per curiam); *Farrington v. Sysco Food Services, Inc.*, 865 S.W.2d 247, 251 (Tex. App.—Houston [1st Dist.] 1993, writ denied).

Source of question and definition. PJC 107.6 is derived from Tex. Lab. Code § 21.051(1), which parallels 42 U.S.C. § 2000e-2(a)(1) and prohibits intentional discriminatory practices. *See also Texas Department of Community Affairs v. Burdine*, 450 U.S. 248 (1981); *International Brotherhood of Teamsters v. United States*, 431 U.S. 324 (1977); *McDonnell Douglas Corp. v. Green*, 411 U.S. 792 (1973) (all discussing title VII's purpose); *see also Quantum Chemical Corp. v. Toennies*, 47 S.W.3d 473 (Tex. 2001). The Committee believes that PJC 107.6 and the definition of "motivating factor" correctly state the ultimate fact-finding necessary to determine liability under the TCHRA; additional instructions may, however, be necessary in a particular case. *See Adams v. Valley Federal Credit Union*, 848 S.W.2d 182 (Tex. App.—Corpus Christi 1992, writ denied); *Lakeway Land Co. v. Kizer*, 796 S.W.2d 820, 825–26 (Tex. App.—Austin 1990, writ denied); *but see Olitsky v. Spencer Gifts, Inc.*, 964 F.2d 1471 (5th Cir. 1992), *cert. denied*, 507 U.S. 909 (1993).

The definition of "motivating factor" is derived from the following: (1) Tex. Lab. Code § 21.125(a), which provides that "an unlawful employment practice is established when the complainant demonstrates that race, color, sex, national origin, religion, age, or disability was a motivating factor for an employment practice, even if other factors also motivated the practice"; and (2) section 709 of the Civil Rights Act of 1991, 42 U.S.C. § 2000e, codifying a portion of the Supreme Court's definition of causation under title VII in *Price Waterhouse v. Hopkins*, 490 U.S. 228 (1989).

Circumstantial evidence. A circumstantial evidence instruction may be appropriate. See PJC 100.8. *See also Quantum Chemical Corp.*, 47 S.W.3d at 481–82.

National origin. For a definition of discrimination because of national origin, see Tex. Lab. Code § 21.110 and *EEOC Guidelines on Discrimination Because of National Origin*, 29 C.F.R. § 1606.1.

Disparate treatment versus disparate impact. There is a difference between disparate treatment (Tex. Lab. Code § 21.051(1)) and disparate impact (Tex. Lab. Code §§ 21.051(2), 21.122) cases. PJC 107.6 submits disparate treatment. In a disparate impact case, an employer may be held liable for unintentional discrimination where an employment practice or criterion, neutral on its face, has a disproportionate effect or impact on a protected group. *Griggs v. Duke Power Co.*, 401 U.S. 424 (1971). The TCHRA defines "disparate impact" as a practice where the employer "limits, segregates, or classifies an employee or applicant for employment in a manner that would deprive or tend to deprive an individual of any employment opportunity or adversely affect in any other manner the status of an employee." Tex. Lab. Code § 21.051(2). For example, height and weight requirements may unlawfully discriminate against women and some ethnic or racial minorities. *Dothard v. Rawlinson*, 433 U.S. 321 (1977). Education requirements may impact impermissibly on historically disadvantaged minority groups. *See Griggs*, 401 U.S. at 431–33. Disparate impact is not restricted to objective criteria or written tests with a discriminatory effect. *Watson v. Fort Worth Bank & Trust*, 487 U.S. 977, 989–91 (1988).

"Business necessity" is an affirmative defense to a disparate impact claim if an employer can show that the job requirement is job-related and justified by a valid business necessity. Tex. Lab. Code § 21.115. "Business necessity" is never a justification, however, for intentional discrimination (disparate treatment). Tex. Lab. Code § 21.123.

Submission of disparate impact cases. Tex. Lab. Code § 21.122 sets forth the elements and burden of proof necessary in a disparate impact case and is the basis of the Committee's following suggested questions and instructions:

QUESTION ______

Did *Don Davis*'s requirement that [*particular employment practice*] have a disparate impact on [*name of protected group, e.g., women, racial minorities, etc.*]?

"Disparate impact" is established if an employer uses a particular employment practice, even if apparently neutral, that has a significant adverse effect on the basis of [*race, color, sex, national origin, etc.*].

Answer: ______________

If you answered "Yes" to Question ______ [*disparate impact question*], then answer the following question. Otherwise, do not answer the following question.

QUESTION ______

Was the employment practice inquired about in Question ______ [*disparate impact question*] job-related to the position in question and consistent with business necessity?

An employment practice is job-related if the practice clearly relates to skills, knowledge, or ability required for successful performance on the job. For an employment practice to be consistent with business necessity, it must be necessary to safe and efficient job performance.

Answer: ______________

If you answered "Yes" to Question ______ [*employment practice question*], then answer the following question. Otherwise, do not answer the following question.

QUESTION _____

Has *Don Davis* refused to adopt an "alternative employment practice" to the job requirement inquired about in Question _____ [*disparate impact question*]?

An "alternative employment practice" is an employment practice that serves the employer's legitimate interest in an equally effective manner, but which does not have a disparate impact on [*name of protected group, e.g., women, racial minorities, etc.*].

Answer: _______________

"Disparate impact" was defined by the Supreme Court in *Albemarle Paper Co. v. Moody*, 422 U.S. 405, 425 (1975). The "significant adverse effect" language originated in *Connecticut v. Teal*, 457 U.S. 440, 448 (1982) (holding that a disparate impact claim under title VII is established when "an employer uses a nonjob-related barrier in order to deny a minority or woman applicant employment or promotion, and that barrier has a significant adverse effect on minorities or women"). That language has not been expressly used by Texas courts. The Austin Court of Appeals has described disparate impact cases as those that involve facially neutral practices "that operate to exclude a disproportionate percentage of persons in a protected group and cannot be justified by business necessity." *Wal-Mart Stores v. Davis*, 979 S.W.2d 30, 44 (Tex. App.—Austin 1998, pet. denied). The requirements of business necessity are set forth in Tex. Lab. Code §§ 21.115, 21.122(a)(1). Tex. Lab. Code § 21.122(a)(2) states the burden of proof with respect to showing an alternative employment practice to be that "in accordance with federal law as that law existed [on] June 4, 1989"—a reference to the 1991 amendments to title VII that codified those burdens following the June 5, 1989, Supreme Court decision in *Wards Cove Packing Co. v. Atonio*, 490 U.S. 642 (1989). Therefore, the burden of proof, on a showing of disparate impact, is on the employer to demonstrate that the practice is "job-related" and consistent with business necessity. *Dothard*, 433 U.S. at 329. The instruction on "job-relatedness" is derived from *Albemarle Paper Co.*, 422 U.S. at 425; *Contreras v. City of Los Angeles*, 656 F.2d 1267 (9th Cir. 1981), *cert. denied*, 455 U.S. 1021 (1982); and 29 C.F.R. § 1607. *See also* Tex. Lab. Code § 21.115; *Davis v. Richmond, Fredericksburg & Potomac Railroad Co.*, 803 F.2d 1322, 1327–28 (4th Cir. 1986); *EEOC v. Rath Packing Co. Creditors' Trust*, 787 F.2d 318, 328 (8th Cir. 1986), *cert. denied*, 479 U.S. 910 (1986). The "alternative employment practice" definition is derived from *Watson*, 487 U.S. at 998.

Disparate impact cases: age. Age is a protected category under the Texas Labor Code. Tex. Lab. Code § 21.051; *see also* Tex. Lab. Code § 21.101. For submission of a disparate impact case based on age discrimination, the Committee recommends the following question and instruction:

QUESTION ______

Did *Don Davis*'s requirement that [*describe specific employment practice*] have a disparate impact on [*name of protected group, e.g., persons over the age of forty*]?

"Disparate impact" is established if the identified and challenged practice has a significantly adverse effect and is not based on reasonable factors other than age discrimination.

Answer: _______________

"Disparate impact" claims based on age discrimination were first recognized by the Supreme Court in *Smith v. City of Jackson*, 544 U.S. 228 (2005). The scope of disparate impact under the ADEA is significantly narrower than disparate impact under title VII. *Smith*, 544 U.S. at 240–41. This is in part because the ADEA includes a narrowing provision that provides that it is not unlawful for an employer "to take any action otherwise prohibited . . . where the differentiation is based on reasonable factors other than age." 29 U.S.C. § 623(f). Unlike the business-necessity test articulated under title VII, the reasonableness inquiry does not inquire whether there are other means by which an employer can accomplish its goals. *Smith*, 544 U.S. at 243.

Damages. See PJC 115.30 for the question submitting actual damages and PJC 115.31 regarding exemplary damages.

After-acquired evidence of employee misconduct. If the employer has pleaded the discovery of evidence of employee misconduct acquired only after the employee's employment was terminated, see PJC 107.7 for the applicable question.

PJC 107.7 Question on After-Acquired Evidence of Employee Misconduct

QUESTION ______

Did *Paul Payne* engage in misconduct for which *Don Davis* would have legitimately discharged him solely on that basis?

Answer "Yes" or "No."

Answer: _______________

COMMENT

When to use. PJC 107.7 should be used if the employer pleads that evidence of the employee's misconduct, acquired after the employee's discharge, should limit the employee's recovery, because the employer either would not have hired or would have terminated the employee on legitimate and lawful grounds had the evidence been discovered before discharge. The Committee believes that PJC 107.7 is appropriate to submit if after-acquired evidence is pleaded by the defendant in any wrongful discharge claim. *See McKennon v. Nashville Banner Publishing Co.*, 513 U.S. 352 (1995) (age discrimination); *Trico Technologies Corp. v. Montiel*, 949 S.W.2d 308 (Tex. 1997) (per curiam) (worker's compensation retaliation); *Norwood v. Litwin Engineers & Constructors, Inc.*, 962 S.W.2d 220 (Tex. App.—Houston [1st Dist.] 1998, pet. denied) (disability discrimination).

PJC 107.8 Instruction on Damages Reduction for After-Acquired Evidence of Employee Misconduct

If you answered "Yes" to Question ______ [*107.7*], do not include any damages suffered past the date *Don Davis* discovered that *Paul Payne* engaged in the conduct you found in answer to Question ______ [*107.7*].

COMMENT

When to use. PJC 107.8 should be predicated on a "Yes" answer to PJC 107.7. It should be used as the last sentence of the preliminary instruction in PJC 115.26–.28 or 115.30.

Source of instruction. PJC 107.8 is derived from *McKennon v. Nashville Banner Publishing Co.*, 513 U.S. 352 (1995); *Trico Technologies Corp. v. Montiel*, 949 S.W.2d 308 (Tex. 1997) (per curiam); and *Norwood v. Litwin Engineers & Constructors, Inc.*, 962 S.W.2d 220 (Tex. App.—Houston [1st Dist.] 1998, pet. denied).

PJC 107.9 Question on Retaliation

QUESTION ______

Did *Don Davis* [*fail or refuse to hire, discharge, or (describe other discriminatory or retaliatory action)*] *Paul Payne* because of *Paul Payne*'s [*opposition to a discriminatory practice; making or filing a charge of discrimination; filing a complaint; or testifying, assisting, or participating in any manner in a discrimination investigation, proceeding, or hearing under the Texas Commission on Human Rights Act*]?

Paul Payne must establish that without his [*opposition to a discriminatory practice; making or filing a charge of discrimination; filing a complaint; or testifying, assisting, or participating in any manner in a discrimination investigation, proceeding, or hearing under the Texas Commission on Human Rights Act*], if any, *Don Davis*'s [*failure or refusal to hire, discharge, or (describe other discriminatory or retaliatory action)*], if any, would not have occurred when it did. There may be more than one cause for an employment decision. *Paul Payne* need not establish that his [*opposition to a discriminatory practice; making or filing a charge of discrimination; filing a complaint; or testifying, assisting, or participating in any manner in a discrimination investigation, proceeding, or hearing under the Texas Commission on Human Rights Act*], if any, was the sole cause of *Don Davis*'s [*failure or refusal to hire, discharge, or (describe other discriminatory or retaliatory action)*], if any.

Answer: ______________

COMMENT

When to use. PJC 107.9 should be used for a claim that an employer retaliated or discriminated against an employee for engaging in conduct protected by Tex. Lab. Code § 21.055. *See also Burlington Northern & Santa Fe Railway Co. v. White*, 548 U.S. 53, 61–64 (2006) (holding antiretaliation provision under title VII not limited to discriminatory actions that affect terms and conditions of employment).

Source of question. PJC 107.9 is derived from Tex. Lab. Code § 21.055.

Causation standard. Tex. Lab. Code § 21.055 contains no express standard of causation in retaliation cases. Courts have adopted a "but for" causation standard. *See Pineda v. United Parcel Service, Inc.*, 360 F.3d 483, 488–89 (5th Cir. 2004) (holding that the "motivating factor" causation standard applicable to claims under Tex. Lab. Code § 21.125 does not apply to retaliation claims under section 21.055); *Herbert v. City of Forest Hill*, 189 S.W.3d 369, 377 (Tex. App.—Fort Worth 2006, no pet.) ("A plaintiff asserting a retaliation claim must establish . . . a 'but for' causal nexus between the protected activity and the employer's prohibited conduct."); *Thomann v. Lakes Regional MHMR Center*, 162 S.W.3d 788, 799 (Tex. App.—Dallas 2005, no pet.) ("To prove a causal connection between her filing the complaint and the termination of her employment, Thomann must show that 'but for' filing the complaint, her employment would not have been terminated when it was."). If there is a dispute about whether an adverse employment action occurred or whether the plaintiff undertook a protected activity, a predicate question may be required on these fact issues.

PJC 107.10 Instruction on Constructive Discharge

An employee is considered to have been discharged when an employer makes conditions so intolerable that a reasonable person in the employee's position would have felt compelled to resign.

COMMENT

When to use. PJC 107.10 should be used with PJC 107.6 if an employee alleges that the conditions of his employment amounted to a constructive discharge. *Pennsylvania State Police v. Suders*, 542 U.S. 129, 141 (2004) (outlining the proper inquiry in a constructive discharge analysis); *Dillard Department Stores v. Gonzales*, 72 S.W.3d 398, 409 (Tex. App.—El Paso 2002, pet. denied) (discussing constructive discharge in sexual harassment case); *Wal-Mart Stores v. Itz*, 21 S.W.3d 456, 475 (Tex. App.—Austin 2000, pet. denied) (same).

Source of instruction. PJC 107.10 is derived from *Suders* and its predecessors, including *Gonzales* and *Itz*. *See also Baylor University v. Coley*, 221 S.W.3d 599, 604–05 (Tex. 2007) (citing PJC 107.10).

Constructive discharge not resulting from an official act. In *Suders*, the Court held that an employer in a hostile work environment constructive discharge case retains its affirmative defense "when an official act does not underlie the constructive discharge[.]" *Suders*, 542 U.S. at 148 (relying on *Burlington Industries, Inc. v. Ellerth*, 524 U.S. 742 (1998), and *Faragher v. City of Boca Raton*, 524 U.S. 775 (1998)). The Court concluded in *Suders* that a court may preclude assertion of the affirmative defense when a plaintiff's decision to resign "resulted, at least in part," from an official action. *Suders*, 542 U.S. at 150 (quoting *Robinson v. Sappington*, 351 F.3d 317, 337 (7th Cir. 2003)). *Suders* does not define an official act or action.

PJC 107.11 Instruction on Disability

"Disability" means:

a. a mental or physical impairment that substantially limits at least one major life activity;

b. a record of mental or physical impairment; or

c. being regarded as having such an impairment.

The term "mental or physical impairment" means any physiological disorder, condition, cosmetic disfigurement, or anatomical loss affecting one or more of the following body systems: neurological; musculoskeletal; special sense organs; respiratory (including speech organs); cardiovascular; reproductive; digestive; genitourinary; hemic; lymphatic; skin; and endocrine; or any mental or psychological disorder, such as mental retardation, organic brain syndrome, emotional or mental illness, and specific learning disabilities.

"Major life activities" means functions such as caring for oneself, performing manual tasks, walking, seeing, hearing, speaking, breathing, learning, or working.

"Substantially limits" (as applied to "major life activities" other than "working") means that an individual is unable to perform a major life activity that the average person in the general population can perform or that an individual is significantly restricted as to the condition, manner, or duration under which an individual can perform a particular major life activity as compared to the condition, manner, or duration under which the average person in the general population can perform that same major life activity.

"Substantially limits" (as applied to the "major life activity" of "working") means that an individual is restricted in the ability to perform either a class of jobs or a broad range of jobs in various classes as compared to the average person having comparable training, skills, and abilities. The inability to perform a single, particular job does not constitute a substantial limitation in the major life activity of working.

"Substantially limits" (as applied to the "major life activity" of "performing manual tasks") means that an individual is prevented or severely restricted from doing activities that are of central importance to most people's daily lives.

"Record of such an impairment" means that an individual has a history of or has been misclassified as having a mental or physical impairment that substantially limits one or more major life activities.

"Being regarded as having such an impairment" means an individual: (a) has a physical or mental impairment that does not substantially limit a major life activity but is perceived by the employer as having such a limitation; (b) has a physical or mental impairment that substantially limits a major life activity only as a result of the attitudes of others toward the impairment; or (c) does not have an impairment at all, but is regarded by the employer as having such a substantially limiting impairment.

Disability is not a motivating factor in an employment decision if an individual's disability impairs the individual's ability to reasonably perform the job in question.

COMMENT

When to use. PJC 107.11 is to be used with PJC 107.6 if disability is alleged to be the basis of an employer's commission of an unlawful employment practice.

Source of instruction. PJC 107.11 is derived from the Americans with Disabilities Act of 1990 (ADA), 42 U.S.C. §§ 12101–12213, and from Tex. Lab. Code §§ 21.002(6), 21.105. The definitions pertaining to disability are contained in the EEOC regulations implementing the equal employment provisions of the ADA, 29 C.F.R. § 1630.2(g)–(*l*). These definitions, first promulgated as part of the Rehabilitation Act of 1973 (29 U.S.C. § 31 *et seq.*), were interpreted by the U.S. Supreme Court in *School Board of Nassau County, Florida v. Arline*, 480 U.S. 273 (1987), and *Southeastern Community College v. Davis*, 442 U.S. 397 (1979). *See also Toyota Motor Manufacturing, Kentucky, Inc. v. Williams*, 534 U.S. 184 (2002); *Rodriguez v. ConAgra Grocery Products Co.*, 436 F.3d 468, 475–76 (5th Cir. 2006) (discussing the requirements under the TCHRA for establishing that an employer discriminated against an employee "regarded as" having a disability); *Little v. Texas Department of Criminal Justice*, 148 S.W.3d 374 (Tex. 2004).

Additional instruction: substance addiction or communicable disease status. In the appropriate case, use the following instruction:

> "Disability" does not include [*a current condition of addiction to the use of alcohol, a drug, an illegal substance, or a federally controlled substance*] [*a currently communicable disease or infection, including, but not limited to, acquired immune deficiency syndrome or infection with the human immunodeficiency virus, that constitutes a direct threat to the health or safety of other persons or that makes the affected person unable to perform the duties of the person's employment*].

See Tex. Lab. Code § 21.002(6).

Additional instruction—effect of mitigating measures on disability determination. Pursuant to *Sutton v. United Air Lines, Inc.*, 527 U.S. 471 (1999), mitigating measures must be taken into account in determining whether an impairment constitutes a substantial limitation on a major life activity. Therefore, in circumstances where mitigating measures impact major life activities, the jury should be instructed as follows:

> In determining whether an individual has an impairment that substantially limits a major life activity, you must consider the effect, positive or negative, that corrective measures, devices, or medications have on the impairment in question and whether in light of such corrective measures, devices, or medications, such impairment substantially limits a major life activity.

PJC 107.12 Instruction on Failure to Make Reasonable Workplace Accommodation

Disability is a motivating factor when an employer refuses or fails to make a reasonable workplace accommodation to a known physical or mental limitation of an otherwise qualified individual with a disability.

The term "reasonable workplace accommodation" means [*select one or more as applicable*]:

a. modifications or adjustments to a job application process that enables an applicant with a disability to be considered for the position that the applicant desires;

b. modifications or adjustments to the work environment, or to the manner or circumstances in which the position held or desired is customarily performed, that enables an individual with a disability to perform the essential functions of that position; or

c. modifications or adjustments that enable an employee with a disability to enjoy equal benefits and privileges of employment as are enjoyed by other similarly situated employees without disabilities.

There may be more than one reasonable workplace accommodation.

COMMENT

When to use. PJC 107.12 is to be used in conjunction with PJC 107.6 and the definition of "disability" in PJC 107.11 if the discrimination alleged is a claim that the employer refused or failed to make a reasonable workplace accommodation to a known disability.

Source of instruction. PJC 107.12 is derived from Tex. Lab. Code § 21.128 and 29 C.F.R. § 1630.2(o) (EEOC regulations implementing the equal employment provisions of the Americans with Disabilities Act).

PJC 107.13 Question and Instruction on Undue Hardship Defense

If you answered Question ______ [*107.6*] "Yes," then answer the following question. Otherwise, do not answer the following question.

QUESTION ______

Would a reasonable workplace accommodation to *Paul Payne*'s known disability have caused undue hardship to the operation of *Don Davis*'s business?

> "Reasonable workplace accommodation" is defined in Question ______ [*107.12*].
>
> "Undue hardship" means a significant difficulty or expense incurred by an employer in light of the reasonableness of the costs of any necessary workplace accommodation considered in light of the availability of all alternatives or other appropriate relief.

Answer: ______________

COMMENT

When to use. PJC 107.13 should be used if the employer presents evidence of undue hardship in defense to a claim of lack of reasonable workplace accommodation under Tex. Lab. Code § 21.128.

Source of question and instructions. PJC 107.13 is derived from Tex. Lab. Code § 21.128 and 29 C.F.R. § 1630.2(p) (EEOC regulations implementing the equal employment provisions of the Americans with Disabilities Act).

PJC 107.14 Question on Good-Faith Effort to Make Reasonable Workplace Accommodation

If you answered Question ______ [*107.6*] "Yes," then answer the following question. Otherwise, do not answer the following question.

QUESTION ______

Did *Don Davis* consult with *Paul Payne* in good faith in an effort to identify and make a reasonable workplace accommodation to *Paul Payne*'s disability that would not cause an undue hardship to the operation of *Don Davis*'s business?

"Reasonable workplace accommodation" and "undue hardship" are defined in Questions ______ [*107.12*] and ______ [*107.13*].

Answer: _______________

COMMENT

When to use. PJC 107.14 should be used if the employer presents evidence that it has made a good-faith effort to identify and accommodate a known disability in defense to a claim of lack of reasonable accommodation under Tex. Lab. Code § 21.128. The inquiry in PJC 107.14 is for use by the judge in entry of a judgment. *See* Tex. Lab. Code §§ 21.258, 21.2585, 21.259.

Source of question. PJC 107.14 is derived from Tex. Lab. Code § 21.128(c). The employer bears the burden of proof on the issue.

PJC 107.15 Instruction on Sex Discrimination

In determining whether sex was a motivating factor, "sex" includes discrimination because of or on the basis of pregnancy, childbirth, or a related medical condition.

COMMENT

When to use. PJC 107.15 is to be used with PJC 107.6 if pregnancy, childbirth, or a related medical condition is alleged to be the basis of an employer's commission of an unlawful employment practice.

Source of instruction. PJC 107.15 is derived from Tex. Lab. Code § 21.106.

PJC 107.16 Instruction on Religious Observance or Practice

Religion is a motivating factor if the decision to [*fail or refuse to hire, discharge, or (describe other discriminatory action)*] *Paul Payne* was made because of or on the basis of any aspect of religious [*observance, practice, or belief*].

COMMENT

When to use. PJC 107.16 is to be used with PJC 107.6 if some aspect of observance of a religion, such as inability to work on a Sabbath, is alleged to be the basis of an employer's commission of an unlawful employment practice. This instruction, however, should not be used if religious preference alone is at issue. See PJC 107.6.

Source of instruction. PJC 107.16 is derived from Tex. Lab. Code § 21.108.

PJC 107.17 Question and Instruction on Defense of Undue Hardship to Accommodate Religious Observances or Practices

QUESTION ______

Was *Don Davis* unable to reasonably accommodate *Paul Payne*'s religious observance or practice without undue hardship to the conduct of *his* business?

A reasonable accommodation to an employee's religious observances or practices constitutes an undue hardship when it requires the employer to bear more than a minimal cost, such cost including both monetary costs and burdens in conducting business.

COMMENT

When to use. PJC 107.17 should be used if the employer alleges that reasonable accommodation to religious observances or practices would cause undue hardship.

Source of question and instruction. PJC 107.17 is derived from Tex. Lab. Code § 21.108 and *Trans World Airlines, Inc. v. Hardison*, 432 U.S. 63, 84–85 & n.15 (1977).

PJC 107.18 Question Limiting Relief in Unlawful Employment Practices

If you answered "Yes" to Question ______ [*107.6*], then answer the following question. Otherwise, do not answer the following question.

QUESTION ______

Would *Don Davis* have taken the same action inquired about in Question ______ [*107.6*] when *he* did, in the absence of the impermissible motivating factor?

Answer: _______________

COMMENT

When to use. PJC 107.18 should be used if an employer claims that its employment decision would have been made in the absence of an impermissible motive. Tex. Lab. Code § 21.125(b); *see also Quantum Chemical Corp. v. Toennies*, 47 S.W.3d 473, 475–76 (Tex. 2001). In such a mixed-motive case, a plaintiff may be entitled to declaratory or injunctive relief, attorney's fees, and costs, although not entitled to back pay or reinstatement. Tex. Lab. Code § 21.125(b); *see also* 42 U.S.C. § 2000e-5(g)(2)(B). PJC 107.18 should not be submitted to the jury based on after-acquired evidence. *See McKennon v. Nashville Banner Publishing Co.*, 513 U.S. 352 (1995).

Source of question. PJC 107.18 is derived from Tex. Lab. Code § 21.125(b).

PJC 107.19 Question and Instruction on Bona Fide Occupational Qualification Defense

QUESTION ______

Was *Don Davis*'s [*failure or refusal to hire, discharge, or (describe other discriminatory action)*] *Paul Payne* based on a bona fide occupational qualification reasonably necessary to the normal operation of *Don Davis*'s business?

"Bona fide occupational qualification" means a qualification (1) reasonably related to the satisfactory performance of the duties of a job, and (2) for which a factual basis exists for the belief that no person of an excluded group would be able to satisfactorily perform the duties of the job with safety or efficiency.

Answer: _______________

COMMENT

When to use. PJC 107.19 is to be used if an employer asserts a bona fide occupational qualification as the basis for any discrimination based on disability, religion, sex, national origin, or age of an employee. Tex. Lab. Code § 21.119.

Source of instruction. PJC 107.19 is derived from Tex. Lab. Code §§ 21.002(1), 21.119.

PJC 107.20 Question on Harassment

QUESTION ______

Was *Paul Payne* subjected to harassment based on [*sex, national origin, race, age, or other protected category*] by *Don Davis*?

[Insert appropriate instruction.]

Answer: _______________

COMMENT

When to use. PJC 107.20 should be used if there is an allegation of actionable harassment.

Source of question and instruction. PJC 107.20 is derived from the principles recognized in *Union Pacific Railroad Co. v. Loa*, 153 S.W.3d 162, 168–69 (Tex. App.—El Paso 2004, no pet.), and *Nagel Manufacturing & Supply Co. v. Ulloa*, 812 S.W.2d 78, 80–81 (Tex. App.—Austin 1991, writ denied). *See also Harris v. Forklift Systems, Inc.*, 510 U.S. 17 (1993); *Meritor Savings Bank, FSB v. Vinson*, 477 U.S. 57 (1986); *Benavides v. Moore*, 848 S.W.2d 190 (Tex. App.—Corpus Christi 1992, writ denied).

Accompanying instructions. Instructions to accompany PJC 107.20 are at PJC 107.21–.23. If more than one instruction is used, each should be separated by the word *or*.

PJC 107.21 Instruction on Sexual Harassment by Supervisor Involving Tangible Employment Action (*Quid Pro Quo*)

"Sexual harassment" occurred if:

1. *Paul Payne* was subjected to unwelcome sexual advance(s) or demand(s);

2. submission to or refusal to submit to the unwelcome sexual advance(s) or demand(s) resulted in [*discharge, demotion, undesirable reassignment, or (describe other tangible employment action)*]; and

3. the conduct was committed by an employee who had authority over hiring, advancement, dismissals, discipline, or other employment decisions affecting *Paul Payne*.

[*or*]

COMMENT

When to use. PJC 107.21 should be used with PJC 107.20 if it is alleged that the employee was subjected to what has traditionally been referred to as *quid pro quo* sexual harassment, which involves harassment by a supervisor of the employee and a tangible employment action.

Source of instruction. PJC 107.21 is derived from the principles recognized in *Wal-Mart Stores v. Itz*, 21 S.W.3d 456, 471 (Tex. App.—Austin 2000, pet. denied).

Tangible employment action. The U.S. Supreme Court in *Burlington Industries, Inc. v. Ellerth*, 524 U.S. 742, 761 (1998), defined "tangible employment action" as "a significant change in employment status, such as hiring, firing, failing to promote, reassignment with significantly different responsibilities, or a decision causing a significant change in benefits."

Vicarious liability. If a supervisor's harassment culminates in tangible employment action, the employer is vicariously liable for the supervisor's conduct. *Faragher v. City of Boca Raton*, 524 U.S. 775, 807–08 (1998). In that instance, the affirmative defense in PJC 107.24 is not available.

Constructive discharge not resulting from an official act. The U.S. Supreme Court held that an employer in a hostile work environment constructive discharge case retains its affirmative defense "when an official act does not underlie the constructive discharge[.]" *Pennsylvania State Police v. Suders*, 542 U.S. 129, 148 (2004) (relying on *Ellerth*, 524 U.S. 742, and *Faragher*, 524 U.S. 775). The Court concluded in *Suders* that a court may preclude assertion of the affirmative defense when a plaintiff's decision to resign "resulted, at least in part," from an official action. *Suders*, 542 U.S. at 150 (quoting *Robinson v. Sappington*, 351 F.3d 317, 337 (7th Cir. 2003)).

PJC 107.22 Instruction on Harassment by Nonsupervisory Employee (Hostile Environment)

"Harassment based on [*sex, national origin, race, age, or other protected category*]" occurred if:

1. *Paul Payne* [*was subjected to ridicule or insult and/or other improper conduct*] based on *Paul Payne*'s [*sex, national origin, race, age, or other appropriate protected category*] that was unwelcome and undesirable or offensive to *Paul Payne*; and

2. the harassment complained of altered a term, condition, or privilege of employment; and

3. *Don Davis* knew or should have known of the harassment and *Don Davis* failed to take prompt, remedial action to eliminate the harassment.

Harassment alters a term, condition, or privilege of employment when a reasonable person would find that the harassment created an abusive working environment. In determining whether an abusive working environment existed, consider the following: the frequency of the conduct; its severity; whether it was physically threatening or humiliating or a mere offensive utterance; and whether it unreasonably interferes with an employee's work performance.

[*or*]

COMMENT

When to use. PJC 107.22 should be used with PJC 107.20 if it is alleged that the plaintiff has been subjected to what is commonly referred to as "a hostile environment" that involves harassment by an employee who is not a supervisor of the employee.

Source of instruction. PJC 107.22 is derived from *Burlington Industries, Inc. v. Ellerth*, 524 U.S. 742, 753–54 (1998); *Faragher v. City of Boca Raton*, 524 U.S. 775, 781–88 (1998); *Harris v. Forklift Systems, Inc.*, 510 U.S. 17, 23 (1993); and *Meritor Savings Bank, FSB v. Vinson*, 477 U.S. 57 (1986). *See also Nash v. Electrospace System, Inc.*, 9 F.3d 401, 404 (5th Cir. 1993); *Jones v. Flagship International*, 793 F.2d 714, 719–20 (5th Cir. 1986), *cert. denied*, 479 U.S. 1065 (1987); *Ewald v. Wornick Family Foods Corp.*, 878 S.W.2d 653, 659 (Tex. App.—Corpus Christi 1994, writ denied).

Constructive discharge not resulting from an official act. The U.S. Supreme Court held that an employer in a hostile work environment constructive discharge case retains its affirmative defense "when an official act does not underlie the constructive discharge[.]" *Pennsylvania State Police v. Suders*, 542 U.S. 129, 148 (2004) (relying on

Ellerth, 524 U.S. 742, and *Faragher*, 524 U.S. 775). The Court concluded in *Suders* that a court may preclude assertion of the affirmative defense when a plaintiff's decision to resign "resulted, at least in part," from an official action. *Suders*, 542 U.S. at 150 (quoting *Robinson v. Sappington*, 351 F.3d 317, 337 (7th Cir. 2003)).

PJC 107.23 Instruction on Harassment by Supervisory Employee Not Involving Tangible Employment Action (Hostile Environment)

"Harassment based on [*sex, national origin, race, age, or other protected category*]" occurred if:

1. *Paul Payne* [*was subjected to ridicule or insult and/or other improper conduct*] based on *Paul Payne*'s [*sex, national origin, race, age, or other appropriate category*] that was unwelcome and undesirable or offensive to *Paul Payne*; and

2. the harassment complained of altered a term, condition, or privilege of employment; and

3. the conduct was committed by a supervisor who had authority over hiring, advancement, dismissals, discipline, or other employment decisions affecting *Paul Payne*.

Harassment alters a term, condition, or privilege of employment when a reasonable person would find that the harassment created an abusive working environment. In determining whether an abusive working environment existed, consider the following: the frequency of the conduct; its severity; whether it was physically threatening or humiliating or a mere offensive utterance; and whether it unreasonably interferes with an employee's work performance.

[*or*]

COMMENT

When to use. PJC 107.23 should be used with PJC 107.20 if it is alleged that the plaintiff has been subjected to what is commonly referred to as "a hostile environment" that involves harassment by a supervisor of the employee but no tangible employment action. In sexual harassment cases, it may be proper to substitute the following for paragraph 1 above:

> "Harassment based on sex" occurred if:
>
> 1. *Paul Payne* [*was subjected to sexual advances, requests for sexual favors, and/or other conduct of a sexual nature*] that was unwelcome and undesirable or offensive to *Paul Payne*; and

Source of instruction. PJC 107.23 is derived from *Faragher v. City of Boca Raton*, 524 U.S. 775, 787–88 (1998); *Burlington Industries, Inc. v. Ellerth*, 524 U.S. 742, 753–

54 (1998); *Harris v. Forklift Systems, Inc.*, 510 U.S. 17, 23 (1993); *Meritor Savings Bank, FSB v. Vinson*, 477 U.S. 57 (1986); *City of Houston v. Fletcher*, 166 S.W.3d 479, 490–91 (Tex. App.—Eastland 2005, pet. denied) (claim of hostile work environment based on age); *Union Pacific Railroad Co. v. Loa*, 153 S.W.3d 162, 169 (Tex. App.—El Paso 2004, no pet.); *Dillard Department Stores v. Gonzales*, 72 S.W.3d 398, 407 (Tex. App.—El Paso 2002, pet. denied); and *Wal-Mart Stores v. Itz*, 21 S.W.3d 456, 472–73 (Tex. App.—Austin 2000, pet. denied).

Affirmative defense. An employer is entitled to submission of the affirmative defense of reasonable care under PJC 107.24 if the supervisor's harassment does not culminate in a tangible employment action. *Ellerth*, 524 U.S. at 765; *Faragher*, 524 U.S. at 807. If the existence of a tangible employment action is in dispute, a separate question may need to be submitted.

Constructive discharge not resulting from an official act. The U.S. Supreme Court held that an employer in a hostile work environment constructive discharge case retains its affirmative defense "when an official act does not underlie the constructive discharge[.]" *Pennsylvania State Police v. Suders*, 542 U.S. 129, 148 (2004) (relying on *Ellerth*, 524 U.S. 742, and *Faragher*, 524 U.S. 775). The Court concluded in *Suders* that a court may preclude assertion of the affirmative defense when a plaintiff's decision to resign "resulted, at least in part," from an official action. *Suders*, 542 U.S. at 150 (quoting *Robinson v. Sappington*, 351 F.3d 317, 337 (7th Cir. 2003)).

PJC 107.24 Question on Affirmative Defense to Harassment Where No Tangible Employment Action Occurred

If your answer to Question ______ [*107.20*] is "Yes," then answer the following question. Otherwise, do not answer the following question.

QUESTION ______

Is *Don Davis* legally excused from responsibility for the conduct of [*insert name(s) of supervisor(s)*] found in Question ______ [*107.20*]?

Don Davis is legally excused if—

1. *Don Davis* exercised reasonable care to prevent and correct promptly any harassment behavior; and
2. *Paul Payne* unreasonably failed to take advantage of any preventive or corrective opportunities by *his* employer or to avoid harm otherwise.

Answer "Yes" or "No."

Answer: ______________

COMMENT

When to use. PJC 107.24 should be used if the defendant employer alleges the affirmative defense of reasonable care and there has been no tangible employment action taken by the employer against the employee alleging harassment. Tangible employment action includes discharge, demotion, or undesirable reassignment. *Dillard Department Stores v. Gonzales*, 72 S.W.3d 398, 410 (Tex. App.—El Paso 2002, pet. denied); *Wal-Mart Stores v. Itz*, 21 S.W.3d 456, 472–73 (Tex. App.—Austin 2000, pet. denied) (quoting *Faragher v. City of Boca Raton*, 524 U.S. 775, 808 (1998)).

Source of question. PJC 107.24 is derived from *Burlington Industries, Inc. v. Ellerth*, 524 U.S. 742, 765 (1998); and *Faragher*, 524 U.S. at 807–08; *see also Padilla v. Flying J, Inc.*, 119 S.W.3d 911, 915 (Tex. App.—Dallas 2003, no pet.); *Gulf States Toyota, Inc. v. Morgan*, 89 S.W.3d 766, 770–71 (Tex. App.—Houston [1st Dist.] 2002, no pet.); *Dillard Department Stores*, 72 S.W.3d at 410–11.

Constructive discharge not resulting from an official act. The U.S. Supreme Court held that an employer in a hostile work environment constructive discharge case retains its affirmative defense "when an official act does not underlie the constructive discharge[.]" *Pennsylvania State Police v. Suders*, 542 U.S. 129, 148 (2004) (relying on *Ellerth*, 524 U.S. 742, and *Faragher*, 524 U.S. 775). The Court concluded in *Suders* that a court may preclude assertion of the affirmative defense when a plaintiff's decision to resign "resulted, at least in part," from an official action. *Suders*, 542 U.S. at 150 (quoting *Robinson v. Sappington*, 351 F.3d 317, 337 (7th Cir. 2003)).

PJC 108.1 Basic Question

QUESTION ______

Is *Don Davis* responsible for the conduct of [*name of corporation*]?

Don Davis is "responsible" for the conduct of [*name of corporation*] if:

[Insert appropriate instruction(s); see PJC 108.2–.7.]

Answer "Yes" or "No."

Answer: _______________

COMMENT

When to use. PJC 108.1 is a basic question that is appropriate to submit when the claimant seeks to disregard the corporate fiction and pierce the corporate veil.

Accompanying instructions. PJC 108.1 should be accompanied by appropriate instructions and definitions informing the jury of the applicable bases for disregarding the corporate fiction. Disregarding the corporate fiction is "an equitable doctrine [that] takes a flexible fact-specific approach focusing on equity." *Castleberry v. Branscum*, 721 S.W.2d 270, 273, 274–76 (Tex. 1986); *see also Stewart & Stevenson Services, Inc. v. Serv-Tech, Inc.*, 879 S.W.2d 89, 110 (Tex. App.—Houston [14th Dist.] 1994, writ denied). Instructions to accompany PJC 108.1, informing the jury what type of conduct should be considered under the question, are at PJC 108.2–.7.

Use of "or." If more than one instruction is used, each must be separated by the word *or*, because a finding of any one of the theories for disregarding the corporate fiction defined in the instructions would support an affirmative answer to the question.

PJC 108.2 Instruction on Alter Ego

[*Name of corporation*] was organized and operated as a mere tool or business conduit of *Don Davis*; there was such unity between [*name of corporation*] and *Don Davis* that the separateness of [*name of corporation*] had ceased and holding only [*name of corporation*] responsible would result in injustice; and *Don Davis* caused [*name of corporation*] to be used for the purpose of perpetuating and did perpetuate an actual fraud on *Paul Payne* primarily for the direct personal benefit of *Don Davis*.

In deciding whether there was such unity between [*name of corporation*] and *Don Davis* that the separateness of [*name of corporation*] had ceased, you are to consider the total dealings of [*name of corporation*] and *Don Davis*, including:

1. the degree to which [*name of corporation*]'s property had been kept separate from that of *Don Davis*;
2. the amount of financial interest, ownership, and control *Don Davis* maintained over [*name of corporation*]; and
3. whether [*name of corporation*] had been used for personal purposes of *Don Davis*.

[*or*]

COMMENT

When to use. PJC 108.2 should be used as an instruction accompanying the question in PJC 108.1 if it is alleged that a holder of shares, an owner of any beneficial interest in shares, a subscriber for shares whose subscription has been accepted, any of their affiliates, or affiliates of the corporation is the alter ego of the corporation, in a case relating to or arising from a contractual obligation. See comment below, "Cases not covered by statute," for charge language to be used in other cases.

Use of "or." If used with other instructions (see PJC 108.3 –.7), PJC 108.2 must be followed by the word *or*, because a finding of any one of the theories for disregarding the corporate fiction defined in the instructions would support an affirmative answer to the question.

Source of instruction. PJC 108.2 is based on the supreme court's discussion of alter ego in *Castleberry v. Branscum*, 721 S.W.2d 270, 272 (Tex. 1986). The language of *Castleberry* has been modified to reflect the enactment of Tex. Bus. Corp. Act art. 2.21(A) (the "Act") (subsequently codified as Tex. Bus. Orgs. Code § 21.223(a)), which eliminated constructive fraud as a consideration for piercing the corporate veil in contract-based claims against holders, owners, subscribers, or affiliates. *See Willis v. Donnelly*, 199 S.W.3d 262, 271–72 & n.12 (Tex. 2006). The Act further modified *Castleberry* by eliminating the failure to observe corporate formalities as a consideration for piercing the corporate veil in all claims against holders, owners, subscribers, or affiliates. Tex. Bus. Corp. Act art. 2.21(A)(3); *see also Aluminum Chemicals (Bolivia), Inc. v. Bechtel Corp.*, 28 S.W.3d 64, 67 n.3 (Tex. App.—Texarkana 2000, no pet.).

"Injustice." No Texas case has stated whether *injustice* must be defined in alter ego cases. For a case discussing the term *injustice* in an alter ego context, see *Mancorp, Inc. v. Culpepper*, 836 S.W.2d 844 (Tex. App.—Houston [1st Dist.] 1992), *on remand from* 802 S.W.2d 226 (Tex. 1990).

"Actual fraud." The term *actual fraud* appearing in Tex. Bus. Corp. Act art. 2.21(A)(2) and Tex. Bus. Orgs. Code § 21.223(b) is not defined in either statute. In *Castleberry*, decided before article 2.21(A)(2) and section 21.223(b), the supreme court defined actual fraud in the context of piercing the corporate veil as "involv[ing] dishonesty of purpose or intent to deceive." 721 S.W.2d at 273 (quoting *Archer v. Griffith*, 390 S.W.2d 735, 740 (Tex. 1964)). Some courts have held that the fraud must relate to the transaction at issue. *See, e.g.*, *Menetti v. Chavers*, 974 S.W.2d 168, 175 (Tex. App.—San Antonio 1998, no pet.); *Rutherford v. Atwood*, No. 01-00-00113-CV, 2003 WL 22053687, at *4 (Tex. App.—Houston [1st Dist.] Nov. 13, 2003, no pet.) (mem. op.). For issues relating to the definition and submission of actual fraud, see *Country Village Homes, Inc. v. Patterson*, 236 S.W.3d 413, 432 (Tex. App.—Houston [1st Dist.] 2007, pet. dism'd, judgm't vacated by agr.) (rejecting contention that article 2.21 requires submission of common-law fraud as an independent ground of recovery in a veil-piercing action based on alter ego); *McCarthy v. Wani Venture, A.S.*, 251 S.W.3d 573, 584–85 (Tex. App.—Houston [1st Dist.] 2007, pet. denied) (approving "actual fraud" definition that did not require a material misrepresentation but only the "concealment of material facts or the failure to disclose a material fact" (emphasis omitted)); *Huff v. Harrell*, 941 S.W.2d 230, 237 (Tex. App.—Corpus Christi 1996, writ denied); *Bates v. de Tournillon*, No. 07-03-0257-CV, 2006 WL 265474, at *2 (Tex. App.—Amarillo 2006, no pet.) (mem. op.) (using a definition of fraud that requires a material misrepresentation) (citing *Harco Energy, Inc. v. Re-Entry People, Inc.*, 23 S.W.3d 389, 393 (Tex. App.—Amarillo 2000, no pet.)).

Cases not covered by statute. For cases not involving contract-based claims against holders, owners, subscribers, or affiliates, use the following instruction:

> [*Name of corporation*] was organized and operated as a mere tool or business conduit of *Don Davis* and there was such unity between [*name of corporation*] and *Don Davis* that the separateness of [*name of corporation*] had ceased and holding only [*name of corporation*] responsible would result in injustice.

In deciding whether there was such unity between [*name of corporation*] and *Don Davis* that the separateness of [*name of corporation*] had ceased, you are to consider the total dealings of [*name of corporation*] and *Don Davis*, including—

1. the degree to which [*name of corporation*]'s property had been kept separate from that of *Don Davis*;
2. the amount of financial interest, ownership, and control *Don Davis* maintained over [*name of corporation*]; and
3. whether [*name of corporation*] had been used for personal purposes of *Don Davis*.

This instruction is derived from *Castleberry*, 721 S.W.2d at 271–73. By their terms, the actual fraud requirements of Tex. Bus. Corp. Act art. 2.21(A)(2) and Tex. Bus. Orgs. Code § 21.223(a)(2) apply only to claims relating to or arising from contractual obligations. *See Farr v. Sun World Savings Ass'n*, 810 S.W.2d 294, 296 (Tex. App.—El Paso 1991, no writ); *see also Menetti*, 974 S.W.2d at 173–74 (discussing when a showing of actual fraud is necessary after the 1997 amendments to the Texas Business Corporation Act); *Stewart & Stevenson Services, Inc. v. Serv-Tech, Inc.*, 879 S.W.2d 89, 110 (Tex. App.—Houston [14th Dist.] 1994, writ denied) (recommending that trial courts follow an alter ego instruction that came verbatim from *Castleberry*).

If the corporation whose veil is sought to be pierced is a close corporation organized under Tex. Bus. Corp. Act arts. 12.01–.54, one or more of the indicia of unity may not apply.

1997 amendments to Business Corporation Act. Tex. Bus. Corp. Act art. 2.21 was amended in 1997 as follows:

1. the list of persons or entities protected from liability (except for actual fraud) was expanded to include "affiliates" (Tex. Bus. Corp. Act art. 2.21);
2. not only contractual obligations of the corporation but "matter[s] relating to or arising from" contractual obligations were excluded as grounds for disregarding the corporate fiction unless actual fraud was proved (Tex. Bus. Corp. Act art. 2.21(A)(2)); and
3. failure of the corporation to observe a corporate formality is no longer a ground for piercing the corporate veil in any case, not just contract cases (Tex. Bus. Corp. Act art. 2.21(A)(3)).

The Act further preempted liability "under common law or otherwise" for holders, owners, subscribers, and affiliates by providing the exclusive mechanism for imposing liability upon such persons for obligations limited by the Act, subject to the exceptions stated in the Act. Tex. Bus. Corp. Act art. 2.21(B). This preemption has been carried over into the Code. *See* Tex. Bus. Orgs. Code §§ 21.224–.225; *see also Willis*, 199 S.W.3d at 272–73 (refusing to impose liability against shareholders under a common-law theory of implied ratification where doing so would contravene statute precluding shareholder liability for contractual obligations of the corporation in the absence of actual fraud or an express agreement to assume personal liability); *Southern Union Co. v. City of Edinburg*, 129 S.W.3d 74, 87 (Tex. 2003) (article 2.21 controls action based on single business enterprise theory); *Country Village Homes, Inc.*, 236 S.W.3d at 430 (finding of actual fraud is required to prove single business enterprise theory).

2003 adoption of Texas Business Organizations Code. In 2003, Texas enacted the Texas Business Organizations Code, which codified the Texas Business Corporation Act. Corporations formed after January 1, 2006, are governed by the Code rather than the Act. Tex. Bus. Orgs. Code § 402.001. Corporations formed before January 1, 2006, may elect to be governed by the Code rather than the Act. Tex. Bus. Orgs. Code § 402.003. After January 1, 2010, all Texas corporations are governed by the Code, regardless of when the corporation was formed. Tex. Bus. Orgs. Code § 402.005.

PJC 108.3 Instruction on Sham to Perpetrate a Fraud

Don Davis used [*name of corporation*] for the purpose of perpetrating and did perpetrate an actual fraud on *Paul Payne* primarily for the direct personal benefit of *Don Davis*.

[*or*]

COMMENT

When to use. PJC 108.3 should be used as an instruction accompanying the question in PJC 108.1 if it is alleged that a corporation has been used by a holder of shares, an owner of any beneficial interest in shares, a subscriber for shares whose subscription has been accepted, any of their affiliates, or affiliates of the corporation as a sham to perpetrate a fraud in a case relating to or arising from a contractual obligation. Tex. Bus. Corp. Act art. 2.21(A)(2); Tex. Bus. Orgs. Code § 21.223(a)(2), (b). See comment below, "Cases not covered by statute," for charge language to be used in other cases.

Use of "or." If used with other instructions (see PJC 108.2 and 108.4–.7), PJC 108.3 must be followed by the word *or*, because a finding of any one of the theories for disregarding the corporate fiction defined in the instructions would support an affirmative answer to the question.

Source of instruction. PJC 108.3 is based on the supreme court's discussion of the theories for disregarding the corporate fiction in *Castleberry v. Branscum*, 721 S.W.2d 270, 271–73 (Tex. 1986). The language of *Castleberry* has been modified to reflect the enactment of Tex. Bus. Corp. Act art. 2.21(A) (the "Act") (subsequently codified as Tex. Bus. Orgs. Code § 21.223(a)), which eliminated constructive fraud as a consideration for piercing the corporate veil in contract-based claims against holders, owners, subscribers, or affiliates. *See Willis v. Donnelly*, 199 S.W.3d 262, 271–72 & n.12 (Tex. 2006). The Act further modified *Castleberry* by eliminating the failure to observe corporate formalities as a consideration for piercing the corporate veil in all claims against holders, owners, subscribers, or affiliates. Tex. Bus. Corp. Act art. 2.21(A)(3); *see also Aluminum Chemicals (Bolivia), Inc. v. Bechtel Corp.*, 28 S.W.3d 64, 67–68 nn.3, 4 (Tex. App.—Texarkana 2000, no pet.).

"Actual fraud." The term *actual fraud* appearing in Tex. Bus. Corp. Act art. 2.21(A) and Tex. Bus. Orgs. Code § 21.223(b) is not defined in either statute. In *Castleberry*, decided before article 2.21(A)(2) and section 21.223(b), the supreme court defined actual fraud in the context of piercing the corporate veil as "involv[ing] dishonesty of purpose or intent to deceive." 721 S.W.2d at 273 (quoting *Archer v. Griffith*, 390 S.W.2d 735, 740 (Tex. 1964)). Some courts have held that the fraud must relate to the transaction at issue. *See, e.g., Menetti v. Chavers*, 974 S.W.2d 168, 175 (Tex. App.—San

Antonio 1998, no pet.); *Rutherford v. Atwood*, No. 01-00-00113-CV, 2003 WL 22053687, at *4 (Tex. App.—Houston [1st Dist.] Nov. 13, 2003, no pet.) (mem. op.). For issues relating to the definition and submission of actual fraud, see *Country Village Homes, Inc. v. Patterson*, 236 S.W.3d 413, 432 (Tex. App.—Houston [1st Dist.] 2007, pet. dism'd, judgm't vacated by agr.) (rejecting contention that article 2.21 requires submission of common-law fraud as an independent ground of recovery in a veil-piercing action based on alter ego); *McCarthy v. Wani Venture, A.S.*, 251 S.W.3d 573, 584–85 (Tex. App.—Houston [1st Dist.] 2007, pet. denied) (approving "actual fraud" definition that did not require a material misrepresentation but only the "concealment of material facts or the failure to disclose a material fact" (emphasis omitted)); *Huff v. Harrell*, 941 S.W.2d 230, 237 (Tex. App.—Corpus Christi 1996, writ denied); *Bates v. de Tournillon*, No. 07-03-0257-CV, 2006 WL 265474, at *2 (Tex. App.—Amarillo 2006, no pet.) (mem. op.) (using a definition of fraud that requires a material misrepresentation) (citing *Harco Energy, Inc. v. Re-Entry People, Inc.*, 23 S.W.3d 389, 393 (Tex. App.—Amarillo 2000, no pet.)).

Cases not covered by statute. For cases not involving contract-based claims against holders, owners, subscribers, or affiliates, use the following instruction:

> *Don Davis* used [*name of corporation*] as a sham to perpetrate a fraud, and holding only [*name of corporation*] responsible would result in injustice.

This instruction is derived from *Castleberry*, 721 S.W.2d at 271–73, 275. "[C]onstructive fraud, not intentional fraud, is the standard for disregarding the corporate fiction on the basis of a sham to perpetrate a fraud" in cases not covered by Tex. Bus. Corp. Act art. 2.21(A)(2) or Tex. Bus. Orgs. Code §21.223(a)(2). *Castleberry*, 721 S.W.2d at 275. *See also Menetti*, 974 S.W.2d at 173–74 (discussing when a showing of actual fraud is necessary after the 1997 amendments to the Texas Business Corporation Act); *Farr v. Sun World Savings Ass'n*, 810 S.W.2d 294, 296 (Tex. App.—El Paso 1991, no writ). Under *Castleberry*, "constructive fraud is the breach of some legal or equitable duty which, irrespective of moral guilt, the law declares fraudulent because of its tendency to deceive others, to violate confidence, or to injure public interests." *Castleberry*, 721 S.W.2d at 273 (quoting *Archer*, 390 S.W.2d at 740); *see also Seaside Industries, Inc. v. Cooper*, 766 S.W.2d 566, 568 (Tex. App.—Dallas 1989, no writ). The standard for disregarding the corporate fiction is flexible in this context, and additional questions, instructions, or definitions may be needed depending on the facts in dispute. *See Castleberry*, 721 S.W.2d at 273 ("Because disregarding the corporate fiction is an equitable doctrine, Texas takes a flexible fact-specific approach focusing on equity.")

"Injustice." No Texas case has stated whether *injustice* must be defined in cases of the type covered by this instruction. For a case discussing the term *injustice* in the context of piercing the corporate veil, see *Mancorp, Inc. v. Culpepper*, 836 S.W.2d 844 (Tex. App.—Houston [1st Dist.] 1992), *on remand from* 802 S.W.2d 226 (Tex. 1990).

1997 amendments to Business Corporation Act. Tex. Bus. Corp. Act art. 2.21 was amended in 1997 as follows:

1. the list of persons or entities protected from liability (except for actual fraud) was expanded to include "affiliates" (Tex. Bus. Corp. Act art. 2.21);
2. not only contractual obligations of the corporation but "matter[s] relating to or arising from" contractual obligations were excluded as grounds for disregarding the corporate fiction unless actual fraud was proved (Tex. Bus. Corp. Act art. 2.21(A)(2)); and
3. failure of the corporation to observe a corporate formality is no longer a ground for piercing the corporate veil in any case, not just contract cases (Tex. Bus. Corp. Act art. 2.21(A)(3)).

The Act further preempted liability "under common law or otherwise" for holders, owners, subscribers, and affiliates by providing the exclusive mechanism for imposing liability upon such persons for obligations limited by the Act, subject to the exceptions stated in the Act. Tex. Bus. Corp. Act art. 2.21(B). This preemption has been carried over into the Code. *See* Tex. Bus. Orgs. Code §§ 21.224–.225; *see also Willis*, 199 S.W.3d at 272–73 (refusing to impose liability against shareholders under a common-law theory of implied ratification where doing so would contravene statute precluding shareholder liability for contractual obligations of the corporation in the absence of actual fraud or an express agreement to assume personal liability); *Southern Union Co. v. City of Edinburg*, 129 S.W.3d 74, 87 (Tex. 2003) (article 2.21 controls action based on single business enterprise theory); *Country Village Homes, Inc.*, 236 S.W.3d at 430 (finding of actual fraud is required to prove single business enterprise theory).

2003 adoption of Texas Business Organizations Code. In 2003, Texas enacted the Texas Business Organizations Code, which codified the Texas Business Corporation Act. Corporations formed after January 1, 2006, are governed by the Code rather than the Act. Tex. Bus. Orgs. Code § 402.001. Corporations formed before January 1, 2006, may elect to be governed by the Code rather than the Act. Tex. Bus. Orgs. Code § 402.003. After January 1, 2010, all Texas corporations are governed by the Code, regardless of when the corporation was formed. Tex. Bus. Orgs. Code § 402.005.

PJC 108.4 Instruction on Evasion of Existing Legal Obligation

Don Davis used [*name of corporation*] as a means of evading an existing legal obligation for the purpose of perpetrating and did perpetrate an actual fraud on *Paul Payne* primarily for the direct personal benefit of *Don Davis*.

[*or*]

COMMENT

When to use. PJC 108.4 should be used as an instruction accompanying the question in PJC 108.1 if it is alleged that a corporation has been used by a holder of shares, an owner of any beneficial interest in shares, a subscriber for shares whose subscription has been accepted, any of their affiliates, or affiliates of the corporation to evade an existing legal obligation in a case relating to or arising from a contractual obligation. Tex. Bus. Corp. Act art. 2.21(A)(2); Tex. Bus. Orgs. Code § 21.223(a)(2), (b). See comment below, "Cases not covered by statute," for charge language to be used in other cases.

Use of "or." If used with other instructions (see PJC 108.2–.3 and 108.5–.7), PJC 108.4 must be followed by the word *or*, because a finding of any one of the theories for disregarding the corporate fiction defined in the instructions would support an affirmative answer to the question.

Source of instruction. PJC 108.4 is based on the supreme court's discussion of the theories for disregarding the corporate fiction in *Castleberry v. Branscum*, 721 S.W.2d 270, 271–73 (Tex. 1986). The language of *Castleberry* has been modified to reflect the enactment of Tex. Bus. Corp. Act art. 2.21(A) (the "Act") (subsequently codified as Tex. Bus. Orgs. Code § 21.223(a), (b)), which eliminated constructive fraud as a consideration for piercing the corporate veil in contract-based claims against holders, owners, subscribers, or affiliates. *See Willis v. Donnelly*, 199 S.W.3d 262, 271–72 & n.12 (Tex. 2006). The Act further modified *Castleberry* by eliminating the failure to observe corporate formalities as a consideration for piercing the corporate veil in all claims against holders, owners, subscribers, or affiliates. Tex. Bus. Corp. Act art. 2.21(A)(3); *see also Aluminum Chemicals (Bolivia), Inc. v. Bechtel Corp.*, 28 S.W.3d 64, 67–68 nn.3, 4 (Tex. App.—Texarkana 2000, no pet.).

"Actual fraud." The term *actual fraud* appearing in Tex. Bus. Corp. Act art. 2.21(A) and Tex. Bus. Orgs. Code § 21.223(b) is not defined in either statute. In *Castleberry*, decided before article 2.21(A)(2) and section 21.223(b), the supreme court defined actual fraud in the context of piercing the corporate veil as "involv[ing] dishonesty of purpose or intent to deceive." 721 S.W.2d at 273 (quoting *Archer v. Griffith*, 390 S.W.2d 735, 740 (Tex. 1964)). Some courts have held that the fraud must relate to the transaction at issue. *See, e.g., Menetti v. Chavers*, 974 S.W.2d 168, 175 (Tex. App.—San

Antonio 1998, no pet.); *Rutherford v. Atwood*, No. 01-00-00113-CV, 2003 WL 22053687, at *4 (Tex. App.—Houston [1st Dist.] Nov. 13, 2003, no pet.) (mem. op.). For issues relating to the definition and submission of actual fraud, see *Country Village Homes, Inc. v. Patterson*, 236 S.W.3d 413, 432 (Tex. App.—Houston [1st Dist.] 2007, pet. dism'd, judgm't vacated by agr.) (rejecting contention that article 2.21 requires submission of common-law fraud as an independent ground of recovery in a veil-piercing action based on alter ego); *McCarthy v. Wani Venture, A.S.*, 251 S.W.3d 573, 584–85 (Tex. App.—Houston [1st Dist.] 2007, pet. denied) (approving "actual fraud" definition that did not require a material misrepresentation but only the "concealment of material facts or the failure to disclose a material fact" (emphasis omitted)); *Huff v. Harrell*, 941 S.W.2d 230, 237 (Tex. App.—Corpus Christi 1996, writ denied); *Bates v. de Tournillon*, No. 07-03-0257-CV, 2006 WL 265474, at *2 (Tex. App.—Amarillo 2006, no pet.) (mem. op.) (using a definition of fraud that requires a material misrepresentation) (citing *Harco Energy, Inc. v. Re-Entry People, Inc.*, 23 S.W.3d 389, 393 (Tex. App.—Amarillo 2000, no pet.)).

Cases not covered by statute. For cases not involving contract-based claims against holders, owners, subscribers, or affiliates, use the following instruction:

> *Don Davis* used [*name of corporation*] as a means of evading an existing legal obligation, and holding only [*name of corporation*] responsible would result in injustice.

This instruction is derived from *Castleberry*, 721 S.W.2d at 271–73. By their terms, the actual fraud requirements of Tex. Bus. Corp. Act art. 2.21(A)(2) and Tex. Bus. Orgs. Code § 21.223(a)(2) apply only to claims relating to or arising from contractual obligations against holders, owners, subscribers, and affiliates. *See Menetti*, 974 S.W.2d at 173–74 (discussing when a showing of actual fraud is necessary after the 1997 amendments to the Texas Business Corporation Act).

"Injustice." No Texas case has stated whether *injustice* must be defined in cases of the type covered by this instruction. For a case discussing the term *injustice* in the context of piercing the corporate veil, see *Mancorp, Inc. v. Culpepper*, 836 S.W.2d 844 (Tex. App.—Houston [1st Dist.] 1992), *on remand from* 802 S.W.2d 226 (Tex. 1990).

1997 amendments to Business Corporation Act. Tex. Bus. Corp. Act art. 2.21 was amended in 1997 as follows:

1. the list of persons or entities protected from liability (except for actual fraud) was expanded to include "affiliates" (Tex. Bus. Corp. Act art. 2.21);
2. not only contractual obligations of the corporation but "matter[s] relating to or arising from" contractual obligations were excluded as grounds for disregarding the corporate fiction unless actual fraud was proved (Tex. Bus. Corp. Act art. 2.21(A)(2)); and

3. failure of the corporation to observe a corporate formality is no longer a ground for piercing the corporate veil in any case, not just contract cases (Tex. Bus. Corp. Act art. 2.21(A)(3)).

The Act further preempted liability "under common law or otherwise" for holders, owners, subscribers, and affiliates by providing the exclusive mechanism for imposing liability upon such persons for obligations limited by the Act, subject to the exceptions stated in the Act. Tex. Bus. Corp. Act art. 2.21(B). This preemption has been carried over into the Code. *See* Tex. Bus. Orgs. Code §§ 21.224–.225; *see also Willis*, 199 S.W.3d at 272–73 (refusing to impose liability against shareholders under a common-law theory of implied ratification where doing so would contravene statute precluding shareholder liability for contractual obligations of the corporation in the absence of actual fraud or an express agreement to assume personal liability); *Southern Union Co. v. City of Edinburg*, 129 S.W.3d 74, 87 (Tex. 2003) (article 2.21 controls action based on single business enterprise theory); *Country Village Homes, Inc.*, 236 S.W.3d at 430 (finding of actual fraud is required to prove single business enterprise theory).

2003 adoption of Texas Business Organizations Code. In 2003, Texas enacted the Texas Business Organizations Code, which codified the Texas Business Corporation Act. Corporations formed after January 1, 2006, are governed by the Code rather than the Act. Tex. Bus. Orgs. Code § 402.001. Corporations formed before January 1, 2006, may elect to be governed by the Code rather than the Act. Tex. Bus. Orgs. Code § 402.003. After January 1, 2010, all Texas corporations are governed by the Code, regardless of when the corporation was formed. Tex. Bus. Orgs. Code § 402.005.

PJC 108.5 Instruction on Circumvention of a Statute

Don Davis used [*name of corporation*] to circumvent a statute for the purpose of perpetrating and did perpetrate an actual fraud on *Paul Payne* primarily for the direct personal benefit of *Don Davis*.

[*or*]

COMMENT

When to use. PJC 108.5 should be used as an instruction accompanying the question in PJC 108.1 if it is alleged that a corporation has been used by a holder of shares, an owner of any beneficial interest in shares, a subscriber for shares whose subscription has been accepted, any of their affiliates, or affiliates of the corporation to circumvent a statute in a case relating to or arising from a contractual obligation. Tex. Bus. Corp. Act art. 2.21(A)(2); Tex. Bus. Orgs. Code § 21.223(a)(2), (b). See comment below, "Cases not covered by statute," for charge language to be used in other cases.

Use of "or." If used with other instructions (see PJC 108.2–.4 and 108.6–.7), PJC 108.5 must be followed by the word *or*, because a finding of any one of the theories for disregarding the corporate fiction defined in the instructions would support an affirmative answer to the question.

Source of instruction. PJC 108.5 is based on the supreme court's discussion of the theories for disregarding the corporate fiction in *Castleberry v. Branscum*, 721 S.W.2d 270, 271–73 (Tex. 1986). The language of *Castleberry* has been modified to reflect the enactment of Tex. Bus. Corp. Act art. 2.21(A) (the "Act") (subsequently codified as Tex. Bus. Orgs. Code § 21.223(a), (b)), which eliminated constructive fraud as a consideration for piercing the corporate veil in contract-based claims against holders, owners, subscribers, or affiliates. *See Willis v. Donnelly*, 199 S.W.3d 262, 271–72 & n.12 (Tex. 2006). The Act further modified *Castleberry* by eliminating the failure to observe corporate formalities as a consideration for piercing the corporate veil in all claims against holders, owners, subscribers, or affiliates. Tex. Bus. Corp. Act art. 2.21(A)(3); *see also Aluminum Chemicals (Bolivia), Inc. v. Bechtel Corp.*, 28 S.W.3d 64, 67–68 nn.3, 4 (Tex. App.—Texarkana 2000, no pet.).

"Actual fraud." The term *actual fraud* appearing in Tex. Bus. Corp. Act art. 2.21(A) and Tex. Bus. Orgs. Code § 21.223(b) is not defined in either statute. In *Castleberry*, decided before article 2.21(A)(2) and section 21.223(b), the supreme court defined actual fraud in the context of piercing the corporate veil as "involv[ing] dishonesty of purpose or intent to deceive." 721 S.W.2d at 273 (quoting *Archer v. Griffith*, 390 S.W.2d 735, 740 (Tex. 1964)). Some courts have held that the fraud must relate to the transaction at issue. *See, e.g.*, *Menetti v. Chavers*, 974 S.W.2d 168, 175 (Tex. App.—San

Antonio 1998, no pet.); *Rutherford v. Atwood*, No. 01-00-00113-CV, 2003 WL 22053687, at *4 (Tex. App.—Houston [1st Dist.] Nov. 13, 2003, no pet.) (mem. op.). For issues relating to the definition and submission of actual fraud, see *Country Village Homes, Inc. v. Patterson*, 236 S.W.3d 413, 432 (Tex. App.—Houston [1st Dist.] 2007, pet. dism'd, judgm't vacated by agr.) (rejecting contention that article 2.21 requires submission of common-law fraud as an independent ground of recovery in a veil-piercing action based on alter ego); *McCarthy v. Wani Venture, A.S.*, 251 S.W.3d 573, 584–85 (Tex. App.—Houston [1st Dist.] 2007, pet. denied) (approving "actual fraud" definition that did not require a material misrepresentation but only the "concealment of material facts or the failure to disclose a material fact" (emphasis omitted)); *Huff v. Harrell*, 941 S.W.2d 230, 237 (Tex. App.—Corpus Christi 1996, writ denied); *Bates v. de Tournillon*, No. 07-03-0257-CV, 2006 WL 265474, at *2 (Tex. App.—Amarillo 2006, no pet.) (mem. op.) (using a definition of fraud that requires a material misrepresentation) (citing *Harco Energy, Inc. v. Re-Entry People, Inc.*, 23 S.W.3d 389, 393 (Tex. App.—Amarillo 2000, no pet.)).

Cases not covered by statute. For cases not involving contract-based claims against holders, owners, subscribers, or affiliates, use the following instruction:

> *Don Davis* used [*name of corporation*] as a means of circumventing a statute, and holding only [*name of corporation*] responsible would result in injustice.

This instruction is derived from *Castleberry*, 721 S.W.2d at 271–73. By their terms, the actual fraud requirements of Tex. Bus. Corp. Act art. 2.21(A)(2) and Tex. Bus. Orgs. Code § 21.223(a)(2) apply only to claims relating to or arising from contractual obligations against holders, owners, subscribers, and affiliates. *See Menetti*, 974 S.W.2d at 173–74 (discussing when a showing of actual fraud is necessary after the 1997 amendments to the Texas Business Corporation Act).

"Injustice." No Texas case has stated whether *injustice* must be defined in cases of the type covered by this instruction. For a case discussing the term *injustice* in the context of piercing the corporate veil, see *Mancorp, Inc. v. Culpepper*, 836 S.W.2d 844 (Tex. App.—Houston [1st Dist.] 1992), *on remand from* 802 S.W.2d 226 (Tex. 1990).

1997 amendments to Business Corporation Act. Tex. Bus. Corp. Act art. 2.21 was amended in 1997 as follows:

1. the list of persons or entities protected from liability (except for actual fraud) was expanded to include "affiliates" (Tex. Bus. Corp. Act art. 2.21);
2. not only contractual obligations of the corporation but "matter[s] relating to or arising from" contractual obligations were excluded as grounds for disregarding the corporate fiction unless actual fraud was proved (Tex. Bus. Corp. Act art. 2.21(A)(2)); and

3. failure of the corporation to observe a corporate formality is no longer a ground for piercing the corporate veil in any case, not just contract cases (Tex. Bus. Corp. Act art. 2.21(A)(3)).

The Act further preempted liability "under common law or otherwise" for holders, owners, subscribers, and affiliates by providing the exclusive mechanism for imposing liability upon such persons for obligations limited by the Act, subject to the exceptions stated in the Act. Tex. Bus. Corp. Act art. 2.21(B). This preemption has been carried over into the Code. *See* Tex. Bus. Orgs. Code §§ 21.224–.225; *see also Willis*, 199 S.W.3d at 272–73 (refusing to impose liability against shareholders under a common-law theory of implied ratification where doing so would contravene statute precluding shareholder liability for contractual obligations of the corporation in the absence of actual fraud or an express agreement to assume personal liability); *Southern Union Co. v. City of Edinburg*, 129 S.W.3d 74, 87 (Tex. 2003) (article 2.21 controls action based on single business enterprise theory); *Country Village Homes, Inc.*, 236 S.W.3d at 430 (finding of actual fraud is required to prove single business enterprise theory).

2003 adoption of Texas Business Organizations Code. In 2003, Texas enacted the Texas Business Organizations Code, which codified the Texas Business Corporation Act. Corporations formed after January 1, 2006, are governed by the Code rather than the Act. Tex. Bus. Orgs. Code § 402.001. Corporations formed before January 1, 2006, may elect to be governed by the Code rather than the Act. Tex. Bus. Orgs. Code § 402.003. After January 1, 2010, all Texas corporations are governed by the Code, regardless of when the corporation was formed. Tex. Bus. Orgs. Code § 402.005.

PJC 108.6 Instruction on Protection of Crime or Justification of Wrong

Don Davis used [*name of corporation*] to protect a crime or to justify a wrong for the purpose of perpetrating and did perpetrate an actual fraud on *Paul Payne* primarily for the direct personal benefit of *Don Davis*.

[*or*]

COMMENT

When to use. PJC 108.6 should be used as an instruction accompanying the question in PJC 108.1 if it is alleged that a corporation has been used by a holder of shares, an owner of any beneficial interest in shares, a subscriber for shares whose subscription has been accepted, any of their affiliates, or affiliates of the corporation to protect a crime or to justify a wrong in a case relating to or arising from a contractual obligation. Tex. Bus. Corp. Act art. 2.21(A)(2); Tex. Bus. Orgs. Code § 21.223(a)(2), (b). See comment below, "Cases not covered by statute," for charge language to be used in other cases.

Use of "or." If used with other instructions (see PJC 108.2–.5 and 108.7), PJC 108.6 must be followed by the word *or*, because a finding of any one of the theories for disregarding the corporate fiction defined in the instructions would support an affirmative answer to the question.

Source of instruction. PJC 108.6 is based on the supreme court's discussion of the theories for disregarding the corporate fiction in *Castleberry v. Branscum*, 721 S.W.2d 270, 271–73 (Tex. 1986). The language of *Castleberry* has been modified to reflect the enactment of Tex. Bus. Corp. Act art. 2.21(A) (the "Act") (subsequently codified as Tex. Bus. Orgs. Code § 21.223(a), (b)), which eliminated constructive fraud as a consideration for piercing the corporate veil in contract-based claims against holders, owners, subscribers, or affiliates. *See Willis v. Donnelly*, 199 S.W.3d 262, 271–72 & n.12 (Tex. 2006). The Act further modified *Castleberry* by eliminating the failure to observe corporate formalities as a consideration for piercing the corporate veil in all claims against holders, owners, subscribers, or affiliates. Tex. Bus. Corp. Act art. 2.21(A)(3); *see also Aluminum Chemicals (Bolivia), Inc. v. Bechtel Corp.*, 28 S.W.3d 64, 67–68 nn.3, 4 (Tex. App.—Texarkana 2000, no pet.).

"Actual fraud." The term *actual fraud* appearing in Tex. Bus. Corp. Act art. 2.21(A) and Tex. Bus. Orgs. Code § 21.223(b) is not defined in either statute. In *Castleberry*, decided before article 2.21(A)(2) and section 21.223(b), the supreme court defined actual fraud in the context of piercing the corporate veil as "involv[ing] dishonesty of purpose or intent to deceive." 721 S.W.2d at 273 (quoting *Archer v. Griffith*, 390 S.W.2d 735, 740 (Tex. 1964)). Some courts have held that the fraud must relate to the transaction at issue. *See, e.g.*, *Menetti v. Chavers*, 974 S.W.2d 168, 175 (Tex. App.—San Antonio 1998, no pet.); *Rutherford v. Atwood*, No. 01-00-00113-CV, 2003 WL 22053687, at *4 (Tex. App.—Houston [1st Dist.] Nov. 13, 2003, no pet.) (mem. op.). For issues relating to the definition and submission of actual fraud, see *Country Village Homes, Inc. v. Patterson*, 236 S.W.3d 413, 432 (Tex. App.—Houston [1st Dist.] 2007, pet. dism'd, judgm't vacated by agr.) (rejecting contention that article 2.21 requires submission of common-law fraud as an independent ground of recovery in a veil-piercing action based on alter ego); *McCarthy v. Wani Venture, A.S.*, 251 S.W.3d 573, 584–85 (Tex. App.—Houston [1st Dist.] 2007, pet. denied) (approving "actual fraud" definition that did not require a material misrepresentation but only the "concealment of material facts or the failure to disclose a material fact" (emphasis omitted)); *Huff v. Harrell*, 941 S.W.2d 230, 237 (Tex. App.—Corpus Christi 1996, writ denied); *Bates v. de Tournillon*, No. 07-03-0257-CV, 2006 WL 265474, at *2 (Tex. App.—Amarillo 2006, no pet.) (mem. op.) (using a definition of fraud that requires a material misrepresentation) (citing *Harco Energy, Inc. v. Re-Entry People, Inc.*, 23 S.W.3d 389, 393 (Tex. App.—Amarillo 2000, no pet.)).

"Protection of crime." "Protection of crime" is one of the grounds given by the supreme court in *Castleberry* for disregarding the corporate fiction. This phrase appears to include but not be limited to "perpetration of crime." Its scope includes, therefore, not only those situations where the party commits a crime but also situations where a crime has been abetted or the criminal has otherwise received assistance. The practitioner should amend this question as appropriate to reflect the facts of the case.

Cases not covered by statute. For cases not involving contract-based claims against holders, owners, subscribers, or affiliates, use the following instruction:

> *Don Davis* used [*name of corporation*] to protect a crime or to justify a wrong, and holding only [*name of corporation*] responsible would result in injustice.

This instruction is derived from *Castleberry*, 721 S.W.2d at 271–73. By their terms, the actual fraud requirements of Tex. Bus. Corp. Act art. 2.21(A)(2) and Tex. Bus. Orgs. Code § 21.223(a)(2) apply only to claims relating to or arising from contractual obligations against holders, owners, subscribers, and affiliates. *See Menetti*, 974 S.W.2d at 173–74 (discussing when a showing of actual fraud is necessary after the 1997 amendments to the Texas Business Corporation Act).

"Injustice." No Texas case has stated whether *injustice* must be defined in cases of the type covered by this instruction. For a case discussing the term *injustice* in the context of piercing the corporate veil, see *Mancorp, Inc. v. Culpepper*, 836 S.W.2d 844 (Tex. App.—Houston [1st Dist.] 1992), *on remand from* 802 S.W.2d 226 (Tex. 1990).

1997 amendments to Business Corporation Act. Tex. Bus. Corp. Act art. 2.21 was amended in 1997 as follows:

1. the list of persons or entities protected from liability (except for actual fraud) was expanded to include "affiliates" (Tex. Bus. Corp. Act art. 2.21);
2. not only contractual obligations of the corporation but "matter[s] relating to or arising from" contractual obligations were excluded as grounds for disregarding the corporate fiction unless actual fraud was proved (Tex. Bus. Corp. Act art. 2.21(A)(2)); and
3. failure of the corporation to observe a corporate formality is no longer a ground for piercing the corporate veil in any case, not just contract cases (Tex. Bus. Corp. Act art. 2.21(A)(3)).

The Act further preempted liability "under common law or otherwise" for holders, owners, subscribers, and affiliates by providing the exclusive mechanism for imposing liability upon such persons for obligations limited by the Act, subject to the exceptions stated in the Act. Tex. Bus. Corp. Act art. 2.21(B). This preemption has been carried over into the Code. *See* Tex. Bus. Orgs. Code §§ 21.224–.225; *see also Willis*, 199 S.W.3d at 272–73 (refusing to impose liability against shareholders under a common-law theory of implied ratification where doing so would contravene statute precluding shareholder liability for contractual obligations of the corporation in the absence of actual fraud or an express agreement to assume personal liability); *Southern Union Co. v. City of Edinburg*, 129 S.W.3d 74, 87 (Tex. 2003) (article 2.21 controls action based on single business enterprise theory); *Country Village Homes, Inc.*, 236 S.W.3d at 430 (finding of actual fraud is required to prove single business enterprise theory).

2003 adoption of Texas Business Organizations Code. In 2003, Texas enacted the Texas Business Organizations Code, which codified the Texas Business Corporation Act. Corporations formed after January 1, 2006, are governed by the Code rather than the Act. Tex. Bus. Orgs. Code § 402.001. Corporations formed before January 1, 2006, may elect to be governed by the Code rather than the Act. Tex. Bus. Orgs. Code § 402.003. After January 1, 2010, all Texas corporations are governed by the Code, regardless of when the corporation was formed. Tex. Bus. Orgs. Code § 402.005.

PJC 108.7 Instruction on Monopoly

Don Davis used [*name of corporation*] to achieve a monopoly for the purpose of perpetrating and did perpetrate an actual fraud on *Paul Payne* primarily for the direct personal benefit of *Don Davis*.

[*or*]

COMMENT

When to use. PJC 108.7 should be used as an instruction accompanying the question in PJC 108.1 if it is alleged that a corporation has been used by a holder of shares, an owner of any beneficial interest in shares, a subscriber for shares whose subscription has been accepted, any of their affiliates, or affiliates of the corporation to achieve or perpetrate a monopoly in a case relating to or arising from a contractual obligation. Tex. Bus. Corp. Act art. 2.21(A)(2); Tex. Bus. Orgs. Code § 21.223(a)(2), (b). See comment below, "Cases not covered by statute," for charge language to be used in other cases.

Use of "or." If used with other instructions (see PJC 108.2–.6), PJC 108.7 must be followed by the word *or*, because a finding of any one of the theories for disregarding the corporate fiction defined in the instructions would support an affirmative answer to the question.

Source of instruction. PJC 108.7 is based on the supreme court's discussion of the theories for disregarding the corporate fiction in *Castleberry v. Branscum*, 721 S.W.2d 270, 271–73 (Tex. 1986). The language of *Castleberry* has been modified to reflect the enactment of Tex. Bus. Corp. Act art. 2.21(A) (the "Act") (subsequently codified as Tex. Bus. Orgs. Code § 21.223(a), (b)), which eliminated constructive fraud as a consideration for piercing the corporate veil in contract-based claims against holders, owners, subscribers, or affiliates. *See Willis v. Donnelly*, 199 S.W.3d 262, 271–72 & n.12 (Tex. 2006). The Act further modified *Castleberry* by eliminating the failure to observe corporate formalities as a consideration for piercing the corporate veil in all claims against holders, owners, subscribers, or affiliates. Tex. Bus. Corp. Act art. 2.21(A)(3); *see also Aluminum Chemicals (Bolivia), Inc. v. Bechtel Corp.*, 28 S.W.3d 64, 67–68 nn.3, 4 (Tex. App.—Texarkana 2000, no pet.).

"Actual fraud." The term *actual fraud* appearing in Tex. Bus. Corp. Act art. 2.21(A) and Tex. Bus. Orgs. Code § 21.223(b) is not defined in either statute. In *Castleberry*, decided before article 2.21(A)(2) and section 21.223(b), the supreme court defined actual fraud in the context of piercing the corporate veil as "involv[ing] dishonesty of purpose or intent to deceive." 721 S.W.2d at 273 (quoting *Archer v. Griffith*, 390 S.W.2d 735, 740 (Tex. 1964)). Some courts have held that the fraud must relate to the transaction at issue. *See, e.g., Menetti v. Chavers*, 974 S.W.2d 168, 175 (Tex. App.—San

Antonio 1998, no pet.); *Rutherford v. Atwood*, No. 01-00-00113-CV, 2003 WL 22053687, at *4 (Tex. App.—Houston [1st Dist.] Nov. 13, 2003, no pet.) (mem. op.). For issues relating to the definition and submission of actual fraud, see *Country Village Homes, Inc. v. Patterson*, 236 S.W.3d 413, 432 (Tex. App.—Houston [1st Dist.] 2007, pet. dism'd, judgm't vacated by agr.) (rejecting contention that article 2.21 requires submission of common-law fraud as an independent ground of recovery in a veil-piercing action based on alter ego); *McCarthy v. Wani Venture, A.S.*, 251 S.W.3d 573, 584–85 (Tex. App.—Houston [1st Dist.] 2007, pet. denied) (approving "actual fraud" definition that did not require a material misrepresentation but only the "concealment of material facts or the failure to disclose a material fact" (emphasis omitted)); *Huff v. Harrell*, 941 S.W.2d 230, 237 (Tex. App.—Corpus Christi 1996, writ denied); *Bates v. de Tournillon*, No. 07-03-0257-CV, 2006 WL 265474, at *2 (Tex. App.—Amarillo 2006, no pet.) (mem. op.) (using a definition of fraud that requires a material misrepresentation) (citing *Harco Energy, Inc. v. Re-Entry People, Inc.*, 23 S.W.3d 389, 393 (Tex. App.—Amarillo 2000, no pet.)).

Cases not covered by statute. For cases not involving contract-based claims against holders, owners, subscribers, or affiliates, use the following instruction:

> *Don Davis* used [*name of corporation*] to achieve or perpetrate a monopoly, and holding only [*name of corporation*] liable would result in injustice.

This instruction is derived from *Castleberry*, 721 S.W.2d at 271–73. By their terms, the actual fraud requirements of Tex. Bus. Corp. Act art. 2.21(A)(2) and Tex. Bus. Orgs. Code § 21.223(a)(2) apply only to claims relating to or arising from contractual obligations against holders, owners, subscribers, and affiliates. *See Menetti*, 974 S.W.2d at 173–74 (discussing when a showing of actual fraud is necessary after the 1997 amendments to the Texas Business Corporation Act).

"Injustice." No Texas case has stated whether *injustice* must be defined in cases of the type covered by this instruction. For a case discussing the term *injustice* in the context of piercing the corporate veil, see *Mancorp, Inc. v. Culpepper*, 836 S.W.2d 844 (Tex. App.—Houston [1st Dist.] 1992), *on remand from* 802 S.W.2d 226 (Tex. 1990).

1997 amendments to Business Corporation Act. Tex. Bus. Corp. Act art. 2.21 was amended in 1997 as follows:

1. the list of persons or entities protected from liability (except for actual fraud) was expanded to include "affiliates" (Tex. Bus. Corp. Act art. 2.21);
2. not only contractual obligations of the corporation but "matter[s] relating to or arising from" contractual obligations were excluded as grounds for disregarding the corporate fiction unless actual fraud was proved (Tex. Bus. Corp. Act art. 2.21(A)(2)); and

3. failure of the corporation to observe a corporate formality is no longer a ground for piercing the corporate veil in any case, not just contract cases (Tex. Bus. Corp. Act art. 2.21(A)(3)).

The Act further preempted liability "under common law or otherwise" for holders, owners, subscribers, and affiliates by providing the exclusive mechanism for imposing liability upon such persons for obligations limited by the Act, subject to the exceptions stated in the Act. Tex. Bus. Corp. Act art. 2.21(B). This preemption has been carried over into the Code. *See* Tex. Bus. Orgs. Code §§ 21.224–.225; *see also Willis*, 199 S.W.3d at 272–73 (refusing to impose liability against shareholders under a common-law theory of implied ratification where doing so would contravene statute precluding shareholder liability for contractual obligations of the corporation in the absence of actual fraud or an express agreement to assume personal liability); *Southern Union Co. v. City of Edinburg*, 129 S.W.3d 74, 87 (Tex. 2003) (article 2.21 controls action based on single business enterprise theory); *Country Village Homes, Inc.*, 236 S.W.3d at 430 (finding of actual fraud is required to prove single business enterprise theory).

2003 adoption of Texas Business Organizations Code. In 2003, Texas enacted the Texas Business Organizations Code, which codified the Texas Business Corporation Act. Corporations formed after January 1, 2006, are governed by the Code rather than the Act. Tex. Bus. Orgs. Code § 402.001. Corporations formed before January 1, 2006, may elect to be governed by the Code rather than the Act. Tex. Bus. Orgs. Code § 402.003. After January 1, 2010, all Texas corporations are governed by the Code, regardless of when the corporation was formed. Tex. Bus. Orgs. Code § 402.005.

PJC 109.1 Question and Instruction on Conspiracy

QUESTION ______

[Conditioned on findings of a statutory violation or a tort (other than negligence) that proximately caused damages.]

Was *Connie Conspirator* part of a conspiracy that damaged *Paul Payne*?

To be part of a conspiracy, *Connie Conspirator* and another person or persons must have had knowledge of, agreed to, and intended a common objective or course of action that resulted in the damages to *Paul Payne*. One or more persons involved in the conspiracy must have performed some act or acts to further the conspiracy.

Answer: ______________

COMMENT

When to use. PJC 109.1 submits the question of conspiracy to accomplish the unlawful objective of harming another by committing a statutory violation or a tort (other than negligence). See comment below, "Conspiracy to accomplish lawful objective by unlawful means," for the situation involving a conspiracy to employ an unlawful means to accomplish a lawful objective. Civil conspiracy to unlawfully harm another is a derivative tort. Liability must be dependent on participation in some underlying statutory violation or a tort (other than negligence). *Chu v. Hong*, 249 S.W.3d 441, 444 n.4 (Tex. 2008). It is a means for imposing joint and several liability on persons in addition to the actual perpetrator(s) of the underlying tort.

Source of question and instruction. A civil conspiracy is "a combination by two or more persons to accomplish an unlawful purpose or to accomplish a lawful purpose by unlawful means." *Firestone Steel Products Co. v. Barajas*, 927 S.W.2d 608, 614 (Tex. 1996). The elements of civil conspiracy have been stated as "(1) two or more persons; (2) an object to be accomplished; (3) a meeting of minds on the object or course of action; (4) one or more unlawful, overt acts; and (5) damages as a proximate result." *Tri v. J.T.T.*, 162 S.W.3d 552, 556 (Tex. 2005); *Juhl v. Airington*, 936 S.W.2d 640, 644 (Tex. 1996); *see also Triplex Communications, Inc. v. Riley*, 900 S.W.2d 716, 719–20 (Tex. 1995); *Schlumberger Well Surveying Corp. v. Nortex Oil & Gas Corp.*, 435 S.W.2d 854, 856 (Tex. 1968).

Knowledge, intent, and agreement. To be liable for conspiracy, a party must be shown to have intended to do more than engage in the conduct that resulted in the injury. It must be shown that from the inception of the combination or agreement the party intended to cause the injury or was aware of the harm likely to result from the wrongful conduct. *Triplex Communications, Inc.*, 900 S.W.2d at 720; *Great National Life Insurance Co. v. Chapa*, 377 S.W.2d 632, 635 (Tex. 1964). Thus, a party must be shown to have known the object and purpose of the conspiracy and to have had a meeting of the minds with the other conspirators to accomplish that object and purpose, intending to bring about the resulting injury. *Nortex Oil & Gas Corp.*, 435 S.W.2d at 857.

Unlawful act. A defendant's liability for conspiracy is based on participation in the statutory violation or underlying tort (other than negligence) that would have been actionable against at least one of the conspirators individually. *Tilton v. Marshall*, 925 S.W.2d 672, 681 (Tex. 1996); *International Bankers Life Insurance Co. v. Holloway*, 368 S.W.2d 567, 581 (Tex. 1963). An act or declaration by a conspirator not in pursuance of the common objective is not actionable against coconspirators. *Chapa*, 377 S.W.2d at 635. Likewise, an improper motive in performing a lawful action will not support liability for conspiracy. *Kingsbery v. Phillips Petroleum Co.*, 315 S.W.2d 561, 576 (Tex. Civ. App.—Austin 1958, writ ref'd n.r.e.). The injury must have been caused by the tort or statutory violation that the conspirator agreed with the perpetrator to bring about while intending the resulting harm. *Triplex Communications, Inc.*, 900 S.W.2d at 720; *Nortex Oil & Gas Corp.*, 435 S.W.2d at 857. Once a civil conspiracy is found, each coconspirator is responsible for the actions of any coconspirator in furtherance of the conspiracy. Thus, each element of the underlying tort or violation is imputed to each participant. *Akin v. Dahl*, 661 S.W.2d 917, 921 (Tex. 1983), *cert. denied*, 466 U.S. 938 (1984).

Conspiracy to accomplish lawful objective by unlawful means. PJC 109.1 submits the proper question if a court or jury has established the existence of an unlawful objective, that is, a statutory violation or a tort (other than negligence). The supreme court's opinions regarding conspiracy also define a conspiracy cause of action arising when the conspirators pursue a lawful objective by unlawful means. *Triplex Communications, Inc.*, 900 S.W.2d at 719–20; *Massey v. Armco Steel Co.*, 652 S.W.2d 932, 934 (Tex. 1983); *Chapa*, 377 S.W.2d at 635; *Berry v. Golden Light Coffee Co.*, 327 S.W.2d 436, 438 (Tex. 1959); *State v. Standard Oil Co.*, 107 S.W.2d 550, 559 (Tex. 1937). The Committee believes PJC 109.1 can be used to submit either theory but that it may need modification in some instances depending on the facts of the case.

Damages. The damages recoverable in an action for civil conspiracy are those damages resulting from the commission of the wrong, not the conspiratorial agreement. *Carroll v. Timmers Chevrolet, Inc.*, 592 S.W.2d 922, 925 (Tex. 1979); *see also Triplex Communications, Inc.*, 900 S.W.2d at 720. Therefore, the Committee recommends that PJC 109.1 be submitted after, and conditioned on, an affirmative finding of damages caused by the statutory violation or underlying tort (other than negligence).

Exemplary damages. An affirmative finding on an underlying cause of action that includes a finding sufficient to impose exemplary damages may be imputed to all participants in the conspiracy on an affirmative conspiracy finding. *Akin*, 661 S.W.2d at 921.

For questions submitting exemplary damages, see PJC 115.36 and 115.37 and the Comments accompanying those questions.

PJC 110.1 Libel and Slander (Comment on Broad Form)

Explanatory note. Chapter 110 governs submission of libel and slander cases. The following general comments should be considered when using the patterns in chapter 110.

Libel and slander distinguished. Defamation includes both libel and slander. Libel is a publication by writing or some other graphic means (including broadcasting). *See* Tex. Civ. Prac. & Rem. Code § 73.001; *Christy v. Stauffer Publications, Inc.*, 437 S.W.2d 814, 815 (Tex. 1969) ("[T]he broadcasting of defamatory statements read from a script is libel rather than slander."). Slander is orally communicated defamatory words. *Randall's Food Markets, Inc. v. Johnson*, 891 S.W.2d 640, 646 (Tex. 1995). Libel in Texas, when the common law still prevailed in the libel area, was codified in a statute, now Tex. Civ. Prac. & Rem. Code § 73.001 *et seq.* Slander remains controlled by the common law, subject to constitutional standards in an appropriate case. *Cain v. Hearst Corp.*, 878 S.W.2d 577, 580 (Tex. 1994).

Broad-form submission. Tex. R. Civ. P. 277 provides that "the court shall, whenever feasible, submit the cause upon broad-form questions." *See also Texas Department of Human Services v. E.B.*, 802 S.W.2d 647, 649 (Tex. 1990). Defamation claims involve multiple elements and defenses, all of which may not apply to every case, and many publications give rise to multiple allegedly defamatory statements. That many defamation cases involve constitutional issues further complicates the trial court's task in crafting a jury charge. Therefore, the drafting of a broad-form pattern charge in defamation cases was deemed not feasible by the Committee. Instead, the questions and instructions in chapter 110 assume as their subject a single allegedly defamatory statement and provide patterns from which to select those elements or defenses that apply in a particular case. Broad-form submission, however, may be feasible in some cases, and the questions and instructions in chapter 110 may be combined as appropriate.

PJC 110.2 Question and Instruction on Publication

QUESTION ______

Did *Don Davis* publish the following: [*insert the alleged defamatory matter*]?

"Publish" means intentionally or negligently to communicate the matter to a person other than *Paul Payne* who is capable of understanding its meaning.

Answer: ______________

COMMENT

When to use. "To maintain a defamation cause of action, the plaintiff must prove that the defendant: (1) published a statement; (2) that was defamatory concerning the plaintiff; (3) while acting with either actual malice, if the plaintiff was a public official or public figure, or negligence, if the plaintiff was a private party, regarding the truth of the statement." *WFAA-TV, Inc. v. McLemore*, 978 S.W.2d 568, 571 (Tex. 1998). The allegedly defamatory statement must be directed at the plaintiff; that is, it must appear that the plaintiff is the person with reference to whom the allegedly defamatory statement was made. *Huckabee v. Time Warner Entertainment Co.*, 19 S.W.3d 413, 429 (Tex. 2000); *Newspapers, Inc. v. Matthews*, 339 S.W.2d 890, 893 (Tex 1960). The plaintiff frequently has the burden of proving falsity. See PJC 110.4. PJC 110.2 submits the element of publication if it is in dispute.

Source of definition. The definition of "publish" is derived from *Kelley v Rinkle*, 532 S.W.2d 947, 948 (Tex. 1976), and *AccuBanc Mortgage Corp. v. Drummonds*, 938 S.W.2d 135, 147 (Tex. App.—Fort Worth 1996, writ denied).

Self-defamation. Self-defamation is frequently raised by the plaintiff in response to the defense contemplated by PJC 110.8. The plaintiff argues that the publication was required by the circumstances and was not truly voluntary on the plaintiff's part. The Texas Supreme Court has not decided whether a publication may occur by "self-defamation." The courts of appeals that have addressed the issue differ about whether the plaintiff must establish that he was unaware of the defamatory nature of the matter published at the time of publication. *See AccuBanc Mortgage Corp.*, 938 S.W.2d at 147–50 (plaintiff's judgment for self-defamation reversed where plaintiff knew of the defamatory implications of termination letter and there was no evidence its contents were published by plaintiff); *Doe v. SmithKline Beecham Corp.*, 855 S.W.2d 248 (Tex. App.—Austin 1993, writ granted), *aff'd*, 903 S.W.2d 347 (Tex. 1995) (defendant's summary judgment affirmed where plaintiff knew the defamatory implications of the statement at the time plaintiff published it); *Chasewood Construction Co. v. Rico*, 696 S.W.2d 439 (Tex.

App.—San Antonio 1985, writ ref'd n.r.e.) (plaintiff subcontractor who repeated general contractor's accusations of theft to plaintiff's employees in explanation for abrupt termination of job permitted to recover for defamation where jury found a prudent person would have reasonably expected such accusations would be communicated to others by plaintiff subcontractor); *First State Bank of Corpus Christi v. Ake*, 606 S.W.2d 696 (Tex. Civ. App.—Corpus Christi 1980, writ ref'd n.r.e.) (trial court did not err in refusing to instruct jury that defendant was not liable for damages resulting from plaintiff's publication of the defamatory matter since defendant was aware of the likelihood of communication to third party).

PJC 110.3 Question and Instructions on Defamatory

If your answer to Question ______ [*110.2*] is "Yes," then answer the following question. Otherwise, do not answer the following question.

QUESTION ______

Do you find that the statement in Question ______ [*110.2*] was defamatory concerning Paul Payne?

> "Defamatory" means an ordinary person would interpret the statement in a way that tends to injure a living person's reputation and thereby expose the person to public hatred, contempt or ridicule, or financial injury or to impeach the person's honesty, integrity, virtue, or reputation.

In deciding whether a statement is defamatory, you must construe the [*article/broadcast/other context*] as a whole and in light of the surrounding circumstances based upon how a person of ordinary intelligence would perceive it.

Answer: _______________

COMMENT

When to use. Whether a statement is capable of a defamatory meaning is a threshold question for the court. *Turner v. KTRK Television, Inc.*, 38 S.W.3d 103, 114 (Tex. 2000); *Gartman v. Hedgpeth*, 157 S.W.2d 139, 141 (Tex. 1941). Only when the court determines that the language is ambiguous or of doubtful meaning should the jury determine the statement's meaning and effect on an ordinary person. *Musser v. Smith Protective Services, Inc.*, 723 S.W.2d 653, 655 (Tex. 1987). This question submits the element of whether the matter was defamatory concerning the plaintiff.

Conditioning. If publication is not in dispute and PJC 110.2 is not submitted, the conditioning language should be deleted and the question should be modified as follows:

> Was the following defamatory concerning *Paul Payne*: [*insert the alleged defamatory matter*]?

Source of definition and instruction. The definition of "defamatory" is taken from Tex. Civ. Prac. & Rem. Code § 73.001 and *Turner*, 38 S.W.3d at 115. Although section 73.001 includes the phrase "blacken the memory of the dead," that phrase has not been included in light of authority holding that the legislature did not intend merely by codifying a definition to create by implication a cause of action for defaming the dead. *See Renfro Drug Co. v. Lawson*, 160 S.W.2d 246, 249 (Tex. 1942); *see also Channel 4,*

KGBT v. Briggs, 759 S.W.2d 939, 940 n.1 (Tex. 1988) ("While one cannot bring a cause of action for the defamation of a person already dead, one who is alive while he was defamed and later dies, has a cause of action for defamation which survives his death."). The instruction on construing the statement is taken from *New York Times Co. v. Sullivan*, 376 U.S. 254, 285 (1964); *New Times, Inc. v. Isaacks*, 146 S.W.3d 144, 154 (Tex. 2004); and *Turner*, 38 S.W.3d at 113–15.

Corporations. Corporations may bring actions for defamation. *See General Motors Acceptance Corp. v. Howard*, 487 S.W.2d 708, 712–13 (Tex. 1972). In cases involving a corporate plaintiff, the definition of "defamatory" should be adjusted by changing "living person" to an appropriate descriptive term.

Natural defects. Libel encompasses the publication of "natural defects" of an individual when that publication exposes the individual to public hatred, ridicule, or financial injury. Tex. Civ. Prac. & Rem. Code § 73.001. The few cases addressing "natural defects" involve accusations of a mental problem. *See, e.g.*, *Enterprise Co. v. Ellis*, 98 S.W.2d 452 (Tex. Civ. App.—Beaumont 1936, no writ) (accusation that plaintiff was "goofey" or suffering from mental imbalance); *Hibdon v. Moyer*, 197 S.W. 1117 (Tex. Civ. App.—El Paso 1917, no writ) (accusation that plaintiff suffered from "brainstorms"); *see also Raymer v. Doubleday & Co., Inc.*, 615 F.2d 241, 243 (5th Cir. 1980) (accusation involving physical appearance, i.e., baldness or pudginess, did not implicate a natural defect according to the court). Because this category of defamation remains viable but has rarely been used as the basis for a cause of action, the Committee removed reference to "natural defects" from the statutory definition of "defamatory" in the pattern instruction.

PJC 110.4 Question and Instruction on Falsity

If your answer to Question ______ [*110.3*] is "Yes," then answer the following question. Otherwise, do not answer the following question.

QUESTION ______

Do you find that the statement [*insert matter alleged to be defamatory*] was false at the time it was made as it related to *Paul Payne*?

> "False" means that a statement is not literally true or not substantially true. A statement is not "substantially true" if, in the mind of the average person, the gist of the statement is more damaging to the person affected by it than a literally true statement would have been.

Answer: _______________

COMMENT

When to use. The question and instruction in PJC 110.4 should be used when the plaintiff is required to establish that the publication is false. At common law, in a case against a nonmedia defendant not involving a matter of public concern, a private plaintiff enjoys a presumption of falsity. *See* Tex. Civ. Prac. & Rem. Code § 73.005 ("The truth of the statement in the publication on which an action for libel is based is a defense to the action."); *Randall's Food Markets, Inc. v. Johnson*, 891 S.W.2d 640, 646 (Tex. 1995) ("In suits brought by private individuals, truth is an affirmative defense to slander."); *see also Bentley v. Bunton*, 94 S.W.3d 561, 586 n.62 (Tex. 2002). A public official or public figure, however, must prove that defamatory statements made about him were false. *Bentley*, 94 S.W.3d at 587 (citing *New York Times Co. v. Sullivan*, 376 U.S. 254, 279–280 (1964)). If the defamatory speech is of public concern and the defendant is a member of the media, the plaintiff must prove falsity. *Bentley*, 94 S.W.3d at 587 n.62 (citing *Philadelphia Newspapers, Inc. v. Hepps*, 475 U.S. 767, 777 (1986)). The Texas Supreme Court has also held that public officials and public figures must prove falsity when suing a nonmedia defendant if the matter involves a matter of public concern. *Bentley*, 94 S.W.3d at 586; *see also Casso v. Brand*, 776 S.W.2d 551, 555 n.3 (Tex. 1989). Falsity must be proven by a preponderance of the evidence. *Bentley*, 94 S.W.3d at 587; *Turner v. KTRK Television, Inc.*, 38 S.W.3d 103, 117 (Tex. 2000).

Questions of law. Whether a publication is false presents a question of law "[i]f the underlying facts as to the gist of the defamatory charge are undisputed." *McIlvain v. Jacobs*, 794 S.W.2d 14, 16 (Tex. 1990). Whether a plaintiff is a public figure or public official is a question of constitutional law to be decided by the court. *WFAA-TV, Inc. v. McLemore*, 978 S.W.2d 568, 571 (Tex. 1998) (citing *Rosenblatt v. Baer*, 383 U.S. 75, 88

(1966)). At least one court has held that whether the subject matter of a publication is a matter of public concern is a question of law for the court. *See Texas Beef Group v. Winfrey*, 11 F. Supp. 2d 858, 862 (N.D. Tex. 1998), *aff'd*, 201 F.3d 680 (5th Cir. 2000) (citing *Connick v. Myers*, 461 U.S. 138, 146 (1983)); *see also Dallas County v. Gonzales*, 183 S.W.3d 94, 110 (Tex. App.—Dallas 2006, pet. denied).

Statements of opinion, fair comment, and rhetorical hyperbole are protected by both the state and federal constitutions. *Bentley*, 94 S.W.3d at 579–80 (citing *Milkovich v. Lorain Journal Co.*, 497 U.S. 1, 19–21 (1990)). Determination of whether a statement is protected as opinion, fair comment, or rhetorical hyperbole is generally a question of law for the court. *Bentley*, 94 S.W.3d at 580. *But see Restatement (Second) of Torts* § 566 cmt. c (noting uncertain treatment of opinion in private party cases not involving matters of public concern). The protection for statements of opinion in *Bentley* and *Milkovich* appear to be broader than the "fair comment" statutory privilege in Tex. Civ. Prac. & Rem. Code § 73.002(b)(2).

Source of definition. The definition of falsity is based on *McIlvain*, 794 S.W.2d at 16. A statement is "substantially true" if the gist of the statement is no more damaging to the person than the literal truth would be. *McIlvain*, 794 S.W.2d at 16.

PJC 110.5 Question and Instruction on Negligence

If your answer to Question ______ [*110.4*] is "Yes," then answer the following question. Otherwise, do not answer the following question.

QUESTION ______

Did *Don Davis* know or should he have known, in the exercise of ordinary care, that the [*article/broadcast/other context*] contained in Question ______ [*110.3*] was false and had the potential to be defamatory?

> "Ordinary care" concerning the truth of the statement and its potential to be defamatory means that degree of care that would be used by a person of ordinary prudence under the same or similar circumstances.

Answer: ______________

COMMENT

When to use. PJC 110.5 should be submitted in the following cases: (1) when a private figure sues a media defendant about a statement that involves a private or public issue or (2) when a public official, who is not a public figure, sues a media defendant about a statement unrelated to his performance or fitness for office. *Foster v. Laredo Newspapers, Inc.*, 541 S.W.2d 809, 819–20 (Tex. 1976).

It is uncertain whether a private party plaintiff is required to establish negligence when the case involves a matter of exclusively private concern. *See Philadelphia Newspapers, Inc. v. Hepps*, 475 U.S. 767, 775 (1986) ("When the speech is of exclusively private concern and the plaintiff is a private figure . . . the constitutional requirements do not necessarily force any change in at least some of the features of the common-law landscape."); *see also Leyendecker & Associates v. Wechter*, 683 S.W.2d 369 (Tex. 1985) (affirming plaintiff's verdict and applying common-law principles to private parties in a purely private concern case without discussion of constitutional issues); *Peshak v. Greer*, 13 S.W.3d 421, 425–26 (Tex. App.—Corpus Christi 2000, no pet.); *Snead v. Redland Aggregates Ltd.*, 998 F.2d 1325, 1329–30 (5th Cir. 1993). *But see Restatement (Second) of Torts* §§ 558, 580A, 580B (1977); Robert D. Sack, *Sack on Defamation: Libel, Slander, and Related Problems* §§ 6.5, 6.6 (3d ed. 1999).

To establish negligence, the plaintiff must prove that (1) the defendant knew or should have known that the statement was false and (2) the content of the publication would warn a reasonably prudent person of its defamatory potential. *Foster*, 541 S.W.2d at 819–20.

"Defamatory" should be defined in this question or elsewhere in the charge as appropriate. See PJC 110.3. If the case involves a defamatory impression created by the defendant, use PJC 110.9.

Source of instruction. This instruction is based on *Foster*, 541 S.W.2d at 819–20 (quoting *Gertz v. Robert Welch, Inc.*, 418 U.S. 323, 348 (1974)) ("We hold that a private individual may recover damages from a publisher or broadcaster of a defamatory falsehood as compensation for actual injury upon a showing that the publisher or broadcaster knew or should have known that the defamatory statement was false. In addition, the liability of a publisher or broadcaster of a defamatory falsehood about a private individual may not be predicated upon 'a factual misstatement whose content [would] not warn a reasonably prudent editor or broadcaster of its defamatory potential.'").

PJC 110.6 Question and Instructions on Actual Malice

If you answered "Yes" to Question ______ [*110.5*] , then answer the following question. Otherwise, do not answer the following question.

QUESTION ______

Do you find by clear and convincing evidence that, at the time *Don Davis* made the statement in Question ______ [*110.3*],

1. *Don Davis* knew it was false as it related to *Paul Payne*, or
2. *Don Davis* made the statement with a high degree of awareness that it was probably false, to an extent that *Don Davis* in fact had serious doubts as to the truth of the statement?

"Clear and convincing evidence" is that measure or degree of proof that will produce in the mind of the jury a firm belief or conviction as to the truth of the allegations sought to be established.

Answer: ______________

COMMENT

When to use. PJC 110.6 should be submitted in cases in which the plaintiff is required to prove a defamatory statement was made with actual malice. Because the U.S. Supreme Court has expressed remorse over the use of "actual malice" to describe the standard, and chapter 41 of the Texas Civil Practices and Remedies Code uses "malice" in connection with exemplary damages, the instruction avoids the use of the phrases "actual malice" and "reckless disregard." *See Harte-Hanks Communications, Inc. v. Connaughton*, 491 U.S. 657, 666 n.7 (1989); Tex. Civ. Prac. & Rem. Code § 41.003.

In a case brought by a public figure or public official, the plaintiff must prove actual malice by clear and convincing evidence. *Bentley v. Bunton*, 94 S.W.3d 561, 596–97 (Tex. 2002) (citing *Rosenbloom v. Metromedia, Inc.*, 403 U.S. 29, 55 (1971)). In a case brought by a private figure involving a matter of public concern, the plaintiff must prove actual malice by clear and convincing evidence to recover exemplary damages. *See Dun & Bradstreet, Inc. v. Greenmoss Builders, Inc.*, 472 U.S. 749, 760–61 (1985) (citing *Gertz v. Robert Welch, Inc.*, 418 U.S. 323 (1974)). Actual malice may also be a fact issue in a case involving a qualified privilege defense. *Dun & Bradstreet, Inc. v. O'Neil*, 456 S.W.2d 896, 900 (Tex. 1970).

Questions of law. Determination of whether the plaintiff is a public official or public figure is a matter of law for the court to decide. *WFAA-TV, Inc. v. McLemore*, 978 S.W.2d 568, 571 (Tex. 1998). Whether the subject matter of a publication is a matter of public concern has been held to be a question of law for the court. *Texas Beef Group v. Winfrey*, 11 F. Supp. 2d 858, 862 (N.D. Tex. 1998), *aff'd*, 201 F.3d 680 (5th Cir. 2000) (citing *Connick v. Myers*, 461 U.S. 138, 146 (1983)).

Source of definition and instruction. The instruction is derived from *Bentley*, 94 S.W.3d at 591, 600. *See also St. Amant v. Thompson*, 390 U.S. 727 (1968). The definition of clear and convincing evidence is based on *Bentley*, 94 S.W.3d at 596–97. *See also* Tex. Civ. Prac. & Rem. Code § 41.001(2).

Organizations. When an organization is accused of defamation in a case requiring proof of actual malice, an instruction directing the jury to those persons within the organization whose state of mind is at issue may be appropriate. In determining whether an organization had actual malice, the United States Supreme Court observed in *New York Times Co. v. Sullivan*, 376 U.S. 254 (1964), that it was not enough that the *New York Times* had stories in its files showing that a proposed advertisement was false. The court instead noted that "[t]here was testimony that the persons handling the advertisement saw nothing in it that would render it unacceptable." *New York Times Co.*, 376 U.S. at 287. Accordingly, for the organization to be liable, "the state of mind required for actual malice would have to be brought home to the persons in the Times' organization having responsibility for the publication of the advertisement." *New York Times Co.*, 376 U.S. at 287.

PJC 110.7 Actual Malice in Cases of Qualified Privilege (Comment)

When the facts are undisputed and the language used in the publication is not ambiguous, the question whether a publication is protected by a qualified privilege is one of law for the court. Once the qualified privilege is shown to exist, the burden is on the plaintiff to show the privilege is lost. Privilege is an affirmative defense in the nature of confession and avoidance; and, except where the plaintiff's petition shows on its face that the alleged defamatory publication is protected by a privilege, the defendant has the burden of pleading and proving that the publication is privileged. *Denton Publishing Co. v. Boyd*, 460 S.W.2d 881, 884 (Tex. 1970).

The plaintiff may overcome the qualified privilege only by establishing that the publication was made with actual malice. *Randall's Food Markets, Inc. v. Johnson*, 891 S.W.2d 640, 646 (Tex. 1995); *Dun & Bradstreet, Inc. v. O'Neil*, 456 S.W.2d 896, 900–01 (Tex. 1970). It is unclear whether the plaintiff's burden of proof to defeat the privilege by showing actual malice is by a preponderance of the evidence or by clear and convincing evidence. *Compare Hagler v. Proctor & Gamble Manufacturing Co.*, 884 S.W.2d 771 (Tex. 1994) (actual malice in qualified privilege context requires knowing falsity or reckless disregard for truth, citing cases indicating that such matters must be proved by clear and convincing evidence), *with Ellis County State Bank v. Keever*, 888 S.W.2d 790, 792–93 n.5 (Tex. 1994) (stating that preponderance of the evidence standard is firmly established in Texas civil cases; a more onerous burden is required only in extraordinary circumstances, such as when mandated by the United States Supreme Court). If the court concludes that actual malice provides the standard, the question in PJC 110.6 would be appropriate. If the court concludes that a preponderance burden of proof applies, the question in PJC 110.6 should be modified accordingly.

Whether a qualified privilege exists can depend on whether the publication of the alleged defamation was limited to certain persons. *See Randall's Food Markets, Inc.*, 891 S.W.2d at 646 ("The privilege remains intact as long as communications pass only to persons having an interest or duty in the matter to which the communications relate."). If the evidence raises a fact issue whether the defendant communicated the statement to persons not covered by the privilege, the court should submit that issue to the jury. *Mitre v. Brooks Fashion Stores Inc.*, 840 S.W.2d 612, 619 (Tex. App.—Corpus Christi 1992, writ denied), *overruled on other grounds by Cain v. Hearst Corp.*, 878 S.W.2d 577 (Tex. 1994).

PJC 110.8 Question and Instructions on Defense of Substantial Truth

QUESTION ______

Do you find that the statement in Question ______ [*110.3*] was substantially true at the time it was made as it related to *Paul Payne*?

> A statement is "substantially true" if it varies from the literal truth in only minor details or if, in the mind of the average person, the gist of it is no more damaging to the person affected by it than a literally true statement would have been.

In connection with this question, you are instructed that *Don Davis* has the burden to prove substantial truth by a preponderance of the evidence.

Answer: ______________

COMMENT

When to use. PJC 110.8 should be submitted only in cases involving a private party plaintiff regarding a matter of exclusively private concern when the defendant pleads truth as an affirmative defense and there is evidence of truth. *See* Tex. Civ. Prac. & Rem. Code § 73.005; *Randall's Food Markets, Inc. v. Johnson*, 891 S.W.2d 640, 646 (Tex. 1995) (slander); *McIlvain v. Jacobs*, 794 S.W.2d 14, 15–16 (Tex. 1990) (libel). The statutory privileges for newspapers and other periodicals provided in Tex. Civ. Prac. & Rem. Code § 73.002(b)(1) contemplate a submission as to the truth of the publication at issue. When truth is an affirmative defense, the burden of proof rests on the defendant. *Grotti v. Belo Corp.*, 188 S.W.3d 768, 774–75 (Tex. App.—Fort Worth, 2006, pet. denied); *see also Randall's Food Markets, Inc.*, 891 S.W.2d at 646.

Source of instruction. The definition of falsity is based on *McIlvain*, 794 S.W.2d at 16. A statement is "substantially true" if the gist of the statement is no more damaging to the person than the literal truth would be. *McIlvain*, 794 S.W.2d at 16.

PJC 110.9 Question and Instructions on Defamatory False Impression

QUESTION ______

Did the [*article/broadcast/other context*] as a whole and not merely individual statements contained in it, either by omitting material facts or suggestively juxtaposing facts in a misleading way, create the substantially false and defamatory impression that *Paul Payne* [*insert alleged false and defamatory impression*]?

> "False" means that the impression created, if any, is not literally true or not substantially true. An impression is not "substantially true" if, in the mind of the average person, the gist of the impression is more damaging to the person affected by it than a literally true impression would have been.
>
> "Defamatory" means that an ordinary person would be left with an impression that tends to injure a living person's reputation and thereby expose the person to public hatred, contempt or ridicule, or financial injury or to impeach the person's honesty, integrity, virtue, or reputation.

In deciding whether an impression is defamatory, you must construe the [*article/broadcast/other context*] as a whole and in light of the surrounding circumstances based upon how a person of ordinary intelligence would perceive it.

Answer: _______________

COMMENT

When to use. A defendant may defame a person where all the statements in a publication are true when read in isolation but the publication conveys a substantially false and defamatory impression by omitting material facts or suggestively juxtaposing true facts. *See Turner v. KTRK Television, Inc.*, 38 S.W.3d 103, 113–14 (Tex. 2000). Since defamation by an otherwise accurate publication requires that the publication create both "a substantially false and defamatory impression," a private party plaintiff in a case involving an exclusively private matter must establish the falsity of the impression by a preponderance of the evidence. *Turner*, 38 S.W.3d at 113–14. This question submits the basic inquiry in a false impression case about whether the publication created the false and defamatory impression complained of.

Source of definition and instruction. The definitions and instructions in PJC 110.9 are adapted from *Turner,* 38 S.W.3d at 113–14.

Corporations. Corporations may bring actions for defamation. *See General Motors Acceptance Corp. v. Howard*, 487 S.W.2d 708, 712–13 (Tex. 1972). In cases involving a corporate plaintiff, the definition of "defamatory" should be adjusted by changing "living person" to an appropriate descriptive term.

Natural defects. Libel encompasses the publication of "natural defects" of an individual when that publication exposes the individual to public hatred, ridicule, or financial injury. Tex. Civ. Prac. & Rem. Code § 73.001. The few cases addressing "natural defects" involve accusations of a mental problem. *See, e.g., Enterprise Co. v. Ellis*, 98 S.W.2d 452 (Tex. Civ. App.—Beaumont 1936, no writ) (accusation that plaintiff was "goofey" or suffering from mental imbalance); *Hibdon v. Moyer*, 197 S.W. 1117 (Tex. Civ. App.—El Paso 1917, no writ) (accusation that plaintiff suffered from "brainstorms"); *see also Raymer v. Doubleday & Co., Inc.*, 615 F.2d 241, 243 (5th Cir. 1980) (accusation involving physical appearance, i.e., baldness or pudginess, did not implicate a natural defect according to the court). Because this category of defamation remains viable but has rarely been used as the basis for a cause of action, the Committee removed reference to "natural defects" from the statutory definition of "defamatory" in the pattern instruction.

PJC 110.10 Question and Instruction on Negligence (Defamatory False Impression)

If your answer to Question ______ [*110.9*] is "Yes," then answer the following question. Otherwise, do not answer the following question.

QUESTION ______

Did *Don Davis* know or should he have known, in the exercise of ordinary care, that the impression created by the [*article/broadcast/other context*] contained in Question ______ [*110.9*] was false and had the potential to be defamatory?

> "Ordinary care" concerning the truth of the impression and its potential to be defamatory means that degree of care that would be used by a person of ordinary prudence under the same or similar circumstances.

Answer: ______________

COMMENT

When to use. PJC 110.10 should be submitted in the following cases in which the negligence standard of care is submitted to the jury regarding a defendant's knowledge of a false and defamatory impression of the plaintiff created by the defendant, as opposed to a defamatory statement made by the defendant: (1) when a private figure sues a media defendant about an impression that involves a private or public issue or (2) when a public official, who is not a public figure, sues a media defendant about an impression unrelated to his performance or fitness for office. *Turner v. KTRK Television, Inc.*, 38 S.W.3d 103, 113–14 (Tex. 2000) (recognizing defamation by false impression); *Foster v. Laredo Newspapers, Inc.*, 541 S.W.2d 809, 819–20 (Tex. 1976).

It is uncertain whether a private party plaintiff is required to establish negligence when the case involves a matter of exclusively private concern. *See Philadelphia Newspapers, Inc. v. Hepps*, 475 U.S. 767, 775 (1986) ("When the speech is of exclusively private concern and the plaintiff is a private figure . . . the constitutional requirements do not necessarily force any change in at least some of the features of the common-law landscape."); *see also Leyendecker & Associates v. Wechter*, 683 S.W.2d 369 (Tex. 1985) (affirming plaintiff's verdict and applying common-law principles to private parties in a purely private concern case without discussion of constitutional issues); *Peshak v. Greer*, 13 S.W.3d 421, 425–26 (Tex. App.—Corpus Christi 2000, no pet.); *Snead v. Redland Aggregates Ltd.*, 998 F.2d 1325, 1332–33 (5th Cir. 1993). *But see Restatement (Second) of Torts* §§ 558, 580A, 580B (1977); Robert D. Sack, *Sack on Defamation: Libel, Slander, and Related Probl*ems §§ 6.5, 6.6 (3d ed. 1999).

To establish negligence, the plaintiff must prove that (1) the defendant knew or should have known that the impression was false and (2) the content of the publication would warn a reasonably prudent person of its defamatory potential. *Foster*, 541 S.W.2d at 819–20.

"Defamatory" should be defined in this question or elsewhere in the charge as appropriate. See PJC 110.9 (defamatory impression).

Source of instruction. This instruction is based on *Foster*, 541 S.W.2d at 819–20 (quoting *Gertz v. Robert Welch, Inc.*, 418 U.S. 323, 348 (1974)) ("We hold that a private individual may recover damages from a publisher or broadcaster of a defamatory falsehood as compensation for actual injury upon a showing that the publisher or broadcaster knew or should have known that the defamatory statement was false. In addition, the liability of a publisher or broadcaster of a defamatory falsehood about a private individual may not be predicated upon 'a factual misstatement whose content [would] not warn a reasonable prudent editor or broadcaster of its defamatory potential.'").

PJC 110.11 Question and Instructions on Actual Malice (Defamatory False Impression)

If your answer to Question ______ [*110.9*] is "Yes," then answer the following question. Otherwise, do not answer the following question.

QUESTION ______

Do you find by clear and convincing evidence that at the time *Don Davis* [*published/broadcast/made*] the [*article/broadcast/other context*] in Question ______ [*110.9*] that *Don Davis* knew or strongly suspected that the [*article/broadcast/other context*] presented a substantially false and defamatory impression?

"Strongly suspected" means had a high degree of awareness.

"Clear and convincing evidence" is that measure or degree of proof that will produce in the mind of the jury a firm belief or conviction as to the truth of the allegations sought to be established.

Answer: ______________

COMMENT

When to use. When a case involves a claim of a false and defamatory impression arising from an otherwise accurate publication, the Texas Supreme Court has recognized the necessity of adjusting the inquiries as to falsity and actual malice. *See Turner v. KTRK Television, Inc.*, 38 S.W.3d 103, 119–20 (Tex. 2000). Because the U.S. Supreme Court has expressed remorse over the use of "actual malice" to describe the standard, and chapter 41 of the Texas Civil Practices and Remedies Code uses "malice" in connection with exemplary damages, the instruction avoids the use of the phrases "actual malice" and "reckless disregard." *See Harte-Hanks Communications, Inc. v. Connaughton*, 491 U.S. 657, 666 n.7 (1989); *see also* Tex. Civ. Prac. & Rem. Code § 41.003.

In a case brought by a public figure or public official, the plaintiff must prove actual malice by clear and convincing evidence to establish liability. *WFAA-TV, Inc. v. McLemore*, 978 S.W.2d 568, 571 (Tex. 1998). PJC 110.11 should be submitted in cases in which the plaintiff is required to prove actual malice regarding a defamatory impression of the plaintiff created by the defendant.

Questions of law. Determination of whether the plaintiff is a public official or public figure is a matter of law for the court to decide. *WFAA-TV, Inc.*, 978 S.W.2d at 571. Whether the subject matter of a publication is a matter of public concern has been held to be a question of law for the court. *Texas Beef Group v. Winfrey*, 11 F. Supp. 2d 858, 862

(N.D. Tex. 1998), *aff'd*, 201 F.3d 680 (5th Cir. 2000) (citing *Connick v. Myers*, 461 U.S. 138, 146 (1983)).

Source of definition and instruction. The instruction is derived from *Bentley v. Bunton*, 94 S.W.3d 561, 587 n.62 (Tex. 2002), and *Turner*, 38 S.W.3d at 120–21. The phrase "strongly suspected," instead of "serious doubts," is used based on the holding in *Turner*, 38 S.W.3d at 120–21. The definition of clear and convincing evidence is based on *Bentley*, 94 S.W.3d at 596–97. *See also* Tex. Civ. Prac. & Rem. Code § 41.001(2).

Organizations. When an organization is accused of defamation in a case requiring proof of actual malice, an instruction directing the jury to those persons within the organization whose state of mind is at issue may be appropriate. In determining whether an organization had actual malice, the United States Supreme Court observed in *New York Times Co. v. Sullivan*, 376 U.S. 254 (1964), that it was not enough that the *New York Times* had stories in its files showing that a proposed advertisement was false. The court instead noted that "[t]here was testimony that the persons handling the advertisement saw nothing in it that would render it unacceptable." *New York Times Co.*, 376 U.S. at 287. Accordingly, for the organization to be liable, "the state of mind required for actual malice would have to be brought home to the persons in the Times' organization having responsibility for the publication of the advertisement." *New York Times Co.*, 376 U.S. at 287.

PJC 110.12 Question on Defamatory Parody or Satire

QUESTION ______

Do you find that the [*article/broadcast/other context*], in context and as a whole, would be reasonably understood by a person of ordinary intelligence as stating as actual fact that *Paul Payne* [*insert alleged false and defamatory fact*]?

Answer: _______________

COMMENT

When to use. A defendant may defame a person by satire or parody where the complained of matter is defamatory and may reasonably be interpreted as stating actual fact concerning the plaintiff. *New Times, Inc. v. Isaacks*, 146 S.W.3d 144, 156–58 (Tex. 2004). PJC 110.12 submits the issue of whether the allegedly defamatory matter may reasonably be interpreted as stating actual fact concerning the plaintiff. All remaining contested fact issues also should be submitted. See PJC 110.2 (publication), 110.3 (defamatory), and comments to 110.12–13 (concerning falsity) as applicable.

Source of instruction. The instruction is adapted from *Isaacks*, 146 S.W.3d at 158.

PJC 110.13 Question and Instruction on Negligence (Defamatory Parody or Satire)

If your answer to Question ______ [*110.12*] is "Yes," then answer the following question. Otherwise, do not answer the following question.

QUESTION ______

Did *Don Davis* know or should he have known, in the exercise of ordinary care, that the [*article/broadcast/other context*] contained in Question ______ [*110.12*] would be reasonably understood by a person of ordinary intelligence as stating actual fact and that the [*article/broadcast/other context*] had the potential to be defamatory?

> "Ordinary care" means that degree of care that would be used by a person of ordinary prudence under the same or similar circumstances.

Answer: _______________

COMMENT

When to use. PJC 110.13 should be submitted in the following cases in which the negligence standard of care is submitted to the jury regarding the false and defamatory satire or parody: (1) when a private figure sues a media defendant about an impression that involves a private or public issue or (2) when a public official, who is not a public figure, sues a media defendant about an impression unrelated to his performance or fitness for office. *Foster v. Laredo Newspapers, Inc.*, 541 S.W.2d 809, 819–20 (Tex. 1976); *see New Times, Inc. v. Isaacks*, 146 S.W.3d 144, 156–58 (Tex. 2004) (recognizing defamation by parody or satire).

It is uncertain whether a private party plaintiff is required to establish negligence when the case involves a matter of exclusively private concern. *See Philadelphia Newspapers, Inc. v. Hepps*, 475 U.S. 767, 775 (1986) ("When the speech is of exclusively private concern and the plaintiff is a private figure . . . the constitutional requirements do not necessarily force any change in at least some of the features of the common-law landscape."); *see also Leyendecker & Associates v. Wechter*, 683 S.W.2d 369 (Tex. 1985) (affirming plaintiff's verdict and applying common-law principles to private parties in a purely private concern case without discussion of constitutional issues); *Peshak v. Greer*, 13 S.W.3d 421, 425–26 (Tex. App.—Corpus Christi 2000, no pet.); *Snead v. Redland Aggregates Ltd.*, 998 F.2d 1325, 1329–30 (5th Cir. 1993). *But see Restatement (Second) of Torts* §§ 558, 580A, 580B (1977); Robert D. Sack, *Sack on Defamation: Libel, Slander, and Related Problems* §§ 6.5, 6.6 (3d ed. 1999).

To establish negligence, the plaintiff must prove that (1) the defendant knew or should have known that the statement was false and (2) the content of the publication would warn a reasonably prudent person of its defamatory potential. *See Foster*, 541 S.W.2d at 819–20.

"Defamatory" should be defined in this question or elsewhere in the charge as appropriate. See PJC 110.3.

Falsity. PJC 110.13 assumes that falsity is not disputed; however, if falsity is disputed, and the plaintiff is required to prove falsity, substitute the following question:

> Did *Don Davis* know or should he have known, in the exercise of ordinary care, that the [*article/broadcast/other context*] contained in Question ______ [*110.12*] would be reasonably understood by a person of ordinary intelligence as stating actual fact, that the fact was false, and that the [*article/broadcast/other context*] had the potential to be defamatory?

Source of instruction. This instruction is based on *Foster*, 541 S.W.2d at 819–20 (quoting *Gertz v. Robert Welch, Inc.*, 418 U.S. 323, 348 (1974)) ("We hold that a private individual may recover damages from a publisher or broadcaster of a defamatory falsehood as compensation for actual injury upon a showing that the publisher or broadcaster knew or should have known that the defamatory statement was false. In addition, the liability of a publisher or broadcaster of a defamatory falsehood about a private individual may not be predicated upon 'a factual misstatement whose content [would] not warn a reasonable prudent editor or broadcaster of its defamatory potential.'").

PJC 110.14 Question and Instruction on Actual Malice (Defamatory Parody or Satire)

If your answer to Question ______ [*110.12*] is "Yes," then answer the following question. Otherwise, do not answer the following question.

QUESTION ______

Do you find by clear and convincing evidence that at the time *Don Davis* published the [*article/broadcast/other context*] *he* knew or had a high degree of awareness that the [*article/broadcast/other context*] would reasonably be interpreted as stating actual fact?

> "Clear and convincing evidence" is that measure or degree of proof that will produce in the mind of the jury a firm belief or conviction as to the truth of the allegations sought to be established.

Answer: ______________

COMMENT

When to use. PJC 110.14 should be submitted in cases in which a public figure or public official seeks recovery based on satire or parody. *New Times, Inc. v. Isaacks*, 146 S.W.3d 144, 156–58 (Tex. 2004). Because the U.S. Supreme Court has expressed remorse over the use of "actual malice" to describe the standard, and chapter 41 of the Texas Civil Practices and Remedics Code uses "malice" in connection with exemplary damages, the instruction avoids the use of the phrases "actual malice" and "reckless disregard." *See Harte-Hanks Communications, Inc. v. Connaughton*, 491 U.S. 657, 666 n.7 (1989); *see also* Tex. Civ. Prac. & Rem. Code § 41.003. In a case brought by a public figure or public official, the plaintiff must prove actual malice by clear and convincing evidence to establish liability. *WFAA-TV, Inc. v. McLemore*, 978 S.W.2d 568, 571 (Tex. 1998).

Questions of law. Determination of whether the plaintiff is a public official or public figure is a matter of law for the court to decide. *WFAA-TV, Inc.*, 978 S.W.2d at 571. Whether the subject matter of a publication is a matter of public concern has been held to be a question of law for the court. *Texas Beef Group v. Winfrey*, 11 F. Supp. 2d 858, 862 (N.D. Tex. 1998), *aff'd*, 201 F.3d 680 (5th Cir. 2000) (citing *Connick v. Myers*, 461 U.S. 138, 146 (1983)).

Falsity. PJC 110.12 assumes that falsity is not disputed; however, if falsity is disputed, the phrase "and that the fact was false" should be inserted at the end of the question.

Source of definition and instruction. The instruction is taken from *Isaacks*, 146 S.W.3d at 156. The definition of clear and convincing evidence is based on *Bentley v. Bunton*, 94 S.W.3d 561, 596–97 (Tex. 2002). *See also* Tex. Civ. Prac. & Rem. Code § 41.001(2).

Organizations. When an organization is accused of defamation in a case requiring proof of actual malice, an instruction directing the jury to those persons within the organization whose state of mind is at issue may be appropriate. In determining whether an organization had actual malice, the United States Supreme Court observed in *New York Times Co. v. Sullivan*, 376 U.S. 254 (1964), that it was not enough that the *New York Times* had stories in its files showing that a proposed advertisement was false. The court instead noted that "[t]here was testimony that the persons handling the advertisement saw nothing in it that would render it unacceptable." *New York Times Co.*, 376 U.S. at 287. Accordingly, for the organization to be liable, "the state of mind required for actual malice would have to be brought home to the persons in the Times' organization having responsibility for the publication of the advertisement." *New York Times Co.*, 376 U.S. at 287.

PJC 110.15 Business Disparagement

QUESTION ______

Did *Don Davis* disparage the business of *Paul Payne*?

A person disparages the business of another if he publishes a disparaging false statement about the business, and, when he publishes the statement, he [*knows the falsity of the statement or acts with reckless disregard of whether the statement is false/acts with ill will or intends to interfere with the economic interest of Paul Payne*], and his publication of the statement played a substantial part in inducing others not to do business with *Paul* Payne and resulted in a specific pecuniary loss to *Paul Payne*.

A statement is "published" if it is intentionally communicated to a person other than *Paul Payne* who is capable of understanding its meaning.

Answer "Yes" or "No" for each statement listed below.

In answering this question, you may consider only the following statements: [*statements defined by pleadings and proof*]

Answer: _______________

COMMENT

When to use. PJC 110.15 is used for business disparagement instead of defamation. Business disparagement is a species of tort similar to defamation, because both involve the imposition of liability for injury sustained through publication to third parties of a false statement affecting the plaintiff. *Astoria Industries of Iowa, Inc. v. SNF, Inc.*, 223 S.W.3d 616, 624–25 (Tex. App.—Fort Worth 2007, pet. denied). But business disparagement and defamation protect different interests. "The action for defamation is to protect the personal reputation of the injured party, whereas the action for injurious falsehood or business disparagement is to protect the economic interests of the injured party against pecuniary loss." *Hurlbut v. Gulf Atlantic Life Insurance Co.*, 749 S.W.2d 762, 766 (Tex. 1987). The supreme court explained in *Hurlbut* that, unlike in common-law libel, the plaintiff in a business disparagement claim must plead and prove the falsity of the statement as part of his cause of action; the defendant in an action for business disparagement is subject to liability "only if he knew of the falsity or acted with reckless disregard concerning it, or if he acted with ill will or intended to interfere in the economic interest of the plaintiff in an unprivileged fashion"; and the plaintiff must always prove pecuniary loss to establish a cause of action for business disparagement. *Hurlbut*, 749 S.W.2d at 766. Unlike defamation, where the submission of the different elements depends on many variables and may require separate questions, business disparagement lends itself to a global submission.

If the alleged disparaging statement involves a product or service rather than a business, the question and instruction should be modified accordingly.

Source of instruction. This instruction is based on *Prudential Insurance Co. of America v. Financial Review Services, Inc.*, 29 S.W.3d 74, 82 (Tex. 2000), which stated that business disparagement requires proof of "publication by the defendant of the disparaging words, falsity, malice, lack of privilege, and special damages." *See also Hurlbut,* 749 S.W.2d at 766.

Form of publication. The supreme court has not considered whether a negligent publication will suffice for business disparagement. Given the intentional nature of the business disparagement tort, the Committee suggests that only intentional publication will suffice.

Fact vs. opinion. Statements of opinion, fair comment, and rhetorical hyperbole are protected by both the state and federal constitutions. *Bentley v. Bunton*, 94 S.W.3d 561, 579–80 (Tex. 2002) (citing *Milkovich v. Lorain Journal Co.*, 497 U.S. 1, 19–21 (1990)). Whether a statement is protected as opinion, fair comment, or rhetorical hyperbole is generally a question of law for the court. *Bentley*, 94 S.W.3d at 580; *see also MKC Energy Investments, Inc. v. Sheldon*, 182 S.W.3d 372, 377 (Tex. App—Beaumont 2005, no pet.); *Delta Air Lines, Inc. v. Norris*, 949 S.W.2d 422, 426 (Tex. App.—Waco 1997, writ denied).

Business disparagement vs. injurious falsehood. PJC 110.15 is limited to business disparagement. The Texas Supreme Court and courts of appeals have used the terms "business disparagement" and "injurious falsehood" interchangeably. However, these are distinct torts with different elements. Business disparagement requires that the words at issue be disparaging as well as false. *Forbes, Inc. v. Granada Biosciences, Inc.*, 124 S.W.3d 167, 170 (Tex. 2003); *Prudential Insurance Co. of America*, 29 S.W.3d at 82; *Hurlbut*, 749 S.W.2d at 766. This requirement does not appear in the *Restatement*'s description of injurious falsehood, which requires only a false statement that is injurious; the statement need not contain any opprobrium. *See Restatement (Second) of Torts* § 623A (1977) ("One who publishes a false statement harmful to the interests of another is subject to liability for pecuniary loss resulting to the other if [describing the malice requirement]." However, no Texas case has yet recognized a claim for injurious falsehood where the words at issue are not disparaging but are false and, as a result, harm the business of the plaintiff. *See, e,g.*, *Delta Air Lines, Inc.*, 949 S.W.2d 422 (rejecting business disparagement claim where words were not defamatory); *MKC Energy Investments, Inc.*, 182 S.W.3d 372 (same).

Lack of privilege. While lack of privilege is a required element in business disparagement, only absolute privilege is relevant. Because a "Yes" answer to PJC 110.15 requires a finding of malice that defeats qualified privileges, qualified privileges are irrelevant in business disparagement cases. *See Hurlbut,* 749 S.W.2d at 768. The issue of absolute privilege is a legal question that the court will determine as a matter of law before the submission to the jury. *See Galveston County Fair & Rodeo, Inc. v. Glover,* 880 S.W.2d 112, 120 (Tex. App.—Texarkana 1994), *writ denied per curiam,* 940 S.W.2d 585 (Tex. 1996); *Arant v. Jaffe,* 436 S.W.2d 169, 178 (Tex. App.—Dallas 1968, no writ).

Standard of proof of defendant's fault. The common-law standard for business disparagement required a plaintiff to prove the defendant's "malice" in making the statement. As noted above, the malice standard at common law could be met by proof of knowing falsity, reckless disregard of falsity, or acting with ill will or intent to interfere with the plaintiff's interests. *Hurlbut,* 749 S.W.2d at 766; *Restatement (Second) of Torts* § 623A (1977).

With the constitutionalization of speech-related torts when they involve speech on matters of public concern, there is some uncertainty regarding the standard for malice. When the object of the allegedly disparaging speech is a public figure such as a large, publicly traded company, the U.S. Supreme Court precedents point to a constitutional requirement that the plaintiff must prove "actual malice"—knowing falsity or reckless disregard for the truth—to prevail against a media defendant. *See Bose Corp. v. Consumers Union of United States, Inc.,* 466 U.S. 485, 511–14 (1984). Such proof clearly meets some of the alternative proofs of malice—knowing falsity—under the common law. *See Forbes, Inc.,* 124 S.W.3d 167, in which the supreme court assumed, without deciding, "that the *New York Times* actual-malice standard applies in a public figure's business disparagement suit against a media defendant." *Forbes, Inc.,* 124 S.W.3d at 171.

Where the matter discussed is of public concern but the plaintiff is not a public official or public figure, the Texas Supreme Court has not spoken on the standard of fault in business disparagement cases.

It is not clear whether the common-law standard or some different standard will apply when the party allegedly disparaged is not a public figure, the defendant is not a media outlet, or the disparagement does not involve a matter of public concern. Proof of knowing falsity or reckless disregard for the truth will always suffice, since those were ways to prove malice under the common law. *See, e.g., Prudential Insurance Co. of America,* 29 S.W.3d at 82–83 (reviewing summary judgment evidence and finding it sufficient to show that the defendant made a fraud accusation knowing it was baseless). *See also Hurlbut,* 749 S.W.2d at 766 ("In the present case there is evidence to support findings that the statements of Gulf Atlantic were false and malicious in the sense that Gulf Atlantic knew them to be false.").

Ill will. Malice still appears to qualify as a basis for liability in cases where the common law controls. In *Hurlbut* and later in *Forbes, Inc.,* the Texas Supreme Court still recited ill will as part of the "malice" standard. *Hurlbut*, 749 S.W.2d at 766; *Forbes, Inc.*, 124 S.W.3d at 170. *See also Graham Land & Cattle Co. v. The Independent Bankers Bank*, 205 S.W.3d 21, 27 (Tex. App.—Corpus Christi 2006, no pet.). Unless the supreme court chooses to change this standard, it will likely be applied to common-law cases.

Special damages. A business disparagement plaintiff must offer proof of special damages. In *Hurlbut*, the court explained that this element obligated the plaintiff to prove a realized or liquidated pecuniary loss, and "the communication must play a substantial part in inducing others not to deal with the plaintiff." *Hurlbut*, 749 S.W.2d at 767. Given the court's comments, the Committee has included the special damages element in the liability question. While the fact of special damages is submitted in this question, the amount of damages incurred would still be determined in the separate damages question addressing this element. See PJC 115.34.

[Chapters 111–114 are reserved for expansion.]

CHAPTER 115 DAMAGES

PJC 115.1 Predicate—Instruction Conditioning Damages Question on Liability

If your answer to Question _______ [*insert number of appropriate liability question*] is "Yes," then answer the following question. Otherwise, do not answer the following question.

COMMENT

When to use. PJC 115.1 is used to condition answers to damages questions. The damages questions in this chapter assume liability in the question, so this predicate should always precede those questions. The Comments following damages questions in this chapter refer to the corresponding liability questions in other chapters.

PJC 115.1.5 Instruction on Whether Compensatory Damages Are Subject to Income Taxes (Actions Filed on or after September 1, 2003)

You are instructed that any monetary recovery for [*list each element of economic or noneconomic damages that is subject to taxation*] is subject to [*federal or state*] income taxes. Any recovery for [*list each element of economic or noneconomic damages that is not subject to taxation*] is not subject to [*federal or state*] income taxes.

COMMENT

When to use. PJC 115.1.5 should be submitted with the damages question in any action filed on or after September 1, 2003, in which a claimant seeks recovery for loss of earnings, loss of earning capacity, loss of contributions of a pecuniary value, or loss of inheritance. Whether an element of damages is taxable depends on the substantive tax law pertaining to each cause of action.

Source of instruction. Section 18.091 of the Texas Civil Practice and Remedies Code, entitled "Proof of Certain Losses; Jury Instruction," provides:

> (a) Notwithstanding any other law, if any claimant seeks recovery for loss of earnings, loss of earning capacity, loss of contributions of a pecuniary value, or loss of inheritance, evidence to prove the loss must be presented in the form of a net loss after reduction for income tax payments or unpaid tax liability pursuant to any federal income tax law.
>
> (b) If any claimant seeks recovery for loss of earnings, loss of earning capacity, loss of contributions of a pecuniary value, or loss of inheritance, the court shall instruct the jury as to whether any recovery for compensatory damages sought by the claimant is subject to federal or state income taxes.

Tex. Civ. Prac. & Rem. Code § 18.091.

PJC 115.2 Question on Contract Damages

[Insert predicate, PJC 115.1.]

QUESTION ______

What sum of money, if any, if paid now in cash, would fairly and reasonably compensate *Paul Payne* for *his* damages, if any, that resulted from such failure to comply?

Consider the following elements of damages, if any, and none other.

[Insert appropriate instructions. See samples in PJC 115.3 and instructions in PJC 115.4.]

Do not add any amount for interest on damages, if any.

Answer separately in dollars and cents for damages, if any.

a. [*Element A*] sustained in the past.

Answer: ______________

b. [*Element A*] that, in reasonable probability, will be sustained in the future.

Answer: ______________

c. [*Element B*] sustained in the past.

Answer: ______________

d. [*Element B*] that, in reasonable probability, will be sustained in the future.

Answer: ______________

COMMENT

When to use. PJC 115.2 should be predicated on a "Yes" answer to PJC 101.2 and may be adapted for use in most breach-of-contract cases by the addition of appropriate instructions setting out legally available measures of damages. See PJC 115.3 and 115.4. If only one measure of damages is supported by the pleadings and proof, the measure may be incorporated into the question.

Instruction required. PJC 115.2 *may not* be submitted without an instruction on the appropriate measures of damages. *See Jackson v. Fontaine's Clinics, Inc.*, 499 S.W.2d 87, 90 (Tex. 1973). See PJC 115.3 and 115.4 for sample instructions.

Causation. The phrase *resulted from* is derived from *McKnight v. Hill & Hill Exterminators, Inc.*, 689 S.W.2d 206, 209 (Tex. 1985).

Parallel theories. If the breach-of-contract cause of action is only one of several theories of recovery submitted in the charge and any theory has a different legal measure of damages to be applied to a factually similar claim for damages, a separate damages question for each theory may be submitted and the following additional instruction may be included earlier in the charge:

> In answering questions about damages, answer each question separately. Do not increase or reduce the amount in one answer because of the instructions in or your answers to any other questions about damages. Do not speculate about what any party's ultimate recovery may or may not be. Any recovery will be determined by the court when it applies the law to your answers at the time of judgment.

Elements of damages submitted separately. The Committee generally recommends that multiple elements of damages be separately submitted to the jury. *Harris County v. Smith*, 96 S.W.3d 230, 233–34 (Tex. 2002) (broad-form submission of multiple elements of damages may lead to harmful error if there is a proper objection raising insufficiency of the evidence to support one or more of the elements submitted); *see also* Tex. Civ. Prac. & Rem. Code § 41.008(a) ("In an action in which a claimant seeks recovery of damages, the trier of fact shall determine the amount of economic damages separately from the amount of other compensatory damages."). Separating economic from noneconomic damages is required to allow the court to apply the limits on recovery of exemplary damages based on economic and noneconomic damages as required by Tex. Civ. Prac. & Rem. Code § 41.008(b).

Further, "[p]rejudgment interest may not be assessed or recovered on an award of future damages." Tex. Fin. Code § 304.1045 (wrongful death, personal injury, or property damage cases); *see also Johnson & Higgins of Texas, Inc. v. Kenneco Energy, Inc.*, 962 S.W.2d 507, 514, 530 (Tex. 1998) (reconciling equitable prejudgment interest with statutory prejudgment interest); *Perry Roofing Co. v. Olcott*, 744 S.W.2d 929, 931 (Tex. 1988) (unliquidated damages in contract cases); *Cavnar v. Quality Control Parking, Inc.*, 696 S.W.2d 549, 555–56 (Tex. 1985) (personal injury, later extended to other types of cases). Therefore, separation of past and future damages is required.

Elements considered separately. *Golden Eagle Archery, Inc. v. Jackson*, 116 S.W.3d 757, 770 (Tex. 2002), provides an instruction for cases involving undefined or potentially overlapping categories of damages. In those cases, the following language should be substituted for the instruction to consider each element separately:

Consider the following elements of damages, if any, and none other. You shall not award any sum of money on any element if you have otherwise, under some other element, awarded a sum of money for the same loss. That is, do not compensate twice for the same loss, if any.

Prejudgment interest. Instructing the jury not to add interest is suggested because prejudgment interest, if recoverable, will be calculated by the court at the time of judgment. If interest paid on an obligation is claimed as an element of damages, it may be necessary to modify the instruction on interest.

PJC 115.3 Sample Instructions on Direct and Incidental Damages—Contracts

Explanatory note: Damages instructions in contract actions are often necessarily fact-specific. Unlike most other form instructions in this volume, therefore, the following sample instructions are illustrative only, using a hypothetical situation to give a few examples of how instructions may be worded to submit various legal measures of damages for use in connection with the contract damages question, PJC 115.2.

Sample A—Loss of the benefit of the bargain

The difference, if any, between the value of the paint job agreed to by the parties and the value of the paint job performed by *Don Davis*. The difference in value, if any, shall be determined at the time and place the paint job was performed.

Sample B—Remedial damages

The reasonable and necessary cost to repaint *Paul Payne*'s truck.

Sample C—Loss of contractual profit

The difference between the agreed price and the cost *Paul Payne* would have incurred in painting the truck.

Sample D—Loss of contractual profit plus expenses incurred before breach

The amount *Don Davis* agreed to pay *Paul Payne* less the expenses *Paul Payne* saved by not completing the paint job.

Sample E—Damages after mitigation

The difference between the amount paid by *Paul Payne* to *John Jones* for painting the truck and the amount *Paul Payne* had agreed to pay *Don Davis* for that work.

Sample F—Mitigation expenses

Reasonable and necessary expenses incurred in attempting to have the truck repainted.

Sample G—Incidental damages

Reasonable and necessary costs to store *Paul Payne*'s tools while the truck was being repainted.

COMMENT

When to use. See explanatory note above. Because damages instructions in contract suits are necessarily fact-specific, no true "pattern" instructions are given—only samples of some measures of general damages available in contract actions. This list is not exhaustive. The samples are illustrative only, adapted to a hypothetical fact situation, and must be rewritten to fit the particular damages raised by the pleadings and proof and recoverable under a legally accepted theory. The instructions should be drafted in an attempt to make the plaintiff factually whole but not to put the plaintiff in a better position than he would have been in had the defendant fully performed the contract. *See Osoba v. Bassichis*, 679 S.W.2d 119, 122 (Tex. App.—Houston [14th Dist.] 1984, writ ref'd n.r.e.). For a comprehensive discussion of the theories of contract damages, see *Restatement (Second) of Contracts* §§ 346–356 (1981).

Measures generally alternative. The measures outlined here are generally alternatives, although some, particularly incidental damages, may be available in addition to one of the other measures, as may consequential damages (see PJC 115.4).

Direct damages. Since *Hadley v. Baxendale*, 9 Exch. 341, 156 Eng. Rep. 145 (1854), contract damages have been divided into two categories: direct and consequential. *See Arthur Andersen & Co. v. Perry Equipment Corp.*, 945 S.W.2d 812, 816 (Tex. 1997). Direct damages—

> are those which naturally and necessarily flow from a wrongful act, are so usual an accompaniment of the kind of breach alleged that the mere allegation of the breach gives sufficient notice, and are conclusively presumed to have been foreseen or contemplated by the party as a consequence of his breach of contract.

Hess Die Mold, Inc. v. American Plasti-Plate Corp., 653 S.W.2d 927, 929 (Tex. App.—Tyler 1983, no writ). The general or direct nature of a type of damages is a determination of law to be made by the court. No question should be submitted concerning the foreseeability of direct damages; even if the evidence shows that such damages were not factually foreseeable to the parties, recovery is permitted if the damages are properly characterized by the court as direct rather than consequential. *American Bank v. Thompson*, 660 S.W.2d 831, 834 (Tex. App.—Waco 1983, writ ref'd n.r.e.).

Even damages usually not considered recoverable may be deemed direct damages if they stem as a matter of law from the breach of the contract in question. *See Cactus Utility Co. v. Larson*, 709 S.W.2d 709, 716 (Tex. App.—Corpus Christi 1986), *rev'd in part on other grounds*, 730 S.W.2d 640 (Tex. 1987) (expert witness fee, for accountant, recoverable as direct damages for breach of agreement to provide accounting services).

Benefit of the bargain and remedial damages. Whether difference in value or cost of repair is the proper measure of damages depends on the particular facts and circumstances in each case. *Fidelity & Deposit Co. of Maryland v. Stool*, 607 S.W.2d 17, 21

(Tex. Civ. App.—Tyler 1980, no writ); *see also Smith v. Kinslow*, 598 S.W.2d 910 (Tex. Civ. App.—Dallas 1980, no writ); *P.G. Lake, Inc. v. Sheffield*, 438 S.W.2d 952 (Tex. Civ. App.—Tyler 1969, writ ref'd n.r.e.).

Loss of contractual profit. Lost profits from collateral contracts are generally classified as consequential damages. Profits lost from the actual contract in question, however, are direct damages for the seller. *Continental Holdings, Ltd. v. Leahy*, 132 S.W.3d 471, 475 (Tex. App.—Eastland 2003, no pet.).

Lost profit plus capital expenditures. If the plaintiff has incurred expenses in preparation or performance and reasonably expected to recoup that investment as well as make a profit, this lost profit plus capital expenditures may be an appropriate measure of damages. *Houston Chronicle Publishing Co. v. McNair Trucklease, Inc.*, 519 S.W.2d 924, 929–31 (Tex. Civ. App.—Houston [1st Dist.] 1975, writ ref'd n.r.e.).

Reliance damages. The plaintiff may elect to recover expenditures made in preparation or performance instead of claiming lost benefit of the bargain or profit damages. If the plaintiff makes this election because he would have lost money had the contract been completed and the defendant proves the amount of loss avoided as a result of the breach, the jury should also be instructed to deduct those prospective losses from the reliance damages. *Mistletoe Express Service v. Locke*, 762 S.W.2d 637 (Tex. App.—Texarkana 1988, no writ).

Mitigation damages. Although normally raised defensively, the reasonable expenses of mitigating an economic loss are recoverable as actual damages for breach of contract. *Hycel, Inc. v. Wittstruck*, 690 S.W.2d 914, 924 (Tex. App.—Waco 1985, writ dism'd).

Incidental damages. A variety of expenditures and other incidental damages may be recoverable as direct damages, depending on the particular facts and circumstances of each case. *See, e.g.*, *Cactus Utility Co.*, 709 S.W.2d at 716 (accountant's fees); *LaChance v. Hollenbeck*, 695 S.W.2d 618 (Tex. App.—Austin 1985, writ ref'd n.r.e.) (improvements to real property); *Anderson Development Corp. v. Coastal States Crude Gathering Co.*, 543 S.W.2d 402 (Tex. Civ. App.—Houston [14th Dist.] 1976, writ ref'd n.r.e.) (additional salaries and expenses for equipment, maintenance, and supervision). Whether any particular incidental damages are characterized as direct or consequential is, as discussed above, a question for the court. If a claimed expense is deemed consequential, it should be submitted as such, using the form in PJC 115.4.

UCC cases. If the contract is for the sale of goods, the damages instructions should be drafted to incorporate the appropriate damages provisions in Tex. Bus. & Com. Code §§ 2.701–.724 (Tex. UCC). The following examples are illustrative only, using only a few damages provisions in the Uniform Commercial Code.

Sample A—(§ 2.708) Seller's damages for nonacceptance

The difference between the market price of the goods at the time and place *Paul Payne* was to tender them to *Don Davis* and the unpaid contract price.

Sample B—(§ 2.710) Seller's incidental damages

Commercially reasonable charges, expenses, or commissions *Paul Payne* incurred in stopping delivery of goods.

Commercially reasonable charges *Paul Payne* incurred for transportation, care, and custody of goods in connection with their return or resale.

Sample C—(§ 2.713) Buyer's damages for nondelivery

The difference between the market price at the time *Paul Payne* learned of *Don Davis*'s failure to comply and the contract price.

PJC 115.4 Instructions on Consequential Damages—Contracts

Lost profits that were a natural, probable, and foreseeable consequence of *Don Davis*'s failure to comply.

Damage to credit reputation that was a natural, probable, and foreseeable consequence of *Don Davis*'s failure to comply.

COMMENT

When to use. PJC 115.4, with its added element of foreseeability, should be used for recoverable elements of consequential damages that do not, as a matter of law, directly flow from the defendant's breach. *See Stuart v. Bayless*, 964 S.W.2d 920, 921 (Tex. 1998). See PJC 115.3 Comment.

Foreseeability. Consequential damages may be recovered only if proved to be the "natural, probable, and foreseeable consequence" of the defendant's breach. *Mead v. Johnson Group, Inc.*, 615 S.W.2d 685, 687 (Tex. 1981). The instruction does not state to whom the damage must be foreseeable. In *Mead*, 615 S.W.2d at 687, the court indirectly gave conflicting answers to this question, recognizing both the rule in *Hadley v. Baxendale*, 9 Exch. 341, 156 Eng. Rep. 145 (1854) (both parties), and the rule in *Restatement (Second) of Contracts* § 365 (1981) (party in breach).

Caveat. Damages usually characterized as consequential may be deemed direct if they are so directly related to the contract that they stem as a matter of law from the breach. Conversely, not all factually foreseeable damages are legally recoverable. *See Myrtle Springs Reverted Independent School District v. Hogan*, 705 S.W.2d 707, 710 (Tex. App.—Texarkana 1985, writ ref'd n.r.e.), *cert. denied*, 480 U.S. 906 (1987) (loss of earning capacity and mental anguish not recoverable for breach of teaching contract).

Lost profits. If lost profits are not proven with reasonable certainty but are merely speculative, no recovery is allowed as a matter of law, and this instruction should not be included in the damages question. *Texas Instruments, Inc. v. Teletron Energy Management, Inc.*, 877 S.W.2d 276, 278–81 (Tex. 1994). If, however, there is legally sufficient evidence of lost profits, a fact question is raised. *Southwest Battery Corp. v. Owen*, 115 S.W.2d 1097, 1099 (Tex. 1938). The Committee has not found any cases holding that, once this "no evidence" threshold is passed, any additional instructions should be given concerning the quality or amount of evidence necessary to support the jury's findings.

UCC cases. For transactions covered by article 2 of the Uniform Commercial Code, see Tex. Bus. & Com. Code § 2.715(b)(1) (Tex. UCC) (buyer's consequential damages).

PJC 115.5 Question on Promissory Estoppel—Reliance Damages

[Insert predicate, PJC 115.1.]

QUESTION ______

What sum of money, if any, if paid now in cash, would fairly and reasonably compensate *Paul Payne* for *his* damages, if any, that resulted from *his* reliance on *Don Davis*'s promise?

Consider the following elements of damages, if any, and none other.

[Insert appropriate instructions.]

Do not add any amount for interest on damages, if any.

Answer separately in dollars and cents for damages, if any.

a. [*Element A*] sustained in the past.

Answer: _______________

b. [*Element A*] that, in reasonable probability, will be sustained in the future.

Answer: _______________

c. [*Element B*] sustained in the past.

Answer: _______________

d. [*Element B*] that, in reasonable probability, will be sustained in the future.

Answer: _______________

COMMENT

When to use. PJC 115.5 and appropriate instructions tailored to the specific reliance damages alleged by the plaintiff should be submitted following the liability question for promissory estoppel. See PJC 101.41.

Reliance damages only. In a claim based on promissory estoppel, the plaintiff is not entitled to recover expectancy damages or to receive the full benefit of the bargain. Only reliance damages are allowed. *Fretz Construction Co. v. Southern National Bank*, 626 S.W.2d 478, 483 (Tex. 1981); *Wheeler v. White*, 398 S.W.2d 93, 96–97 (Tex. 1965).

Elements of damages submitted separately. The Committee generally recommends that multiple elements of damages be separately submitted to the jury. *Harris County v. Smith*, 96 S.W.3d 230, 233–34 (Tex. 2002) (broad-form submission of multiple elements of damages may lead to harmful error if there is a proper objection raising insufficiency of the evidence to support one or more of the elements submitted); *see also* Tex. Civ. Prac. & Rem. Code § 41.008(a) ("In an action in which a claimant seeks recovery of damages, the trier of fact shall determine the amount of economic damages separately from the amount of other compensatory damages."). Separating economic from noneconomic damages is required to allow the court to apply the limits on recovery of exemplary damages based on economic and noneconomic damages as required by Tex. Civ. Prac. & Rem. Code § 41.008(b).

Further, "[p]rejudgment interest may not be assessed or recovered on an award of future damages." Tex. Fin. Code § 304.1045 (wrongful death, personal injury, or property damage cases); *see also Johnson & Higgins of Texas, Inc. v. Kenneco Energy, Inc.*, 962 S.W.2d 507, 514, 530 (Tex. 1998) (reconciling equitable prejudgment interest with statutory prejudgment interest); *Perry Roofing Co. v. Olcott*, 744 S.W.2d 929, 931 (Tex. 1988) (unliquidated damages in contract cases); *Cavnar v. Quality Control Parking, Inc.*, 696 S.W.2d 549, 555–56 (Tex. 1985) (personal injury, later extended to other types of cases). Therefore, separation of past and future damages is required.

Elements considered separately. *Golden Eagle Archery, Inc. v. Jackson*, 116 S.W.3d 757, 770 (Tex. 2002), provides an instruction for cases involving undefined or potentially overlapping categories of damages. In those cases, the following language should be substituted for the instruction to consider each element separately:

> Consider the following elements of damages, if any, and none other. You shall not award any sum of money on any element if you have otherwise, under some other element, awarded a sum of money for the same loss. That is, do not compensate twice for the same loss, if any.

Prejudgment interest. Instructing the jury not to add interest is suggested because prejudgment interest, if recoverable, will be calculated by the court at the time of judgment. If interest paid on an obligation is claimed as an element of damages, it may be necessary to modify the instruction on interest.

PJC 115.6 Question on Quantum Meruit Recovery

[Insert predicate, PJC 115.1.]

QUESTION ______

What is the reasonable value of such compensable work at the time and place it was performed?

Answer in dollars and cents, if any.

Answer: _______________

COMMENT

When to use. PJC 115.6 submits the measure of recovery for quantum meruit. *Colbert v. Dallas Joint Stock Land Bank*, 150 S.W.2d 771, 776 (Tex. 1941) (ultimate question is reasonable value of work performed); *see, e.g.*, *Texas Delta Upsilon Foundation v. Fehr*, 307 S.W.2d 124, 127 (Tex. Civ. App.—Austin 1957, writ ref'd n.r.e.); *Blalack v. Johnson*, 293 S.W.2d 811, 813 (Tex. Civ. App.—Texarkana 1956, no writ) (jury questions in these cases quoted with approval). The question must be predicated on an affirmative finding that the work is compensable under this theory. See PJC 101.42.

PJC 115.7 Defensive Instruction on Mitigation—Contract Damages

Do not include in your answer any amount that you find *Paul Payne* could have avoided by the exercise of reasonable care.

COMMENT

When to use. If the evidence raises a question about the plaintiff's failure to mitigate damages after the defendant's actionable conduct, an instruction on mitigation should be included with the damages question. *Alexander & Alexander of Texas, Inc. v. Bacchus Industries, Inc.*, 754 S.W.2d 252, 253 (Tex. App.—El Paso 1988, writ denied); *Cook Consultants, Inc. v. Larson*, 700 S.W.2d 231, 238 (Tex. App.—Dallas 1985, writ ref'd n.r.e.).

Defendant's burden of proof. Failure to mitigate is an affirmative defense, and the burden of proof is on the party asserting such a failure. The supreme court has approved the submission of affirmative defenses by instruction, "provided the burden of proof is properly placed." *Cropper v. Caterpillar Tractor Co.*, 754 S.W.2d 646, 651 (Tex. 1998). Where appropriate, the trial court may specifically state the burden of proof by supplementing the above instruction or the general instructions (see PJC 100.3), or the trial court may submit a question on the defense. The defendant must offer evidence showing not just the plaintiff's lack of care but also the amount by which the damages were increased by such failure to mitigate. *Cocke v. White*, 697 S.W.2d 739, 744 (Tex. App.—Corpus Christi 1985, writ ref'd n.r.e.); *R.A. Corbett Transport, Inc. v. Oden*, 678 S.W.2d 172, 176 (Tex. App.—Tyler 1984, no writ); *Copenhaver v. Berryman*, 602 S.W.2d 540, 544 (Tex. Civ. App.—Corpus Christi 1980, writ ref'd n.r.e.).

Settlement offers and expense to plaintiff of mitigation. The supreme court has held that a mere refusal to accept a settlement offer cannot support submission of a mitigation-of-damages instruction and that the long-standing law of this state requires a claimant to mitigate damages only if it can do so with "trifling expense or with reasonable exertions." *Gunn Infinity v. O'Byrne*, 996 S.W.2d 854, 857 (Tex. 1999), quoting *Great American Insurance Co. v. North Austin Municipal Utility District No. 1*, 908 S.W.2d 415, 426 (Tex. 1995), quoting *Walker v. Salt Flat Water Co.*, 96 S.W.2d 231, 232 (Tex. 1936).

DTPA and Insurance Code. Several appellate opinions have cited the duty to mitigate as grounds for allowing DTPA consumers to recover mitigation expenses as actual damages. *Hycel, Inc. v. Wittstruck*, 690 S.W.2d 914, 924 (Tex. App.—Waco 1985, writ dism'd); *Orkin Exterminating Co. v. Lesassier*, 688 S.W.2d 651, 653 (Tex. App.—Beaumont 1985, no writ). At least three courts have allowed the duty to mitigate to be used defensively in DTPA and Insurance Code suits. *Pinson v. Red Arrow Freight Lines, Inc.*, 801 S.W.2d 14 (Tex. App.—Austin 1990, no writ) (DTPA); *Alexander & Alexander of*

Texas, Inc., 754 S.W.2d at 253 (Insurance Code article 21.21); *Town East Ford Sales, Inc. v. Gray*, 730 S.W.2d 796, 806 (Tex. App.—Dallas 1987, no writ) (DTPA).

Mitigation damages. Mitigation may also be the basis for an affirmative recovery of damages for the plaintiff. See PJC 115.3.

UCC cases. A buyer's recovery of consequential damages is limited to those "which could not reasonably be prevented by cover or otherwise." Tex. Bus. & Com. Code § 2.715(b)(1) (Tex. UCC).

PJC 115.8 Question and Instruction on Deceptive Trade Practice Damages

[Insert predicate, PJC 115.1.]

QUESTION ______

What sum of money, if any, if paid now in cash, would fairly and reasonably compensate *Paul Payne* for *his* damages, if any, that resulted from such conduct?

Consider the following elements of damages, if any, and none other.

[Insert appropriate instructions.
See examples in PJC 115.3 and 115.9.]

In answering questions about damages, answer each question separately. Do not increase or reduce the amount in one answer because of your answer to any other question about damages. Do not speculate about what any party's ultimate recovery may or may not be. Any recovery will be determined by the court when it applies the law to your answers at the time of judgment. Do not add any amount for interest on damages, if any.

Answer separately in dollars and cents for damages, if any.

a. [*Element A*] sustained in the past.

Answer: _______________

b. [*Element A*] that, in reasonable probability, will be sustained in the future.

Answer: _______________

c. [*Element B*] sustained in the past.

Answer: _______________

d. [*Element B*] that, in reasonable probability, will be sustained in the future.

Answer: _______________

COMMENT

When to use. PJC 115.8 should be predicated on a "Yes" answer to PJC 102.1, 102.7, or 102.8, finding a violation of section 17.46(b) of the Texas Deceptive Trade Practices–Consumer Protection Act (Tex. Bus. & Com. Code §§ 17.41–.63) (DTPA), a breach of warranty, or an unconscionable action. It may be adapted for use in most DTPA cases by the addition of appropriate instructions setting out legally available measures of damages. See PJC 115.3 and 115.9.

Instruction required. Failure to instruct the jury on appropriate measures of damages is error. *Jackson v. Fontaine's Clinics, Inc.*, 499 S.W.2d 87, 90 (Tex. 1973).

Alternative measures. The DTPA permits the injured consumer to recover the greatest amount of actual damages caused by the wrongful conduct. Thus, the consumer may submit to the jury alternative measures of damages for the same loss and then elect after the verdict the recovery desired by waiving the surplus findings on damages. *Kish v. Van Note*, 692 S.W.2d 463, 466–67 (Tex. 1985). Similarly, if the DTPA claim is only one of several theories of recovery, each cause of action will have its own damages question inquiring about similar claims of damages.

Separating elements of damages. Based on Tex. Civ. Prac. & Rem. Code § 41.008(a), the Committee suggests separating economic from other compensatory damages. Separating economic from noneconomic and past from future damages is required—

1. to allow the court to apply the limits on recovery of exemplary damages based on economic and noneconomic damages as required by Tex. Civ. Prac. & Rem. Code § 41.008(b);
2. to allow calculation of prejudgment interest on damages in cases governed by Tex. Fin. Code § 304.1045 (for final judgments signed or subject to appeal on or after September 1, 2003) or *Cavnar v. Quality Control Parking, Inc.*, 696 S.W.2d 549 (Tex. 1985); and
3. to allow the court to apply the proper standards for recovery of economic, mental anguish, and additional damages under DTPA § 17.50(b).

See PJC 115.9 for sample damages instructions.

In addition, broad-form submission of multiple elements of damages may lead to harmful error if there is a proper objection raising insufficiency of the evidence to support one or more of the elements submitted. *Harris County v. Smith*, 96 S.W.3d 230, 233–34 (Tex. 2002). If there is any question about the sufficiency of the evidence to support one or more of the elements, the Committee recommends that the elements of damages be separately submitted to the jury.

Instruction on considering elements separately. *Golden Eagle Archery, Inc. v. Jackson*, 116 S.W.3d 757, 770 (Tex. 2002), provides an instruction for cases involving undefined or potentially overlapping categories of damages. In those cases, the following language should be substituted for the instruction to consider each element separately:

> Consider the following elements of damages, if any, and none other. You shall not award any sum of money on any element if you have otherwise, under some other element, awarded a sum of money for the same loss. That is, do not compensate twice for the same loss, if any.

Prejudgment interest. Instructing the jury not to add interest is suggested because prejudgment interest, if recoverable, will be calculated by the court at the time of judgment. If interest paid on an obligation is claimed as an element of damages, it may be necessary to modify the instruction on interest.

PJC 115.9 Sample Instructions—Deceptive Trade Practice Damages

Explanatory note: Damages instructions in DTPA actions are necessarily fact-specific. Unlike most other form instructions in this volume, therefore, the following sample instructions are illustrative only, using a hypothetical situation to give a few examples of how instructions may be worded to submit various legal measures of damages for use in connection with the DTPA damages question, PJC 115.8.

Sample A—Loss of the benefit of the bargain

The difference, if any, in the value of the paint job as it was received and the value it would have had if it had been as [*represented*] [*warranted*]. The difference in value, if any, shall be determined at the time and place the paint job was done.

Sample B—Out of pocket

The difference, if any, in the value of the paint job as it was received and the price *Paul Payne* paid for it. The difference, if any, shall be determined at the time and place the paint job was done.

Sample C—Expenses

The reasonable and necessary cost to repaint the truck.

The reasonable and necessary interest expense that *Paul Payne* incurred on the loan *he* received to pay for the paint job.

Sample D—Loss of use

[The reasonable and necessary expense incurred in renting a car.] [The reasonable rental value of a replacement vehicle.]

Sample E—Lost profits

Paul Payne's lost profits sustained in the past.

Paul Payne's lost profits that, in reasonable probability, *he* will sustain in the future.

Sample F—Lost time

The reasonable value of the time spent by *Paul Payne* correcting or attempting to correct the problems with the paint job.

Sample G—Damage to credit

Damage to *Paul Payne*'s credit reputation sustained in the past.

Damage to *Paul Payne*'s credit reputation that, in reasonable probability, *he* will sustain in the future.

Sample H—Medical care

Medical care in the past.

Medical care that, in reasonable probability, *Paul Payne* will sustain in the future.

Sample I—Loss of earning capacity

Loss of earning capacity sustained in the past.

Loss of earning capacity that, in reasonable probability, *Paul Payne* will sustain in the future.

Sample J—Mental anguish

Paul Payne's mental anguish sustained in the past.

Paul Payne's mental anguish that, in reasonable probability, *he* will sustain in the future.

COMMENT

When to use. See explanatory note above. Because damages instructions in DTPA suits are necessarily fact-specific, no true "pattern" instructions are given—only samples of damages available in DTPA actions. This list is not exhaustive. The samples are illustrative only, adapted to a hypothetical fact situation, and must be rewritten to fit the particular damages raised by the pleadings and proof. Instructions on one or more measures of damages must be submitted with the DTPA damages question, PJC 115.8. In addition to the measures outlined above, any of the common-law measures of damages for breach of contract may be available to the plaintiff in a DTPA action. See PJC 115.3.

Instruction required. Failure to instruct the jury on appropriate measures of damages is error. *Jackson v. Fontaine's Clinics, Inc.*, 499 S.W.2d 87, 90 (Tex. 1973).

Separating elements of damages. Based on Tex. Civ. Prac. & Rem. Code § 41.008(a), the Committee suggests separating economic from other compensatory damages. Separating economic from noneconomic and past from future damages is required—

1. to allow the court to apply the limits on recovery of exemplary damages based on economic and noneconomic damages as required by Tex. Civ. Prac. & Rem. Code § 41.008(b);

2. to allow calculation of prejudgment interest on damages in cases governed by Tex. Fin. Code § 304.1045 (for final judgments signed or subject to appeal on or after September 1, 2003) or *Cavnar v. Quality Control Parking, Inc.*, 696 S.W.2d 549 (Tex. 1985); and

3. to allow the court to apply the proper standards for recovery of economic, mental anguish, and additional damages under Tex. Bus. & Com. Code § 17.50(b) (DTPA).

Available measures. Damages available to DTPA plaintiffs are those recoverable at common law. *Brown v. American Transfer & Storage Co.*, 601 S.W.2d 931, 939 (Tex. 1980). Traditional measures of damages for misrepresentation are the out-of-pocket and benefit-of-the-bargain measures, the first two samples listed above. *W.O. Bankston Nissan, Inc. v. Walters*, 754 S.W.2d 127 (Tex. 1988); *Leyendecker & Associates v. Wechter*, 683 S.W.2d 369, 373 (Tex. 1984). Cost of repair is another recognized measure. *Nobility Homes of Texas, Inc. v. Shivers*, 557 S.W.2d 77, 78 n.1 (Tex. 1977). Cost of repair and permanent reduction in market value after repair are cumulative, and both may be recovered in a proper case. *Ludt v. McCollum*, 762 S.W.2d 575 (Tex. 1988). A wide variety of incidental and consequential damages are recoverable. *Henry S. Miller Co. v. Bynum*, 836 S.W.2d 160, 162 (Tex. 1992); *Kish v. Van Note*, 692 S.W.2d 463, 466–67 (Tex. 1985). Except as specifically provided in DTPA § 17.50(b), (h), damages for bodily injury or death or for the infliction of mental anguish are exempted from DTPA coverage. DTPA § 17.49(e).

Alternative measures. The DTPA permits the injured consumer to recover the greatest amount of actual damages caused by the wrongful conduct. Thus, the consumer may submit to the jury alternative measures of damages for the same loss and then elect after the verdict the recovery desired by waiving the surplus findings on damages. *Kish*, 692 S.W.2d at 466–67.

Separate answer for each element. Broad-form submission of multiple elements of damages may lead to harmful error if there is a proper objection raising insufficiency of the evidence to support one or more of the elements submitted. *Harris County v. Smith*, 96 S.W.3d 230, 233–34 (Tex. 2002). If there is any question about the sufficiency of the evidence to support one or more of the elements, the Committee recommends that the elements of damages be separately submitted to the jury.

Loss of use. The consumer does not need to actually incur out-of-pocket expenses to recover for loss of use of an item. Evidence of the reasonable rental value of the substitute is sufficient. *Luna v. North Star Dodge Sales*, 667 S.W.2d 115, 118–19 (Tex. 1984).

Expenses. Recoverable damages include reasonably necessary expenses shown to be factually caused by the defendant's conduct. *Kish*, 692 S.W.2d at 466. In *Jacobs v. Danny Darby Real Estate, Inc.*, 750 S.W.2d 174, 175 n.2 (Tex. 1988), the supreme court raised, but because it was not asserted by point of error, left unanswered, the question of whether those expenses must be proved reasonable and necessary.

Lost time. See *Village Mobile Homes, Inc. v. Porter*, 716 S.W.2d 543, 549–50 (Tex. App.—Austin 1986, writ ref'd n.r.e.), and *Ybarra v. Saldana*, 624 S.W.2d 948, 951–52 (Tex. App.—San Antonio 1981, no writ), for discussion of damages for lost time.

Consideration paid. Another accepted measure of damages is the consumer's net economic loss, determined by subtracting the amount of any benefits received from the consideration the consumer has paid. For example, in *Woo v. Great Southwestern Acceptance Corp.*, 565 S.W.2d 290, 298 (Tex. Civ. App.—Waco 1978, writ ref'd n.r.e.), the consumer recovered as damages the amount paid for a distributorship, less the value of certain materials she had received, and in *Bynum*, 797 S.W.2d 51, 54 (Tex. App.—Houston [1st Dist.] 1990), *aff'd*, 836 S.W.2d 160 (Tex. 1992), the consumer recovered the amounts spent to open a business, less the amount he recouped when the business was sold. If the consumer receives nothing or if what is received is worthless, then the recovery under this measure of damages would be simply the consideration paid. *Vogelsang v. Reece Import Autos, Inc.*, 745 S.W.2d 47, 48 (Tex. App.—Dallas 1987, no writ) (citation omitted). In addition to being a measure of damages, restoration of money paid is available under a theory of rescission and restitution in DTPA § 17.50(b)(3). *Carrow v. Bayliner Marine Corp.*, 781 S.W.2d 691, 696 (Tex. App.—Austin 1989, no writ); *Green Tree Acceptance, Inc. v. Pierce*, 768 S.W.2d 416, 419 (Tex. App.—Tyler 1989, no writ); *Smith v. Kinslow*, 598 S.W.2d 910, 915 (Tex. Civ. App.—Dallas 1980, no writ).

Medical care. If there is a question whether medical expenses are reasonable or medical care is necessary, the phrase *Reasonable expenses for necessary medical care* should be substituted for the phrase *Medical care* in sample *H*.

No foreseeability required. Proof of foreseeability is not required to recover consequential damages, such as lost profits, under the DTPA. *Hycel, Inc. v. Wittstruck*, 690 S.W.2d 914, 922–23 (Tex. App.—Waco 1985, writ dism'd); *cf. Investors, Inc. v. Hadley*, 738 S.W.2d 737 (Tex. App.—Austin 1987, writ denied).

Mental anguish. Mental anguish damages may be recoverable in DTPA actions if the trier of fact finds the conduct was committed knowingly, DTPA § 17.50(b)(1), or if a claimant is granted the right to bring a cause of action under the DTPA by "another law," DTPA § 17.50(h).

[PJC 115.10 is reserved for expansion.]

PJC 115.11 Question on Additional Damages—Deceptive Trade Practices

[Insert predicate, PJC 115.1.]

QUESTION ______

What sum of money, if any, in addition to actual damages, should be awarded to *Paul Payne* against *Don Davis* because *Don Davis*'s conduct was committed knowingly [*intentionally*]?

Answer in dollars and cents, if any.

Answer: _______________

COMMENT

When to use. PJC 115.11 should be predicated on a jury finding that the defendant's deceptive trade practice, breach of warranty, or unconscionable act was committed knowingly or intentionally. See PJC 102.21.

Factors to consider. In light of the constitutional concerns raised in *Transportation Insurance Co. v. Moriel*, 879 S.W.2d 10, 26–30 (Tex. 1994), an instruction on the exemplary damages factors set out at PJC 115.37 should be submitted with the question at PJC 115.11. *See also TXO Production Corp. v. Alliance Resources Corp.*, 509 U.S. 443 (1993); *Pacific Mutual Life Insurance Co. v. Haslip*, 499 U.S. 1 (1991). Some trial courts have, without objection, given instructions similar to the definition of exemplary damages in connection with submission of these DTPA enhancement damages. *Ortiz v. Flintkote Co.*, 761 S.W.2d 531, 537 (Tex. App.—Corpus Christi 1988, writ denied); *Rendon v. Sanchez*, 737 S.W.2d 122, 126 (Tex. App.—San Antonio 1987, no writ).

Treble damages.

A. *DTPA suits.* A finding of knowing or intentional conduct is required for any award of discretionary damages. Tex. Bus. & Com. Code § 17.50(b)(1) (DTPA). See PJC 102.21.

B. *Insurance Code chapter 541 suits.* The Insurance Code makes additional damages discretionary with the trier of fact if the defendant acted knowingly. The plaintiff should submit the question of knowing conduct as in PJC 102.21 and then should ask the jury to determine the amount of additional damages as in PJC 115.11. *See* Tex. Ins. Code § 541.152(b).

Recovery of treble damages is the same whether the claim is brought directly under chapter 541 or is brought through DTPA § 17.50(a)(4). In *Vail v. Texas Farm Bureau*

Mutual Insurance Co., 754 S.W.2d 129, 137 (Tex. 1988), the supreme court held that this DTPA section "incorporates article 21.21 [now chapter 541] . . . in its entirety," including its treble damages provision.

Cap on treble damages. The maximum recovery under DTPA § 17.50(b)(1) is treble damages. *Jim Walter Homes, Inc. v. Valencia*, 690 S.W.2d 239, 241 (Tex. 1985). Rather than submit to the jury the rather convoluted formula in section 17.50(b)(1), it is preferable to have the jury supply whatever amount it wishes as "additional damages" and have the court impose the statutory ceiling on the recovery actually awarded at judgment.

PJC 115.12 Contribution—Deceptive Trade Practices Act and Insurance Code Chapter 541 (Comment)

DTPA and Insurance Code incorporate existing principles. DTPA section 17.555 provides that a DTPA defendant "may seek contribution or indemnity from one who, under the statute law or at common law, may have liability for the damaging event of which the consumer complains." Tex. Bus. & Com. Code § 17.555 (DTPA). No new contribution scheme was created; rather, the section incorporates "existing principles of contribution and indemnity law into DTPA cases." *Plas-Tex, Inc. v. U.S. Steel Corp.*, 772 S.W.2d 442, 446 (Tex. 1989). Though the Insurance Code does not have a section like DTPA § 17.555 incorporating existing contribution principles, the supreme court applied the original statutory pro rata scheme in chapter 32 of the Civil Practice and Remedies Code to an article 21.21 (now chapter 541) case in *Stewart Title Guaranty Co. v. Sterling*, 822 S.W.2d 1, 6 n.7 (Tex. 1991).

1995 DTPA amendments. In DTPA causes of action accruing on or after September 1, 1995, and for all such suits filed on or after September 1, 1996, contribution is governed by chapter 33 of the Texas Civil Practice and Remedies Code. *See* Tex. Civ. Prac. & Rem. Code § 33.002(a)(2); *see also* Acts 1995, 74th Leg., R.S., ch. 414, § 20(b) (H.B. 668), eff. Sept. 1, 1995. For a discussion and a sample submission, see PJC 115.35 comment, "Contribution defendants."

PJC 115.13 Question and Instruction on Actual Damages under Insurance Code Chapter 541

[Insert predicate, PJC 115.1.]

QUESTION ______

What sum of money, if any, if paid now in cash, would fairly and reasonably compensate *Paul Payne* for *his* damages, if any, that were caused by such unfair or deceptive act or practice?

Consider the following elements of damages, if any, and none other.

[Insert appropriate instructions. See examples in PJC 115.9.]

In answering questions about damages, answer each question separately. Do not increase or reduce the amount in one answer because of your answer to any other question about damages. Do not speculate about what any party's ultimate recovery may or may not be. Any recovery will be determined by the court when it applies the law to your answers at the time of judgment. Do not add any amount for interest on damages, if any.

Answer separately in dollars and cents for damages, if any.

a. [*Element A*] sustained in the past.

Answer: _______________

b. [*Element A*] that, in reasonable probability, will be sustained in the future.

Answer: _______________

c. [*Element B*] sustained in the past.

Answer: _______________

d. [*Element B*] that, in reasonable probability, will be sustained in the future.

Answer: _______________

COMMENT

When to use. PJC 115.13 should be used if the insured is claiming damages for a violation of Tex. Ins. Code ch. 541. PJC 115.13 should be predicated on a "Yes" answer to PJC 102.14.

Instruction required. PJC 115.13 *may not* be submitted without an instruction on the appropriate measures of damages. *See Jackson v. Fontaine's Clinics, Inc.*, 499 S.W.2d 87, 90 (Tex. 1973). See PJC 115.9 for sample instructions.

Policy benefits. The supreme court held in *Vail v. Texas Farm Bureau Mutual Insurance Co.*, 754 S.W.2d 129, 136 (Tex. 1988), that policy benefits were recoverable as a matter of law. Subsequent cases have limited *Vail* and held that a causation finding may nonetheless be required. *See Twin City Fire Insurance Co. v. Davis*, 904 S.W.2d 663 (Tex. 1995); *Seneca Resources Corp. v. Marsh & McLennan, Inc.*, 911 S.W.2d 144 (Tex. App.—Houston [1st Dist.] 1995, no writ); *Beaston v. State Farm Life Insurance Co.*, 861 S.W.2d 268 (Tex. App.—Austin 1993), *rev'd on other grounds*, 907 S.W.2d 430 (Tex. 1995). Unless both the amount and causation of policy benefits as damages are conclusively established, the Committee believes it prudent to submit this element of damages to the jury.

Mental anguish. Mental anguish damages may not be recovered under the DTPA or Insurance Code chapter 541 unless a knowing violation is shown. *Beaston*, 907 S.W.2d at 435–36 (former article 21.21).

Elements of damages submitted separately. The Committee generally recommends that multiple elements of damages be separately submitted to the jury. *Harris County v. Smith*, 96 S.W.3d 230, 233–34 (Tex. 2002) (broad-form submission of multiple elements of damages may lead to harmful error if there is a proper objection raising insufficiency of the evidence to support one or more of the elements submitted); *see also* Tex. Civ. Prac. & Rem. Code § 41.008(a) ("In an action in which a claimant seeks recovery of damages, the trier of fact shall determine the amount of economic damages separately from the amount of other compensatory damages."). Separating economic from noneconomic damages is required to allow the court to apply the limits on recovery of exemplary damages based on economic and noneconomic damages as required by Tex. Civ. Prac. & Rem. Code § 41.008(b).

Further, "[p]rejudgment interest may not be assessed or recovered on an award of future damages." Tex. Fin. Code § 304.1045 (wrongful death, personal injury, or property damage cases); *see also Johnson & Higgins of Texas, Inc. v. Kenneco Energy, Inc.*, 962 S.W.2d 507, 514, 530 (Tex. 1998) (reconciling equitable prejudgment interest with statutory prejudgment interest); *Perry Roofing Co. v. Olcott*, 744 S.W.2d 929, 931 (Tex. 1988) (unliquidated damages in contract cases); *Cavnar v. Quality Control Parking, Inc.*, 696 S.W.2d 549, 555–56 (Tex. 1985) (personal injury, later extended to other types of cases). Therefore, separation of past and future damages is required.

Elements considered separately. *Golden Eagle Archery, Inc. v. Jackson*, 116 S.W.3d 757, 770 (Tex. 2002), provides an instruction for cases involving undefined or potentially overlapping categories of damages. In those cases, the following language should be substituted for the instruction to consider each element separately:

> Consider the following elements of damages, if any, and none other. You shall not award any sum of money on any element if you have otherwise, under some other element, awarded a sum of money for the same loss. That is, do not compensate twice for the same loss, if any.

Prejudgment interest. Instructing the jury not to add interest is suggested because prejudgment interest, if recoverable, will be calculated by the court at the time of judgment. If interest paid on an obligation is claimed as an element of damages, it may be necessary to modify the instruction on interest.

PJC 115.14 Question and Instruction on Actual Damages for Breach of Duty of Good Faith and Fair Dealing

[Insert predicate, PJC 115.1.]

QUESTION ______

What sum of money, if any, if paid now in cash, would fairly and reasonably compensate *Paul Payne* for *his* damages, if any, that were proximately caused by such conduct?

[Insert definition of proximate cause, PJC 100.9.]

Consider the following elements of damages, if any, and none other.

[Insert appropriate instructions. See sample instructions in PJC 115.9 for format.]

In answering questions about damages, answer each question separately. Do not increase or reduce the amount in one answer because of your answer to any other question about damages. Do not speculate about what any party's ultimate recovery may or may not be. Any recovery will be determined by the court when it applies the law to your answers at the time of judgment. Do not add any amount for interest on damages, if any.

Answer separately in dollars and cents for damages, if any.

a. [*Element A*] sustained in the past.

Answer: ______________

b. [*Element A*] that, in reasonable probability, will be sustained in the future.

Answer: ______________

c. [*Element B*] sustained in the past.

Answer: ______________

d. [*Element B*] that, in reasonable probability, will be sustained in the future.

Answer: ______________

COMMENT

When to use. PJC 115.14 should be used if the insured is claiming damages other than policy benefits. PJC 115.14 should be predicated on a "Yes" answer to PJC 103.1.

Instruction required. PJC 115.14 *may not* be submitted without an instruction on the appropriate measures of damages. *See Jackson v. Fontaine's Clinics, Inc.*, 499 S.W.2d 87, 90 (Tex. 1973). See PJC 115.9 for sample instructions.

Proximate cause. For a definition of proximate cause, see PJC 100.9.

Policy benefits. Unpaid benefits due under the policy may or may not be recoverable as damages, depending on the circumstances of the case. *See Twin City Fire Insurance Co. v. Davis*, 904 S.W.2d 663 (Tex. 1995); *Seneca Resources Corp. v. Marsh & McLennan, Inc.*, 911 S.W.2d 144 (Tex. App.—Houston [1st Dist.] 1995, no writ). If policy benefits are wrongfully withheld, they are properly submitted as damages. *See Vail v. Texas Farm Bureau Mutual Insurance Co.*, 754 S.W.2d 129, 136 (Tex. 1988) (policy benefits wrongfully withheld recoverable as a matter of law in DTPA or article 21.21 (now chapter 541) case).

Damages other than policy benefits. If there is delay or denial of payment of an insurance claim, there may be personal injury damages, damage to credit, lost profits, and other damages. For sample instructions that may apply, see PJC 115.9.

Elements of damages submitted separately. The Committee generally recommends that multiple elements of damages be separately submitted to the jury. *Harris County v. Smith*, 96 S.W.3d 230, 233–34 (Tex. 2002) (broad-form submission of multiple elements of damages may lead to harmful error if there is a proper objection raising insufficiency of the evidence to support one or more of the elements submitted); *see also* Tex. Civ. Prac. & Rem. Code § 41.008(a) ("In an action in which a claimant seeks recovery of damages, the trier of fact shall determine the amount of economic damages separately from the amount of other compensatory damages."). Separating economic from noneconomic damages is required to allow the court to apply the limits on recovery of exemplary damages based on economic and noneconomic damages as required by Tex. Civ. Prac. & Rem. Code § 41.008(b).

Further, "[p]rejudgment interest may not be assessed or recovered on an award of future damages." Tex. Fin. Code § 304.1045 (wrongful death, personal injury, or property damage cases); *see also Johnson & Higgins of Texas, Inc. v. Kenneco Energy, Inc.*, 962 S.W.2d 507, 514, 530 (Tex. 1998) (reconciling equitable prejudgment interest with statutory prejudgment interest); *Perry Roofing Co. v. Olcott*, 744 S.W.2d 929, 931 (Tex. 1988) (unliquidated damages in contract cases); *Cavnar v. Quality Control Parking, Inc.*, 696 S.W.2d 549, 555–56 (Tex. 1985) (personal injury, later extended to other types of cases). Therefore, separation of past and future damages is required.

Elements considered separately. *Golden Eagle Archery, Inc. v. Jackson*, 116 S.W.3d 757, 770 (Tex. 2002), provides an instruction for cases involving undefined or potentially overlapping categories of damages. In those cases, the following language should be substituted for the instruction to consider each element separately:

> Consider the following elements of damages, if any, and none other. You shall not award any sum of money on any element if you have otherwise, under some other element, awarded a sum of money for the same loss. That is, do not compensate twice for the same loss, if any.

Prejudgment interest. Instructing the jury not to add interest is suggested because prejudgment interest, if recoverable, will be calculated by the court at the time of judgment. If interest paid on an obligation is claimed as an element of damages, it may be necessary to modify the instruction on interest.

PJC 115.15 Remedies for Breach of Fiduciary Duty (Comment)

Jury questions. Whether equitable relief is granted is for the court to decide based on "the equity of the circumstances"; however, the jury must resolve any contested fact issues. *Burrow v. Arce*, 997 S.W.2d 229, 245 (Tex. 1999). Fact disputes for the jury to decide may include the existence of a breach, the agent's culpability, the value of the agent's services, and the existence and amount of any harm to the principal. The court will then decide whether the breach was clear and serious and whether the remedy would be equitable and just. *Burrow*, 997 S.W.2d at 245–46.

Equitable relief generally. Where a fiduciary who breaches his duty has profited or benefited from a transaction with the beneficiary, as described in PJC 104.2, the plaintiff is entitled to equitable relief (such as rescission, constructive trust, profit disgorgement, or fee forfeiture) without having to show that the breach caused damages. *Burrow*, 997 S.W.2d at 238; *Kinzbach Tool Co. v. Corbett-Wallace Corp.*, 160 S.W.2d 509 (Tex. 1942); *see also Restatement (Third) of Agency* § 8.01 cmt. d (2006) (listing remedies).

Rescission. The court may grant rescission of a transaction accomplished by a breach of the defendant's fiduciary duty. *See Allison v. Harrison*, 156 S.W.2d 137, 140 (Tex. 1941) (purchase of land done without full disclosure by the fiduciary was voidable and could be set aside at plaintiff's option, even without proof that the price obtained was unreasonable); *see also Schiller v. Elick*, 240 S.W.2d 997, 1000 (Tex. 1951) (setting aside deed obtained through fiduciary's breach).

Constructive trust. The court may impose a constructive trust to restore property or profits lost through the fiduciary's breach. *Consolidated Gas & Equipment Co. v. Thompson*, 405 S.W.2d 333, 336 (Tex. 1966); *International Bankers Life Insurance Co. v. Holloway*, 368 S.W.2d 567, 577 (Tex. 1963); *Slay v. Burnett Trust*, 187 S.W.2d 377, 388 (Tex. 1945).

Injunction. The court may grant injunctive relief. *Hyde Corp. v. Huffines*, 314 S.W.2d 763, 773 (Tex. 1958) (injunction allowed to prevent damage through abuse of confidence in wrongfully appropriating trade secrets); *Elcor Chemical Corp. v. Agri-Sul, Inc.*, 494 S.W.2d 204, 212 (Tex. Civ. App.—Dallas 1973, writ ref'd n.r.e.) (enjoining unfair use of trade secret by party breaching confidential relationship).

Statutory remedies. Under appropriate circumstances, the court may:

1. compel a trustee to perform the trustee's duties;
2. enjoin the trustee from committing a breach of trust;
3. compel the trustee to redress a breach of trust;
4. order a trustee to account;
5. appoint a receiver to take possession of the trust property and administer the trust;
6. suspend the trustee;

7. remove the trustee when the trustee materially violates a trust, the trustee becomes incompetent, incapacitated, or insolvent, the trustee fails to make a necessary accounting, or the court finds other cause for the trustee's removal;
8. reduce or deny compensation to the trustee;
9. void an act of the trustee, impose a lien or a constructive trust on trust property, or trace trust property of which the trustee wrongfully disposed and recover the property or the proceeds from the property; or
10. "order any other appropriate relief."

Tex. Prop. Code § 114.008(a); *see also* Tex. Civ. Prac. & Rem. Code chs. 64, 65.

Profit disgorgement, fee forfeiture. See PJC 115.16 and 115.17.

Jury questions. Whether equitable relief is granted is for the court to decide based on the equity of the circumstances. However, the jury must resolve any contested fact issues. *Burrow*, 997 S.W.2d at 245. Fact disputes for the jury to decide may include the existence of a breach, the agent's culpability, the value of the agent's services, and the existence and amount of any harm to the principal. The court will then decide whether the breach was clear and serious and whether the remedy would be equitable and just. *Burrow*, 997 S.W.2d at 245–46.

Actual and exemplary damages. In a proper case, in addition to equitable relief, the plaintiff may also recover actual and exemplary damages caused by the fiduciary's breach. *Manges v. Guerra*, 673 S.W.2d 180, 184 (Tex. 1984); *see also Cantu v. Butron*, 921 S.W.2d 344, 351–53 (Tex. App.—Corpus Christi 1996, writ denied). See PJC 115.18 (actual damages for breach of fiduciary duty) and 115.36 and 115.37 (exemplary damages).

PJC 115.16 Question on Profit Disgorgement—Amount of Profit

QUESTION ______

What was the amount of *Don Davis*'s profit in [*describe the transaction in question, e.g., Don Davis's leasing of mineral rights to himself*]?

Answer in dollars and cents, if any.

Answer: _______________

COMMENT

When to use. Profit disgorgement does not present a jury question. If the amount of profit is disputed, however, PJC 115.16 may be used. See PJC 115.15.

Amount of profit. A fiduciary cannot use his position to gain any benefit for himself at the expense of his principal. *Schiller v. Elick*, 240 S.W.2d 997, 999 (Tex. 1951); *Fitz-Gerald v. Hull*, 237 S.W.2d 256, 264–65 (Tex. 1951); *Slay v. Burnett Trust*, 187 S.W.2d 377, 388 (Tex. 1945); *MacDonald v. Follett*, 180 S.W.2d 334, 338 (Tex. 1944). A fiduciary must account for, and yield to the beneficiary, any profit that he makes as a result of a breach of his fiduciary duty. *International Bankers Life Insurance Co. v. Holloway*, 368 S.W.2d 567, 576–77 (Tex. 1963); *Restatement (Third) of Agency* §§ 8.01 cmt. d(1), 8.02, 8.06 (2006).

PJC 115.17 Question on Fee Forfeiture—Amount of Fee

QUESTION ______

What was the amount of *Don Davis*'s fees in [*describe the transaction in question, e.g., Don Davis's brokerage of the real estate transaction*]?

Answer in dollars and cents, if any.

Answer: ______________

COMMENT

When to use. The right to fee forfeiture does not present a jury question. If the amount earned is disputed, however, PJC 115.17 may be used. See PJC 115.15.

Amount of fees forfeited. The traditional rule is that a fiduciary who breaches his fiduciary duties forfeits all fees in the transaction and the right to compensation. *Kinzbach Tool Co. v. Corbett-Wallace Corp.*, 160 S.W.2d 509, 514 (Tex. 1942); *Armstrong v. O'Brien*, 19 S.W. 268, 274 (Tex. 1892); *Murphy v. Canion*, 797 S.W.2d 944, 947 (Tex. App.—Houston [14th Dist.] 1990, no writ); *Russell v. Truitt*, 554 S.W.2d 948, 951 (Tex. Civ. App.—Fort Worth 1977, writ ref'd n.r.e.); *Anderson v. Griffith*, 501 S.W.2d 695, 702 (Tex. Civ. App.—Fort Worth 1973, writ ref'd n.r.e.); *but see Archer v. Griffith*, 390 S.W.2d 735, 741–42 (Tex. 1964) (canceling a contingent fee agreement as exorbitant, but suggesting that quantum meruit recovery might be proper). In *Burrow v. Arce*, 997 S.W.2d 229, 245 (Tex. 1999), the supreme court held that the amount to be forfeited was an equitable determination for the trial court.

Causation not required. It is not necessary to prove that the fiduciary's breach caused damages to have the fiduciary forfeit compensation. *Burrow*, 997 S.W.2d at 240; *Kinzbach Tool Co.*, 160 S.W.2d at 514; *Armstrong*, 19 S.W. at 274.

PJC 115.18 Question on Actual Damages for Breach of Fiduciary Duty

[Insert predicate, PJC 115.1.]

QUESTION ______

What sum of money, if any, if paid now in cash, would fairly and reasonably compensate *Paul Payne* for *his* damages, if any, that were proximately caused by such conduct?

Consider the following elements of damages, if any, and none other.

[Insert appropriate instructions.
See examples in PJC 115.3 and 115.9.]

Do not add any amount for interest on damages, if any.

Answer separately in dollars and cents for damages, if any.

a. [*Element A*] sustained in the past.

Answer: _______________

b. [*Element A*] that, in reasonable probability, will be sustained in the future.

Answer: _______________

c. [*Element B*] sustained in the past.

Answer: _______________

d. [*Element B*] that, in reasonable probability, will be sustained in the future.

Answer: _______________

COMMENT

When to use. Breach of fiduciary duty is an independent tort that will support an award of actual damages. *Manges v. Guerra*, 673 S.W.2d 180, 184 (Tex. 1984). A fiduciary is liable for any loss or damages suffered by the plaintiff. *Slay v. Burnett Trust*, 187 S.W.2d 377, 391 (Tex. 1945); *see also NRC, Inc. v. Huddleston*, 886 S.W.2d 526, 530 (Tex. App.—Austin 1994, no writ); *Restatement (Third) of Trusts* § 205(a) (1992); *Restatement (Third) of Agency* § 8.01 cmt. d (2006). PJC 115.18 may be used when the plaintiff seeks actual damages in addition to equitable relief or as an alternate remedy.

See Cantu v. Butron, 921 S.W.2d 344, 351–53 (Tex. App.—Corpus Christi 1996, writ denied); see also PJC 115.4 and 115.20.

Elements of damages submitted separately. The Committee generally recommends that multiple elements of damages be separately submitted to the jury. *Harris County v. Smith*, 96 S.W.3d 230, 233–34 (Tex. 2002) (broad-form submission of multiple elements of damages may lead to harmful error if there is a proper objection raising insufficiency of the evidence to support one or more of the elements submitted); *see also* Tex. Civ. Prac. & Rem. Code § 41.008(a) ("In an action in which a claimant seeks recovery of damages, the trier of fact shall determine the amount of economic damages separately from the amount of other compensatory damages."). Separating economic from noneconomic damages is required to allow the court to apply the limits on recovery of exemplary damages based on economic and noneconomic damages as required by Tex. Civ. Prac. & Rem. Code § 41.008(b).

Further, "[p]rejudgment interest may not be assessed or recovered on an award of future damages." Tex. Fin. Code § 304.1045 (wrongful death, personal injury, or property damage cases); *see also Johnson & Higgins of Texas, Inc. v. Kenneco Energy, Inc.*, 962 S.W.2d 507, 514, 530 (Tex. 1998) (reconciling equitable prejudgment interest with statutory prejudgment interest); *Perry Roofing Co. v. Olcott*, 744 S.W.2d 929, 931 (Tex. 1988) (unliquidated damages in contract cases); *Cavnar v. Quality Control Parking, Inc.*, 696 S.W.2d 549, 555–56 (Tex. 1985) (personal injury, later extended to other types of cases). Therefore, separation of past and future damages is required.

Elements considered separately. *Golden Eagle Archery, Inc. v. Jackson*, 116 S.W.3d 757, 770 (Tex. 2002), provides an instruction for cases involving undefined or potentially overlapping categories of damages. In those cases, the following language should be substituted for the instruction to consider each element separately:

> Consider the following elements of damages, if any, and none other. You shall not award any sum of money on any element if you have otherwise, under some other element, awarded a sum of money for the same loss. That is, do not compensate twice for the same loss, if any.

Prejudgment interest. Instructing the jury not to add interest is suggested because prejudgment interest, if recoverable, will be calculated by the court at the time of judgment. If interest paid on an obligation is claimed as an element of damages, it may be necessary to modify the instruction on interest.

PJC 115.19 Question and Instruction on Direct Damages Resulting from Fraud

[Insert predicate, PJC 115.1.]

QUESTION ______

What sum of money, if any, if paid now in cash, would fairly and reasonably compensate *Paul Payne* for *his* damages, if any, that resulted from such fraud?

Consider the following elements of damages, if any, and none other.

[Insert appropriate instructions. See sample instructions in PJC 115.3 and 115.9 for format.]

In answering questions about damages, answer each question separately. Do not increase or reduce the amount in one answer because of your answer to any other question about damages. Do not speculate about what any party's ultimate recovery may or may not be. Any recovery will be determined by the court when it applies the law to your answers at the time of judgment. Do not add any amount for interest on damages, if any.

Answer separately in dollars and cents for damages, if any.

a. [*Element A*] sustained in the past.

Answer: ______________

b. [*Element A*] that, in reasonable probability, will be sustained in the future.

Answer: ______________

c. [*Element B*] sustained in the past.

Answer: ______________

d. [*Element B*] that, in reasonable probability, will be sustained in the future.

Answer: ______________

COMMENT

When to use. PJC 115.19 should be predicated on a "Yes" answer to PJC 105.1 or 105.7 and may be adapted for use in most fraud cases by the addition of appropriate instructions setting out legally available measures of direct damages. See PJC 115.3 and 115.9. If only one measure of damages is supported by the pleadings and proof, the measure may be incorporated into the question.

Instruction required. PJC 115.19 *may not* be submitted without an instruction on the appropriate measures of damages. *See Jackson v. Fontaine's Clinics, Inc.*, 499 S.W.2d 87, 90 (Tex. 1973). See PJC 115.3 and 115.9 for sample instructions.

Direct damages. PJC 115.19 should be used only for the submission of direct damages in fraud cases. For a discussion of direct damages, see PJC 115.3 Comment. In fraud cases, direct damages are sometimes referred to as general damages—that is, damages that are the necessary and usual result of the wrong complained of. *Airborne Freight Corp. v. C.R. Lee Enterprises*, 847 S.W.2d 289, 295 (Tex. App.—El Paso 1992, writ denied). The measure of direct damages in fraud cases has been held to be either "out of pocket" or "benefit of the bargain." *Streller v. Hecht*, 859 S.W.2d 114, 116 (Tex. App.—Houston [14th Dist.] 1993, writ denied); *LSR Joint Venture No. 2 v. Callewart*, 837 S.W.2d 693, 701–02 (Tex. App.—Dallas 1992, writ denied); *Matthews v. AmWest Savings Ass'n*, 825 S.W.2d 552, 554 (Tex. App.—Beaumont 1992, writ denied). However, the benefit-of-the-bargain measure is not available for a fraudulent-inducement claim when there is no enforceable contract. *Haase v. Glazner*, 62 S.W.3d 795, 799–800 (Tex. 2001).

PJC 115.20 may be used to submit consequential damages, and PJC 115.37 may be used to submit exemplary damages.

Elements of damages submitted separately. The Committee generally recommends that multiple elements of damages be separately submitted to the jury. *Harris County v. Smith*, 96 S.W.3d 230, 233–34 (Tex. 2002) (broad-form submission of multiple elements of damages may lead to harmful error if there is a proper objection raising insufficiency of the evidence to support one or more of the elements submitted); *see also* Tex. Civ. Prac. & Rem. Code § 41.008(a) ("In an action in which a claimant seeks recovery of damages, the trier of fact shall determine the amount of economic damages separately from the amount of other compensatory damages."). Separating economic from noneconomic damages is required to allow the court to apply the limits on recovery of exemplary damages based on economic and noneconomic damages as required by Tex. Civ. Prac. & Rem. Code § 41.008(b).

Further, "[p]rejudgment interest may not be assessed or recovered on an award of future damages." Tex. Fin. Code § 304.1045 (wrongful death, personal injury, or property damage cases); *see also Johnson & Higgins of Texas, Inc. v. Kenneco Energy, Inc.*, 962 S.W.2d 507, 514, 530 (Tex. 1998) (reconciling equitable prejudgment interest with statutory prejudgment interest); *Perry Roofing Co. v. Olcott*, 744 S.W.2d 929, 931 (Tex.

1988) (unliquidated damages in contract cases); *Cavnar v. Quality Control Parking, Inc.*, 696 S.W.2d 549, 555–56 (Tex. 1985) (personal injury, later extended to other types of cases). Therefore, separation of past and future damages is required.

Elements considered separately. *Golden Eagle Archery, Inc. v. Jackson*, 116 S.W.3d 757, 770 (Tex. 2002), provides an instruction for cases involving undefined or potentially overlapping categories of damages. In those cases, the following language should be substituted for the instruction to consider each element separately:

> Consider the following elements of damages, if any, and none other. You shall not award any sum of money on any element if you have otherwise, under some other element, awarded a sum of money for the same loss. That is, do not compensate twice for the same loss, if any.

Prejudgment interest. Instructing the jury not to add interest is suggested because prejudgment interest, if recoverable, will be calculated by the court at the time of judgment. If interest paid on an obligation is claimed as an element of damages, it may be necessary to modify the instruction on interest.

PJC 115.20 Question and Instruction on Consequential Damages Caused by Fraud

[Insert predicate, PJC 115.1.]

QUESTION ______

What sum of money, if any, if paid now in cash, would fairly and reasonably compensate *Paul Payne* for *his* damages, if any, that were proximately caused by such fraud?

[Insert definition of proximate cause, PJC 100.9.]

Consider the following elements of damages, if any, and none other.

[Insert appropriate instructions. See sample instructions in PJC 115.3 and 115.9 for format, and see PJC 115.4.]

In answering questions about damages, answer each question separately. Do not increase or reduce the amount in one answer because of your answer to any other question about damages. Do not speculate about what any party's ultimate recovery may or may not be. Any recovery will be determined by the court when it applies the law to your answers at the time of judgment. Do not add any amount for interest on damages, if any.

Answer separately in dollars and cents for damages, if any.

a. [*Element A*] sustained in the past.

Answer: ________________

b. [*Element A*] that, in reasonable probability, will be sustained in the future.

Answer: ________________

c. [*Element B*] sustained in the past.

Answer: ________________

d. [*Element B*] that, in reasonable probability, will be sustained in the future.

Answer: ________________

COMMENT

When to use. PJC 115.20 should be predicated on a "Yes" answer to PJC 105.1 or 105.7 and may be adapted for use in most fraud cases by the addition of appropriate instructions setting out legally available measures of damages. See PJC 115.3, 115.4, and 115.9. If only one measure of damages is supported by the pleadings and proof, the measure may be incorporated into the question.

Instruction required. PJC 115.20 *may not* be submitted without an instruction on the appropriate measures of damages. *See Jackson v. Fontaine's Clinics, Inc.*, 499 S.W.2d 87, 90 (Tex. 1973). See PJC 115.3, 115.4, and 115.9 for sample instructions.

Proximate cause—consequential damages. PJC 115.20 should be used only for the submission of consequential or special damages in fraud cases. To be recoverable, such damages must be the "proximate result" of fraud. *Airborne Freight Corp. v. C.R. Lee Enterprises*, 847 S.W.2d 289, 295 (Tex. App.—El Paso 1992, writ denied); *El Paso Development Co. v. Ravel*, 339 S.W.2d 360, 363 (Tex. Civ. App.—El Paso 1960, writ ref'd n.r.e.), *cited and relied on in Trenholm v. Ratcliff*, 646 S.W.2d 927, 933 (Tex. 1983); *see also Morriss-Buick Co. v. Pondrom*, 113 S.W.2d 889, 890 (Tex. 1938) (loss resulting directly and proximately from fraud). For a description of general and special damages, see *Sherrod v. Bailey*, 580 S.W.2d 24, 28 (Tex. Civ. App.—Houston [1st Dist.] 1979, writ ref'd n.r.e.).

PJC 115.19 should be used to submit direct damages, and PJC 115.37 may be used to submit exemplary damages.

Elements of damages submitted separately. The Committee generally recommends that multiple elements of damages be separately submitted to the jury. *Harris County v. Smith*, 96 S.W.3d 230, 233–34 (Tex. 2002) (broad-form submission of multiple elements of damages may lead to harmful error if there is a proper objection raising insufficiency of the evidence to support one or more of the elements submitted); *see also* Tex. Civ. Prac. & Rem. Code § 41.008(a) ("In an action in which a claimant seeks recovery of damages, the trier of fact shall determine the amount of economic damages separately from the amount of other compensatory damages."). Separating economic from noneconomic damages is required to allow the court to apply the limits on recovery of exemplary damages based on economic and noneconomic damages as required by Tex. Civ. Prac. & Rem. Code § 41.008(b).

Further, "[p]rejudgment interest may not be assessed or recovered on an award of future damages." Tex. Fin. Code § 304.1045 (wrongful death, personal injury, or property damage cases); *see also Johnson & Higgins of Texas, Inc. v. Kenneco Energy, Inc.*, 962 S.W.2d 507, 514, 530 (Tex. 1998) (reconciling equitable prejudgment interest with statutory prejudgment interest); *Perry Roofing Co. v. Olcott*, 744 S.W.2d 929, 931 (Tex. 1988) (unliquidated damages in contract cases); *Cavnar v. Quality Control Parking, Inc.*, 696 S.W.2d 549, 555–56 (Tex. 1985) (personal injury, later extended to other types of cases). Therefore, separation of past and future damages is required.

Elements considered separately. *Golden Eagle Archery, Inc. v. Jackson*, 116 S.W.3d 757, 770 (Tex. 2002), provides an instruction for cases involving undefined or potentially overlapping categories of damages. In those cases, the following language should be substituted for the instruction to consider each element separately:

> Consider the following elements of damages, if any, and none other. You shall not award any sum of money on any element if you have otherwise, under some other element, awarded a sum of money for the same loss. That is, do not compensate twice for the same loss, if any.

Prejudgment interest. Instructing the jury not to add interest is suggested because prejudgment interest, if recoverable, will be calculated by the court at the time of judgment. If interest paid on an obligation is claimed as an element of damages, it may be necessary to modify the instruction on interest.

PJC 115.21 Question and Instruction on Monetary Loss Caused by Negligent Misrepresentation

[Insert predicate, PJC 115.1.]

QUESTION ______

What sum of money, if any, if paid now in cash, would fairly and reasonably compensate *Paul Payne* for *his* damages, if any, that were proximately caused by such negligent misrepresentation?

[Insert definition of proximate cause, PJC 100.9.]

Consider the following elements of damages, if any, and none other. Do not add any amount for interest on past damages, if any.

Answer separately in dollars and cents for damages, if any.

The difference, if any, between the value of what *Paul Payne* received in the transaction and the purchase price or value given.

Answer: _______________

The economic loss, if any, otherwise suffered in the past as a consequence of *Paul Payne*'s reliance on the misrepresentation.

Answer: _______________

The economic loss, if any, that in reasonable probability will be sustained in the future as a consequence of *Paul Payne*'s reliance on the misrepresentation.

Answer: _______________

COMMENT

When to use. PJC 115.21 should be predicated on a "Yes" answer to PJC 105.16. If only one measure of damages is supported by the pleadings and proof, the measure may be incorporated into the question.

Instruction required. PJC 115.21 *may not* be submitted without an instruction on the appropriate measures of damages. *See Jackson v. Fontaine's Clinics, Inc.*, 499 S.W.2d 87, 90 (Tex. 1973).

Source of instructions. The measures of damages set forth in the instructions are prescribed by *Restatement (Second) of Torts* § 552B (1977) and have been adopted by the Supreme Court of Texas. *Federal Land Bank Ass'n of Tyler v. Sloane*, 825 S.W.2d 439, 442–43 (Tex. 1991); *see also D.S.A., Inc. v. Hillsboro Independent School District*, 973 S.W.2d 662, 663–64 (Tex. 1998). In *D.S.A., Inc.*, the court also recognized that under *Restatement (Second) of Torts* § 311 (1965), a party could recover damages for risk of physical harm if actual physical harm had resulted from negligent misrepresentation. *D.S.A., Inc.*, 973 S.W.2d at 664; *but see Sloane*, 825 S.W.2d at 443 n.4.

Elements of damages submitted separately. The Committee generally recommends that multiple elements of damages be separately submitted to the jury. *Harris County v. Smith*, 96 S.W.3d 230, 233–34 (Tex. 2002) (broad-form submission of multiple elements of damages may lead to harmful error if there is a proper objection raising insufficiency of the evidence to support one or more of the elements submitted); *see also* Tex. Civ. Prac. & Rem. Code § 41.008(a) ("In an action in which a claimant seeks recovery of damages, the trier of fact shall determine the amount of economic damages separately from the amount of other compensatory damages."). Separating economic from noneconomic damages is required to allow the court to apply the limits on recovery of exemplary damages based on economic and noneconomic damages as required by Tex. Civ. Prac. & Rem. Code § 41.008(b).

Further, "[p]rejudgment interest may not be assessed or recovered on an award of future damages." Tex. Fin. Code § 304.1045 (wrongful death, personal injury, or property damage cases); *see also Johnson & Higgins of Texas, Inc. v. Kenneco Energy, Inc.*, 962 S.W.2d 507, 514, 530 (Tex. 1998) (reconciling equitable prejudgment interest with statutory prejudgment interest); *Perry Roofing Co. v. Olcott*, 744 S.W.2d 929, 931 (Tex. 1988) (unliquidated damages in contract cases); *Cavnar v. Quality Control Parking, Inc.*, 696 S.W.2d 549, 555–56 (Tex. 1985) (personal injury, later extended to other types of cases). Therefore, separation of past and future damages is required.

Elements considered separately. *Golden Eagle Archery, Inc. v. Jackson*, 116 S.W.3d 757, 770 (Tex. 2002), provides an instruction for cases involving undefined or potentially overlapping categories of damages. In those cases, the following language should be substituted for the instruction to consider each element separately:

> Consider the following elements of damages, if any, and none other. You shall not award any sum of money on any element if you have otherwise, under some other element, awarded a sum of money for the same loss. That is, do not compensate twice for the same loss, if any.

Parallel theories. If the negligent misrepresentation cause of action is only one of several theories of recovery submitted in the charge and any theory has a different legal measure of damages to be applied to a factually similar claim for damages, a separate damages question for each theory may be submitted and the following additional instruction may be included earlier in the charge:

> In answering questions about damages, answer each question separately. Do not increase or reduce the amount in one answer because of

> the instructions in or your answers to any other questions about damages. Do not speculate about what any party's ultimate recovery may or may not be. Any recovery will be determined by the court when it applies the law to your answers at the time of judgment.

Prejudgment interest. Instructing the jury not to add interest is suggested because prejudgment interest, if recoverable, will be calculated by the court at the time of judgment. If interest paid on an obligation is claimed as an element of damages, it may be necessary to modify the instruction on interest.

PJC 115.22 Question on Damages for Intentional Interference with Existing Contract or for Wrongful Interference with Prospective Contractual Relations

[Insert predicate, PJC 115.1.]

QUESTION ______

What sum of money, if any, if paid now in cash, would fairly and reasonably compensate *Paul Payne* for *his* damages, if any, proximately caused by such interference?

[Insert definition of proximate cause, PJC 100.9.]

Consider the following elements of damages, if any, and none other.

[Insert appropriate instructions. See examples in PJC 115.3 and instructions in PJC 115.4.]

Do not add any amount for interest on damages, if any.

Answer separately in dollars and cents for damages, if any.

a. [*Element A*] sustained in the past.

Answer: ______________

b. [*Element A*] that, in reasonable probability, will be sustained in the future.

Answer: ______________

c. [*Element B*] sustained in the past.

Answer: ______________

d. [*Element B*] that, in reasonable probability, will be sustained in the future.

Answer: ______________

COMMENT

When to use. PJC 115.22 should be predicated on a "Yes" answer to PJC 106.1 finding interference with an existing contract or to a question appropriately submitting tortious interference with prospective contractual relations (see the Comment to PJC 106.2). PJC 115.22 is used to establish the proximate cause and actual damages elements of intentional interference with an existing contract as set forth in the comments to PJC 106.1 and of wrongful interference with prospective contractual relations as stated in the comments to PJC 106.2.

Instruction required. PJC 115.22 *may not* be submitted without an instruction on the appropriate measures of damages. *See Jackson v. Fontaine's Clinics, Inc.*, 499 S.W.2d 87, 90 (Tex. 1973). See PJC 115.3 and 115.4 for sample instructions.

Damages. PJC 115.22 submits actual damages in interference cases. For questions submitting exemplary damages, see PJC 115.36 and 115.37 and the Comments accompanying those questions.

The basic measure of damages is the same as for breach of contract. *American Natural Petroleum Co. v. Transcontinental Gas Pipe Line Corp.*, 798 S.W.2d 274, 278 (Tex. 1990) (the "basic measure of actual damages for tortious interference with contract is the same as the measure of damages for breach of the contract interfered with, to put the plaintiff in the same economic position he would have been in had the contract [or relationship] interfered with been actually performed."). Thus, damages for interference with an existing contract or prospective contractual relations include the pecuniary loss of the contract's benefit and consequential losses. *American Natural Petroleum Co.*, 798 S.W.2d at 278. Damages for mental anguish may not be recoverable for an interference claim. *See Creditwatch, Inc. v. Jackson*, 157 S.W.3d 814, 818 (Tex. 2005) (stating that tortious interference does not allow mental anguish damages). *But see Exxon Corp. v. Allsup*, 808 S.W.2d 648, 660 (Tex. App.—Corpus Christi 1991, writ denied) (following *Restatement (Second) of Torts* § 774A (1977), holding loss incurred does not have to be one contemplated by the parties when the contract was made, and allowing recovery for mental anguish).

Elements of damages submitted separately. The Committee generally recommends that multiple elements of damages be separately submitted to the jury. *Harris County v. Smith*, 96 S.W.3d 230, 233–34 (Tex. 2002) (broad-form submission of multiple elements of damages may lead to harmful error if there is a proper objection raising insufficiency of the evidence to support one or more of the elements submitted); *see also* Tex. Civ. Prac. & Rem. Code § 41.008(a) ("In an action in which a claimant seeks recovery of damages, the trier of fact shall determine the amount of economic damages separately from the amount of other compensatory damages."). Separating economic from noneconomic damages is required to allow the court to apply the limits on recovery of exemplary damages based on economic and noneconomic damages as required by Tex. Civ. Prac. & Rem. Code § 41.008(b).

Further, "[p]rejudgment interest may not be assessed or recovered on an award of future damages." Tex. Fin. Code § 304.1045 (wrongful death, personal injury, or property damage cases); *see also Johnson & Higgins of Texas, Inc. v. Kenneco Energy, Inc.*,

962 S.W.2d 507, 514, 530 (Tex. 1998) (reconciling equitable prejudgment interest with statutory prejudgment interest); *Perry Roofing Co. v. Olcott*, 744 S.W.2d 929, 931 (Tex. 1988) (unliquidated damages in contract cases); *Cavnar v. Quality Control Parking, Inc.*, 696 S.W.2d 549, 555–56 (Tex. 1985) (personal injury, later extended to other types of cases). Therefore, separation of past and future damages is required.

Elements considered separately. *Golden Eagle Archery, Inc. v. Jackson*, 116 S.W.3d 757, 770 (Tex. 2002), provides an instruction for cases involving undefined or potentially overlapping categories of damages. In those cases, the following language should be substituted for the instruction to consider each element separately:

> Consider the following elements of damages, if any, and none other. You shall not award any sum of money on any element if you have otherwise, under some other element, awarded a sum of money for the same loss. That is, do not compensate twice for the same loss, if any.

Parallel theories. If theories of recovery other than those addressed in PJC 115.22 are submitted in the charge and any theory has a different legal measure of damages to be applied to a factually similar claim for damages, a separate damages question for each theory may be submitted and the following additional instruction may be included earlier in the charge:

> In answering questions about damages, answer each question separately. Do not increase or reduce the amount in one answer because of the instructions in or your answers to any other questions about damages. Do not speculate about what any party's ultimate recovery may or may not be. Any recovery will be determined by the court when it applies the law to your answers at the time of judgment.

Prejudgment interest. Instructing the jury not to add interest is suggested because prejudgment interest, if recoverable, will be calculated by the court at the time of judgment. If interest paid on an obligation is claimed as an element of damages, it may be necessary to modify the instruction on interest.

[PJC 115.23 is reserved for expansion.]

PJC 115.24 Sample Instructions on Direct and Incidental Damages—Breach of Employment Agreement

Explanatory note: Damages instructions in a breach of an employment agreement case, like contract actions, are necessarily fact-specific and can vary with the circumstances of each case. The elements listed below are those commonly used in employment contract cases but do not represent an exhaustive list. These instructions are to be used in conjunction with the contract damages question, PJC 115.2.

Sample A—Lost earnings

"Lost earnings" equal the present cash value of the employment agreement to the employee had it not been breached, less amounts actually earned.

Sample B—Lost employee benefits other than earnings

"Benefits" include [*sick-leave pay, vacation pay, cost of living increases, profit-sharing benefits, stock options, pension fund benefits, health insurance, life insurance, housing or transportation subsidies, bonuses*].

Sample C—Loss of insurance coverage

Losses incurred as a result of the loss of health, life, dental, or similar insurance coverage.

Sample D—Mitigation expenses

Reasonable and necessary expenses in obtaining other employment.

COMMENT

When to use. See explanatory note above. Because damages instructions are necessarily fact-specific, no true "pattern" instructions are given—only samples of general damages available in employment contract actions. This list is not exhaustive. The samples are illustrative only and must be rewritten to fit the particular damages raised by the pleadings and proof and recoverable under a legally accepted theory.

Measure of damages. The legal measure of damages for the breach of an employment agreement is the present cash value of the agreement to the employee had it not been breached, less any amounts the employee should in the exercise of reasonable diligence be able to earn through other employment. *Gulf Consolidated International, Inc. v.*

Murphy, 658 S.W.2d 565, 566 (Tex. 1983); *Greater Fort Worth & Tarrant County Community Action Agency v. Mims*, 627 S.W.2d 149, 151 (Tex. 1982); *see also Southwest Airlines Co. v. Jaeger*, 867 S.W.2d 824, 835 (Tex. App.—El Paso 1993, writ denied) (approving jury question and instructions on damages for breach of employment contract); *Lone Star Steel Co. v. Wahl*, 636 S.W.2d 217, 221 (Tex. App.—Texarkana 1982, no writ) (measure of damages is all wages past due and all future promised wages less what can be earned by reasonable effort in similar employment). There may be elements of actual damages that are recoverable other than those listed in PJC 115.24.

Separate answer for each element. Broad-form submission of multiple elements of damages may lead to harmful error if there is a proper objection raising insufficiency of the evidence to support one or more of the elements submitted. *Harris County v. Smith*, 96 S.W.3d 230, 233–34 (Tex. 2002). If there is any question about the sufficiency of the evidence to support one or more of the elements, the Committee recommends that the elements of damages be separately submitted to the jury.

Consequential damages. If foreseeability is at issue, see PJC 115.4 and make appropriate modifications.

PJC 115.25 Defensive Instruction on Mitigation—Breach of Employment Agreement Damages

Do not include in your answer any amount that you find *Paul Payne* could have earned by exercising reasonable diligence in seeking other employment.

COMMENT

When to use. PJC 115.25 should be included with the damages question (see PJC 115.2) if the evidence raises a question about the employee's failure to mitigate damages after the employer's actionable conduct. *Gulf Consolidated International, Inc. v. Murphy*, 658 S.W.2d 565, 566 (Tex. 1983); *Southwest Airlines Co. v. Jaeger*, 867 S.W.2d 824, 835 (Tex. App.—El Paso 1993, writ denied).

The general rules concerning mitigation found in the Comment to PJC 115.7 are also applicable to mitigation in employment contracts.

Source of instruction. PJC 115.25 is derived from *Gulf Consolidated International, Inc.*, 658 S.W.2d at 566, and *Lee-Wright, Inc. v. Hall*, 840 S.W.2d 572, 581 (Tex. App.—Houston [1st Dist.] 1992, no writ). See also PJC 115.7.

PJC 115.26 Question and Instruction on Damages for Wrongful Discharge for Refusing to Perform an Illegal Act

QUESTION ______

What sum of money, if any, if paid now in cash, would fairly and reasonably compensate *Paul Payne* for *his* damages, if any, that resulted from such conduct?

Consider the following elements of damages, if any, and none other. Answer separately in dollars and cents for damages, if any.

a. Lost earnings that were sustained in the past.

Answer: _______________

b. Lost earnings that, in reasonable probability, will be sustained in the future.

Answer: _______________

c. Lost employee benefits other than earnings that were sustained in the past.

Answer: _______________

d. Lost employee benefits other than earnings that, in reasonable probability, will be sustained in the future.

Answer: _______________

"Benefits" include [*sick-leave pay, vacation pay, profit-sharing benefits, stock options, pension fund benefits, housing or transportation subsidies, bonuses, monetary losses incurred as a result of the loss of health, life, dental, or similar insurance coverage*].

COMMENT

When to use. PJC 115.26 should be predicated on a "Yes" answer to PJC 107.3, finding wrongful discharge for refusing to perform an illegal act.

Source of question and instruction. No Texas court has specifically addressed the measure of damages under *Sabine Pilot Service, Inc. v. Hauck*, 687 S.W.2d 733 (Tex. 1985); however, the concurring opinion in *Sabine Pilot* suggests that article 8307c (now codified at Tex. Lab. Code § 451.001), prohibiting firing an employee for filing a worker's compensation claim, should serve as a guide. *Sabine Pilot Service, Inc.*, 687

S.W.2d at 736; *see also Worsham Steel Co. v. Arias*, 831 S.W.2d 81, 84 (Tex. App.—El Paso 1992, no writ) (approving above as measures of damages in article 8307c case). There may be other elements of common-law damages, e.g., mental anguish, that are recoverable other than those listed in PJC 115.26. The Committee expresses no opinion concerning the recoverability of these common-law damages.

Mitigation. For a defensive instruction on mitigation, see PJC 115.7 and 115.25.

Elements of damages submitted separately. The Committee generally recommends that multiple elements of damages be separately submitted to the jury. *Harris County v. Smith*, 96 S.W.3d 230, 233–34 (Tex. 2002) (broad-form submission of multiple elements of damages may lead to harmful error if there is a proper objection raising insufficiency of the evidence to support one or more of the elements submitted); *see also* Tex. Civ. Prac. & Rem. Code § 41.008(a) ("In an action in which a claimant seeks recovery of damages, the trier of fact shall determine the amount of economic damages separately from the amount of other compensatory damages."). Separating economic from noneconomic damages is required to allow the court to apply the limits on recovery of exemplary damages based on economic and noneconomic damages as required by Tex. Civ. Prac. & Rem. Code § 41.008(b).

Further, "[p]rejudgment interest may not be assessed or recovered on an award of future damages." Tex. Fin. Code § 304.1045 (wrongful death, personal injury, or property damage cases); *see also Johnson & Higgins of Texas, Inc. v. Kenneco Energy, Inc.*, 962 S.W.2d 507, 514, 530 (Tex. 1998) (reconciling equitable prejudgment interest with statutory prejudgment interest); *Perry Roofing Co. v. Olcott*, 744 S.W.2d 929, 931 (Tex. 1988) (unliquidated damages in contract cases); *Cavnar v. Quality Control Parking, Inc.*, 696 S.W.2d 549, 555–56 (Tex. 1985) (personal injury, later extended to other types of cases). Therefore, separation of past and future damages is required.

Elements considered separately. *Golden Eagle Archery, Inc. v. Jackson*, 116 S.W.3d 757, 770 (Tex. 2002), provides an instruction for cases involving undefined or potentially overlapping categories of damages. In those cases, the following language should be substituted for the instruction to consider each element separately:

> Consider the following elements of damages, if any, and none other. You shall not award any sum of money on any element if you have otherwise, under some other element, awarded a sum of money for the same loss. That is, do not compensate twice for the same loss, if any.

Exemplary damages. No Texas case has established whether exemplary damages are recoverable in a *Sabine Pilot* case. The predicate state of mind or conduct for an award of exemplary damages is set out in Tex. Civ. Prac. & Rem. Code § 41.003(a). See PJC 115.36. *Cf. Azar Nut Co. v. Caille*, 734 S.W.2d 667, 669 (Tex. 1987) (exemplary damages are within article 8307c "reasonable damages suffered by employee" terminated in a retaliatory manner). If exemplary damages are recoverable, see PJC 115.37.

After-acquired evidence of employee misconduct. If the employer has pleaded the discovery of evidence of employee misconduct acquired only after the employee's employment was terminated, see PJC 107.8 for the applicable instruction.

PJC 115.27 Question and Instructions on Damages for Retaliation under Texas Whistleblower Act

QUESTION ______

What sum of money, if any, if paid now in cash, would fairly and reasonably compensate *Paul Payne* for *his* damages, if any, that resulted from such conduct?

Consider the following elements of damages, if any, and none other.

Do not include interest on any amount of damages you may find.

Do not include back pay or interest in calculating compensatory damages, if any.

Answer separately in dollars and cents for damages, if any.

a. Lost wages during the period of suspension or termination.

Answer: ______________

b. Lost employee benefits other than loss of earnings.

"Benefits" include [*sick-leave pay, vacation pay, profit-sharing benefits, stock options, pension fund benefits, housing or transportation subsidies, bonuses, monetary losses incurred as a result of the loss of health, life, dental, or similar insurance coverage*].

Answer: ______________

c. Compensatory damages in the past, which include [*emotional pain and suffering, inconvenience, mental anguish, loss of enjoyment of life, and other noneconomic losses*].

Answer: ______________

d. Compensatory damages in the future, which include [*economic losses, emotional pain and suffering, inconvenience, mental anguish, loss of enjoyment of life, and other noneconomic losses*].

Answer: ______________

COMMENT

When to use. PJC 115.27 should be predicated on a "Yes" answer to PJC 107.4, finding retaliation under the Texas Whistleblower Act, Tex. Gov't Code §§ 554.001–.010.

Source of question and instructions. PJC 115.27 is derived from Tex. Gov't Code § 554.003 and *City of Ingleside v. Kneuper*, 768 S.W.2d 451, 454 (Tex. App.—Austin 1989, writ denied). *See also Texas Department of Human Services v. Green*, 855 S.W.2d 136, 150–51 (Tex. App.—Austin 1993, writ denied).

Statutory relief. Tex. Gov't Code § 554.003 provides for recovery of actual damages and attorney's fees for a violation of the Whistleblower Act. The statute, however, does not define "actual damages." The elements given above are not meant to be exclusive, but rather are those most commonly allowed in employment cases.

The statute also provides for equitable relief in the nature of an injunction or reinstatement of employment and/or benefits, which is to be determined by the trial court. Tex. Gov't Code § 554.003; *see Caballero v. Central Power & Light Co.*, 858 S.W.2d 359 (Tex. 1993) (equitable relief under Texas Commission on Human Rights Act is to be determined by judge).

Mitigation. For a defensive instruction on mitigation, see PJC 115.7 and 115.25.

Attorney's fees. For submission of attorney's fees, see PJC 115.46.

Exemplary damages unavailable, post–June 15, 1995, cases. Exemplary damages are not available under the Texas Whistleblower Act. Tex. Gov't Code § 554.003(a).

Elements of damages submitted separately. The Committee generally recommends that multiple elements of damages be separately submitted to the jury. *Harris County v. Smith*, 96 S.W.3d 230, 233–34 (Tex. 2002) (broad-form submission of multiple elements of damages may lead to harmful error if there is a proper objection raising insufficiency of the evidence to support one or more of the elements submitted); *see also* Tex. Civ. Prac. & Rem. Code § 41.008(a) ("In an action in which a claimant seeks recovery of damages, the trier of fact shall determine the amount of economic damages separately from the amount of other compensatory damages."). Separating economic from noneconomic damages is required to allow the court to apply the limits on recovery of exemplary damages based on economic and noneconomic damages as required by Tex. Civ. Prac. & Rem. Code § 41.008(b).

Further, "[p]rejudgment interest may not be assessed or recovered on an award of future damages." Tex. Fin. Code § 304.1045 (wrongful death, personal injury, or property damage cases); *see also Johnson & Higgins of Texas, Inc. v. Kenneco Energy, Inc.*, 962 S.W.2d 507, 514, 530 (Tex. 1998) (reconciling equitable prejudgment interest with statutory prejudgment interest); *Perry Roofing Co. v. Olcott*, 744 S.W.2d 929, 931 (Tex.

1988) (unliquidated damages in contract cases); *Cavnar v. Quality Control Parking, Inc.*, 696 S.W.2d 549, 555–56 (Tex. 1985) (personal injury, later extended to other types of cases). Therefore, separation of past and future damages is required.

Elements considered separately. *Golden Eagle Archery, Inc. v. Jackson*, 116 S.W.3d 757, 770 (Tex. 2002), provides an instruction for cases involving undefined or potentially overlapping categories of damages. In those cases, the following language should be substituted for the instruction to consider each element separately:

> Consider the following elements of damages, if any, and none other. You shall not award any sum of money on any element if you have otherwise, under some other element, awarded a sum of money for the same loss. That is, do not compensate twice for the same loss, if any.

Prejudgment interest. Instructing the jury not to add interest is suggested because prejudgment interest, if recoverable, will be calculated by the court at the time of judgment. If interest paid on an obligation is claimed as an element of damages, it may be necessary to modify the instruction on interest.

After-acquired evidence of employee misconduct. If the employer has pleaded the discovery of evidence of employee misconduct acquired only after the employee's employment was terminated, see PJC 107.8 for the applicable instruction.

PJC 115.28 Question and Instruction on Damages—Retaliation for Seeking Worker's Compensation Benefits

QUESTION ______

What sum of money, if any, if paid now in cash, would fairly and reasonably compensate *Paul Payne* for *his* damages, if any, that resulted from such conduct?

Consider the following elements of damages, if any, and none other.

Do not include interest on any amount of damages you may find.

Do not include back pay or interest in calculating compensatory damages, if any.

Reduce lost wages, if any, by wages earned, if any, in the past and wages, if any, which in reasonable probability will be earned in the future.

Answer separately in dollars and cents for damages, if any.

a. Lost earnings and employee benefits in the past (between date of [*discharge or discriminatory event*] and today).

Answer: _______________

b. Lost earnings and employee benefits that in reasonable probability will be lost in the future.

Answer: _______________

c. Compensatory damages in the past, which include [*emotional pain and suffering, inconvenience, mental anguish, loss of enjoyment of life, and other noneconomic losses*].

Answer: _______________

d. Compensatory damages in the future, which include [*emotional pain and suffering, inconvenience, mental anguish, loss of enjoyment of life, and other noneconomic losses*].

Answer: _______________

COMMENT

When to use. PJC 115.28 should be predicated on a "Yes" answer to PJC 107.5.

Source of question and instructions. Tex. Lab. Code § 451.002 provides for recovery of reasonable damages. The elements of damages given in PJC 115.28 are not meant to be exclusive, but rather are those most commonly allowed in employment cases. *See, e.g.*, *Carnation Co. v. Borner*, 610 S.W.2d 450, 453–54 (Tex. 1980) (permitting recovery for future lost wages, retirement benefits, and other benefits ascertainable with reasonable certainty); *Pacesetter Corp. v. Barrickman*, 885 S.W.2d 256, 259 (Tex. App.—Tyler 1994, no writ) (award of past and future employee benefits); *Worsham Steel Co. v. Arias*, 831 S.W.2d 81, 85–86 (Tex. App.—El Paso 1992, no writ) (mental anguish as a compensable injury); *DeFord Lumber Co. v. Roys*, 615 S.W.2d 235, 237–38 (Tex. Civ. App.—Dallas 1981, no writ) (award of damages for lost wages in the past). In this instruction, damages for "lost earnings" subsumes the elements of lost earnings and loss of earning capacity. *See Texas Department of Human Services v. Hinds*, 860 S.W.2d 893, 900–901 (Tex. App.—El Paso 1993), *rev'd on other grounds*, 904 S.W.2d 629 (Tex. 1995) (discussing distinction between lost earning capacity and loss of actual earnings).

Equitable relief. In addition to the reasonable damages allowed under Tex. Lab. Code § 451.002, the trial court may reinstate the employee (Tex. Lab. Code § 451.002(b)) or restrain for cause a violation of section 451.001 (Tex. Lab. Code § 451.003).

Mitigation. For a defensive instruction on mitigation, see PJC 115.7 and 115.25.

Exemplary damages. See PJC 115.29 and 115.37.

After-acquired evidence of employee misconduct. If the employer has pleaded the discovery of evidence of employee misconduct acquired only after the employee's employment was terminated, see PJC 107.8 for the applicable instruction. *See Trico Technologies Corp. v. Montiel*, 949 S.W.2d 308 (Tex. 1997).

Elements of damages submitted separately. The Committee generally recommends that multiple elements of damages be separately submitted to the jury. *Harris County v. Smith*, 96 S.W.3d 230, 233–34 (Tex. 2002) (broad-form submission of multiple elements of damages may lead to harmful error if there is a proper objection raising insufficiency of the evidence to support one or more of the elements submitted); *see also* Tex. Civ. Prac. & Rem. Code § 41.008(a) ("In an action in which a claimant seeks recovery of damages, the trier of fact shall determine the amount of economic damages separately from the amount of other compensatory damages."). Separating economic from noneconomic damages is required to allow the court to apply the limits on recovery of exemplary damages based on economic and noneconomic damages as required by Tex. Civ. Prac. & Rem. Code § 41.008(b).

Further, "[p]rejudgment interest may not be assessed or recovered on an award of future damages." Tex. Fin. Code § 304.1045 (wrongful death, personal injury, or property damage cases); *see also Johnson & Higgins of Texas, Inc. v. Kenneco Energy, Inc.*, 962 S.W.2d 507, 514, 530 (Tex. 1998) (reconciling equitable prejudgment interest with statutory prejudgment interest); *Perry Roofing Co. v. Olcott*, 744 S.W.2d 929, 931 (Tex. 1988) (unliquidated damages in contract cases); *Cavnar v. Quality Control Parking, Inc.*, 696 S.W.2d 549, 555–56 (Tex. 1985) (personal injury, later extended to other types of cases). Therefore, separation of past and future damages is required.

Elements considered separately. *Golden Eagle Archery, Inc. v. Jackson*, 116 S.W.3d 757, 770 (Tex. 2002), provides an instruction for cases involving undefined or potentially overlapping categories of damages. In those cases, the following language should be substituted for the instruction to consider each element separately:

> Consider the following elements of damages, if any, and none other. You shall not award any sum of money on any element if you have otherwise, under some other element, awarded a sum of money for the same loss. That is, do not compensate twice for the same loss, if any.

Prejudgment interest. Instructing the jury not to add interest is suggested because prejudgment interest, if recoverable, will be calculated by the court at the time of judgment. If interest paid on an obligation is claimed as an element of damages, it may be necessary to modify the instruction on interest.

PJC 115.29 Predicate Question and Instruction on Exemplary Damages—Retaliation for Seeking Worker's Compensation Benefits—Causes of Action Accruing before September 1, 1997

If you answered "Yes" to Question _____ [*107.5*], then answer the following question. Otherwise, do not answer the following question.

QUESTION ______

Do you find that the harm to *Paul Payne* resulted from actual malice?

"Actual malice" means ill will, spite, evil motive, or purpose to injure another.

Answer "Yes" or "No."

Answer: _______________

COMMENT

When to use. PJC 115.29 should be used for a claim for exemplary damages if the plaintiff alleges retaliation for seeking worker's compensation benefits and the claim accrued before September 1, 1997. For causes accruing after September 1, 1997, see PJC 115.37.

Bifurcation. On timely motion, the trial court must bifurcate the determination of the amount of exemplary damages from the remaining issues. *Transportation Insurance Co. v. Moriel*, 879 S.W.2d 10, 30 (Tex. 1994).

Modification of "factors to consider" in PJC 115.37. Use PJC 115.37 as the question asking the jury to fix the amount of exemplary damages, modifying the "factors to consider" in awarding exemplary damages to read as follows:

a. The nature of the wrong.

b. The frequency of the wrongs committed.

c. The character of the conduct involved.

d. The degree of culpability of *Don Davis*.

e. The situation and sensibilities of the parties involved.

f. The extent to which such conduct offends a public sense of justice and propriety.

g. The size of the award needed to deter similar wrongs in the future.

Moriel, 879 S.W.2d at 27 n.22.

Source of question and instruction. The question and instruction are derived from *Continental Coffee Products Co. v. Cazarez*, 937 S.W.2d 444, 452 (Tex. 1996), and *Clements v. Withers*, 437 S.W.2d 818, 822 (Tex. 1969). Note that Tex. Civ. Prac. & Rem. Code ch. 41 does not apply to any cause of action brought under title 5 of the Texas Labor Code (worker's compensation) that accrued before September 1, 1997.

PJC 115.30 Question and Instruction on Unlawful Employment Practices Damages

QUESTION ______

What sum of money, if any, if paid now in cash, would fairly and reasonably compensate *Paul Payne* for *his* damages, if any, that resulted from such conduct?

Consider the following elements of damages, if any, and none other.

Do not include interest on any amount of damages you may find.

Do not include back pay or interest in calculating compensatory damages, if any.

Answer in dollars and cents for damages, if any.

a. Back pay.

"Back pay" is that amount of wages and employment benefits that *Paul Payne* would have earned if *he* had not been subjected to *his* employer's unlawful conduct less any wages, unemployment compensation benefits or worker's compensation benefits *he* received in the interim.

"Employment benefits" include [*sick-leave pay, vacation pay, profit-sharing benefits, stock options, pension fund benefits, housing or transportation subsidies, bonuses, monetary losses incurred as a result of the loss of health, life, dental, or similar insurance coverage*].

Answer: ______________

b. Compensatory damages in the past, which include [*emotional pain and suffering, inconvenience, mental anguish, loss of enjoyment of life, and other noneconomic losses*].

Answer: ______________

c. Compensatory damages in the future, which include [*economic losses, emotional pain and suffering, inconvenience, mental anguish, loss of enjoyment of life, and other noneconomic losses*].

Answer: ______________

COMMENT

When to use. PJC 115.30 should be predicated on a "Yes" answer to PJC 107.6.

Source of question and instruction. PJC 115.30 is based on Tex. Lab. Code §§ 21.258, 21.2585. *See also Speer v. Presbyterian Children's Home & Service Agency*, 847 S.W.2d 227, 228 (Tex. 1993) (Texas Commission on Human Rights Act specifically allows for compensatory relief).

Equitable relief. In addition to actual and exemplary damages allowed under Tex. Lab. Code § 21.2585 and attorney's fees under Tex. Lab. Code § 21.259, on a finding that an employer has engaged in unlawful employment practices, the trial court may order an injunction or additional equitable relief under Tex. Lab. Code § 21.258. *See also Caballero v. Central Power & Light Co.*, 858 S.W.2d 359, 361 (Tex. 1993) (equitable relief under TCHRA is to be determined by judge).

Attorney's fees. See PJC 115.46.

Front pay. Front pay, money awarded for future lost compensation, is recognized as a substitute for reinstatement when reinstatement is not feasible. *Pollard v. E.I. du Pont de Nemours & Co.*, 532 U.S. 843, 846 (2001); *Julian v. City of Houston*, 314 F.3d 721, 728 (5th Cir. 2002). Although the United States Supreme Court has determined in *Pollard*, 532 U.S. at 848, that "front pay" is not a future pecuniary loss subject to the statutory cap on damages under 42 U.S.C. § 1981a, the federal counterpart to Texas Labor Code section 21.2585, courts considering front-pay awards have not been uniform in determining who decides such awards. *Compare Mota v. University of Texas Health Science Center*, 261 F.3d 512 (5th Cir. 2001) (court determines front pay), *with Hansard v. Pepsi Cola*, 865 F.2d 1461, 1469 (5th Cir.) (jury determines front pay), *cert. denied*, 493 U.S. 842 (1989). The Committee expresses no opinion on whether front pay is determined by the court or the jury.

After-acquired evidence of employee misconduct. If the employer has pleaded the discovery of evidence of employee misconduct acquired only after the employee's employment was terminated, see PJC 107.8 for the applicable instruction.

Elements of damages submitted separately. The Committee generally recommends that multiple elements of damages be separately submitted to the jury. *Harris County v. Smith*, 96 S.W.3d 230, 233–34 (Tex. 2002) (broad-form submission of multiple elements of damages may lead to harmful error if there is a proper objection raising insufficiency of the evidence to support one or more of the elements submitted); *see also* Tex. Civ. Prac. & Rem. Code § 41.008(a) ("In an action in which a claimant seeks recovery of damages, the trier of fact shall determine the amount of economic damages separately from the amount of other compensatory damages."). Separating economic from noneconomic damages is required to allow the court to apply the limits on recovery of exemplary damages based on economic and noneconomic damages as required by Tex. Civ. Prac. & Rem. Code § 41.008(b).

Further, "[p]rejudgment interest may not be assessed or recovered on an award of future damages." Tex. Fin. Code § 304.1045 (wrongful death, personal injury, or property damage cases); *see also Johnson & Higgins of Texas, Inc. v. Kenneco Energy, Inc.*, 962 S.W.2d 507, 514, 530 (Tex. 1998) (reconciling equitable prejudgment interest with statutory prejudgment interest); *Perry Roofing Co. v. Olcott*, 744 S.W.2d 929, 931 (Tex. 1988) (unliquidated damages in contract cases); *Cavnar v. Quality Control Parking, Inc.*, 696 S.W.2d 549, 555–56 (Tex. 1985) (personal injury, later extended to other types of cases). Therefore, separation of past and future damages is required.

Elements considered separately. *Golden Eagle Archery, Inc. v. Jackson*, 116 S.W.3d 757, 770 (Tex. 2002), provides an instruction for cases involving undefined or potentially overlapping categories of damages. In those cases, the following language should be substituted for the instruction to consider each element separately:

> Consider the following elements of damages, if any, and none other. You shall not award any sum of money on any element if you have otherwise, under some other element, awarded a sum of money for the same loss. That is, do not compensate twice for the same loss, if any.

Prejudgment interest. Instructing the jury not to add interest is suggested because prejudgment interest, if recoverable, will be calculated by the court at the time of judgment. If interest paid on an obligation is claimed as an element of damages, it may be necessary to modify the instruction on interest.

PJC 115.31 Predicate Question and Instruction on Exemplary Damages for Unlawful Employment Practices

PJC 115.31A Instruction for Actions Filed before September 1, 2003

QUESTION ______

Do you find by clear and convincing evidence that *Don Davis* engaged in the discriminatory practice that you have found in answer to Question _____ [*107.6*] with malice or with reckless indifference to the right of *Paul Payne* to be free from such practices?

"Clear and convincing evidence" means the measure or degree of proof that produces a firm belief or conviction of the truth of the allegations sought to be established.

"Malice" means:

(a) a specific intent by *Don Davis* to cause substantial injury to *Paul Payne*; or

(b) an act or omission by *Don Davis*,

(i) which when viewed objectively from the standpoint of *Don Davis* at the time of its occurrence involves an extreme degree of risk, considering the probability and magnitude of the potential harm to others; and

(ii) of which *Don Davis* has actual, subjective awareness of the risk involved, but nevertheless proceeds with conscious indifference to the rights, safety, or welfare of others.

Answer "Yes" or "No."

Answer: _______________

PJC 115.31B Instruction for Actions Filed on or after September 1, 2003

Answer the following question regarding *Don Davis* only if you unanimously answered "Yes" to Question ______ [*or Question ______, or Question ______*]. Otherwise, do not answer the following question.

To answer "Yes" to [*any part of*] the following question, your answer must be unanimous. You may answer "No" to [*any part of*] the following question only upon a vote of ten or more jurors. Otherwise, you must not answer [*that part of*] the following question.

QUESTION ______

Do you find by clear and convincing evidence that *Don Davis* engaged in the discriminatory practice that you have found in answer to Question ______ [*107.6*] with malice or with reckless indifference to the right of *Paul Payne* to be free from such practices?

> "Clear and convincing evidence" means the measure or degree of proof that produces a firm belief or conviction of the truth of the allegations sought to be established.
>
> "Malice" means a specific intent by *Don Davis* to cause substantial injury or harm to *Paul Payne*.

Answer "Yes" or "No."

Answer: ______________

COMMENT

When to use. PJC 115.31 should be used for a claim for punitive damages under the Texas Commission on Human Rights Act, Tex. Lab. Code §§ 21.001–.556, when—

1. the evidence indicates that the discriminatory employment practice was motivated by malice or reckless indifference, Tex. Lab. Code § 21.2585(b); and
2. the cause of action arose on or after September 1, 1995, the effective date of Tex. Lab. Code § 21.2585.

Use PJC 115.31A for actions filed before September 1, 2003. For actions filed on or after September 1, 2003, use PJC 115.31B.

Source of question and instruction. PJC 115.31A is derived from former Tex. Lab. Code § 21.2585 and former Tex. Civ. Prac. & Rem. Code § 41.001(2), (7) (Acts 1987, 70th Leg., 1st C.S., ch. 2, § 2.12 (S.B. 5), eff. Sept. 2, 1987, *amended by* Acts 1995, 74th Leg., R.S., ch. 19, § 1 (S.B. 25), eff. Sept. 1, 1995). PJC 115.31B is derived from Tex. Lab. Code § 21.2585 and Tex. Civ. Prac. & Rem. Code § 41.001(2), (7). Under Tex. Civ. Prac. & Rem. Code § 41.003(d) and the supreme court's January 27, 2005, order under Tex. R. Civ. P. 226a, unanimity is required on the exemplary damages question and the applicable liability question. PJC 115.31B is conditioned accordingly. The unanimity instruction is adapted from the instruction in Tex. Civ. Prac. & Rem.

Code § 41.003(e) and the supreme court's January 27, 2005, order under Tex. R. Civ. P. 226a.

Unanimity. For actions filed on or after September 1, 2003, "[e]xemplary damages may be awarded only if the jury was unanimous in regard to finding liability for and the amount of exemplary damages." Tex. Civ. Prac. & Rem. Code § 41.003(d). Section 41.003(e) of the Code mandates that the jury be instructed that its answer regarding the amount of exemplary damages must be unanimous. By the supreme court's January 27, 2005, order under Tex. R. Civ. P. 226a, the supreme court requires unanimity on the exemplary damages question and the applicable liability question in cases governed by Tex. Civ. Prac. & Rem. Code § 41.003(d). PJC 115.31B is conditioned accordingly.

Multiple defendants. The following conditioning instruction may be substituted in a case involving claims against multiple defendants:

> Answer the following question regarding a defendant only if you unanimously answered "Yes" to Question ______ [*or Question ______, or Question ______*] regarding that defendant. Otherwise, do not answer the following question regarding that defendant.

PJC 115.32 Question on Employer Liability for Exemplary Damages for Conduct of Supervisor

QUESTION ______

Did *Don Davis* make a good-faith effort to prevent [*race, color, disability, religious, sex, national origin, or age*] [*discrimination or harassment*] in *his* workplace?

Answer "Yes" or "No."

Answer: ______________

COMMENT

When to use. PJC 115.32 should be used for claims of exemplary damages under the Texas Commission on Human Rights Act, Tex. Lab. Code §§ 21.001–.556, where there is evidence that an employer made good-faith efforts to comply with the antidiscrimination laws and a manager or agent acted contrary to such efforts.

Source of question. PJC 115.32 is derived from *Kolstad v. American Dental Ass'n*, 527 U.S. 526 (1999), and *Deffenbaugh-Williams v. Wal-Mart Stores*, 188 F.3d 278 (5th Cir. 1999).

PJC 115.33 Question and Instructions—Defamation General Damages

QUESTION ______

What sum of money, if paid now in cash, would fairly and reasonably compensate *Paul Payne* for *his* injuries, if any, that were proximately caused by [*the statement*]?

Consider the elements of damages listed below and none other. Consider each element separately. Do not award any sum of money on any element if you have otherwise, under some other element, awarded a sum of money for the same loss. That is, do not compensate twice for the same loss, if any. Do not include interest on any amount of damages you find.

Answer separately in dollars and cents for damages, if any.

a. Injury to reputation sustained in the past.

Answer: _______________

b. Injury to reputation that, in reasonable probability, *Paul Payne* will sustain in the future.

Answer: _______________

c. Mental anguish sustained in the past.

Answer: _______________

d. Mental anguish that, in reasonable probability, *Paul Payne* will sustain in the future.

Answer: _______________

COMMENT

When to use. PJC 115.33 is to be used in a defamation case involving a claim of general damages.

Source of instruction. In defamation cases, "[o]nce injury to reputation is established, a person defamed may recover general damages without proof of other injury." *Leyendecker & Associates v. Wechter*, 683 S.W.2d 369, 374 (Tex. 1984). General damages include damages for loss of reputation and mental anguish in the past and in the future. *Peshak v. Greer*, 13 S.W.3d 421, 427 (Tex. App.—Corpus Christi 2000, no pet.); *First State Bank of Corpus Christi v. Ake*, 606 S.W.2d 696, 702–03 (Tex. App.—Corpus

Christi 1980, writ ref'd n.r.e.); *Winkel v. Hankins*, 585 S.W.2d 889, 899–90 (Tex. Civ. App.—Eastland 1979, writ dism'd). Mental anguish damages include humiliation. *Parkway Co. v. Woodruff*, 901 S.W.2d 434, 444 (Tex. 1995).

Defamatory per se. In common-law cases where the court (or in some cases, the jury) has found the matter to be defamatory per se, the following instruction may be used in the common-law defamation case that does not involve constitutional requirements. Texas law presumes that statements that are defamatory per se injure the victim's reputation and entitle him to recover general damages, including damages for loss of reputation and mental anguish. *Bentley v. Bunton*, 94 S.W.3d 561, 604 (Tex. 2002); *see also Leyendecker & Associates*, 683 S.W.2d at 374 (party defamed by a writing libelous per se allowed recovery at common law without proof of injury). Where the statement is defamatory per se, the following instruction should be given with the question:

> You must award at least nominal damages for injury to reputation in the past.

This instruction comes from *Express Publishing Co. v. Hormuth*, 5 S.W.2d 1025, 1027 (Tex. Civ. App.—El Paso 1928, writ ref'd) (where article was false and defamatory, jury was properly instructed to find at least nominal damages for plaintiff).

Except under very limited circumstances, this instruction should not be used in cases involving public officials, public figures, or matters of public concern, even if the matter at issue is defamatory per se. In *Gertz v. Robert Welch, Inc.*, 418 U.S. 323, 349 (1974), the U.S. Supreme Court held that states are not free to presume damages in libel cases with constitutional implications unless there is a finding of actual malice (knowing falsity). In a case where these prerequisites—defamation per se and actual malice—have been met, one court has held that the jury should be instructed concerning this presumption. *Texas Disposal Systems Landfill, Inc. v. Waste Management Holdings, Inc.*, 219 S.W.3d 563, 582–83 (Tex. App.—Austin 2007, pet. denied).

Multiple statements. Chapter 110 of this volume assumes a single allegedly defamatory statement. If multiple statements are at issue, separate submissions may be required. For example, as a matter of common law and constitutional law damages are recoverable only for false and defamatory statements. *See Philadelphia Newspapers, Inc. v. Hepps*, 475 U.S. 767, 777 (1986) (libel plaintiff "must bear the burden of showing that the speech at issue is false before recovering damages for defamation from a media defendant."); *NAACP v. Claiborne Hardware Co.*, 458 U.S. 886, 918 (1982) (no damages can be awarded for economic losses caused by expression protected by First Amendment); *Bell Publishing Co. v. Garrett Engineering Co.*, 170 S.W.2d 197, 206 (Tex. 1943) (under common law, where affirmative defense of substantial truth has been submitted to jury, damages are recoverable only for defamatory statements that are not found to be true: "[W]here some of the defamatory charges are found to be true and others false, the jury should be instructed to consider only such damages as resulted from the false . . . ."). Further, submitting a single damages question for multiple statements may be error if liability for one or more of the statements is not supported by the law or the evidence. *See, e.g.*, *Romero v. KPH Consolidation, Inc.*, 166 S.W.3d 212, 215, 225–28 (Tex. 2005); *Harris County v. Smith*, 96 S.W.3d 230, 233–34 (Tex. 2002); *Crown Life Insurance Co. v. Casteel*, 22 S.W.3d 378, 388–89 (Tex. 2000).

Elements considered separately. The instruction not to compensate twice for the same loss is taken from *Golden Eagle Archery, Inc. v. Jackson*, 116 S.W.3d 757, 770 (Tex. 2003) and is proper in cases involving undefined or potentially overlapping categories of damages. In other cases, the following instruction may be substituted:

Consider the following elements of damages, if any, and none other.

Past and future damages submitted separately. Separation of past and future damages is required because "[p]rejudgment interest may not be assessed or recovered on an award of future damages." Tex. Fin. Code § 304.1045 (wrongful death, personal injury, or property damage cases); *see also Johnson & Higgins of Texas, Inc. v. Kenneco Energy, Inc.*, 962 S.W.2d 507, 514, 530 (Tex. 1998) (reconciling equitable prejudgment interest with statutory prejudgment interest); *Perry Roofing Co. v. Olcott*, 744 S.W.2d 929, 931 (Tex. 1988) (unliquidated damages in contract cases); *Cavnar v. Quality Control Parking, Inc.*, 696 S.W.2d 549, 555–56 (Tex. 1985) (personal injury, later extended to other types of cases).

PJC 115.34 Question and Instruction—Defamation Special Damages

QUESTION ______

What sum of money, if paid now in cash, would fairly and reasonably compensate *Paul Payne* for *his* actual pecuniary loss, if any, that was proximately caused by [*the statement*]?

Consider the elements of damages listed below and none other. Consider each element separately. Do not award any sum of money on any element if you have otherwise, under some other element, awarded a sum of money for the same loss. That is, do not compensate twice for the same loss, if any. Do not include interest on any amount of damages you find.

Answer separately in dollars and cents for damages, if any.

a. [*Element A*] sustained in the past.

Answer: _______________

b. [*Element A*] that, in reasonable probability, will be sustained in the future.

Answer: _______________

c. [*Element B*] sustained in the past.

Answer: _______________

d. [*Element B*] that, in reasonable probability, will be sustained in the future.

Answer: _______________

[Insert additional elements as may be appropriate for items of special damages.]

COMMENT

When to use. Special damages in defamation claims are the actual pecuniary losses arising from a defamation. *Hurlbut v. Gulf Atlantic Life Insurance Co.*, 749 S.W.2d 762, 766–67 (Tex. 1987). Courts have recognized a variety of special damages in defamation cases. *Brown v. Petrolite Corp.*, 965 F.2d 38, 46 (5th Cir. 1992) (increased advertising costs to respond to defamation); *Peshak v. Greer*, 13 S.W.3d 421, 427 (Tex. App.—Corpus Christi 2000, no pet.) (loss of earning capacity); *Shearson Lehman Hutton, Inc. v.*

Tucker, 806 S.W.2d 914, 922 (Tex. App.—Corpus Christi 1991, writ dism'd w.o.j.) (lost past and future profits); *Wenco of El Paso/Las Cruces, Inc. v. Nazario*, 783 S.W.2d 663, 667 (Tex. App.—El Paso 1989, no writ) (past and future loss of wages); *Houston Belt & Terminal Railway Co. v. Wherry*, 548 S.W.2d 743, 753 (Tex. App.—Houston [1st Dist.] 1976, writ ref'd n.r.e.) (loss of employment).

The submission of special damages should be adapted to the individual facts of the case. This question may be combined with a question on general damages where no presumption of damages arises. Special damages should be submitted separately where, because the statement is defamatory per se, damages are presumed.

Source of instruction. This question is based on *Hurlbut*, 749 S.W.2d at 766–67.

Multiple statements. Chapter 110 of this volume assumes a single allegedly defamatory statement. If multiple statements are at issue, separate submissions may be required. For example, as a matter of common law and constitutional law damages are recoverable only for false and defamatory statements. *See Philadelphia Newspapers, Inc. v. Hepps*, 475 U.S. 767, 777 (1986) (libel plaintiff "must bear the burden of showing that the speech at issue is false before recovering damages for defamation from a media defendant."); *NAACP v. Claiborne Hardware Co.*, 458 U.S. 886, 918 (1982) (no damages can be awarded for economic losses caused by expression protected by First Amendment); *Bell Publishing Co. v. Garrett Engineering Co.*, 170 S.W.2d 197, 206 (Tex. 1943) (under common law, where affirmative defense of substantial truth has been submitted to jury, damages are recoverable only for defamatory statements that are not found to be true: "[W]here some of the defamatory charges are found to be true and others false, the jury should be instructed to consider only such damages as resulted from the false . . . ."). Further, submitting a single damages question for multiple statements may be error if liability for one or more of the statements is not supported by the law or the evidence. *See, e.g., Romero v. KPH Consolidation, Inc.*, 166 S.W.3d 212, 215, 225–28 (Tex. 2005); *Harris County v. Smith*, 96 S.W.3d 230, 233–34 (Tex. 2002); *Crown Life Insurance Co. v. Casteel*, 22 S.W.3d 378, 388–89 (Tex. 2000).

Elements considered separately. The instruction not to compensate twice for the same loss is taken from *Golden Eagle Archery, Inc. v. Jackson*, 116 S.W.3d 757, 770 (Tex. 2003) and is proper in cases involving undefined or potentially overlapping categories of damages. In other cases, the following instruction may be substituted:

Consider the following elements of damages, if any, and none other.

Past and future damages submitted separately. Separation of past and future damages is required because "[p]rejudgment interest may not be assessed or recovered on an award of future damages." Tex. Fin. Code § 304.1045 (wrongful death, personal injury, or property damage cases); *see also Johnson & Higgins of Texas, Inc. v. Kenneco Energy, Inc.*, 962 S.W.2d 507, 514, 530 (Tex. 1998) (reconciling equitable prejudgment interest with statutory prejudgment interest); *Perry Roofing Co. v. Olcott*, 744 S.W.2d 929, 931 (Tex. 1988) (unliquidated damages in contract cases); *Cavnar v. Quality Con-*

trol Parking, Inc., 696 S.W.2d 549, 555–56 (Tex. 1985) (personal injury, later extended to other types of cases).

PJC 115.35 Proportionate Responsibility

If you answered "Yes" to Questions ______ and ______ [*applicable questions*] for more than one of those named below, then answer the following question. Otherwise, do not answer the following question.

Assign percentages of responsibility only to those you found caused or contributed to cause the [*harm*] [*damages*]. The percentages you find must total 100 percent. The percentages must be expressed in whole numbers. The percentage of responsibility attributable to any one is not necessarily measured by the number of acts or omissions found.

QUESTION ______

For each person you found caused or contributed to cause the [*harm*] [*damages*] to *Paul Payne*, find the percentage of responsibility attributable to each:

a. *Don Davis* ______________%

b. *Paul Payne* ______________%

c. *Sam Settlor* ______________%

d. *Responsible Ray* ______________%

Total ______100______%

COMMENT

When to use. Tex. R. Civ. P. 277 requires a percentage question "[i]n any cause in which the jury is required to apportion the loss among the parties." For causes of action based on tort accruing on or after September 1, 1995, and in all such suits filed on or after September 1, 1996, the trier of fact must determine the percentage of responsibility of each defendant, claimant, settling person, or responsible third party with respect to each person's causing or contributing to cause the harm for which damages are sought. Tex. Civ. Prac. & Rem. Code § 33.003. The responsibility to be determined must arise from a negligent act or omission, a defective or unreasonably dangerous product, or other conduct or activity that violates an applicable legal standard. Tex. Civ. Prac. & Rem. Code § 33.003.

PJC 115.35 should be used if the case involves "any cause of action based on tort" or any action brought under the DTPA. Tex. Civ. Prac. & Rem. Code § 33.002(a). Before the 1995 changes to the proportionate responsibility statute, intentional tort claims, including fraud, were not subject to apportionment. *See Stewart Title Guaranty Co. v.*

Sterling, 822 S.W.2d 1, 6 n.7 (Tex. 1991); *Trenholm v. Ratcliff*, 646 S.W.2d 927, 933 (Tex. 1983). The current version of the proportionate responsibility statute has done away with this statutory exclusion. Several courts have concluded that fraud is subject to apportionment, while others have not. *Compare JCW Electronics, Inc. v. Garza*, 176 S.W.3d 618, 626 & n.3 (Tex. App.—Corpus Christi 2005, no pet. h.), *and JHC Ventures, L.P. v. Fast Trucking, Inc.*, 94 S.W.3d 762, 773–74 (Tex. App.—San Antonio 2002, no pet.), *with Mayes v. Stewart*, 11 S.W.3d 440, 451–52 (Tex. App.—Houston [14th Dist.] 2000, pet. denied) (holding that only actual knowledge of fraud—not "should have known" negligence standard—will defeat claim for fraud), *and Davis v. Estridge*, 85 S.W.3d 308, 311–12 (Tex. App.—Tyler 2002, pet. denied) ("Traditionally, negligence has never been a defense to fraud.").

A proportionate responsibility submission has been found improper where the plaintiff asserted claims for conversion under the UCC. *Southwest Bank v. Information Support Concepts, Inc.*, 149 S.W.3d 104, 111 (Tex. 2004).

Use of "harm" or "damages." Depending on the type of cause submitted to the jury, the term "harm" or "damages" should be used as appropriate. See also the current editions of State Bar of Texas, *Texas Pattern Jury Charges—General Negligence & Intentional Personal Torts* and *Texas Pattern Jury Charges—Malpractice, Premises & Products* for instances in which "occurrence," "injury," or "occurrence or injury" may be appropriate.

Conditioned on responsibility of more than one person. PJC 115.35 is conditioned on findings that the acts or omissions of more than one person caused the damages or injury, because otherwise no comparison is possible.

Multiple liability theories. When multiple liability theories are submitted and the parties dispute whether one theory is legally valid or supported by legally sufficient evidence, it may not be feasible to submit a single proportionate responsibility question predicated on all liability theories. *See Romero v. KPH Consolidation, Inc.*, 166 S.W.3d 212, 215, 225–28 (Tex. 2005) (reversible error to allow jury, in apportioning responsibility, to consider claim on which there was no evidence).

Plaintiff submitted only if plaintiff violated legal standard. The plaintiff (*Paul Payne*) should be submitted in this question only if the law governing the cause of action provides an "applicable legal standard" by which the plaintiff's conduct is measured and the jury is asked in a predicate question whether *Paul Payne* violated that standard. Tex. Civ. Prac. & Rem. Code § 33.003. Otherwise, the question should not include the plaintiff.

If there is more than one responsible person. If more than one responsible person has been found liable in a liability question, separate percentage answers should be sought for each person. For example:

a. *Don Davis* _______________%

b. *Davis Corporation* ______________%

c. *Paul Payne* ______________%

d. *Sam Settlor* ______________%

e. *Responsible Ray* ______________%

Settling persons. The proportionate responsibility statute requires the responsibility of a settling person (*Sam Settlor*) to be determined by the trier of fact. Tex. Civ. Prac. & Rem. Code §§ 33.003, 33.011. "Settling person" is defined as a person—

> who has, at any time, paid or promised to pay money or anything of monetary value to a claimant in consideration of potential liability with respect to the personal injury, property damage, death, or other harm for which recovery of damages is sought.

Tex. Civ. Prac. & Rem. Code § 33.011(5). To include a settling person, that person's name must be included in a basic liability question.

Responsible third parties—causes of action filed before July 1, 2003. The liability of a "responsible third party" (*Responsible Ray*) should be inquired into only if that party is joined under former Tex. Civ. Prac. & Rem. Code § 33.004. Acts 1995, 74th Leg., R.S., ch. 136, § 1 (S.B. 28), eff. Sept. 1, 1995. A "responsible third party" is defined in former Tex. Civ. Prac. & Rem. Code § 33.011(6). Acts 1985, 69th Leg., R.S., ch. 959, § 1 (S.B. 797), eff. Sept. 1, 1985, *amended by* Acts 1987, 70th Leg., 1st C.S., ch. 2, § 2.07 (S.B. 5), eff. Sept. 2, 1987; Acts 1995, 74th Leg., R.S., ch. 136, § 1 (S.B. 28), eff. Sept. 1, 1995. Under former Tex. Civ. Prac. & Rem. Code § 33.003, if a responsible third party is submitted in a basic liability question, the responsible third party should also be submitted in the proportionate responsibility question. Acts 1987, 70th Leg., 1st C.S., ch. 2, § 2.06 (S.B. 5), eff. Sept. 2, 1987, *amended by* Acts 1995, 74th Leg., R.S., ch. 136, § 1 (S.B. 28), eff. Sept. 1, 1995.

Responsible third parties—causes of action filed on or after July 1, 2003. In 2003 the legislature changed responsible third party practice from one of joinder to one of designation. Tex. Civ. Prac. & Rem. Code § 33.004. The legislature also expanded the category of responsible third parties. Tex. Civ. Prac. & Rem. Code §§ 33.004, 33.011(6). "'Responsible third party' means any person who is alleged to have caused or contributed to causing in any way the harm for which recovery of damages is sought, whether by negligent act or omission, by any defective or unreasonably dangerous product, by other conduct or activity that violates an applicable legal standard, or by any combination of these." Tex. Civ. Prac. & Rem. Code § 33.011(6). Section 33.003(b) provides that a question regarding conduct by any person may not be submitted to the jury without evidence to support the submission. Tex. Civ. Prac. & Rem. Code § 33.003(b).

Contribution defendants.

A. *Inclusion in liability question.* If there is a contribution defendant (*Connie Contributor*), that party's liability should be determined in a separate liability question. *See* Tex. Civ. Prac. & Rem. Code §§ 33.003, 33.011, 33.016. "Contribution defendant" is defined as "any defendant, counterdefendant, or third-party defendant from whom any party seeks contribution with respect to any portion of damages for which that party may be liable, but from whom the claimant seeks no relief at the time of submission." Tex. Civ. Prac. & Rem. Code § 33.016(a).

B. *Separate comparative question necessary.* The responsibility of the contribution defendant should *not* be included in the question comparing the responsibility of the plaintiff with that of the other defendants. Tex. Civ. Prac. & Rem. Code § 33.016(c). A separate comparative question is necessary. An example of a question on comparative responsibility of a contribution defendant is as follows:

> If you answered "Yes" to Questions ______ and ______ [*applicable questions*] for more than one of those named below, then answer the following question. Otherwise, do not answer the following question.
>
> Assign percentages only to those you found caused or contributed to cause the [*harm*]. The percentages you find must total 100 percent. The percentages must be expressed in whole numbers. The percentage of responsibility attributable to any one named below is not necessarily measured by the number of acts or omissions found.
>
> QUESTION ______
>
> For each person you found caused or contributed to cause the [*harm*] to *Paul Payne*, find the percentage of responsibility attributable to each:
>
> | | | |
> |---|---|---|
> | a. | *Don Davis* | ______________% |
> | b. | *Connie Contributor* | ______________% |
> | | Total | 100 % |

Exceptions to the limitations on joint and several liability. The limitations on joint and several liability set forth in chapter 33 of the Civil Practice and Remedies Code do not apply in certain instances:

Actions filed before July 1, 2003. See former section 33.002 of the Civil Practice and Remedies Code (Acts 1987, 70th Leg., 1st C.S., ch. 2, § 2.05 (S.B. 5), eff. Sept. 2, 1987, *amended by* Acts 1989, 71st Leg., R.S., ch. 380, § 4 (S.B. 437), eff. Sept. 1, 1989; Acts 1995, 74th Leg., R.S., ch. 136, § 1 (S.B. 28), eff. Sept. 1, 1995; Acts 1995, 74th

Leg., R.S., ch. 414, § 17 (H.B. 668), eff. Sept. 1, 1995; Acts 2001, 77th Leg., R.S., ch. 643, § 2 (H.B. 2087), eff. Sept. 1, 2001).

Actions filed on or after July 1, 2003. *See* Tex. Civ. Prac. & Rem. Code § 33.013.

Several of the examples of criminal conduct constituting exceptions to the limitations on joint and several liability also constitute exceptions to the cap or limitation on exemplary damages, such as forgery, securing execution of a document by deception, fraudulent removal of a document, or theft. See PJC 115.39–.45 for examples of those charges and for applicable comments. Note, however, that a jury question seeking to establish conduct sufficient to lift the limitation on joint and several liability must ask whether the defendant, with the specific intent to do harm to others, acted in concert with another person to engage in the conduct described in the applicable Penal Code section. Tex. Civ. Prac. & Rem. Code § 33.002(b). These elements are not contained in the charges found at PJC 115.39–.45.

PJC 115.36 Predicate Question and Instruction on Award of Exemplary Damages

PJC 115.36A Question and Instruction for Actions Filed before September 1, 2003

If you answered "Yes" to Question ______ [*103.1, 106.1, or other applicable liability question*], then answer the following question. Otherwise, do not answer the following question.

QUESTION ______

Do you find by clear and convincing evidence that the harm to *Paul Payne* resulted from [*malice* or *fraud*]?

"Clear and convincing evidence" means the measure or degree of proof that produces a firm belief or conviction of the truth of the allegations sought to be established.

"Malice" means:

(a) a specific intent by *Don Davis* to cause substantial injury to *Paul Payne*; or

(b) an act or omission by *Don Davis*,

(i) which when viewed objectively from the standpoint of *Don Davis* at the time of its occurrence involves an extreme degree of risk, considering the probability and magnitude of the potential harm to others; and

(ii) of which *Don Davis* has actual, subjective awareness of the risk involved, but nevertheless proceeds with conscious indifference to the rights, safety, or welfare of others.

[And/or use appropriate definition for "fraud"; see comment below, "Fraud as a ground for exemplary damages."]

Answer "Yes" or "No."

Answer: ______________

PJC 115.36B Question and Instruction for Actions Filed on or after September 1, 2003

Answer the following question only if you unanimously answered "Yes" to Question ______ [*or Question* ______, *or Question* ______]. Otherwise, do not answer the following question.

To answer "Yes" to [*any part of*] the following question, your answer must be unanimous. You may answer "No" to [*any part of*] the following question only upon a vote of ten or more jurors. Otherwise, you must not answer [*that part of*] the following question.

QUESTION ______

Do you find by clear and convincing evidence that the harm to *Paul Payne* resulted from [*malice*, *fraud*, or *gross negligence*]?

> "Clear and convincing evidence" means the measure or degree of proof that produces a firm belief or conviction of the truth of the allegations sought to be established.
>
> "Malice" means a specific intent by *Don Davis* to cause substantial injury or harm to *Paul Payne*.

[And/or use appropriate definition for "fraud" or "gross negligence"; see comments below, "Fraud as a ground for exemplary damages" and "Gross negligence as a ground for exemplary damages."]

COMMENT

When to use. PJC 115.36 is used as a predicate question to PJC 115.37, the question for exemplary damages. It is based on an affirmative finding to a liability question such as PJC 103.1 (tort duty of good faith and fair dealing) or 106.1 (interference with existing contract). PJC 115.36A applies only to causes of action arising on or after September 1, 1995, and filed before September 1, 2003. PJC 115.36B applies to actions filed on or after September 1, 2003.

In a case where a defendant has requested a bifurcated trial pursuant to Tex. Civ. Prac. & Rem. Code § 41.009, PJC 115.36 should be answered in the first phase of the trial.

Source of question. PJC 115.36A is derived from Acts 1987, 70th Leg., 1st C.S., ch. 2, § 2.12 (S.B. 5), eff. Sept. 2, 1987, *amended by* Acts 1995, 74th Leg., R.S., ch. 19, § 1 (S.B. 25), eff. Sept. 1, 1995; Acts 1997, 75th Leg., R.S., ch. 165, § 4.01 (S.B. 898), eff. Sept. 1, 1997. (Note: In the remainder of this Comment, citations to the Texas Civil Practice and Remedies Code as set out in the preceding session laws will be made to "former Tex. Civ. Prac. & Rem. Code § ____.") PJC 115.36B is derived from Tex. Civ. Prac. & Rem. Code §§ 41.001(7), (11), 41.003(a)(1), (2), (3), (d), 41.004(a). By the supreme court's January 27, 2005, order under Tex. R. Civ. P. 226a, the supreme court requires unanimity on the exemplary damages question and the applicable liability question in cases governed by Tex. Civ. Prac. & Rem. Code § 41.003(d). PJC 115.36B is conditioned accordingly. The unanimity instruction is adapted from the instruction in Tex. Civ. Prac. & Rem. Code § 41.003(e) and the supreme court's January 27, 2005, order under Tex. R. Civ. P. 226a.

Actual damages generally required. In general, exemplary damages may be awarded only if damages other than nominal damages are awarded. However, in actions filed before September 1, 2003, if the jury finds that the harm suffered by the plaintiff was caused by a specific intent by the defendant to cause substantial injury to the plaintiff (the first definition of "malice" in the question above), then an award of nominal damages will support an award of exemplary damages. Former Tex. Civ. Prac. & Rem. Code § 41.004. Actions filed on or after September 1, 2003, are governed by the 2003 amendments to the Civil Practice and Remedies Code that provide that a claimant may not recover exemplary damages if the jury awards only nominal damages. Tex. Civ. Prac. & Rem. Code § 41.004(a).

Fraud as a ground for exemplary damages. Fraud, as well as malice, is a ground for recovery of exemplary damages. Tex. Civ. Prac. & Rem. Code § 41.003(a)(1). As a predicate for recovery of exemplary damages, fraud is defined as "fraud other than constructive fraud." Tex. Civ. Prac. & Rem. Code § 41.001(6). In an appropriate case, substitute "fraud" for "malice" in the question proper and insert a definition for "fraud" conforming to the pleadings and evidence of the case, using the definitions for fraud found at PJC 105.2–.11 as a guide.

Gross negligence as a ground for exemplary damages. In actions filed on or after September 1, 2003, gross negligence is also a ground for recovery of exemplary damages. Tex. Civ. Prac. & Rem. Code § 41.003(a)(3). As a predicate for recovery of exemplary damages, the following instruction should be given:

> "Gross negligence" means an act or omission by *Don Davis*,
>
> (a) which when viewed objectively from the standpoint of *Don Davis* at the time of its occurrence involves an extreme degree of risk, considering the probability and magnitude of the potential harm to others; and
>
> (b) of which *Don Davis* has actual, subjective awareness of the risk involved, but nevertheless proceeds with con-

> scious indifference to the rights, safety, or welfare of others.

Tex. Civ. Prac. & Rem. Code § 41.001(11). In an appropriate case, substitute this statutory definition of "gross negligence" for "malice" in the question proper.

Recovery of exemplary damages in a wrongful death case. In a wrongful death case brought before September 1, 2003, by or on behalf of the decedent's spouse or heir of the decedent's body under a statute enacted pursuant to Tex. Const. art. XVI, § 26, exemplary damages may be recovered on a showing that the claimant's damages resulted from willful act, omission, or gross neglect. "Gross neglect" has the same definition as "malice" in former Tex. Civ. Prac. & Rem. Code § 41.001(7)(B). Former Tex. Civ. Prac. & Rem. Code § 41.003(a)(3). That statutory definition is the source of the second definition of "malice" in PJC 115.36A. See former Tex. Civ. Prac. & Rem. Code § 71.001 *et seq.* (Acts 1985, 69th Leg., R.S., ch. 959, § 1 (S.B. 797), eff. Sept 1, 1985, *amended by* Acts 1993, 73d Leg., R.S., ch. 4, § 1 (S.B. 2), eff. Aug. 30, 1993; Acts 1995, 74th Leg., R.S., ch. 567, § 1 (S.B. 400), eff. Sept. 1, 1995; Acts 1997, 75th Leg., R.S., ch. 424, §§ 1, 3 (S.B. 220), eff. May 29, 1997; Acts 1999, 76th Leg., R.S., ch. 382, §§ 1, 2 (H.B. 3477), eff. May 29, 1999) for applicable statutes concerning wrongful death, and the current edition of State Bar of Texas, *Texas Pattern Jury Charges—Malpractice, Premises & Products* ch. 81, for pattern jury charges in wrongful death cases.

Unanimity. For actions filed on or after September 1, 2003, "[e]xemplary damages may be awarded only if the jury was unanimous in regard to finding liability for and the amount of exemplary damages." Tex. Civ. Prac. & Rem. Code § 41.003(d). Section 41.003(e) of the Code mandates that the jury be instructed that its answer regarding the amount of exemplary damages must be unanimous. By the supreme court's January 27, 2005, order under Tex. R. Civ. P. 226a, the supreme court requires unanimity on the exemplary damages question and the applicable liability question in cases governed by Tex. Civ. Prac. & Rem. Code § 41.003(d). PJC 115.36B is conditioned accordingly.

Multiple defendants. The following conditioning instruction may be substituted in a case involving claims against multiple defendants:

> Answer the following question regarding a defendant only if you unanimously answered "Yes" to Question ______ [*or Question ______, or Question ______*] regarding that defendant. Otherwise, do not answer the following question regarding that defendant.

PJC 115.37 Question and Instruction on Exemplary Damages

Answer the following question only if you unanimously answered "Yes" to Question ______ [*or Question* ______, *or Question* ______]. Otherwise, do not answer the following question.

You must unanimously agree on the amount of any award of exemplary damages.

QUESTION ______

What sum of money, if any, if paid now in cash, should be assessed against *Don Davis* and awarded to *Paul Payne* as exemplary damages, if any, for the conduct found in response to Question ______ [*question authorizing potential recovery of exemplary damages*]?

"Exemplary damages" means an amount that you may in your discretion award as a penalty or by way of punishment.

Factors to consider in awarding exemplary damages, if any, are—

a. The nature of the wrong.

b. The character of the conduct involved.

c. The degree of culpability of *Don Davis*.

d. The situation and sensibilities of the parties concerned.

e. The extent to which such conduct offends a public sense of justice and propriety.

f. The net worth of *Don Davis*.

[Insert additional instructions if appropriate. See, e.g., PJC 115.38.]

Answer in dollars and cents, if any.

Answer: ______________

COMMENT

When to use. PJC 115.37 is used to submit exemplary damages. It should be predicated on a finding justifying the award of exemplary damages. See comments below. Chapter 41 of the Texas Civil Practice and Remedies Code does not apply to most suits brought under the DTPA and Texas Insurance Code chapter 541. Tex. Civ. Prac. & Rem. Code § 41.002(d). Nor does chapter 41 apply to cases brought under title 5 of the Texas

Labor Code (worker's compensation) that accrued before September 1, 1997. Acts 1995, 74th Leg., R.S., ch. 19, § 1 (S.B. 25), eff. Sept. 1, 1995; *see also Continental Coffee Products Co. v. Cazarez*, 937 S.W.2d 444, 452 n.4 (Tex. 1996). There may be reason, however, to use the "factors to consider" listed in PJC 115.37 in such cases. See PJC 115.11 for the "additional damages" question in DTPA cases, and PJC 115.29 for worker's compensation retaliation cases accruing before September 1, 1997.

Source of instructions. Tex. Civ. Prac. & Rem. Code §§ 41.001(5), 41.003(d), (e), § 41.011(a), and the supreme court's January 27, 2005, order under Tex. R. Civ. P. 226a.

Actions filed before September 1, 2003. A unanimous decision as to the amount of exemplary damages is not required for actions filed before September 1, 2003. In such cases, substitute the following instruction:

> If you answered "Yes" to Question ______ [*predicate finding*], then answer the following question. Otherwise, do not answer the following question.

Predicate finding. Section 41.003 of the Civil Practice and Remedies Code requires a predicate finding before an award of exemplary damages may be made. Tex. Civ. Prac. & Rem. Code § 41.003. Those predicate questions are found at PJC 105.1, 115.31, and 115.36. If a defendant has requested a bifurcated trial pursuant to Tex. Civ. Prac. & Rem. Code § 41.009, predicate questions should be submitted in the first phase of the trial. By the supreme court's January 27, 2005, order under Tex. R. Civ. P. 226a, the supreme court requires unanimity on the exemplary damages question and the applicable liability question in cases governed by Tex. Civ. Prac. & Rem. Code § 41.003(d) that are filed after September 1, 2003. PJC 115.31B and 115.36B are conditioned accordingly.

Multiple defendants. There should be a separate question and answer blank for each defendant against whom exemplary damages are sought. Tex. Civ. Prac. & Rem. Code § 41.006; *Norton Refrigerated Express, Inc. v. Ritter Bros. Co.*, 552 S.W.2d 910, 913 (Tex. Civ. App.—Texarkana 1977, writ ref'd n.r.e.). In a case involving multiple defendants against whom exemplary damages are sought, the following instruction on unanimity may be substituted:

> Answer the following question regarding a defendant only if you unanimously answered "Yes" to Question ______ [*or Question ______, or Question ______*] regarding that defendant. Otherwise, do not answer the following question regarding that defendant.

Multiple plaintiffs. For multiple plaintiffs, consideration may be given to an additional question asking the jury to apportion the exemplary damages among them. Tex. Civ. Prac. & Rem. Code § 71.010; *Burk Royalty Co. v. Walls*, 596 S.W.2d 932, 939 (Tex. Civ. App.—Fort Worth 1980), *aff'd on other grounds*, 616 S.W.2d 911 (Tex. 1981).

Prejudgment interest not recoverable. Prejudgment interest on exemplary damages is not recoverable. Tex. Civ. Prac. & Rem. Code § 41.007; *Cavnar v. Quality Control Parking, Inc.*, 696 S.W.2d 549, 555–56 (Tex. 1985).

Bifurcation. For actions filed before September 1, 2003, no predicating instruction is necessary if the court has granted a timely motion to bifurcate trial of the amount of punitive damages. *See* Tex. Civ. Prac. & Rem. Code § 41.009; *Transportation Insurance Co. v. Moriel*, 879 S.W.2d 10, 29–30 (Tex. 1994). For actions filed on or after September 1, 2003, the instruction on unanimity must be given in the bifurcated phase.

If in the first phase of the trial the jury finds facts establishing a predicate for an award of exemplary damages, then a separate jury charge should be prepared for the second phase of the trial. See the comments above regarding predicate-finding and PJC 115.36. In such a second-phase jury charge, PJC 115.37 should be submitted with both PJC 100.3 and 100.4.

Factors to consider in determining amount of award. The "factors to consider" listed in PJC 115.37 are from Tex. Civ. Prac. & Rem. Code § 41.011(a).

Limits on conduct to be considered. When there is a significant risk that a jury may seek to punish a defendant for a constitutionally improper reason, the Due Process Clause requires that an additional instruction be given to protect against that risk. *Philip Morris USA v. Williams*, 127 S. Ct. 1057, 1064–65 (2007).

For example, the defendant's lawful out-of-state conduct may be probative on some issues in a punitive damages case in certain circumstances. *State Farm Mutual Automobile Insurance Co. v. Campbell*, 538 U.S. 408, 422 (2003). When such evidence is admitted, "[a] jury must be instructed . . . that it may not use evidence of out-of-state conduct to punish a defendant for action that was lawful in the jurisdiction where it occurred." *Campbell*, 538 U.S. at 422.

In addition, evidence that the defendant's conduct risked harm to persons who are not before the court may be probative in determining the reprehensibility of that conduct. But when such evidence is admitted, the jury should be instructed that it may not punish the defendant for any harm it may have caused to persons who are not parties to the litigation. *Williams*, 127 S. Ct. at 1060, 1064–65.

Limitation on amount of recovery. Section 41.008 of the Civil Practice and Remedies Code limits recovery of exemplary damages. However, these limitations will not apply in favor of a defendant found to have "knowingly" or "intentionally" committed conduct described as a felony in specified sections of the Texas Penal Code. *See* Tex. Civ. Prac. & Rem. Code § 41.008(c), (d) and PJC 115.39–.45.

PJC 115.38 Question and Instruction for Imputing Liability for Exemplary Damages

PJC 115.38A Question and Instruction Imputing Malice to a Corporation—Causes of Action Accruing on or after September 1, 1995, and Filed before September 1, 2003

If you answered "Yes" to Question ______ [*applicable liability question*], and you inserted a sum of money in answer to Question ______ [*applicable damages question*], then answer the following question. Otherwise, do not answer the following question.

QUESTION ______

Do you find by clear and convincing evidence that the harm to *Paul Payne* resulted from malice attributable to *ABC Corporation*?

> "Clear and convincing evidence" means the measure or degree of proof that produces a firm belief or conviction of the truth of the allegations sought to be established.
>
> "Malice" means:
>
> (a) a specific intent by *Don Davis* to cause substantial injury to *Paul Payne*; or
>
> (b) an act or omission by *Don Davis*,
>
> (i) which when viewed objectively from the standpoint of *Don Davis* at the time of its occurrence involves an extreme degree of risk, considering the probability and magnitude of the potential harm to others; and
>
> (ii) of which *Don Davis* has actual, subjective awareness of the risk involved, but nevertheless proceeds with conscious indifference to the rights, safety, or welfare of others.

You are further instructed that malice may be attributable to *ABC Corporation* because of an act by *Don Davis* if, but only if—

a. *ABC Corporation* authorized the doing and the manner of the act, or

b. *Don Davis* was unfit and *ABC Corporation* was reckless in employing *him*, or

c. *Don Davis* was employed [*as a vice-principal*] [*in a managerial capacity*] and was acting in the scope of employment, or

d. *ABC Corporation* or a vice-principal of *ABC Corporation* ratified or approved the act.

Answer "Yes" or "No."

Answer: _______________

PJC 115.38B Question and Instruction Imputing Gross Negligence to a Corporation—Actions Filed on or after September 1, 2003

Answer the following question regarding *ABC Corporation* only if you unanimously answered "Yes" to Question ______ [*applicable liability question*] regarding *ABC Corporation*. Otherwise, do not answer the following question regarding *ABC Corporation*.

To answer "Yes" to [*any part of*] the following question, your answer must be unanimous. You may answer "No" to [*any part of*] the following question only upon a vote of ten or more jurors. Otherwise, you must not answer [*that part of*] the following question.

QUESTION ______

Do you find by clear and convincing evidence that the harm to *Paul Payne* resulted from gross negligence attributable to *ABC Corporation*?

"Clear and convincing evidence" means the measure or degree of proof that produces a firm belief or conviction of the truth of the allegations sought to be established.

"Gross negligence" means an act or omission by *Don Davis*,

(a) which when viewed objectively from the standpoint of *Don Davis* at the time of its occurrence involves an extreme degree of risk, considering the probability and magnitude of the potential harm to others; and

(b) of which *Don Davis* has actual, subjective awareness of the risk involved, but nevertheless proceeds with conscious indifference to the rights, safety, or welfare of others.

You are further instructed that *ABC Corporation* may be grossly negligent because of an act by *Don Davis* if, but only if—

a. *ABC Corporation* authorized the doing and the manner of the act, or

b. *Don Davis* was unfit and *ABC Corporation* was reckless in employing *him*, or

c. *Don Davis* was employed as a vice-principal and was acting in the scope of employment, or

d. *ABC Corporation* or a vice-principal of *ABC Corporation* ratified or approved the act.

Answer "Yes" or "No."

Answer: _______________

COMMENT

When to use. PJC 115.38 may be used if a plaintiff seeks to impute the gross negligence or malice of a defendant employee to his corporate employer. The grounds listed in this instruction are alternatives, and any of the listed grounds not in issue in the case should be deleted. PJC 115.38 is not designed for use when the plaintiff seeks to establish corporate liability for exemplary damages based on corporate policies.

Source of instruction. The supreme court adopted the doctrine set out in *Restatement (Second) of Torts* § 909 (1979) in *King v. McGuff*, 234 S.W.2d 403 (Tex. 1950); *see also Fisher v. Carrousel Motor Hotel, Inc.*, 424 S.W.2d 627 (Tex. 1967). Section 909 sets out four distinct reasons to impute the gross negligence or malice of an employee to a corporate employer. As the court in *Fisher* set out:

> The rule in Texas is that a principal or master is liable for exemplary or punitive damages because of the acts of his agent, but only if:
>
> (a) the principal authorized the doing and the manner of the act, or
>
> (b) the agent was unfit and the principal was reckless in employing him, or
>
> (c) the agent was employed in a managerial capacity and was acting in the scope of employment, or
>
> (d) the employer or a manager of the employer ratified or approved the act.

Fisher, 424 S.W.2d at 630; *see also Hammerly Oaks, Inc. v. Edwards*, 958 S.W.2d 387, 391 (Tex. 1997); *Fort Worth Elevators Co. v. Russell*, 70 S.W.2d 397, 406 (Tex. 1934), *disapproved on other grounds by Wright v. Gifford-Hill & Co.*, 725 S.W.2d 712, 714

(Tex. 1987). In *Fort Worth Elevators Co.*, the court held that the gross negligence of a "vice-principal" could be imputed to a corporation and listed the elements of "vice-principal" as above. *Fort Worth Elevators Co.*, 70 S.W.2d at 406. The court also discussed "absolute or nondelegable duties" for which "the corporation itself remains responsible for the manner of their performance." *Fort Worth Elevators Co.*, 70 S.W.2d at 401.

Definition of vice-principal. One or more of the following definitions should be used if the grounds include an element where the term "vice-principal" is used. Only the applicable elements of vice-principal should be included in the definition as submitted to the jury.

> The term "vice-principal" means:
>
> (a) A corporate officer.
>
> (b) A person who has authority to employ, direct, and discharge an employee of *ABC Corporation*.
>
> (c) A person engaged in the performance of nondelegable or absolute duties of *ABC Corporation*.
>
> (d) A person to whom *ABC Corporation* has confided the management of the whole or a department or division of the business of *ABC Corporation*.

See Fort Worth Elevators Co., 70 S.W.2d at 406.

Punitive damages based on criminal act by another person. Subject to certain exceptions, a court may not award exemplary damages against a defendant because of the harmful criminal act of another. *See* Tex. Civ. Prac. & Rem. Code § 41.005(a), (b). For causes of action accruing on or after September 1, 1995, an employer may be liable for punitive damages arising out of a criminal act by an employee but only if—

> (1) the principal authorized the doing and the manner of the act;
>
> (2) the agent was unfit and the principal acted with malice in employing or retaining him;
>
> (3) the agent was employed in a managerial capacity and was acting in the scope of employment; or
>
> (4) the employer or a manager of the employer ratified or approved the act.

Tex. Civ. Prac. & Rem. Code § 41.005(c).

Malice as a ground for exemplary damages in actions filed on or after September 1, 2003. Malice is also a ground for recovery of exemplary damages. *See* Tex. Civ. Prac. & Rem. Code § 41.003(a)(3).

Definitions of "gross negligence" and "malice." See PJC 115.36.

Definition of nondelegable or absolute duties. If the evidence on vice-principal requires the submission of the element that includes the term "nondelegable or absolute duties," further definitions may be necessary.

Nondelegable and absolute duties of a vice-principal are (1) the duty to provide rules and regulations for the safety of employees and to warn them as to the hazards of their positions or employment; (2) the duty to furnish reasonably safe machinery or instrumentalities with which its employees are to labor; (3) the duty to furnish its employees with a reasonably safe place to work; and (4) the duty to exercise ordinary care to select careful and competent coemployees. *See Fort Worth Elevators Co.*, 70 S.W.2d at 401.

Caveat. The decision to define nondelegable or absolute duties may need to be balanced against the consideration that this definition may constitute an impermissible comment on the weight of the evidence. In any event, only those elements of the definition raised by the evidence should be submitted.

Unanimity instructions. The unanimity instructions in PJC 115.38B come from the supreme court's January 27, 2005, order under Tex. R. Civ. P. 226a effective February 1, 2005, in all cases filed on or after September 1, 2003.

PJC 115.39 Question and Instructions—Securing Execution of Document by Deception as a Ground for Removing Limitation on Exemplary Damages (Tex. Civ. Prac. & Rem. Code § 41.008(c)(11))

Answer the following question only if you unanimously answered "Yes" to Question ______ [*115.36*]. Otherwise, do not answer the following question.

To answer "Yes" to [*any part of*] the following question, your answer must be unanimous. You may answer "No" to [*any part of*] the following question only upon a vote of ten or more jurors. Otherwise, you must not answer [*that part of*] the following question.

QUESTION ______

Did *Don Davis* secure the execution of a document by deception [*and was the value of the property affected $1,500 or more*]?

> "Securing the execution of a document by deception" occurs when a person causes another person to *sign* any document affecting *property*, and does so by deception, with the intent to defraud or harm any person.
>
> A person acts with intent with respect to the nature of *his* conduct or to a result of *his* conduct when it is the conscious objective or desire to engage in the conduct or cause the result.
>
> "Deception" means creating or confirming by words or conduct a false impression of law or fact that is likely to affect the judgment of another in the transaction, and that the actor does not believe to be true.
>
> *"Property" means: (a) real property; (b) tangible or intangible personal property, including anything severed from land; or (c) a document, including money, that represents or embodies anything of value.*

Answer "Yes" or "No."

Answer: ______________

COMMENT

When to use. PJC 115.39 should be used in a case where (1) exemplary damages are sought, (2) the harm to the plaintiff resulted from conduct described as a felony in

Tex. Penal Code § 32.46, and (3) the jury has previously found that the defendant committed conduct authorizing recovery of exemplary damages as set out in Tex. Civ. Prac. & Rem. Code § 41.003. *See* Tex. Civ. Prac. & Rem. Code § 41.008(c)(11). This statute applies to causes of action accruing on or after September 1, 1995. If the jury finds conduct that violates Tex. Penal Code § 32.46, and the conduct rises to the level of a felony, the limitations on exemplary damages awards set out in Tex. Civ. Prac. & Rem. Code § 41.008(b) do not apply. Tex. Civ. Prac. & Rem. Code § 41.008(c).

Bifurcation. If a defendant has requested a bifurcated trial pursuant to Tex. Civ. Prac. & Rem. Code § 41.009, PJC 115.39 should be answered in the first phase of the trial.

Alternative language for "sign." In an appropriate case, the word *execute* may be substituted for the word *sign*. Tex. Penal Code § 32.46(a).

Alternative language for "property." In an appropriate case, the term *service* or *the pecuniary interest of any person* may be substituted for the word *property*. Tex. Penal Code § 32.46(a)(1). If *service* is substituted for *property*, the following definition should be substituted:

> "Service" includes: (a) labor and professional service; (b) telecommunication, public utility, and transportation service; (c) lodging, restaurant service, and entertainment; and (d) the supply of a motor vehicle or other property for use.

Tex. Penal Code § 32.01(3).

"Deception." The definition of "deception" in PJC 115.39 is taken from Tex. Penal Code § 31.01(1) and *Goldstein v. State*, 803 S.W.2d 777, 790 (Tex. App.—Dallas 1991, pet. ref'd). See Tex. Penal Code § 31.01(1) for alternative definitions of "deception."

"Value" and requirement that conduct be described as a felony. Tex. Civ. Prac. & Rem. Code § 41.008(c) requires that the limitation or cap on exemplary damages may be lifted only if the plaintiff's damages are based on conduct "described as a felony" in Tex. Penal Code § 32.46. The criterion for felony status is that the property or service have a value of $1,500 or higher. Tex. Penal Code § 32.46(b)(4). The optional language in the basic question in PJC 115.39 establishes whether the defendant's conduct rises to the status of a felony, if there is a dispute about the value of the property in question.

Unanimity. For actions filed on or after September 1, 2003, "[e]xemplary damages may be awarded only if the jury was unanimous in regard to finding liability for and the amount of exemplary damages." Tex. Civ. Prac. & Rem. Code § 41.003(d). The jury must be instructed that its answer regarding the amount of exemplary damages must be unanimous. Tex. Civ. Prac. & Rem. Code § 41.003(e). By the supreme court's January 27, 2005, order under Tex. R. Civ. P. 226a, the supreme court requires unanimity on the applicable liability question as well as the exemplary damages question in cases governed by Tex. Civ. Prac. & Rem. Code § 41.003(d). Section 41.008 of the Civil Practice and Remedies Code limits the amount of exemplary damages and then lists exceptions that remove these limitations or caps. Tex. Civ. Prac. & Rem. Code § 41.008. The Committee considers these exceptions to be findings that establish "liability for and the amount of exemplary damages"; therefore, these questions are conditioned on, and require, unanimous findings. See PJC 115.40–.45.

Actions filed before September 1, 2003. A unanimous decision on liability for and the amount of exemplary damages is not required for actions filed before September 1, 2003. In such cases, substitute the following conditioning instruction:

> If you answered "Yes" to Question ______ [*115.36*], then answer the following question. Otherwise, do not answer the following question.

Source of instruction and definition. The question and instructions are derived from Tex. Penal Code §§ 31.01(1), 31.08, 32.01(2), (3), 32.46; Tex. Civ. Prac. & Rem. Code § 41.008.

PJC 115.40 Question and Instruction—Fraudulent Destruction, Removal, Alteration, or Concealment of Writing as a Ground for Removing Limitation on Exemplary Damages (Tex. Civ. Prac. & Rem. Code § 41.008(c)(12))

Answer the following question only if you unanimously answered "Yes" to Question ______ [*115.36*]. Otherwise, do not answer the following question.

To answer "Yes" to [*any part of*] the following question, your answer must be unanimous. You may answer "No" to [*any part of*] the following question only upon a vote of ten or more jurors. Otherwise, you must not answer [*that part of*] the following question.

QUESTION ______

Did *Don Davis alter* [*describe the writing in question, e.g., Terry Testator's will dated February 29, 1992*] with intent to defraud or harm another?

> A person acts with intent with respect to the nature of *his* conduct or to a result of *his* conduct when it is the conscious objective or desire to engage in the conduct or cause the result.

Answer "Yes" or "No."

Answer: ______________

COMMENT

When to use. PJC 115.40 should be used in a case where (1) exemplary damages are sought, (2) the harm to the plaintiff resulted from conduct described as a felony in Tex. Penal Code § 32.47, and (3) the jury has previously found that the defendant committed conduct authorizing recovery of exemplary damages as set out in Tex. Civ. Prac. & Rem. Code § 41.003. *See* Tex. Civ. Prac. & Rem. Code § 41.008(c)(12). This statute applies to causes of action accruing on or after September 1, 1995. If the jury finds conduct that violates Tex. Penal Code § 32.47, and that conduct rises to the level of a felony, the limitations on exemplary damages awards set out in Tex. Civ. Prac. & Rem. Code § 41.008(b) do not apply. Tex. Civ. Prac. & Rem. Code § 41.008(c). See comment below, "Felonious conduct," for a discussion of the requirements needed to establish that the conduct in question was felonious.

Bifurcation. If a defendant has requested a bifurcated trial pursuant to Tex. Civ. Prac. & Rem. Code § 41.009, PJC 115.40 should be answered in the first phase of the trial.

Alternative language for "alter." In an appropriate case, the terms *remove, conceal, destroy, substitute,* or *impair the verity (legibility) (availability) of* may be substituted for the word *alter.* Tex. Penal Code § 32.47(a).

Not applicable to governmental records. Because Tex. Penal Code § 32.47 does not apply to writings that are "governmental records," PJC 115.40 is not applicable in a case where the writing in question is such a record. *See* Tex. Penal Code § 32.47(a). See Tex. Penal Code § 37.01(2) for a definition of "governmental record."

Definition of "writing." In an appropriate case, use a definition of "writing" as provided in Tex. Penal Code § 32.47(b).

Felonious conduct. Tex. Civ. Prac. & Rem. Code § 41.008(c) provides that the limitation or cap on exemplary damages may be lifted only if the plaintiff's damages are based on conduct "described as a felony" in Tex. Penal Code § 32.47. The criminal conduct described in Tex. Penal Code § 32.47 rises to felonious conduct only in the following situations:

1. the writing is a will or codicil of another, whether or not the maker is alive or dead and whether or not it has been admitted to probate; or
2. the writing is a deed, mortgage, deed of trust, security instrument, security agreement, or other writing for which the law provides public recording or filing, whether or not the writing has been acknowledged.

Tex. Penal Code § 32.47(d).

Unanimity. For actions filed on or after September 1, 2003, "[e]xemplary damages may be awarded only if the jury was unanimous in regard to finding liability for and the amount of exemplary damages." Tex. Civ. Prac. & Rem. Code § 41.003(d). The jury must be instructed that its answer regarding the amount of exemplary damages must be unanimous. Tex. Civ. Prac. & Rem. Code § 41.003(e). By the supreme court's January 27, 2005, order under Tex. R. Civ. P. 226a, the supreme court requires unanimity on the applicable liability question as well as the exemplary damages question in cases governed by Tex. Civ. Prac. & Rem. Code § 41.003(d). Section 41.008 of the Civil Practice and Remedies Code limits the amount of exemplary damages and then lists exceptions that remove these limitations or caps. Tex. Civ. Prac. & Rem. Code § 41.008. The Committee considers these exceptions to be findings that establish "liability for and the amount of exemplary damages"; therefore, these questions are conditioned on, and require, unanimous findings. See PJC 115.39, 115.41–.45.

Actions filed before September 1, 2003. A unanimous decision as to the liability for and the amount of exemplary damages is not required for actions filed before September 1, 2003. In such cases, substitute the following conditioning instruction:

> If you answered "Yes" to Question ______ [*115.36*], then answer the following question. Otherwise, do not answer the following question.

Source of instruction and definition. The question and instructions are derived from Tex. Penal Code §§ 6.03(a), 32.47; Tex. Civ. Prac. & Rem. Code § 41.008.

PJC 115.41 Question and Instructions—Forgery as a Ground for Removing Limitation on Exemplary Damages (Tex. Civ. Prac. & Rem. Code § 41.008(c)(8))

Answer the following question only if you unanimously answered "Yes" to Question ______ [*115.36*]. Otherwise, do not answer the following question.

To answer "Yes" to [*any part of*] the following question, your answer must be unanimous. You may answer "No" to [*any part of*] the following question only upon a vote of ten or more jurors. Otherwise, you must not answer [*that part of*] the following question.

QUESTION ______

Did *Don Davis* commit forgery with the intent to defraud or harm another?

> "Forgery" means that a person *alters, makes, completes, executes, or authenticates* a writing so that it purports to *be the act of another who did not authorize that act.*
>
> A person acts with intent with respect to the nature of *his* conduct or to a result of *his* conduct when it is the conscious objective or desire to engage in the conduct or cause the result.

Answer "Yes" or "No."

Answer: ______________

COMMENT

When to use. PJC 115.41 should be used in a case where (1) exemplary damages are sought, (2) the harm to the plaintiff is alleged to have resulted from conduct described as a felony in Tex. Penal Code § 32.21, and (3) the jury has previously found that the defendant committed conduct authorizing recovery of exemplary damages as set out in Tex. Civ. Prac. & Rem. Code § 41.003. *See* Tex. Civ. Prac. & Rem. Code § 41.008(c)(8). This statute applies to causes of action accruing on or after September 1, 1995. If the jury finds conduct that violates Tex. Penal Code § 32.21, and that conduct rises to the level of a felony, the limitations on exemplary damages awards set out in Tex. Civ. Prac. & Rem. Code § 41.008(b) do not apply. Tex. Civ. Prac. & Rem. Code § 41.008(c)(8). See comment below, "Felonious conduct," for a discussion of the requirements needed to establish that the conduct in question was felonious.

Bifurcation. If a defendant has requested a bifurcated trial pursuant to Tex. Civ. Prac. & Rem. Code § 41.009, PJC 115.41 should be answered in the first phase of the trial.

Alternative language for issuance or possession of a forged writing. Tex. Penal Code § 32.21(a)(1)(B) defines "forgery" alternatively as occurring when a person issues, transfers, registers the transfer of, passes, publishes, or otherwise utters a forged writing as defined in Tex. Penal Code § 32.21(a)(1)(A). Also, Tex. Penal Code § 32.21(a)(1)(C) gives another alternative definition of "forgery" as occurring when a person possesses a forged writing (as defined in Tex. Penal Code § 32.21(a)(1)(A)) with the intent to utter it (as defined in Tex. Penal Code § 32.21(a)(1)(B)). In an appropriate case, an alternative definition of "forgery" may be substituted.

Definition of "writing." In an appropriate case, use an applicable definition of "writing" as found in Tex. Penal Code § 32.21(a)(2).

Alternative language for "be the act of another who did not authorize that act." In an appropriate case, the language *have been executed at a time (at a place) (in a numbered sequence) other than was in fact the case*, or *be a copy of an original when no such original existed* may be substituted for the original language of the charge. Tex. Penal Code § 32.21(a)(1)(A).

Felonious conduct. Tex. Civ. Prac. & Rem. Code § 41.008(c) provides that the limitation or cap on exemplary damages may be lifted only if the plaintiff's damages are based on conduct "described as a felony" in Tex. Penal Code § 32.21. The criminal conduct described in Tex. Penal Code § 32.21 rises to felonious conduct only when the writing—

1. is or purports to be a will, codicil, deed, deed of trust, mortgage, security instrument, security agreement, credit card, check, authorization to debit an account at a financial institution, or similar sight order for payment of money, contract, release, or other commercial instrument;
2. is part of an issue of money, securities, postage, or revenue stamps;
3. is a license, certificate, permit, seal, title, letter of patent, or similar document issued by a government; or
4. is another instrument issued by a state or national government or by a subdivision of either, or part of an issue of stock, bonds, or other instruments representing interests in or claims against another person.

Tex. Penal Code § 32.21(d), (e).

Unanimity. For actions filed on or after September 1, 2003, "[e]xemplary damages may be awarded only if the jury was unanimous in regard to finding liability for and the amount of exemplary damages." Tex. Civ. Prac. & Rem. Code § 41.003(d). The jury must be instructed that its answer regarding the amount of exemplary damages must be unanimous. Tex. Civ. Prac. & Rem. Code § 41.003(e). By the supreme court's January

27, 2005, order under Tex. R. Civ. P. 226a, the supreme court requires unanimity on the applicable liability question as well as the exemplary damages question in cases governed by Tex. Civ. Prac. & Rem. Code § 41.003(d). Section 41.008 of the Civil Practice and Remedies Code limits the amount of exemplary damages and then lists exceptions that remove these limitations or caps. Tex. Civ. Prac. & Rem. Code § 41.008. The Committee considers these exceptions to be findings that establish "liability for and the amount of exemplary damages"; therefore, these questions are conditioned on, and require, unanimous findings. See PJC 115.39, 115.40, 115.42–.45.

Actions filed before September 1, 2003. A unanimous decision as to the liability for and the amount of exemplary damages is not required for actions filed before September 1, 2003. In such cases, substitute the following conditioning instruction:

> If you answered "Yes" to Question ______ [*115.36*], then answer the following question. Otherwise, do not answer the following question.

Source of instruction and definition. The question and instructions are derived from Tex. Penal Code §§ 6.03(a), 32.21(a), (b); Tex. Civ. Prac. & Rem. Code § 41.008.

PJC 115.42 Question and Instructions—Theft as a Ground for Removing Limitation on Exemplary Damages (Tex. Civ. Prac. & Rem. Code § 41.008(c)(13))

Answer the following question only if you unanimously answered "Yes" to Question ______ [*115.36*]. Otherwise, do not answer the following question.

To answer "Yes" to [*any part of*] the following question, your answer must be unanimous. You may answer "No" to [*any part of*] the following question only upon a vote of ten or more jurors. Otherwise, you must not answer [*that part of*] the following question.

QUESTION ______

Did *Don Davis* commit theft [*and was the value of the stolen property $20,000 or greater*]?

"Theft" means that a person unlawfully appropriates *property* with the intent to deprive the owner of property. Appropriating *property* is unlawful if it is without the owner's effective consent.

A person acts with intent with respect to the nature of *his* conduct or to a result of *his* conduct when it is the conscious objective or desire to engage in the conduct or cause the result.

"Deprive" means *to withhold property from the owner permanently or for so extended a period of time that a major portion of the value or enjoyment of the property is lost to the owner.*

"Owner" means a person who has title to the property, possession of the property, whether lawful or not, or a greater right to possession of the property than *Don Davis*.

"Property" means: (a) real property; (b) tangible or intangible personal property, including anything severed from land; or (c) a document, including money, that represents or embodies anything of value.

"Consent" means assent in fact, whether express or implied.

"Effective consent" includes *consent by a person legally authorized to act for the owner. Consent is not effective if induced by deception or coercion.*

Answer "Yes" or "No."

Answer: ______________

COMMENT

When to use. PJC 115.42 should be used in a case where (1) exemplary damages are sought, (2) the harm to the plaintiff is alleged to have resulted from conduct described as a third-degree felony in Tex. Penal Code § 31.03, and (3) the jury has previously found that the defendant committed conduct authorizing recovery of exemplary damages as set out in Tex. Civ. Prac. & Rem. Code § 41.003. *See* Tex. Civ. Prac. & Rem. Code § 41.008(c)(13). This statute applies to causes of action accruing on or after September 1, 1995. If the jury finds conduct that violates Tex. Penal Code ch. 31, and that conduct rises to the level of a third-degree felony, the limitations on exemplary damages awards set out in Tex. Civ. Prac. & Rem. Code § 41.008(b) do not apply. Tex. Civ. Prac. & Rem. Code § 41.008(c). See comment below, " 'Value' and requirement that conduct be described as a third-degree felony," for a discussion of the requirements needed to establish that the conduct in question was felonious.

Bifurcation. If a defendant has requested a bifurcated trial pursuant to Tex. Civ. Prac. & Rem. Code § 41.009, PJC 115.42 should be answered in the first phase of the trial.

Alternative definition for "unlawful appropriation of property." "Unlawful appropriation of property" also occurs when the property is stolen and the actor appropriates the property knowing it was stolen by another. Tex. Penal Code § 31.03(b)(2). In an appropriate case, this definition should be substituted for the one shown above, and the Penal Code's definition of "knowing conduct," found at Tex. Penal Code § 6.03(b), should be given as well.

Alternative definitions for "deprive." In an appropriate case, one or more of the following definitions of "deprive" may be substituted for the one shown above.

> to restore property only upon payment of reward or other compensation.

or—

> to dispose of property in a manner that makes recovery of the property by the owner unlikely.

Tex. Penal Code § 31.01(2)(B), (C).

Effective consent. In an appropriate case, the language *Consent is not effective if induced by deception or coercion* may be replaced with any of the following alternatives:

> [Consent is not effective if]
>
> (a) given by a person *Don Davis* knows is not legally authorized to act for the owner;

(b) given by a person who by reason of youth, mental disease or defect, or intoxication is known by *Don Davis* to be unable to make reasonable property dispositions; or

(c) given solely to detect the commission of an offense.

Tex. Penal Code § 31.01(3). If the defendant's knowledge of a fact is in issue (as in option (a) above), the definition of "knowing conduct" found at Tex. Penal Code § 6.03(b) should be given.

Theft of services and trade secrets. Tex. Penal Code § 31.04 should be consulted if the alleged theft was of services rather than of property, and Tex. Penal Code § 31.05 should be consulted if the alleged theft was of a trade secret.

"Value" and requirement that conduct be described as a third-degree felony. Tex. Civ. Prac. & Rem. Code § 41.008(c)(13) requires that the theft be at a level of a third-degree felony or higher in order to lift the limitation or cap on exemplary damages awards. The general criterion for a third-degree felony is that the property or service have a value of $20,000 or higher. Tex. Penal Code § 31.03(e)(5). The optional language in the basic question in PJC 115.42 makes this inquiry, if there is a dispute about the value of what was stolen. Tex. Penal Code § 31.08 contains additional criteria for ascertaining value to determine the level of the offense, and Tex. Penal Code § 31.03 contains additional, nonmonetary criteria for ascertaining the level of punishment.

Unanimity. For actions filed on or after September 1, 2003, "[e]xemplary damages may be awarded only if the jury was unanimous in regard to finding liability for and the amount of exemplary damages." Tex. Civ. Prac. & Rem. Code § 41.003(d). The jury must be instructed that its answer regarding the amount of exemplary damages must be unanimous. Tex. Civ. Prac. & Rem. Code § 41.003(e). By the supreme court's January 27, 2005, order under Tex. R. Civ. P. 226a, the supreme court requires unanimity on the applicable liability question as well as the exemplary damages question in cases governed by Tex. Civ. Prac. & Rem. Code § 41.003(d). Section 41.008 of the Civil Practice and Remedies Code limits the amount of exemplary damages and then lists exceptions that remove these limitations or caps. Tex. Civ. Prac. & Rem. Code § 41.008. The Committee considers these exceptions to be findings that establish "liability for and the amount of exemplary damages"; therefore, these questions are conditioned on, and require, unanimous findings. See PJC 115.39–.41, 115.43–.45.

Actions filed before September 1, 2003. A unanimous decision as to the liability for and the amount of exemplary damages is not required for actions filed before September 1, 2003. In such cases, substitute the following conditioning instruction:

If you answered "Yes" to Question ______ [*115.36*], then answer the following question. Otherwise, do not answer the following question.

Source of instruction and definition. The question and instructions are derived from Tex. Penal Code §§ 1.07(a)(11), (35), 6.03, 31.01(2), (3), (4), (5), 31.03, 31.08; Tex. Civ. Prac. & Rem. Code § 41.008.

PJC 115.43 Question and Instruction—Commercial (Fiduciary) Bribery as a Ground for Removing Limitation on Exemplary Damages (Tex. Civ. Prac. & Rem. Code § 41.008(c)(9))

Answer the following question only if you unanimously answered "Yes" to Question ______ [*115.36*]. Otherwise, do not answer the following question.

To answer "Yes" to [*any part of*] the following question, your answer must be unanimous. You may answer "No" to [*any part of*] the following question only upon a vote of ten or more jurors. Otherwise, you must not answer [*that part of*] the following question.

QUESTION ______

Did *Don Davis*, without *Paul Payne*'s consent, intentionally solicit, accept, or agree to accept any benefit from another person on the agreement or understanding that the benefit would influence *his* conduct in relation to the affairs of *Paul Payne*?

> A person acts with intent with respect to the nature of *his* conduct or to a result of *his* conduct when it is the conscious objective or desire to engage in the conduct or cause the result.

Answer "Yes" or "No."

Answer: ______________

COMMENT

When to use. PJC 115.43 should be used in a case where (1) exemplary damages are sought, (2) the harm to the plaintiff is alleged to have resulted from conduct described in Tex. Penal Code § 32.43, and (3) the jury has previously found that the defendant committed conduct authorizing recovery of exemplary damages as set out in Tex. Civ. Prac. & Rem. Code § 41.003. *See* Tex. Civ. Prac. & Rem. Code § 41.008(c)(9). This statute applies to causes of action accruing on or after September 1, 1995. If the jury finds conduct that violates Tex. Penal Code § 32.43, the limitations on exemplary damages awards set out in Tex. Civ. Prac. & Rem. Code § 41.008(b) do not apply. Tex. Civ. Prac. & Rem. Code § 41.008(c).

Bifurcation. If a defendant has requested a bifurcated trial pursuant to Tex. Civ. Prac. & Rem. Code § 41.009, PJC 115.43 should be answered in the first phase of the trial.

Consent. If a definition of "consent" is required, use the following:

> "Consent" means assent in fact, whether express or apparent.

Tex. Penal Code § 1.07(a)(11).

Benefit. If a definition of "benefit" is required, use the following:

> "Benefit" means anything reasonably regarded as economic gain or advantage, including benefit to any other person in whose welfare the beneficiary is interested.

Tex. Penal Code § 1.07(a)(7).

Knowing standard of conduct. Tex. Civ. Prac. & Rem. Code § 41.008(c) authorizes elimination of the limitation on exemplary damages awards if the conduct described in the applicable Penal Code section was committed either knowingly or intentionally. If knowing instead of intentional conduct is alleged, use the following definition:

> A person acts knowingly with respect to the nature of *his* conduct or to circumstances surrounding *his* conduct when *he* is aware of the nature of *his* conduct or that the circumstances exist. A person acts knowingly with respect to a result of *his* conduct when *he* is aware that *his* conduct is reasonably certain to cause the result.

Tex. Penal Code § 6.03(b).

Offering bribe also criminal conduct. A person who, for an improper purpose, intentionally offers, confers, or agrees to confer a benefit to a fiduciary also commits commercial bribery. Tex. Penal Code § 32.43(c). In an appropriate case, the question should read:

> Did *Don Davis* intentionally offer, confer, or agree to confer a benefit on *Fred Fiduciary* on the agreement that the benefit would influence *Fred Fiduciary*'s conduct in relation to the affairs of *Paul Payne*?

Fiduciary. The defendant must be a fiduciary for the conduct described in Tex. Penal Code § 32.43 to apply. "Fiduciary" is defined there as (1) an agent or employee; (2) a trustee, guardian, custodian, administrator, executor, conservator, receiver, or similar fiduciary; (3) a lawyer, physician, accountant, appraiser, or other professional advisor; or (4) an officer, director, partner, manager, or other participant in the direction of the affairs of a corporation or association. Tex. Penal Code § 32.43(a). If the existence of such a fiduciary relationship is disputed, a preliminary question should be submitted, and PJC 115.43 should be made conditional on a "Yes" answer to that question. *See Schiller v. Elick*, 240 S.W.2d 997, 999 (Tex. 1951) (dispute whether defendant was plaintiff's agent). See chapter 104 of this volume regarding fiduciary and confidential relationships.

Beneficiary. For purposes of the commercial bribery statute, a "beneficiary" is the person for whom a fiduciary acts. Tex. Penal Code § 32.43(a)(1). PJC 115.43 assumes that the plaintiff is the beneficiary.

Unanimity. For actions filed on or after September 1, 2003, "[e]xemplary damages may be awarded only if the jury was unanimous in regard to finding liability for and the amount of exemplary damages." Tex. Civ. Prac. & Rem. Code § 41.003(d). The jury must be instructed that its answer regarding the amount of exemplary damages must be unanimous. Tex. Civ. Prac. & Rem. Code § 41.003(e). By the supreme court's January 27, 2005, order under Tex. R. Civ. P. 226a, the supreme court requires unanimity on the applicable liability question as well as the exemplary damages question in cases governed by Tex. Civ. Prac. & Rem. Code § 41.003(d). Section 41.008 of the Civil Practice and Remedies Code limits the amount of exemplary damages and then lists exceptions that remove these limitations or caps. Tex. Civ. Prac. & Rem. Code § 41.008. The Committee considers these exceptions to be findings that establish "liability for and the amount of exemplary damages"; therefore, these questions are conditioned on, and require, unanimous findings. See PJC 115.39–.42, 115.44, 115.45.

Actions filed before September 1, 2003. A unanimous decision as to the liability for and the amount of exemplary damages is not required for actions filed before September 1, 2003. In such cases, substitute the following conditioning instruction:

> If you answered "Yes" to Question ______ [*115.36*], then answer the following question. Otherwise, do not answer the following question.

Source of instruction and definition. Tex. Penal Code § 32.43; Tex. Civ. Prac. & Rem. Code § 41.008.

PJC 115.44 Question and Instructions—Misapplication of Fiduciary Property as a Ground for Removing Limitation on Exemplary Damages (Tex. Civ. Prac. & Rem. Code § 41.008(c)(10))

Answer the following question only if you unanimously answered "Yes" to Question ______ [*115.36*]. Otherwise, do not answer the following question.

To answer "Yes" to [*any part of*] the following question, your answer must be unanimous. You may answer "No" to [*any part of*] the following question only upon a vote of ten or more jurors. Otherwise, you must not answer [*that part of*] the following question.

QUESTION ______

Did *Don Davis* intentionally misapply [*identify property defendant held as a fiduciary, e.g., 300 shares of ABC Corporation common stock*] in a manner that involved substantial risk of loss to *Paul Payne* [*and was the value of the property $1,500 or greater*]?

> "Misapply" means a person deals with property [*or money*] contrary to *an agreement under which the person holds the property* [*or money*].
>
> "Substantial risk of loss" means it is more likely than not that loss will occur.
>
> A person acts with intent with respect to the nature of *his* conduct or to a result of *his* conduct when it is the conscious objective or desire to engage in the conduct or cause the result.

Answer "Yes" or "No."

Answer: ______________

COMMENT

When to use. PJC 115.44 should be used in a case where (1) exemplary damages are sought, (2) the harm to the plaintiff is alleged to have resulted from conduct described in Tex. Penal Code § 32.45, and (3) the jury has previously found that the defendant committed conduct authorizing recovery of exemplary damages as set out in Tex. Civ. Prac. & Rem. Code § 41.003. *See* Tex. Civ. Prac. & Rem. Code § 41.008(c)(10). This statute applies to causes of action accruing on or after September

1, 1995. If the jury finds conduct that violates Tex. Penal Code § 32.45, the limitations on exemplary damages awards set out in Tex. Civ. Prac. & Rem. Code § 41.008(b) do not apply. Tex. Civ. Prac. & Rem. Code § 41.008(c).

Bifurcation. If a defendant has requested a bifurcated trial pursuant to Tex. Civ. Prac. & Rem. Code § 41.009, PJC 115.44 should be answered in the first phase of the trial.

Knowing standard of conduct. Tex. Civ. Prac. & Rem. Code § 41.008(c) authorizes elimination of the limitation on exemplary damages awards if the conduct described in the applicable Penal Code section was committed either knowingly or intentionally. If knowing instead of intentional conduct is alleged, use the following definition:

> A person acts knowingly with respect to the nature of *his* conduct or to circumstances surrounding *his* conduct when *he* is aware of the nature of *his* conduct or that the circumstances exist. A person acts knowingly with respect to a result of *his* conduct when *he* is aware that *his* conduct is reasonably certain to cause the result.

Tex. Penal Code § 6.03(b).

Agreement. If a definition of "agreement" is required, use the following:

> "Agreement" means the act of agreement or coming to an agreement; a harmonious understanding; or an arrangement as to a course of action.

Bynum v. State, 711 S.W.2d 321, 323 (Tex. App.—Amarillo 1986), *aff'd*, 767 S.W.2d 769 (Tex. Crim. App. 1989) (applying ordinary, dictionary definition of "agreement").

Property. Tex. Penal Code § 32.01(2) defines "property" broadly to include tangible or intangible property as well as money. Because the jury may not understand money to be "property," the word "money" should be used if money is involved in the case.

Acting contrary to a law governing disposition of property. In an appropriate case, the phrase *a law prescribing the custody or disposition of the property* may be substituted for, or added to, the phrase *an agreement under which the person holds the property*. Tex. Penal Code § 32.45(a)(2).

Fiduciary. The defendant must be a fiduciary for the conduct described in Tex. Penal Code § 32.45 to apply. "Fiduciary" is defined there as including (1) "a trustee, guardian, administrator, executor, conservator, and receiver"; (2) "an attorney in fact or agent appointed under a durable power of attorney" as provided by chapter 12 of the Texas Probate Code; (3) "any other person acting in a fiduciary capacity, but not a commercial bailee unless the commercial bailee is a party in a motor fuel sales agreement with a distributor or supplier," as those terms are defined in Tex. Tax Code § 162.001; and (4) "an officer, manager, employee, or agent carrying on fiduciary functions on behalf of a fiduciary." Tex. Penal Code § 32.45(a)(1). "[A]ny other person acting in a fiduciary capacity" embraces all fiduciaries, not just the categories of fiduciaries enumerated in Tex. Penal Code § 32.45(a)(1). *Coplin v. State*, 585 S.W.2d 734, 735 (Tex. Crim. App. 1979); *Showery v. State*, 678 S.W.2d 103, 107–08 (Tex. App.—El Paso 1984, pet. ref'd).

If the existence of such a fiduciary relationship is disputed, a preliminary question should be submitted, and PJC 115.44 should be made conditional on a "Yes" answer to that question. *See Schiller v. Elick*, 240 S.W.2d 997, 999 (Tex. 1951) (dispute whether defendant was plaintiff's agent). See chapter 104 of this volume regarding fiduciary and confidential relationships.

Substantial risk of loss. The definition of "substantial risk of loss" is derived from *Bynum*, 767 S.W.2d at 774–75, and *Casillas v. State*, 733 S.W.2d 158, 163–64 (Tex. Crim. App. 1986), *appeal dismissed*, 484 U.S. 918 (1987).

Misapplication of property of financial institution. If the defendant is alleged to have misapplied property of a financial institution instead of fiduciary property, the question should be amended to read as follows:

QUESTION ______

Did *Don Davis* intentionally misapply property of *ABC Bank* in a manner that involved substantial risk of loss to *ABC Bank* [*and was the value of the misapplied property $1,500 or greater*]?

"Misapply" means to deal with property contrary to a law prescribing the custody or disposition of the property.

"Substantial risk of loss" means it is more likely than not that loss will occur.

A person acts with intent with respect to the nature of *his* conduct or to a result of *his* conduct when it is the conscious objective or desire to engage in the conduct or cause the result.

"Value" and requirement that conduct be described as a felony. Tex. Civ. Prac. & Rem. Code § 41.008(c) provides that the limitation or cap on exemplary damages may be lifted only if the plaintiff's damages are based on conduct "described as a felony" in Tex. Penal Code § 32.45. The criminal conduct described in Tex. Penal Code § 32.45 rises to felonious conduct only when the value of the property misapplied is $1,500 or higher. Tex. Penal Code § 32.45(c). The optional language in the basic question in PJC 115.44 establishes whether the defendant's conduct rises to the status of a felony, if there is a dispute about the value of the misapplied property.

Unanimity. For actions filed on or after September 1, 2003, "[e]xemplary damages may be awarded only if the jury was unanimous in regard to finding liability for and the amount of exemplary damages." Tex. Civ. Prac. & Rem. Code § 41.003(d). The jury must be instructed that its answer regarding the amount of exemplary damages must be unanimous. Tex. Civ. Prac. & Rem. Code § 41.003(e). By the supreme court's January 27, 2005, order under Tex. R. Civ. P. 226a, the supreme court requires unanimity on the applicable liability question as well as the exemplary damages question in cases governed by Tex. Civ. Prac. & Rem. Code § 41.003(d). Section 41.008 of the Civil Practice and Remedies Code limits the amount of exemplary damages and then lists exceptions that remove these limitations or caps. Tex. Civ. Prac. & Rem. Code § 41.008. The Committee considers these exceptions to be findings that establish "liability for and the amount of exemplary damages"; therefore, these questions are conditioned on, and require, unanimous findings. See PJC 115.39–.43, 115.45.

Actions filed before September 1, 2003. A unanimous decision as to the liability for and the amount of exemplary damages is not required for actions filed before September 1, 2003. In such cases, substitute the following conditioning instruction:

> If you answered "Yes" to Question ______ [*115.36*], then answer the following question. Otherwise, do not answer the following question.

Source of instruction and definition. Tex. Penal Code §§ 31.08, 32.45; Tex. Civ. Prac. & Rem. Code § 41.008.

PJC 115.45 Other Conduct of Defendant Authorizing Removal of Limitation on Exemplary Damages Award (Comment)

In addition to the actions described in PJC 115.39–.44, nine other instances of the defendant's conduct, listed in Tex. Civ. Prac. & Rem. Code § 41.008(c), will support a removal of the limitation on exemplary damages awards set out in Tex. Civ. Prac. & Rem. Code § 41.008(b). They are:

- murder (Tex. Penal Code § 19.02);
- capital murder (Tex. Penal Code § 19.03);
- aggravated kidnapping (Tex. Penal Code § 20.04);
- aggravated assault (Tex. Penal Code § 22.02);
- sexual assault (Tex. Penal Code § 22.011);
- aggravated sexual assault (Tex. Penal Code § 22.021);
- injury to a child, elderly individual, or disabled individual (Tex. Penal Code § 22.04), but for actions filed on or after September 1, 2003, "not if the conduct occurred while providing health care as defined by [Texas Civil Practice and Remedies Code] Section 74.001" (Tex. Civ. Prac. & Rem. Code § 41.008(c)(7));
- intoxication assault (Tex. Penal Code § 49.07); and
- intoxication manslaughter (Tex. Penal Code § 49.08).

When to use. A question asking whether the defendant engaged in the conduct described in the Penal Code provisions set out above should be used in a case where (1) exemplary damages are sought, (2) the harm to the plaintiff is alleged to have resulted from the felonious conduct described in the Penal Code provision, and (3) the jury has previously found that the defendant committed conduct authorizing recovery of exemplary damages as set out in Tex. Civ. Prac. & Rem. Code § 41.003. *See* Tex. Civ. Prac. & Rem. Code § 41.008(c). This statute applies to causes of action accruing on or after September 1, 1995. If the jury answers "Yes" to such a question, the limitations on exemplary damages awards set out in Tex. Civ. Prac. & Rem. Code § 41.008(b) do not apply. Tex. Civ. Prac. & Rem. Code § 41.008(c).

Drafting of question. A jury question regarding one or more of the acts set out in the Penal Code sections listed above should follow the pattern set out in PJC 115.39–.44. See also Paul J. McClung & W. Scott Carpenter, *Texas Criminal Jury Charges* (2004).

Standard of conduct—"intentionally" or "knowingly." Tex. Civ. Prac. & Rem. Code § 41.008(c) authorizes elimination of the limitation on exemplary damages awards if the conduct described in the applicable Penal Code section was committed either knowingly or intentionally. "Knowingly" is defined as follows:

> A person acts knowingly, or with knowledge, with respect to the nature of his conduct or to circumstances surrounding his conduct when he is aware of the nature of his conduct or that the circumstances exist. A person acts knowingly, or with knowledge, with respect to a result of his conduct when he is aware that his conduct is reasonably certain to cause the result.

Tex. Penal Code § 6.03(b).

"Intentionally" is defined as follows:

> A person acts intentionally, or with intent, with respect to the nature of his conduct or to a result of his conduct when it is his conscious objective or desire to engage in the conduct or cause the result.

Tex. Penal Code § 6.03(a).

Felonious conduct. Tex. Civ. Prac. & Rem. Code § 41.008(c) provides that the limitation or cap on exemplary damages may be lifted only if the plaintiff's damages are based on conduct "described as a felony" in the applicable Penal Code section, unless the conduct is intoxication assault or intoxication manslaughter.

Unanimity. For actions filed on or after September 1, 2003, "[e]xemplary damages may be awarded only if the jury was unanimous in regard to finding liability for and the amount of exemplary damages." Tex. Civ. Prac. & Rem. Code § 41.003(d). The jury must be instructed that its answer regarding the amount of exemplary damages must be unanimous. Tex. Civ. Prac. & Rem. Code § 41.003(e). By the supreme court's January 27, 2005, order under Tex. R. Civ. P. 226a, the supreme court requires unanimity on the applicable liability question as well as the exemplary damages question in cases governed by Tex. Civ. Prac. & Rem. Code § 41.003(d). Section 41.008 of the Civil Practice and Remedies Code limits the amount of exemplary damages and then lists exceptions that remove these limitations or caps. Tex. Civ. Prac. & Rem. Code § 41.008. The Committee considers these exceptions to be findings that establish "liability for and the amount of exemplary damages"; therefore, these questions are conditioned on, and require, unanimous findings. See PJC 115.39–.44.

PJC 115.46 Question on Attorney's Fees

If you answered "Yes" to Question _____ [*applicable liability question*], then answer the following question. Otherwise, do not answer the following question.

QUESTION ______

What is a reasonable fee for the necessary services of *Paul Payne*'s attorney, stated in dollars and cents?

Answer with an amount for each of the following:

a. For preparation and trial.

Answer: _______________

b. For an appeal to the Court of Appeals.

Answer: _______________

c. For an appeal to the Supreme Court of Texas.

Answer: _______________

COMMENT

When to use. Attorney's fees are recoverable in contracts, DTPA, Insurance Code, Texas Whistleblower Act, and Texas Commission on Human Rights Act (TCHRA) claims. Tex. Civ. Prac. & Rem. Code § 38.001; Tex. Bus. & Com. Code § 17.50(d) (DTPA); Tex. Ins. Code ch. 541; Tex. Gov't Code § 554.003(a); Tex. Lab. Code § 21.259. PJC 115.46 is to be used regardless of the terms of the fee agreement.

In *Arthur Andersen & Co. v. Perry Equipment Corp.*, 945 S.W.2d 812, 817–19 (Tex. 1997), the supreme court held that a percentage award question should not be used; *see also Lubbock County v. Strube*, 953 S.W.2d 847, 858 (Tex. App.—Austin 1997, no writ) (Whistleblower Act case). Although a contingent fee is proper, the jury's award must be stated in dollars and cents.

Factors to consider. In *Arthur Andersen & Co.*, the supreme court held that the following factors must be considered in determining the reasonableness of an attorney's fees award:

- the time and labor involved, the novelty and difficulty of the questions involved, and the skill required to perform the legal services properly;
- the likelihood that the acceptance of the particular employment will preclude other employment by the lawyer;

- the fee customarily charged in the locality for similar legal services;
- the amount involved and the results obtained;
- the time limitations imposed by the client or the circumstances;
- the nature and length of the professional relationship with the client;
- the experience, reputation, and ability of the lawyer or lawyers performing the services; and
- whether the fee is fixed or contingent on results obtained or uncertainty of collection before the legal services have been rendered.

Arthur Andersen & Co., 945 S.W.2d at 818. *See also* Tex. Disciplinary R. Prof'l Conduct 1.04, *reprinted in* Tex. Gov't Code Ann., tit. 2, subtit. G app. A (Vernon 2005) (Tex. State Bar R. art. X, § 9).

In an appropriate case, one or more of these factors may be included as additional jury instructions.

Attorney's fees awarded to a prevailing plaintiff. To recover attorney's fees under chapter 38 of the Civil Practice and Remedies Code, a party must (1) prevail on a cause of action for which attorney's fees are recoverable, and (2) recover actual damages. *Green International, Inc. v. Solis*, 951 S.W.2d 384, 390 (Tex. 1997); *see also Mustang Pipeline Co. v. Driver Pipeline Co.*, 134 S.W.3d 195, 201 (Tex. 2004) (per curiam); *but see McKinley v. Drozd*, 685 S.W.2d 7 (Tex. 1985) (net recovery not required to obtain attorney's fees under article 2226 (now chapter 38 of the Civil Practice and Remedies Code) or DTPA).

The phrase *if any* should not be included in the questions for fees. The jury determines the amount of reasonable and necessary fees, not whether fees should be recovered. Attorney's fees in some amount are required to be awarded to a prevailing party if authorized by law or contract and supported by some evidence. *See Tony Gullo Motors I, L.P. v. Chapa*, 212 S.W.3d 299, 310 (Tex. 2006); *Brown v. Bank of Galveston, N.A.*, 963 S.W.2d 511 (Tex. 1998).

Segregating claims. If any attorney's fees relate solely to a claim for which such fees are unrecoverable, a claimant must segregate recoverable from unrecoverable fees. Intertwined facts do not make unrecoverable fees recoverable; it is only when discrete legal services advance both a recoverable and unrecoverable claim that they are so intertwined that they need not be segregated. *Tony Gullo Motors I, L.P.*, 212 S.W.3d at 313–14. A party, however, may recover attorney's fees incurred in overcoming defenses or counterclaims to a claim for which attorney's fees are recoverable. *Varner v. Cardenas*, 218 S.W.3d 68, 69 (Tex. 2007). Any error in failing to segregate attorney's fees may be waived by a failure to object to the lack of segregation. *Hruska v. First State Bank*, 747 S.W.2d 783, 785 (Tex. 1988); *Hawkins v. Walker*, 233 S.W.3d 380, 398 (Tex. App.—Fort Worth 2007, no pet.). The question to be submitted may vary from PJC 115.46 in cases involving multiple claims where fees are not recoverable under one or more of the claims.

Defendant's attorney's fees. This question may be modified to submit the defendant's attorney's fees as well, if recoverable under contract law or under DTPA §§ 17.50(c) or 17.506.

APPENDIX

Following are the tables of contents of the other volumes in the *Texas Pattern Jury Charges* series. These tables represent the 2008 editions of these volumes, which were the current editions when this book was published. Other topics may be added in future editions.

Contents of *TEXAS PATTERN JURY CHARGES—GENERAL NEGLIGENCE & INTENTIONAL PERSONAL TORTS* (2008 Ed.)

PJC 8.10	Personal Injury Damages—Child's Loss of Consortium—Question about Parent's Injury
PJC 8.11	Personal Injury Damages—Child's Loss of Consortium—Damages Question
CHAPTER 9	WRONGFUL DEATH DAMAGES
PJC 9.1	Wrongful Death Damages—Instruction Conditioning Damages Questions on Liability
PJC 9.1.5	Wrongful Death Damages—Instruction on Whether Compensatory Damages Are Subject to Income Taxes—Actions Filed on or after September 1, 2003
PJC 9.2	Wrongful Death Damages—Claim of Surviving Spouse
PJC 9.3	Wrongful Death Damages—Claim of Surviving Child
PJC 9.4	Wrongful Death Damages—Claim of Surviving Parents of Minor Child
PJC 9.5	Wrongful Death Damages—Claim of Surviving Parents of Adult Child
PJC 9.5	Wrongful Death Damages—Exemplary Damages
PJC 9.7	Wrongful Death Damages—Apportionment of Exemplary Damages
CHAPTER 10	SURVIVAL DAMAGES
PJC 10.1	Survival Damages—Instruction Conditioning Damages Questions on Liability
PJC 10.1.5	Survival Damages—Instruction on Whether Compensatory Damages Are Subject to Income Taxes—Actions Filed on or after September 1, 2003
PJC 10.2	Survival Damages—Compensatory Damages
PJC 10.3	Survival Damages—Exemplary Damages
CHAPTER 11	PROPERTY DAMAGES
PJC 11.1	Property Damages—Instruction Conditioning Damages Questions on Liability
PJC 11.1.5	Property Damages—Instruction on Whether Compensatory Damages Are Subject to Income Taxes—Actions Filed on or after September 1, 2003

Contents of
***TEXAS PATTERN JURY CHARGES—MALPRACTICE, PREMISES & PRODUCTS* (2008 Ed.)**

[Chapters 62–64 are reserved for expansion.]

Contents of
***TEXAS PATTERN JURY CHARGES—FAMILY* (2008 Ed.)**

STATUTES AND RULES CITED

[Decimal references are to PJC numbers.]

Texas Constitution

Texas Revised Civil Statutes

Texas Agriculture Code

Texas Business & Commerce Code

Texas Business & Commerce Code—*continued*

Texas Business Corporation Act

Texas Business Organizations Code

Texas Civil Practice & Remedies Code

Texas Election Code

Texas Family Code

Texas Finance Code

Texas Government Code

Texas Health & Safety Code

Texas Insurance Code

Texas Labor Code

Texas Local Government Code

Texas Occupations Code

Texas Penal Code

Miscellaneous—*continued*

CASES CITED

[Decimal references are to PJC numbers.]

A

B

D

E

F

G

H

M

Q

R

S

T

U

SUBJECT INDEX

[Decimal references are to PJC numbers.]

C

E

DISK DOCUMENTATION

Texas Pattern Jury Charges—Business, Consumer, Insurance & Employment on Disk, v. 1.4

This complimentary CD-ROM contains the entire text of *Texas Pattern Jury Charges—Business, Consumer, Insurance & Employment* (2008 edition). A copy of this documentation including the license agreement can be found in the file named "StartHere" located on the CD. If you have questions or problems with this product not covered in the documentation below, please contact the State Bar of Texas, TexasBarBooks, P.O. Box 12487, Austin, TX 78711, telephone (800) 204-2222, ext. 1499, or direct line (512) 427-1499, fax (512) 427-4158, e-mail **books@texasbar.com**.

The current owner of this book may purchase additional and bulk entity licenses for the CD. Each additional license is for one additional lawyer and that lawyer's support team only. Additional and bulk entity licenses are subject to the terms of the original license concerning permitted users of the printed book and CD materials. Please visit **www.TexasBarCLE.com/CLE/PMBooks2.asp?sProductType=J** for details.

Contents of the CD

The PDF file "PJC Business 2008" is an exact representation of the printed book. The file is fully word-searchable, and all PJCs and Comments, Texas case citations (S.W.2d & S.W.3d), Texas statutory citations, tables of contents, internal cross-references, and indexes are hyperlinked to allow for easy, rapid navigation to substantive topics of interest.

The text files contain the charge language from the book, including all alternate and additional charge language contained in the PJC Comments, and are intended to be used only in conjunction with the Comments to ease the task of preparing a jury charge in your office. The text files are in Rich Text Format (RTF), which should be compatible with any word-processing software.

New with this 2008 edition: All Texas statute citations are linked to the main Code section cited via Casemaker online. (Read more about this in the section below titled "Usage Tips for the PDF File.")

Contents of the CD's Texas PJC Business 2008 folder: Following are explanations of each folder and file in the Texas PJC Business 2008 folder:

- Codes and Cases folder: Texas cases cited (S.W.2d & S.W.3d) as PDF files and the full text of the Texas Business and Commerce Code, the Texas Civil Practice and Remedies Code, the Texas Insurance Code (Chapter 541), the Texas Labor Code, and the Texas Penal Code (current to the 80th Legislature) as both Word files and fully bookmarked PDF files, all accessible via links in the "PJC Business 2008" PDF file

- PJC files folder: charge language files in RTF, accessible via links in the "PJC Business 2008" PDF file and the "Table of contents by chapter" PDF file
- "PJC Business 2008" PDF file: the entire printed book as a single, fully hyperlinked, word-searchable PDF file
- "StartHere" PDF file: this disk documentation as a single PDF file
- "Table of contents by chapter" PDF file: list of charge language files by chapter hyperlinked to launch the charge language files in your word-processing application

Automatic Installation

On insertion of the CD in your CD drive, a setup program should automatically launch. If the setup program does not launch, go to the Start menu, select Run, type D:\setup (assuming that D:\ is your CD drive), and click OK. The setup program should then launch. You may cancel the operation at any time during the installation process.

Note: The setup program will not run on a Macintosh computer. If you want to install the book and text files to a Macintosh computer, proceed to the manual installation instructions below.

Manual Installation

Note that, although you may rename the Texas PJC Business 2008 folder anything you like after copying it to your hard drive, you should not rename any files or folders within the Texas PJC Business 2008 folder or alter their file structure, or some of the book's links will not work.

To install the book's folders and files to your hard drive, follow the instructions below.

Windows (these instructions assume that C:\ is your hard drive and D:\ is your CD drive):

1. Insert the CD in your CD drive, and if the setup program window appears, click Exit to close the window.
2. Start Windows Explorer or My Computer, single-click (highlight) D:\, right-click, and select Explore.
3. Single-click (highlight) the Texas PJC Business 2008 folder and, from the menu bar, select Edit, Copy.
4. Navigate up one level using the Back button in Windows Explorer or My Computer; double-click C:\; navigate to the desired location on your hard drive; and from the menu bar, select Edit, Paste.

Macintosh:

1. Insert the CD in your CD drive and double-click the disk icon.
2. Single-click (highlight) the CD's Texas PJC Business 2008 folder.
3. Drag the folder to the desired location on your hard drive.

Accessing Text Files from a Word Processor

To access the text files from your word-processing software, execute that software's File, Open command; locate and open the folder named Texas PJC Business 2008; within that folder, select and open the PJC files folder; select and open the appropriate chapter subfolder; and finally, select and open the desired file.

Text File Organization and Format

The text files on the CD replicate the PJC language contained in the printed version, including italic designations, phrases, and bracketed instructions that are intended to be replaced or deleted; additional wording changes may be needed for particular situations. **In every case, consult the Comment following the jury charge for instructions on choosing the correct language for a particular jury charge.** For general instructions about the hypothetical examples, see paragraph f. in section 4. (Principles of Style) of the Introduction to the book.

The name of each electronic document corresponds to the *number* of the printed PJC containing the charge language, except that the decimal point in the PJC number is replaced by a hyphen. For example, "105-3A" is the document name for PJC 105.3A. If the main PJC is divided into parts identified by a letter following the number, each part constitutes a separate electronic document. The PDF file named "Table of contents by chapter" contains a table of contents listing each file on this disk and the corresponding jury charge title. For alternate and additional charge language contained in PJC Comments, the file name specifies the PJC number the language is related to along with a brief description of its purpose (e.g., "101-2 alternate question").

Usage Tips for the PDF File

To use the bookmarks: The bookmarks navigation pane appears on the left side of the Adobe Acrobat/Reader window and displays all chapter and PJC titles. Each item is a link and can be clicked to jump to that portion of the book. The bookmarks navigation pane can be toggled on or off by clicking the Bookmarks button at the left side of the Acrobat/Reader window. You may also use function key F4. The vertical bar separating the navigation pane from the main body of the book can be dragged to resize the navigation pane.

To follow a link within the text: Each link in the text is highlighted in blue, red, or green. Blue-highlighted text links internally to all cross-references in the main PDF file of the book and externally to RTF files of charge language, Internet URLs, and e-mail addresses. Red-highlighted case citations link to PDF files of the cases produced from the Casemaker database. Green-highlighted case names link to search results via Casemaker online; green-highlighted statute citations link to the main Code section cited, also via Casemaker online. Please note that you must be a registered user of TexasBarCLE's Web site and logged on to access Casemaker via the green case name and statute citation links. If you are not already a registered user, once you click on the green link you will be prompted to complete a quick, free registration.

To open charge language files in your word processor: The charge language in the book is hyperlinked from each PJC in the PDF file to a text file in RTF. Click the blue PJC numbers to launch the main charge language files in your default word processor. Alternate or additional charge language is also hyperlinked from relevant PJC Comments. Click the blue first few words of alternate or additional charge language to launch those files in your default word processor.

To return to your previous view after following an internal link: While holding down your keyboard's Alt key, press the left arrow key.

To search the text: Choose Search from the Edit menu (at the top of the Acrobat/Reader window) or click the Search This Book bookmark.

To copy text for use in other programs: Make certain that the Select tool is active instead of the Hand tool. Then use the cursor to highlight the text you want to copy and choose Edit, Copy. The selected text has now been copied and can be pasted into your word processor or other compatible software by executing that software's Edit, Paste command.

USE OF THE MATERIAL ON THE CD IS SUBJECT TO THE FOLLOWING LICENSE AGREEMENT.

License and Limited Warranty

Grant of license: The material on this disk and in the documentation is copyrighted by the State Bar of Texas ("State Bar"). The State Bar grants you a nonexclusive license to use this material as long as you abide by the terms of this agreement.

Ownership: You own the disk on which the material is recorded, but the State Bar retains title and ownership of the material on the original disk and in the documentation and all subsequent copies of the material regardless of the form or media in which or on which the original and other copies may exist. This license is not a sale of the material or any copy. The terms of this agreement apply to derivative works.

Permitted users: The material on this disk is licensed to you for use by one lawyer and that lawyer's support team only. At any given time, the material on this disk may be installed only on the computers used by that lawyer and that lawyer's support team. That lawyer may be the individual purchaser or the lawyer designated by the firm that purchased this product. You may not permit other lawyers to use this material unless you purchase additional licenses. **Lawyers, law firms, and law firm librarians are specifically prohibited from using one disk to distribute these materials to more than one lawyer. A separate license must be purchased for each lawyer who uses these materials.** For information about special bulk discount pricing for law firms, please call 1-800-204-2222, ext. 1402, or 512-427-1402. Libraries not affiliated with firms may permit reading of this material by patrons of the library through installation on one or more computers owned by the library but may not lend or sell the disk itself. The library may not allow patrons to print or copy any of this material in any way.

Copies: You may make a copy of the disk for backup purposes. Otherwise, you may copy the material on the disk only as necessary to allow use by the users permitted under the license you purchased. Copyright notices should be included on copies. You may copy the documentation, including any copyright notices, as needed for reference by authorized users, but not otherwise.

Transfer: You may not transfer any copy of the material on the disk or in the documentation to any other person or entity unless the transferee first accepts this agreement in writing and you transfer all copies, wherever located or installed, of the material and documentation, including the original provided with this agreement. You may not rent, loan, lease, sublicense, or otherwise make the material available for use by any person other than the permitted users except as provided in this paragraph.

Limited warranty and limited liability: If the disk contained in this package is physically defective, the State Bar will replace it if you return it within 30 days of purchase. **THE STATE BAR MAKES NO OTHER WARRANTIES, EXPRESS OR IMPLIED,**

CONCERNING THE MATERIAL ON THIS DISK, THE DOCUMENTATION, OR THIS AGREEMENT. THE STATE BAR EXPRESSLY DISCLAIMS ALL IMPLIED WARRANTIES, INCLUDING THE IMPLIED WARRANTIES OF MERCHANTABILITY AND OF FITNESS FOR A PARTICULAR PURPOSE. THE MATERIAL ON THE DISK AND IN THE DOCUMENTATION IS PROVIDED "AS IS."

THE STATE BAR SHALL NOT BE LIABLE FOR THE LEGAL SUFFICIENCY OR LEGAL ACCURACY OF ANY OF THE MATERIAL CONTAINED ON THIS DISK. NEITHER THE STATE BAR NOR ANY OF THE CONTRIBUTORS TO THE MATERIAL MAKES EITHER EXPRESS OR IMPLIED WARRANTIES WITH REGARD TO THE USE OR FREEDOM FROM ERROR OF THE MATERIAL. EACH USER IS SOLELY RESPONSIBLE FOR THE LEGAL EFFECT OF ANY USE OR MODIFICATION OF THE MATERIAL.

IN NO EVENT SHALL THE STATE BAR BE LIABLE FOR LOSS OF PROFITS OR FOR INDIRECT, SPECIAL, CONSEQUENTIAL, OR PUNITIVE DAMAGES, EVEN IF THE STATE BAR HAS BEEN ADVISED OF THE POSSIBILITY OF THOSE DAMAGES. THE STATE BAR'S AGGREGATE LIABILITY ARISING FROM OR RELATING TO THIS AGREEMENT OR THE MATERIAL ON THE DISK OR IN THE DOCUMENTATION IS LIMITED TO THE PURCHASE PRICE YOU PAID FOR THE LICENSED COPYRIGHTED PRODUCT. THIS AGREEMENT DEFINES YOUR SOLE REMEDY.

General provisions: This agreement contains the entire agreement between you and the State Bar concerning the license to use the material on the disk contained in the package. The waiver of any breach of any provision of this agreement does not waive any other breach of that or any other provision. If any provision is for any reason found to be unenforceable, all other provisions nonetheless remain enforceable.